THE GAME OF LIFE

COLLEGE SPORTS
AND EDUCATIONAL VALUES

James L. Shulman and William G. Bowen

IN COLLABORATION WITH

Lauren A. Meserve and Roger C. Schonfeld

PRINCETON UNIVERSITY PRESS   PRINCETON AND OXFORD

Library of Congress Cataloging-in-Publication Data

Shulman, James Lawrence, 1965–
The game of life: college sports and educational values /
James L. Shulman and William G. Bowen.
p.   cm.
Includes bibliographical references and index.
ISBN 0-691-07075-X (alk. paper)
1. College sports—United States. 2. Education, Higher—Aims and
objectives—United States. 1. Bowen, William G. II. Title.
GV351 .S48   2001
796.04′3′0973—dc21   00-061146

This book has been composed in Adobe New Baskerville by
Princeton Editorial Associates, Inc., Scottsdale, Arizona,
and Roosevelt, New Jersey

The paper used in this publication meets the requirements of
ANSI/NISO Z39.48-1992 (R1997) (*Permanence of Paper*)

www.pup.princeton.edu

Printed in the United States of America

10 9 8 7 6 5 4 3 2

Contents

Chapter 1

Chapter 2

A "MONEY MACHINE"? THE 1999 ATHLETICS BUDGET
AT THE UNIVERSITY OF MICHIGAN

THE 1998–99 YEAR was not a bad one for the University of Michigan's athletic department. The football team shared the Big Ten title, won the Citrus Bowl, and finished the season ranked 12th in the nation. The men's ice hockey team (having won the national championship the year before) made it to the second round of the NCAA tournament before losing in overtime. The women's basketball team went 18–11, the men's gymnastics team won the national championship, and the University finished 6th in the Sears Cup competition (an annual ranking that compares all the schools in the country on the basis of the range and success of their men's and women's programs). But when the fiscal year ended in June, the athletic department was projecting a deficit of $2 million. By September, when audited statements came out, the operating deficit had risen to $2.8 million; when capital expenditures and transfers are included, the shortfall was $3.8 million. "In fiscal year 1999," the authors of a University committee report wrote, "the music has stopped."

How was it possible that—in the same year that the football team set a national attendance record, with an average of 110,965 fans attending six home games—the athletic department could show a net loss of $2.8 million? In the previous year, when Michigan's football team had won the national title, revenues from apparel sales—sweatshirts, hats, and umbrellas emblazoned with Michigan blue and a big M—had provided $5.7 million to the department. Even after having projected a decline in the merchandising line of the 1999 budget, athletic director Tom Goss was surprised to learn that Michigan's apparel royalties had fallen to $3.6 million. Other universities experienced similar sharp declines, as they learned that being part of the world of fashion meant depending on a revenue stream that was driven by the whimsical clothing tastes of teenagers and young adults. "People are wearing Tommy Hilfiger sweatshirts," Goss noted, "rather than collegiate logos." The vagaries of fashion had taken their toll. But avoiding other market temptations, President Lee Bollinger pointed out, had also exacted a financial penalty; unlike other Big Ten schools, Michigan had steadfastly resisted installing the high-priced luxury skyboxes that bring in additional revenues, and it had also prohibited all advertising in the football stadium.

And while revenues had grown 30 percent between 1994 and 1999, expenses had increased 70 percent. In the years when a Rose Bowl appearance could provide additional revenue, balance could be achieved. But in 1999, when the school worked to upgrade brick and mortar facilities and also spent $500,000 to launch a state-of-the-art Web site—at the same time that the men's basketball team had lost key players who had opted to join the NBA rather than finish their college careers—the budget gap widened. Recognizing the incongruity between steadily rising costs and wildly fluctuating sources of revenue, an internal review committee took issue with "the broadly held perception that we are insulated from the national trends, that the Athletic Department is a 'money machine,' and that any financial challenges simply reflect unfortunate specific decisions."

The budget gap was covered by drawing upon a $19 million reserve fund that had been built up over the years. Tighter budget controls were implemented, and the internal review committee also urged the department to seek other sources of private donations. But no one was naïve enough to believe that the department would be spared the pulls of market forces. If extraordinary athletic success and an impressive local and national fan base could not prevent a $2.8 million deficit, could any school reasonably expect college sports to produce the pot of gold of sports lore?[1]

"PURE AND SIMPLE": WOMEN'S LACROSSE AT WILLIAMS COLLEGE

> What will the lasting memories, especially for the
> seniors on this exceptional team, be of Williams?
> Many of these women have actually shed blood for
> the Purple and White. What will the motivation be
> for the underclass members next season?
> —A parent of a Williams College
> women's lacrosse player in an
> e-mail to President Harry Payne

On May 18, 1996, while members of the Amherst College women's lacrosse team were in Alabama playing in the NCAA Division III championship tournament, the players from the Williams team were in Williamstown taking their spring term final exams. Williams had defeated Amherst handily in the final game of the year and—despite a 12–0 undefeated season—had turned down an invitation to compete for the national championship. Following the rules of the New England Small Colleges Athletic Conference (NESCAC), the Williams administration had noted that the tournament was scheduled to take place at the same time as final exams and had chosen not to apply to NESCAC for a waiver to allow the team to participate. So while the women at Amherst—where the exam period did not conflict with the tournament—went on to lose to Trenton State College in the first round, the members of the Williams team, ranked number 2 nationally, went back to being full-time students. They had had a perfect season in a league that *Sports Illustrated* had celebrated as "pure and simple." Yet in the end simplicity proved elusive: "Every team dreams of being No. 1 in the country," the local paper reported, "for the Williams women's lacrosse team, it's been a nightmare."

Twenty-five years earlier, seeking refuge from the increasing intensity of intercollegiate athletics, the presidents of a number of small, highly selective colleges in New England—including Middlebury, Bowdoin, Amherst, and Hamilton—had created a league of schools that took the provision of sports for their students seriously, but not too seriously. And lest anyone confuse moderation with neglect, Williams by 1996 sponsored 31 varsity sports and 16 junior varsity teams (at a time when junior varsities across the country seemed headed toward extinction owing to budgetary pressures). So, how did a perfect lacrosse season end up as "a nightmare"?

In 1993, the presidents of the NESCAC schools loosened a long-standing restriction on postseason team play. Individual athletes—a tennis player or a swimmer—had been allowed to compete in postseason championships since the founding of the league. Teams, on the other hand, had been barred from participation out of concern that individual players might feel pressured by teammates or coaches to compete even though extending the season might interfere with their own academic priorities. The presidents of NESCAC changed this policy by endorsing a three-year experiment that delegated the initial decision concerning teams to the individual schools, although it still required a school to apply for a waiver if a tournament interfered with the school's exam schedule.

As the fall of 1995 came to a close, Williams recognized that the spring exam schedule would make it impossible for four teams (men's and women's lacrosse, women's softball, and men's baseball) to participate in postseason play, if they were to be invited. President Harry Payne and the faculty committee on educational priorities discussed whether the institution should apply to the league for a waiver and decided that it should not. "I think that there is real merit," Payne would later write, "to the idea that seasons come to an end at the examination time, and I think that asking the faculty to negotiate examination formats and schedules with the several dozen athletes would endanger the extraordinary tolerance which faculty have already shown in our unusually expansive athletics environment." The spring seasons were launched, and, as everyone hoped, the teams were extremely successful. The success of the women's lacrosse team, however, reopened the question of participation in the national championship tournament.

The administration was bombarded with e-mail, letters, and anger. "My passion for this cause," one of the lacrosse players wrote to Payne, "and my love of the sport of lacrosse, my teammates, and my coaches far outweighs my desire to demonstrate an attitude of courtesy and respect which is not in my heart. . . . You have made a poor decision. You have crushed a dream. You have denied myself, my teammates, and my coaches the opportunity of a lifetime." At a meeting in the president's office, when President Payne suggested that this was one of those times that everyone, having heard the other side's reasoning, would simply have to agree to disagree, one of the players responded: "President Payne, I've heard your reasons, and your reasons are shit!"

When NESCAC was formed in the early 1970s, the Williams president at the time, John Sawyer, recognized the strain of allowing schools to decide for themselves the question of postseason competition. He wrote to the president of Bowdoin to express his relief that the presidents were in agreement about postseason team play: "While there is minor grumbling from time to time, we have weathered the major storm on this question and I, for one, am not eager to invite it annually."

But thirty years later, the storm clouds had reappeared. For the talented women relegated to watching as teams they had defeated were allowed to advance simply because the other institutions in the league had set different priorities or simply had different exam schedules, the spring of 1996 was a time of great disappointment. Parents who had watched their daughters strive for success, and achieve it, saw the ultimate prize denied them: "I respectfully request," wrote one, "that you change your mind so as to avert the serious negative consequences of your inaction. Please decide to decide." Other parents and lacrosse alumnae wrote to trustees calling for the ouster of President Payne for his unwillingness to apply for the waiver. On campus, petitions were signed urging an exception to the rule, and the students on the team obtained signatures from all of their professors indicating that they would allow the players to make alternative exam arrangements. The softball team had also made the playoffs, and it was unclear until the end of the season whether the men's lacrosse team would also qualify. Allowing the women to make their own exam arrangements would open the door to allowing all the teams to do so. "Flexibility is a virtue," President Payne responded to one parent. "But," he added, "principled consistency is also a virtue, especially in an environment where 2,000 young adults are watching and testing boundaries all the time, no matter where those boundaries are drawn."

Despite the threat of lawsuits, the administration held firm, the tempest of the spring passed, and Williams adjourned for the summer. For a few students, the experience tainted their entire college experience, but for most, normalcy was restored. "No matter how you decide," wrote one parent, "I support your right to decide. . . . Moreover, if you decide to let them play, I promise not to write you my thoughts about grade inflation and [the] soft curriculum, which would be term paper length!" Though it subsided quickly, and though many other teams had accepted the administration's rules without protest, this storm had been real.[2]

"THE FUTURE IS NOW": NORTHWESTERN REBUILDS AROUND THE ROSE BOWL

> At Northwestern, an institution founded on a commitment to the highest order of excellence, superior achievement is expected in every aspect of University life. Athletics is no exception. The coaches demand it. The administration supports it. The student-athletes demonstrate it. . . . The future is now.
>
> —Brochure for "The Campaign for Athletic Excellence"

On a cold March morning in 1995, two months into his presidency at Northwestern University, Henry Bienen was given a tour of Dyche Stadium, where the school has been playing football since 1926. "It was a real eye-opener," Bienen later recalled. The stadium was small by contemporary standards, holding only 50,000 fans. Northwestern had been spending approximately $250,000 a year patching holes left by huge chunks of falling concrete. In amassing a $5 million fund for the eventual repair of the stadium, Bienen's predecessor, Arnold Weber, noted that the restrooms were "barely suitable for a third world refugee camp." Nevertheless, a good argument could have been made that letting the stadium complete its arc toward becoming a ruin would be only appropriate for the home of the Northwestern football team.

Since 1971, the Wildcats had had a combined record of 46 wins, 203 losses, and 4 ties. Included in this history was the infamous 34-game losing streak of the early 1980s and a more recent 0–11 season in 1989. Competing with the University of Chicago in the classroom and with Ohio State on the gridiron was an extremely difficult challenge. With an undergraduate population of only 7,400 students, the Wildcats bore the scars of trying to maintain a team able to compete within the Big Ten and still meet Northwestern's academic standards.

The finances of trying to keep pace were even more daunting. An obvious hurdle—and one that assures that, no matter what level of competitive success is achieved, the athletic program at Northwestern will never be a true money-maker—is the fact that an athletic scholarship at North-western costs the school $30,000 in forgone tuition and fees, while at the public universities scholarships cost the school much less (in most cases around $5,000). Then there are the even larger one-time costs of reserv-ing a seat at the table. By 1989, every school in the Big Ten had an indoor practice facility, many built with bonds issued directly by state legislatures.

Top-quality facilities were not just important for increasingly intense year-round training, they were also weapons in the war to recruit the next star linebacker: "No matter what the adults around him say," Northwest-ern coach Gary Barnett noted, "the athlete can see only four years into the future." With the enthusiasm of a new president and the support of the board of trustees (two of whom pledged multimillion-dollar gifts), the go-ahead was given in the spring of 1995 to launch "The Campaign for Athletic Excellence."

On September 2, 1995, the Northwestern University football team per-formed the highly unlikely act of defeating Notre Dame. This victory, cel-ebrated as "the upset of the century" by the *Chicago Sun-Times*, was only the beginning. Upset after upset followed—including dramatic victories over Ohio State, Michigan, and Penn State. The incredible 10–1 season culminated in Northwestern's first Rose Bowl appearance in 46 years. Such a season seemed impossible to reconcile with the history of a team that only a decade earlier had set a Division IA record for futility by go-ing almost three seasons without a single victory. Three weeks into the miracle season, the campaign to raise $22 million for the new indoor practice facility and for renovating the stadium, which had been quietly launched in May, was formally unveiled. Even with a few miracles to the team's credit, it took fans a little while to warm up to the idea of their team as world-beaters: the home game after the Notre Dame victory did not sell out.

The Rose Bowl season captured the imagination of college sports fans all over the country. Northwestern's backers expected it to play by big-time rules now that it had had a taste of glory. Barnett signed a ten-year contract worth a reported $500,000 a year. And, with such success on the field, the athletics campaign that had been initiated before the dream sea-son began charged full speed ahead. Recognizing that its teams were now competing for entertainment dollars against big-time professional fran-chises, and knowing that corporate fans were used to a high level of lux-ury when watching, say, the Bulls or the Bears, the school added a new Stadium Club with more than 300 indoor theater-type seats, a buffet, and private restrooms.

Some grumbling was inevitable. Longtime fans who had endured years of gray skies, rain, and humbling defeats were now called upon to pay higher prices for the seats they had loyally staked out for years. About

20 percent of the student seats were moved, since students usually stood for almost the whole game and would obscure the view from some of the other seats—seats that had been empty when the team was losing. But, by and large, people were willing—eager, in fact—to help pay for the rejuvenation.

In the end, the entire stadium was renovated, and the good times continued, with a Citrus Bowl appearance in 1996. But along with such success came reminders of the downside of playing big-time sports: two athletes who had been involved in gambling in 1994 (before the Rose Bowl season had even taken place) later lied to a grand jury and were eventually indicted on federal gambling charges in 1997. Reality set in on the field as well, as the team finished 3–9 in 1998 and 3–8 in 1999. Coach Barnett left in 1999 for the University of Colorado. The question of what might have been—of how the campaign might have fared had it not been swept along by two incredible seasons—cannot be answered by looking in Evanston, where the administration had long recognized that it would never be possible to make money on athletics with a stadium with a low seating capacity and the high costs of forgone tuition.

But elsewhere the notion that "you have to spend money to make money" has a storied history, with new chapters added annually. In an article about Tulane's football team, a writer for the *New Orleans Times-Picayune* wrote: "But at least one can look across the landscape and find hope. Northwestern, a university with academic credentials second to none, is headed for the Rose Bowl as the Big Ten champion." The message—Northwestern did it, so why can't we?—illustrates both that hope springs eternal and that the wrong lessons can be learned from a real-time case study. In 1999, Tulane did in fact go undefeated—only to find that it still fell far short of breaking even financially. A commitment to "the highest order of excellence" in all endeavors can be very expensive.[3]

"WRESTLERS ARE DIFFERENT. . . . WRESTLERS ARE FIGHTERS": BUDGET CONSTRAINTS AND TITLE IX AT PRINCETON

On March 17, 1993, Princeton University announced that it would discontinue its varsity wrestling program, citing "constraints on the department's resources, both financial and in terms of admissions."

To many parents paying $25,000 a year in tuition, room, and board, Princeton's decision to act within budgetary constraints probably made good sense. To an admissions department charged with selecting from among the best-prepared high school seniors in the country, the prospect of not having to reserve a place for a 118-pound competitor who could also fit seamlessly into Princeton's academic community may have been a relief. To faculty members who had watched as the University strained to balance its budget, the decision must have seemed an eminently just sharing of the burden. In fact, on campus the University's decision met with little reaction. But, as one alumnus would later write in a letter to President Harold Shapiro, "Wrestlers are different. . . . Wrestlers are fighters." The emotional and exhausting match that ensued illustrates why decisions related to athletics represent such stressful terrain for colleges and universities of all kinds.

"Why wrestling?" those who cared deeply about Princeton wrestling inevitably asked. Unlike the wrestler who enters the arena with a strategy, knowing his own strengths and weaknesses and those of his opponent but relying on instinct and improvisation to adjust to the situation (literally) at hand, institutions rely on a very different decision-making process. Charged with carrying out a mission—or in truth a wide range of missions—and faced with balancing the interests of students, faculty, and alumni/ae, administrations make decisions deliberately, even laboriously.

At the time of the decision, Princeton (like other Ivy League institutions) offered many more sports than virtually any other school in the country—17 men's sports and 16 for women. Unlike athletic powerhouses that sometimes concentrate their financial resources on the bigtime sports of basketball and football and often sponsor only the NCAA minimum number of 14 teams, the Ivy philosophy has been to sponsor a wide array of sports, from crew and fencing to volleyball and ice hockey. Although the schools adhere to an "old-fashioned" stance of not offering athletic scholarships, this emphasis on broad participation nevertheless requires a tremendous commitment. The costs associated with recruiting, coaching, and equipping the teams and transporting them to their contests around the Northeast and around the country are absorbed by the University. Although Princeton remained committed to this philosophy and to bearing these costs—both the financial costs and the opportunity costs of reserving places in the freshman class for goalies, shortstops, and midfielders—the administration had decided that, in a period of budgetary restraint, it was necessary to establish limits. Moreover, Princeton had an obligation to comply with Title IX, and eliminating one all-male sport would help redress the imbalance in the number of men and women athletes.

To the former wrestlers—who signaled their vehement opposition to the decision by writing letters, waving banners at graduation, and threatening never to support the University again—the decision to drop wrestling seemed cruel. They also argued that certain former Princeton wrestlers (including Trustee Donald Rumsfeld) had achieved prominence in government, business, and other fields.

The media seized upon the story as an opportunity to berate the University and academia in general: "Then again," one columnist sardonically asked, "why should the president of one of the nation's leading universities be expected to have any common sense?" President Shapiro announced that he would review the decision to drop wrestling. He did so, and in June he and the board of trustees backed the decision, despite a renewed bombardment of protest from some wrestling alumni. Subsequently, even as the trustees set out to review every aspect of the University's athletics program, the wrestling issue refused to fade away. The Friends of Princeton Wrestling, a booster group that had historically provided extra support for the program, launched a campaign to raise $2 million that they planned to offer to the University as a separate endowment to fund the wrestling program.

This offer confronted Princeton with a difficult dilemma. Even alumni who cared little about wrestling found it difficult to understand why those who *did* care could not choose to support financially that which the University had decided it could not afford. The reasoning was as follows: Although the University had accepted gifts to endow the costs of other teams, these funds always remained under the direction of the University and were not allowed to steer the course of policy. Bringing back a program that would be financed solely (in terms of coverage of direct costs) with restricted funds represented a fundamentally different approach to the always-difficult issues raised by targeted gifts. To the University, accepting a gift that determined policy outside the framework of the regular decision-making process would set a dangerous precedent. Yet to those who cared about wrestling, the administration's initial rejection of their offer seemed spiteful; it made the original decision to drop the program for budgetary reasons appear to be a ruse—a cover for some deeper hidden agenda.

Frustrations mounted, and what had seemed like a difficult but by no means unprecedented programmatic decision (in fact 20 percent of all NCAA institutions, including Yale and Dartmouth, had dropped wrestling) now demanded a great deal of attention and created no small amount of tension for the president and the trustees. The University faced an attack not from the outside, but from its own alumni. "You can build all the Centers for Human Values you want," one angry alumnus wrote, alluding to the University's prestigious center for ethics, "but if you don't practice what you preach, it will all be for naught." For President Shapiro—who had overseen one of the world's great sports powerhouses as president of the University of Michigan before coming to the non-scholarship environment of Princeton—the intensity of the backlash must have been startling.

Universities are no doubt well served by those who feel passionately, whether as students competing for victory on the playing fields or as alumni/ae thriving in the world. And yet, as Princeton learned, powerful passions can—in a moment—be redirected. One alumnus wrote, "I will not again give to Annual Giving unless and until the sport is restored to full varsity status. I will donate instead to the Brown or Pennsylvania wrestling teams." In that extreme case, loyalty to wrestling clearly outweighed loyalty to the institution. In truth, many of those upset by the decision only wanted Princeton to be the Princeton they knew and loved—a Princeton with a varsity wrestling program. At the same time, other wrestling alumni supported the administration and even sought to have other varsity sports reduced to a simpler state.

In the end, Princeton agreed to offer a "self-funded" varsity wrestling program with no admission slots and no University financial support. That is the status of the program today, and a wary détente prevails.[4]

———

These institutions—the University of Michigan, Williams College, Northwestern University, and Princeton University—represent four of the five types of institutions in our study: Division IA public universities, Division III coeducational liberal arts colleges, Division IA private universities, and Division IAA Ivy League universities. (We also include the selective women's colleges, which have not, at the time of our writing, faced the same tempests over athletics that are portrayed here.) The four snapshots presented in this Prelude provide a starting point for a study of the role that athletic programs play on the campuses of selective colleges and universities. However, stories are by no means the same as organized evidence, and in this book we seek to provide empirical data that could be useful as trustees, alumni/ae, students, applicants, parents, and other interested parties debate how best to retain that which is fun and exciting about college sports while negotiating their way through the inevitable tensions and tradeoffs.

As we have seen in the Prelude, sports are taken very seriously in this country, and not just by those who cheer for professional teams. We recognize, of course, that other countries take their sports very seriously as well. As we began this project in 1994, Colombian soccer star Andres Escobar was murdered after he had inadvertently deflected a ball into his own goal during the World Cup finals. But no other country has anything resembling America's college sports programs. In this book, however, we are less interested in how seriously Americans take sports *as sports* than in the question of how intercollegiate athletic programs affect not only colleges and universities but also the signals that these important institutions send to prospective students and their parents, secondary schools, and society at large.

Our title, *The Game of Life,* is—like "the level playing field," "hitting a home run," or "overcoming hurdles"—one of the many images that link sports and the larger society. Life in general is, in many ways, structured like a game, and although colleges have a major impact on who wins and who loses in this game, they also play a more fundamental role. Beyond admitting students, educating them, and sending them into the world with impressive credentials, these institutions help to shape our collective interpretation of what the game itself is all about, what its rules are, and how we as a society define winning and losing.

INTENT, SCOPE, AND METHODS OF THE STUDY

"Intercollegiate athletics" is not an abstract subject. The story of college sports is an amalgamation of the memories, scars, and passions of thousands upon thousands of teams, players, and fans. For us at least, insight into the questions we examine in this book is conveyed most immediately through episodes like the ones recounted in the Prelude. These episodes crystallize many of the issues that this book explores. We see that intercollegiate athletics programs spark emotionally charged debate at every point in the range: from campus playing fields at Division III colleges like Swarthmore and Oberlin to celebrity programs at Division IA universities like Stanford and UNC–Chapel Hill. The issues vary, but when conflict arises—be it over rescheduling exams to pursue a lacrosse championship or constructing luxury skyboxes—emotions run high, and the school is forced to ask whether the proposed direction is in line with, or in conflict with, its core institutional mission.

These introductory stories also introduce a number of the myths that are associated with athletics. (While in colloquial usage *myth* means a false tale, a "myth" is better understood as a belief that powerfully captures the imagination and may or may not be rooted in fact. Hence, the mythical reputation of Warren Buffet in the investor community is different from the myth of the fountain of youth.) Without getting ahead of the research that we present in the rest of the book, we can see already in the Prelude some of the myths that permeate college sports and the facts that pull those myths back to earthbound realities:

- "College sports programs make money." If the University of Michigan can lose money on sports, this myth certainly deserves a closer look.
- "Playing sports builds character." Many of us admire the integrity, work ethic, and social commitment exemplified by the Bill Bradleys of this world. At the same time, widely publicized incidents of cheating and violent behavior, as well as conflicts like those at Williams and Princeton, remind us to consider exactly what kind of character organized athletics either builds or at least promotes.
- "Schools worry about their sports programs for the sake of the alumni/ae." In the Princeton wrestling episode, we saw that one specific group of alumni/ae does indeed care a great deal about the sports program. But are they representative of the alumni/ae in general?
- "Good schools can play the game differently." The Northwestern experience shows that it is difficult for any school to be insulated from competitive pressures, both on the field and in building and maintaining the field house. The attitudes of former Princeton wrestlers and Williams lacrosse players (and their parents) indicate that sports is taken seriously at all levels of play; intensity is not limited to big-time programs.
- "Gender equity is giving women new opportunities." This statement is unquestionably true, as we see from both the increasing number of women's teams and the highly visible success of outstanding women athletes. The wrestling episode is, however, one reminder of the tensions that arise when a rationing of opportunities is necessary. In the Williams episode, we see that there are two sides to having created new opportunities for women to take sports as seriously as the men have.
- "Today's athletes are like those of the past." This myth, implicit in the defense of their program by former Princeton wrestlers, argues

that the paths followed by athletes of the past can be used to predict the outcomes for a different group of students who play sports today. Since so much else has changed in 50 years, it is worth asking whether the athletes of the past are similar to or different from the athletes of today. Are the values of the "good old days" still evident? And were the "good old days" really so good?

The goal of this book is to present data that bear on these myths, before drawing conclusions about how schools might best take advantage of the positive emotions that sports evoke without endangering the core of their educational missions. These episodes remind us that colleges and universities are dependent upon a broad range of constituencies (students, parents, fans, alumni/ae, staff) and that, over the long term, policy decisions affecting admissions play a crucial role in *creating* one of these constituencies—the alumni/ae of the future. The students who attended a college, had various experiences while they were there, and continue to identify with the school throughout their lives constitute an important reality of the institution, in the same way that the buildings, the faculty, and the fight songs do. In part for this reason, we spend a great deal of time in this book on the students who attended the institutions in our study—from the time that they opened their acceptance letters to the times, long after they left the campus, when they sent either checks or angry letters to the president's office.

In order to understand how intercollegiate athletics, in its various forms, affects the ways in which colleges and universities discharge their missions, we decided to study a set of schools that are, in many ways, similar as educational institutions but that have chosen to compete athletically at different levels of play. A woman interested in studying political science might elect to go to Bryn Mawr or to Duke, and such a choice need not entail any dramatic difference in the curriculum available to her. But if she happens also to want to play basketball, it is clear immediately that the two worlds she is considering are radically different.

The schools that make up the institutional population of our study are all academically selective. Being selective means that they receive many more applications from well-qualified students than they have places in their entering classes and thus must pick and choose among applicants on a variety of criteria, including athletic talent. By national standards, the freshman classes that they admit have very strong academic qualifications (with average SAT scores, for example, that are well above national norms, and with large numbers of high school valedictorians and National Merit Scholarship winners). The 30 schools represented in the study are grouped below by type:[1]

Division IA private universities

Duke University
Georgetown University
   (basketball only)
Northwestern University
Rice University
Stanford University
Tulane University
University of Notre Dame
Vanderbilt University

Division IA public universities

Miami University (Ohio)
Pennsylvania State University
University of Michigan
   (Ann Arbor)
University of North Carolina
   (Chapel Hill)

*Division IAA Ivy
League universities*

Columbia University
Princeton University
University of Pennsylvania
Yale University

*Division III coed
liberal arts colleges*

Denison University
Hamilton College
Kenyon College
Oberlin College
Swarthmore College
Wesleyan University
Williams College

Division III universities

Emory University
Tufts University
Washington University
   (St. Louis)

Division III women's colleges

Barnard College
Bryn Mawr College
Smith College
Wellesley College

   This book focuses on these academically selective schools for several reasons. First, despite the great differences among them, all of these institutions participate in a collegiate athletic culture that is tied to Little League and high school sports and is related as well to the shared sports values of our national culture. Second, whether in terms of debates over "the Great Books" or in discussions of how to provide opportunities to women and minorities, many of these institutions are looked to for leadership within higher education. We believe that athletics provides a portal of sorts into other issues affecting this set of colleges and universities. In the end, this book is as much about educational values and the missions of these institutions as it is about sports.

   There is also a third reason for focusing on these schools. Working intensively with this particular group of academically selective institutions has the important advantage of permitting us to compare the nature and effects of radically different kinds of athletic programs (for example, football at Vanderbilt versus football at Oberlin College) without leaving a world of shared academic expectations and requirements. That is, although the admissions standards and academic programs at these schools differ in many respects, they are sufficiently similar that reasonable comparisons can be made across types of schools and, as it were, "levels of play." Thus we can examine how much it matters if a school elects to compete at the Division IA level or in Division III, and whether the Division IAA Ivies really are an intermediate case. One thesis of the study is that there is more continuity along this gradient than is generally understood, with, for example, patterns of recruitment, admissions, and coaching spreading from the big-time programs to the Ivies, and then on to the Division III coed liberal arts colleges.

But at the same time that we want to emphasize many of these similarities, we also want to recognize that the most wrenching issues that confront presidents and trustees are very different at the different levels of play. As the president emeritus of Northwestern University, Arnold Weber, pointed out in commenting on the manuscript, "The practices and leading issues in the Division IA schools are qualitatively different from those of the other institutions [in the study]." Weber is referring, of course, to the fact that big-time athletic programs involve greater risks of scandals and harm to institutional reputations than the corresponding programs in the Ivies and at the coed liberal arts colleges; on the other hand, the recruitment of large numbers of athletes can have more serious effects on admissions and on campus ethos at the smaller schools. These two themes, of similarity and difference, run through the study.

We are very much aware that these 30 colleges and universities are by no means representative of American higher education. They were not chosen with that aim in mind. One of the enormous advantages of this country's system of higher education is its institutional diversity, and the analysis presented here is relevant only in small part to the large number of academic institutions that are less selective than this group. Many of these other institutions offer excellent academic programs and outstanding athletic programs. One reason for limiting the study to a group of 30 institutions is that sharpening the focus in this way has allowed us to work with extremely detailed data on some 90,000 undergraduate students, athletes and others, who entered these colleges at three points in time: the fall of 1951 (thought of by some as "the good old days"), the fall of 1976 (after the composition of the classes at many of these schools had been altered in the wake of the civil rights movement and the spread of coeducation), and the fall of 1989 (the most recent year for which we could collect data on entering students who then could be followed through college and into the early stages of their careers and post-college lives).

The institutional component of the database was compiled from individual student records and contains detailed data on admissions qualifications, fields of study, grades received, and whether or not a student graduated, as well as such demographic data as race, gender, and family background. For many of these same students, we also have extensive survey data that track graduate education, career choices and earnings, civic involvement, family circumstances, and retrospective expressions of attitudes toward the education they received. All of this information and more is contained in a restricted-access database called "College and Beyond" that was built by The Andrew W. Mellon Foundation with the cooperation of the 30 individual schools and the former students who participated in the survey in very large numbers (overall response rates were over 75 percent).[2] We have also made extensive use of linked sets of data provided by the College Board and by UCLA's Cooperative Institutional Research Program (CIRP), which surveyed many of these same individuals when they entered college in 1976 or 1989.

As is evident from this brief description of the database, this study is highly quantitative. The episode of the angry wrestlers illustrates why this approach is needed. When the crisis erupted, the contestants on both sides naturally sought to frame their arguments in as convincing a manner as they could. What they found was a wellspring of strong emotions, powerful anecdotal testimony, long-accepted mythology—and a surprising dearth of facts, let alone empirically driven analyses. In a realm like sports, where schools compete intensely, there is often a reluctance to share data (and sometimes even to collect them). As a consequence, policy makers have generally had to settle for impressionistic answers to key questions.

From the start, one of our primary objectives has been to test various assumptions and myths against a large set of reliable data not heretofore available. We wanted to do all that we could to move beyond what might be called "the anecdote range." At the same time, we recognize the power of myth in our lives, and certainly in the way all of us think about sports. We have tried, therefore, to combine an empirical analysis of propositions that can be tested[3] with a qualitative examination of ideas and feelings that are no less important because they live in a different realm. Both our interpretation of the data and that of the reader will undoubtedly be shaded by which myths about college sports—and about "the Game of Life"—hold us in their sway. To deny the power of myths and even of their cousin, prejudice, would be foolish, and we certainly do not suggest that, despite all of the data presented, this book contains "just the facts."

In the main part of this book, we examine some (but not all) of the myths that feed our collective passions about college sports by bringing empirical data to bear on the questions at hand. Other myths we simply leave alone since we are unable to prove or disprove their validity. Although we are no more capable than others of checking our personal prejudices at the door before pursuing empirical research, we have done our best to reserve most normative judgments and our proposals for future directions until the last two chapters.

Next, a brief word about language. We have chosen to resist some of the standard terminology associated with college sports. So, for example, whereas the NCAA is adamant about referring to students who play college sports as "student-athletes," we do not use this term, since everyone who is enrolled at a college or university is a student. Also, the sports of football and men's basketball (and sometimes ice hockey) are often referred to as "revenue sports," but since these sports do not always generate revenue (especially at the coed liberal arts colleges in our study), we do not refer to them in this way. Rather, we refer to them as "High Profile" sports and to all of the other sports as "Lower Profile." Of course the characteristics of various sports will change over time, and women's basketball and perhaps both men's and women's soccer give every indication of moving into the High Profile category. Still, during the period covered by this study (the mid-1950s through the early 1990s), football and men's basketball clearly garnered more attention than other sports, and we see in the data clear differences between the athletes who played these sports and other athletes.

ORGANIZATION OF THE STUDY

Chapter 1 reviews the historical development of intercollegiate athletics at the types of colleges and universities represented in the study.

The next three chapters examine the characteristics and experiences of male students at these colleges, comparing those who played football, men's basketball, and men's ice hockey with those who played other sports as well as with the rest of their male classmates. Chapter 2 profiles male athletes and other students at the time of admission (in 1951, 1976, or 1989). It describes the numbers of recruited athletes and includes estimates of the substantial changes over time in the "admissions advantage" enjoyed by recruited athletes as well as the increasing gaps in SAT scores. Chapter 3 analyzes the experiences of these men in college, with special attention paid to how they have fared academically and their choices of major field of study. We also discuss the degree to which athletes are integrated into the campus community or largely isolated from other students. Chapter 4 examines the differences in jobs and earnings of former athletes and other students and explains these differences in terms of both factors present when students were admitted and their ex-

periences in college (including the number of years they played intercollegiate sports and the level at which they competed).

The next group of chapters poses similar questions about women athletes at these schools. Chapter 5 is a short history of opportunities for
women to play college sports. Chapters 6 to 8 chart the admissions
records, the in-college, and post-college experiences of women who entered college in 1976 and 1989. In their totality, these chapters offer a
look at the very early years and adolescence of the gender equity movement. A key question that runs through this section is whether women
athletes are mirroring the experiences of the men who went before them,
or whether the increased emphasis on women's athletics has been
marked by different approaches and different outcomes.

Chapter 9 examines the leadership contributed by the male and female
athletes who attended these colleges and universities, both in their vocations and more generally. Particular attention is paid to the relationship
between self-perceptions of leadership and actual contributions made by
various groups of athletes and their classmates.

Chapter 10, "Giving Back," first examines the gift-giving histories of
alumni/ae who were and were not intercollegiate athletes. It then considers the attitudes toward intercollegiate sports of the small group of
alumni/ae who contribute a very large fraction of the dollars received by
leading colleges and universities. The chapter concludes with an analysis
of the proposition that winning records of football teams affect the overall rates and amounts of giving by graduates.

Chapter 11 addresses the complex but important issues that collectively
define the financial equation for intercollegiate sports. Central questions
include: What does it really cost to mount an intercollegiate program at
different levels of competition (Division IA versus the Ivies versus the coed
liberal arts colleges)? How costly are the Lower Profile sports as compared
with sports like football and basketball, and how do these differences vary
by level of competition? To what extent do additional revenues generated
by big-time programs offset their expenses and even help defray other
costs? How have the sources of revenue changed, and are the financial
prospects of intercollegiate athletics improving or worsening?

The concluding part of the book consists of three interrelated chapters. Chapter 12 summarizes the book's empirical findings that make up
the factual bedrock of the study. In Chapter 13, we step back and take
stock. We begin by providing our interpretation of the meaning of the
underlying patterns, noting especially what we see as growing points of
conflict between the athletic enterprise and educational values. Then we
discuss the underlying forces that, in combination, have led to increasing
intensification of intercollegiate athletics and to an ever-widening "ath-

letic divide." Finally, in Chapter 14, we consider the impediments to making changes of any kind and then, against this backdrop, present a series of propositions describing future directions that we believe deserve consideration.

The first appendix contains a series of detailed "scorecards" to which we refer in presenting data for separate groupings of schools, different types of sports, and different time periods. This level of detail will appeal to some readers (as box scores do!), but not to everyone. A second appendix contains tables of additional supplementary data.

OUR PERSONAL PERSPECTIVE ON SPORTS

Everyone who talks or writes about athletics starts out with certain preconceptions, and we would not want to begin presenting facts and arguments without declaring ourselves. Both of us have long enjoyed sports immensely, as players and as spectators. One of us (Shulman) won the prize for being the most active intramural athlete in his residential college at Yale. The other author (Bowen) was captain of his Denison University tennis team and the winner of various Ohio championships— albeit at a time when the quality of play was nothing like what it is now. Today we share a passion, as spectators, for college basketball, pro football, Mets-Cardinals games, and U.S. Open tennis championships.

One of our great concerns is that some of the directions in which intercollegiate sports have been moving in recent years threaten the pleasures (and the values) that we associate with playing, competing, and—at least on occasion—winning. We recognize, and respect, the different interpretations that can be placed on the data that we assemble, and we recognize too that some readers (perhaps especially recruited athletes) will disagree with our point of view and our conclusions. But we want to be explicit in stating that we think of ourselves as "pro-athletics," not as "anti-athletics" (to the degree that anyone wants to put us in one or another of these oversimplified compartments). In our view, the main threat to the continuing vitality of college sports is its increasing professionalization, not its neglect, and it is our hope that this book will strengthen the role that athletics plays on college campuses. There are, we believe, respects in which current practices and trends should be reconsidered and in some instances modified, but we also believe—and believe strongly— that changes should be made within a framework that recognizes that many people derive great pleasure from throwing balls, working hard as part of a team, glorying in a hard-fought win, and, yes, reflecting on the inevitable disappointments that are also part of competing.

ACKNOWLEDGMENTS

Writing can be a true team sport. We have derived enormous pleasure from working together for six years in building the database, putting it to work in writing an earlier book on the long-term outcomes of race-sensitive admissions (*The Shape of the River*), and thinking through the endless possible directions for this project. Part of the allure of college sports is that playing together is often infinitely more productive—and more fun—than thinking too long by one's self. Work can be play when you enjoy your teammates as thoroughly as we do.

The team required to conduct research of this scope has been large and exceptionally hard working. We begin by thanking our collaborators, Lauren Meserve and Roger Schonfeld. These two multitalented players have been stalwart in their service to the project. Both learned to master the intricacies of the College and Beyond database and survived what must have seemed like endless iterations in working with a mammoth database containing countless nooks, crannies, and quirks. Their willingness to produce streams of data, track down countless half-remembered references, and join in thinking through complex issues has been invaluable. We could not have written this book without their hard work and good spirit.

Among other colleagues at the Mellon Foundation who have been stalwart teammates, we must single out Stacy Berg Dale. Stacy was captain of the women's tennis team at the University of Michigan, and she has helped in countless ways by bringing to the project both the talents of a clear-eyed econometrician and her own experiences as an undergraduate: she has been a relentless advocate for the lessons that sports teaches. We want to record our special thanks to Mary Pat McPherson, Thomas Nygren, Dennis Sullivan, and Harriet Zuckerman. These sturdy souls, along with Lauren, Roger, and Stacy, have not only talked sports with us for over five years, they have also provided excellent counsel on sample sizes, selection bias, opportunities for women, and how intercollegiate athletics relates to the purposes of higher education. Special thanks are also due to three other colleagues: Susan Anderson, who cheerfully accepted the Herculean task of putting the entire manuscript into final form for Princeton University Press after having helped in so many other ways all through the study; Doug Mills, who did very demanding work on statistical problems associated with the database in the earlier stages of the study and helped in the careful formulation and testing of numerous hypotheses; and Sarah Levin, who arrived at the Foundation just in time to participate in the final stages of copyediting the manuscript and correcting as many errors as we could find.

We are fortunate to have benefited from the help provided by an unusual array of college- and university-based scholars. Those who read large parts of the manuscript (in some cases, all of it) include Derek Bok, Nancy Cantor, Tom Kane, Michael McPherson, Harold Shapiro, Arnold Weber, and Gordon Winston. Others who have gone over specific chapters include Paul Benacerraf, Robert Kasdin, Robert K. Merton, Allen Sanderson, John Siegfried, Sarah Turner, Gary Walters, and Gil Whitaker. Readers who contributed telling comments and revealing stories include a number of former and current college presidents (in addition to Presidents Bok, McPherson, Shapiro, and Weber, already mentioned): Henry Bienen, Colin Campbell, Robert Edwards, Sheldon Hackney, Paul Hardin, Richard Lyman, Hank Payne, and Hunter Rawlings.

Over the years that we have been working on this project, countless others have helped us understand the issues better, and their combined knowledge of these questions has vastly exceeded our ability to incorporate their insights into our analysis. These include one former Heisman Trophy winner (Richard Kazmaier); a lawyer and university trustee who has been directly involved in the oversight of intercollegiate athletics (Taylor Reveley); several admissions directors or deans (Fred Hargadon, Janet Lavin-Rapelye, Tom Parker, and Rick Shaw); and those who were or are active in athletic administration and coaching (Jim Balgooyen, Sandy Barbour, David Benjamin, Albert Carlson, William Carmody, Chris Kennedy, Ted Leland, James Litvack, Jeff Orleans, Larry Scheiderer, and Tom Wright). We hasten to add that none of these individuals should be blamed in any way for the shortcomings of the study or for its point of view; indeed, a number of them have been especially helpful precisely because they have been candid in expressing their disagreements with one or more of our principal arguments.

Credit also must be given to the still bigger team of people associated with the participating colleges, without whom the College and Beyond database would never have been built. Neither this book nor *The Shape of the River* would have been possible without them. They worked very hard to create a resource that, we hope, will make a contribution to our understanding of what these institutions have done, are doing, and may consider doing in the future. Among this group, we would like to thank Joe Bray, Tony Broh, Rena Cheskis-Gold, Harry DeMik, Rebecca Dixon, Jennifer Potter Hayes, Martin Israel, Marian Pagano, Ross Peacock, John Pothier, Myrtis Powell, John Romano, Dan Shapiro, Dawn Terkla-Geronimo, Lorett Treese, Leona Urbish, Bill Wieler, Ann Wright, and Lew Wyman. Others whose guidance, assistance, and insights helped us carry out the research and think through tough questions were Tom Burish, Steve Christakos, Royce Flippin, Harry Gotwals, Richard Hiskey, Lynn Imergoot, Rob Oden, Peter Philip, Debbie Prentice, Lloyd Suttle, John Thelin, and Ron Vanden Dorpel. Many other people contributed stories or ideas that have shaped our opinions (including those who participated in telephone interviews), and, although we cannot list them all, we appreciate their contributions to the views that we have developed over the course of the study. We are also grateful to others who nurtured the project: Steve and Janet, and Noel.

Once again, we are grateful for the fine work done by Princeton University Press in bringing this book to publication. The director of the Press, Walter Lippincott, and our editor, Peter Dougherty, have been strong supporters of the project from its earliest days. They have contributed good ideas and demonstrated remarkable forbearance. Their associates at the Press and at Princeton Editorial Associates, including Neil Litt, Peter Strupp, and their respective teams, have attended to the details of production and publication in exemplary fashion.

It is also our pleasure to thank the trustees of The Andrew W. Mellon Foundation for their steady support of our research and for allowing us the privilege of making our own mistakes. The analysis and the conclusions in this book are solely our responsibility.

Because they understood that we were off at the word processors rather than on the tennis court or plugged into the television, our greatest thanks are due to those who may (or may not!) have wished to have us around a little more: Mary Ellen, David, and Karen; and Katie and Kaiulani. They have our thanks for so much—encouragement, humor, curiosity—but above all for patience.

THE GAME OF LIFE

The Institutionalization and Regulation of College Sports in Historical Perspective

Let the good work go on—but who the devil is making you all this trouble? Football, in my opinion, is best at its worst. I do not believe in all this namby-pamby talk, and I hope the game will not be emasculated and robbed of its heroic qualities. People who don't like football as now played might like whist——advise them to try that.
—Frederic Remington, writing to Walter Camp upon the establishment of the Camp Commission on Brutality in Football (1894)

It was once possible for college sports administrators on the one hand, and university presidents and trustees on the other, to evade responsibility for the difficulties of intercollegiate athletics. Each side could plausibly claim the other possessed the authority to act. That claim no longer holds water.
—Knight Commission on Intercollegiate Athletics, *A New Beginning for a New Century* (1993)

SOME PEOPLE love college sports and others hate them. Some who feel passionately about colleges and universities regard their sports programs as their best feature; others regard them as "just part of the scene"—accepted and generally appreciated, but not of primary importance; still others believe that athletic programs are completely irrelevant. One fact is clear to all: however one feels about them, intercollegiate athletic programs have become thoroughly institutionalized within American higher education. How did these programs become such a consequential part of what these colleges do? Has the "fit" between the educational missions of the institutions and the nature of the athletic programs changed over time? How has the place of athletics within the institutional structure of colleges and universities been affected by other trends in the society, and especially by the increasing specialization within athletics, commercial incentives, and the intense competition for admission to the most selective schools?

The historical record—shaped by a myriad of actors, including the entertainment industry, the media, and various regulatory authorities—is of course far more than a mere reference point. As we saw in the Prelude, history and tradition are themselves potent factors in shaping debate and justifying current policies. In this chapter, we provide a context for the rest of the book by examining the changing place of intercollegiate athletics within the institutional fabric of colleges and universities.

THE MISSIONS OF COLLEGES AND UNIVERSITIES AND THE RATIONALE FOR SUPPORTING INTERCOLLEGIATE ATHLETICS

Determining how certain activities fit within an institution depends, of course, on how—and if—the institutional mission is defined. Mission statements of colleges and universities are rarely short and specific. Most go on for a number of pages, with subheadings and bullet points. But two slightly different themes do emerge, as the following excerpts from four mission statements illustrate:[1]

Knowledge for its own sake and for preparing flexible minds:

Kenyon is an academic institution. The virtue of the academic mode is that it deals not with private and particular truths, but with the general and the universal. It enables one to escape the limits of private experience and the tyranny of the present moment. . . . As an undergraduate institution, Kenyon focuses upon those studies which are essential to the intellectual and moral development of its students. The curriculum is not defined by the interest of graduate or professional schools, but by the faculty's understanding of what contributes to liberal education. . . . Ours is the best kind of career preparation, for it develops qualities that are prized in any profession. Far beyond immediate career concerns, however, a liberal education forms the foundation of a fulfilling and valuable life. To that purpose Kenyon College is devoted.

Yale's liberal education is an education meant to increase in young people a sense of the joy that learning for the sake of learning brings, learning whose goal is not professional mastery or technical capacity for commercial advantage, but commencement of a life-long pleasure in the human exercise of our minds, our most human part.

Education for leadership or success in life:

Penn inspires, demands, and thrives on excellence, and will measure itself against the best in every field of endeavor in which it participates. Penn is proudly entrepreneurial, dynamically forging new connections and inspiring learning through problem-solving, discovery-oriented approaches.

The mission of the University of Michigan is to serve the people of Michigan and the world through preeminence in creating, communicating, preserving and applying knowledge, art, and academic values, and in developing leaders and citizens who will challenge the present and enrich the future.

How, then, does intercollegiate athletics relate to such missions? As many faculty critics have pointed out, there is no direct connection between organized athletics and the pursuit of learning for its own sake. It can be said, however, that athletic competition helps provide a more balanced life for some number of students than they would find otherwise. The dictum of a "sound mind in a sound body" captures the idea.

The second theme in the mission statements—which invokes excellence in all pursuits and embraces the training of leaders—casts a wider net. It is much easier to make a straightforward case for intercollegiate athletics under this banner, and there has been no shortage of speeches and statements extolling the ways in which athletic competition fosters learning for life, training for leadership, the ability to work in teams, competitiveness, self-control, and discipline. Perhaps the most famous quotation of this genre is the Duke of Wellington's oft-cited aphorism: "The battle of Waterloo was won on the playing fields of Eton." To test these notions, we will present data on which attributes and actions differentiate athletes from other students; we will also test whether these differences should be attributed to participation in college sports or to differences that were present before students entered college.

At schools with the most extensive intercollegiate athletic programs, where athletes constitute 20 to 30 percent of the student body, athletic programs may have deep effects on the composition of the student body, the distribution of students by field of study, the degree to which various groups of students interact, and the overall emphasis placed on academic achievement. In addition, the presence of large numbers of athletes (who go on to make up equally large proportions of the alumni/ae) may have long-lasting effects on the priorities of the school. In all of these respects, the nature of intercollegiate athletic programs may shape as well as reflect the missions of the colleges and universities that offer them. In such settings, sports are seen as part of the school's core educational mission, and it is on these terms that sports programs should be judged.

A second, often unwritten, justification for college sports programs emphasizes their impact on building a sense of community. In order for Hamilton to have an identity that distinguishes it from Wesleyan, the students (past, present, and future) need to feel part of a cohesive community. Sports can play an important role in creating a campus ethos—in part through public ritual (the Saturday afternoon game), but also through the banner on the dorm room wall and the stories on the back page of the student paper. These "bonding" effects can be important in attracting students and in making the campus a pleasant place for everyone. They are also thought to sustain alumni loyalty and, over the long run, contribute to the financial strength of the institution and to its reputation within its state and beyond. (Athletics can of course lead to negative as well as positive reputational effects. Cheating scandals, for example, can damage an institution's reputation for academic integrity.)

There is a third, but somewhat different, way in which athletic programs may be tied to an institution's mission. The High Profile sports of football and men's basketball, in particular, may be valued because of their potential revenue-generating capacity. Although all of the educational institutions in our study are not-for-profit entities, and as such are prohibited from "making money," they are of course allowed to generate revenues that can be used to support their not-for-profit mission. Indeed, all of these colleges and universities raise substantial amounts of revenue by providing services (products that they make available for a price). Tuition revenues are the largest and most obvious example, but schools also sell sweatshirts and operate a range of auxiliary activities such as bookstores and museum shops.

The potential revenue-generating justification for intercollegiate athletics falls squarely under this heading—schools can be seen as "investing" in an athletic enterprise whose ticket sales, booster donations, and sneaker endorsements may provide dollars that can be used to cover the costs of a range of activities, including of course the costs of the Lower Profile sports. Moreover, successful athletic programs may be thought to benefit the institution financially by generating increased alumni/ae support, encouraging legislators to vote for larger appropriations (in the case of public universities), and providing marketing exposure. The success or failure of athletics seen as an investment should be judged in the same way in which any other investment is assessed—by comparing revenues with costs and calculating a rate of return.

How do athletic programs, justified in these different ways, affect a school's core mission? Hanna Gray has written of the importance of focusing on the educational purposes of a university and understanding how successful pursuit of its core mission confers a wide array of benefits on society at large:

> In the long history of discussion over the responsibilities and purposes of universities, there has been too little emphasis on clarifying the all-important benefit that flows from their own special mission. Such statements make the academic world sound aloof, self-absorbed, and arrogant, as though it cared

not at all about the world and its urgent problems and saw no obligation to help in alleviating social ills or improving the state of society or assisting the country in achieving significant national goals. To reply that the development of human and intellectual capital is in itself an enormous contribution of central social priority strikes those who see major needs immediately at hand as somehow unresponsive, especially given the public resources invested in higher education. . . . [Besides international economic competition] there are, of course, many other ways in which universities serve their communities—for example, in the provision of medical care or through projects carried on by scholars in a variety of fields such as urban studies, poverty, and education. *These grow out of the universities' educational missions, and that should be the test.*[2]

Intercollegiate athletics can be assessed, then, in terms of its direct effects on the core educational mission of a college or university (including its effects on the kinds of students enrolled, the education that they receive as undergraduates, and the lives that they go on to lead). It can also be judged in terms of its impact on campus ethos, alumni/ae loyalty, and institutional reputation. Finally, it can be assessed as an activity that, in some situations, might be expected to earn a measurable financial return that will help to make other things possible. Needless to say, these are far from mutually exclusive perspectives, but it is helpful to distinguish among them in thinking about the rationale for electing to support a particular kind of intercollegiate athletic program.

FROM STUDENT CLUBS TO HIGHLY PROFESSIONALIZED ATHLETIC DEPARTMENTS

The world of college sports garners a great deal of attention on the pages of the leading newspapers and magazines and in radio and television coverage of sports events. There is no denying the attention given to the NCAA basketball tournament, debates over equal opportunity for women to compete at the intercollegiate level, admissions standards for athletes, an array of highly publicized scandals concerning illegal payments to athletes, and methods of ranking football teams for the purposes of postseason competition. It seems clear that our revealed preference, as a society, is for an extensive commitment to sports within higher education. Anyone who wants to claim that sports has no place in a college or university is quickly going to run headlong into both the insatiable appetite for sports that is evident in our daily lives—and the reality of history.

The first intercollegiate athletic contest took place in 1852 when boats from Harvard and Yale raced on Lake Winnipesaukee in New Hampshire.

Though historians record the participants as having thought of the race as "a jolly lark," historian Ronald Smith notes that that first boat race was sponsored by a real estate promoter who was selling land in the area.[3] We should not believe that commercial ties to athletics arose only recently. The race signaled the beginning of an enterprise that would grow rapidly during the second half of the nineteenth century.

In 1859 Williams lost to Amherst in the first intercollegiate baseball contest (by a score of 73–32!), and in 1869 Princeton lost to Rutgers in the first football game. But how did such student-organized athletic competitions become embedded in the very core of the leading educational institutions of the country? The rest of this chapter is devoted to examining the factors that led college sports to become increasingly institutionalized over the course of the 20th century. The record of how athletics were absorbed into the institution is central to understanding the rest of this book, since the policies concerning how many (and which) athletes are admitted and how these athletically inclined students live during their time on campus are shaped by the degree to which institutions have come to claim athletics as their own.

Early Days: The Rise of Football

The new sport of football, akin more to soccer than to the sport we know as football today, developed rapidly in the 1870s and in the process changed dramatically through the absorption of rugby rules (via games between Harvard and McGill). Harvard, Yale, Princeton, and Columbia gradually formulated acceptable common rules, and the last quarter of the 19th century saw a huge rise in the popularity of the championship game, played in New York City on Thanksgiving. By the 1890s, 40,000 fans would watch the contest.[4]

As the historian Frederick Rudolph noted, this exciting new sport not only reverberated with the national character but also foreshadowed what was to come in college sports more generally.[5] Rooting for the team provided a focus for school spirit at a time when the campus had been fragmented by the change from a standard curriculum to one in which students could choose their own courses. At the same time, little-known schools like Notre Dame established name recognition by challenging the eastern giants (like Harvard) in football. But above all else, in this aggressive sport in which the individual and the team fought against a common foe, was another more deep and obvious fact: the sport—as is true of sports in general—was fun, and an exciting outlet for the energy and passions of both participants and fans.

According to an 1895 Harper's Magazine *article about Princeton, sports had a central role in training young men:*

The male of the human species passes through a stage when he has ceased to be a boy and is not yet a man, when his passions are virile and his judgment puerile. In the essentials of life he must at that epoch, in spite of his impatience of restraint, remain under tutelage. But how is he to find play for his growing manhood? Where is he to make his blunders and learn his lessons of experience? In some sphere where he will do the least harm and the greatest good both to himself and the community. This sphere is so manifestly that of his physical exercise and sport that the proposition is self-evident.[6]

The passions, rationalizations, and concerns of college sports at the end of the 19th century were in many ways similar to those of today. But the setting within which sports functioned and competed—the market—was entirely different. The Princeton-Yale football games of the 1890s may have attracted huge crowds, but the crowds had few other options. There were no movies, no television, and no Internet. College sports had the luxury of being the only game in town. When the first baseball World Series took place in 1901, no professional football, basketball, or hockey leagues yet existed, and the rebirth of the Olympic games in Athens began only in 1896, with 245 male competitors from 14 countries. The 25 colleges and universities that played intercollegiate football had the sports-entertainment market to themselves.

By 1905, football was living up to the "larger than life" legend that was building around it. Because passions ran so high and rules were still being improvised and ingeniously manipulated, the game took on a brutal tone—driven by plays such as the Harvard-invented "flying wedge," in which what would be the equivalent of today's offensive line started 25 yards behind the line of scrimmage and ran en masse into (or over) one designated (and stationary) member of the opposing team. People were dying—literally—for their schools; eighteen players died playing football in 1905 alone.

On October 16, 1905, shocked by the level of violence in college football, President Theodore Roosevelt summoned the Harvard, Yale, and Princeton presidents and football coaches to the White House. Historian Ronald Smith has noted that, just as muckraking journalism sniffed out exploitation in industry (Sinclair's *The Jungle* was published in 1905), journalists picked up the criticism of what faculty members called "bacillus athletics," a disease afflicting higher education. No wimp himself, Roosevelt accurately gauged the spirit of the day and expressed his outrage at the idea of dishonor staining an otherwise noble contest. The meeting led to some rule changes (including the invention of the forward pass, which was designed to relieve some of the pressure of the scrum) as well as to a gathering of college presidents who formed the group that would eventually become the NCAA. Although some chose radical moves—Northwestern, Stanford, and NYU joined Columbia in banning football outright—others (notably Harvard, whose faculty had voted for a ban in 1906 but acquiesced to rule changes) worked together to reform the game.

Two issues emerged in addition to the threat to life and limb: alumni/ae and other outside interests placed commercial pressure on student sports, and there were threats to academic integrity. Both of these issues were eminently clear to Howard Savage, the author of a 1929 study commissioned by the Carnegie Foundation for the Advancement of Teaching.[7] Most of the questions that he identified are still with us, and in barely altered forms: whether financial aid should be given on the basis of athletics, whether athletics builds moral character, how institutions should pay for facilities, and how much influence boosters should have in the management of athletics programs. But in the 1929 report we can discern what was at that time a new stage in the management of intercollegiate athletics. The governance of college sports had recently shifted from student-run clubs to institutionally managed ventures (an absolutely key development). The Carnegie report notes that the initial hope on the part of universities—that, by taking control of the clubs, the faculty of the university would provide oversight—was probably overly optimistic:

> The final tests for the presence or absence of true faculty control would seem to be these: First, is the guiding influence that of a man whose chief activities and interests lie in academic fields, or of one to whose income athletics contribute directly or indirectly? Secondly, are the coaches immediately responsible to a faculty representative whose principal concerns are academic, or are they subordinate to another or former coach now elevated to faculty status, or to a former business manager or an alumni secretary who is under academic appointment for the sake of the good that may accrue to athletics from his connection with them? Certainly, in the institutions where faculty control exists at its best there appears to be little truckling to special interests or privileged groups, because the director is not in any way dependent upon athletics for success in his professional career.[8]

While so much of the 1929 report sounds familiar, this concept of faculty control seems today like nothing more than a flight of the imagination. Even at many of the coed liberal arts colleges, coaches and athletic directors have ceased to be tenured faculty (and in many cases have ceased to be considered faculty at all). In most of higher education, athletic directors today are likely to be drawn from the ranks of former coaches, ideally with experience in marketing and management—and with expertise directed at increasing revenues. Control of the athletic enterprise, and the motivations of those who wield that control, have changed greatly over the course of the century; the structured and semiautonomous athletics program has been institutionalized and given its own place on the campus.[9]

No other historical development in intercollegiate athletics has been as influential, or as subtle, as the progressive institutionalization of the athletic clubs that students once ran. In institutionalizing these programs, the schools have, in effect, declared, "this is something that we do." This act of assuming ownership of the enterprise has led to a tacit or explicit sanctioning of the goals, values, and norms associated with college sports in a way that has allowed the athletic enterprise to have access to the inner chambers where the educational mission of the school is defined and pursued.

A few attempts were made to resist the institutionalization of college sports. The most notable of these was undertaken by Robert Maynard Hutchins, who declared in 1939 that the University of Chicago (a charter member of the Big Ten) would drop its football program. While Hutchins decried many of the ongoing abuses, his sharpest insight was that how and why colleges play sports tells us a great deal about how they set their overall agendas:

> Several universities have dropped football; but the reason they have stated shows how little they trust the public to understand a good reason for doing so. Almost all the universities that have given up the game have said that football lost money. As the public is willing to believe that a university may do anything for money, so it is prepared to agree that it may stop doing it if the money is not forthcoming. If the curriculum were rational and intelligible, the students might not run from it in such large numbers to devote themselves to extracurricular activities.[10]

Hutchins was prescient in seeing the ways that sports were being allowed to influence a school's mission: by inducing schools to follow the money instead of the more abstract academic goals that were central to them and by providing the public with something that was more fun, and more easily digestible, than dry academic debates. But Hutchins's view would not win in the debate over athletics outside Chicago. Standing on principle but losing in the war of public opinion, the University of Chicago's attempt at de-emphasis was based on grounds of institutional control over its own mission and the importance of being able to set its own priorities. Yet the public's continued preference for the clarity of the scoreboard over the confusing goals of the curriculum made Hutchins's decision seem idiosyncratic, out of touch, and, in the minds of some, downright wimpy.

Much later, in the 1970s and 1980s, other college presidents chose to take a stand on the appropriate way to conduct athletics. Paul Hardin's tenure as president of SMU ended abruptly after he brought to light corruption in the athletic department, disciplined the coaches who were involved in it, and made it clear that under his administration all conference and NCAA rules would be followed regardless of the standards set by other schools and whether or not violations known to the school were likely to be discovered externally. (Eight years later, the SMU football program was the first to receive the NCAA's "death penalty" and was completely shut down for four years.) In 1990, the Michigan State football coach was also appointed to serve as athletic director, despite President John DiBiaggio's warning to his board that this would be a dangerous arrangement; DiBiaggio subsequently left Michigan State and became president of Tufts. Courage among presidents on questions of athletics rarely portends a long tenure.

The Interest of the Public

Roosevelt's attention to the problems of football and the vigorously voiced concerns of the journalists who cried out for reform of college sports remind us of one of the unique powers of these programs. More than any other aspect of the collegiate enterprise, sports attract the interest of the public—of fans, journalists, and even legislators and other government officials. Over time, such attention contributed to the pressure on schools to solidify the institutionalization of sports programs. What is it about college sports programs that makes them more appealing to the public than much of the academic enterprise?

First and most obviously, sports link campuses to the outside community by the strength of their visual imagery, which is easily translated onto television or into photographs in alumni magazines and admissions marketing brochures. The uniformed hero in his or her mud-splashed splendor is a much more arresting image than a photo of a history major with writer's block or an economist hunched over a problem set. Clear communication goes beyond the visual; for the president visiting the alumni/ae club in a faraway city, the results of the big game or the recitation of how many championships the school has captured generally makes for a more engrossing presentation than the harder-to-portray results of work in classrooms, libraries, and labs. It is also sometimes thought, rightly or wrongly, that talking about athletics will have a broader appeal to the school's constituency than a more "academic" emphasis.

There is also a "larger than life" attitude toward sports. But whereas getting caught up in the passion of a mythical moment is something that many of us are naturally inclined to do, it is worth noting that there are people who earn their living through their ability to fan the flames of the mythical imagination. "Outlined against a blue-gray October sky," Grantland Rice wrote in 1924, "The Four Horsemen rode again. In dramatic lore they are known as Famine, Pestilence, Destruction and Death. These are only aliases. Their real names are Stuhldreher, Miller, Crawly, and Layden."[11] The running backs from Notre Dame did not elevate their ball carrying to a supernatural level; sportswriter Grantland Rice did. Two years earlier, Yale coach Tad Jones had told his team: "Gentlemen, you are about to play for Yale against Harvard in football. You will never again do anything so important in your entire life." Once again, it was not the Yale players who bestowed lifelong significance upon their game, it was their coach. Sports draw upon our passions and our myths in a way that little else does. But in drawing in the public—the alumni/ae, the fans, and government officials—schools set expectations that may be difficult to satisfy and that may encourage outsiders to take a much more active role in policy making than is normally found in academia.

Regulation

Having seen how sports attract the interest of powerful off-campus constituencies—ranging from alumni/ae and local boosters to state legislators and presidents—it is not at all surprising that a recurring theme in the development of intercollegiate athletics is the making and enforcing of rules. Even in war, where winning and losing involve the highest of stakes, there are rules—from the formal boundaries of medieval chivalry to the codes of the Geneva Convention. The existence of such treaties implicitly acknowledges the degree to which combatants realize that unrestrained competition will eventually come back to haunt them. But the rules of war also serve to legitimize warfare, by making it at least remotely palatable. In this way, regulating the rules of the game may at first seem like a way of restraining competition, but in fact such regulation may encourage escalation.

The athletic director of one of the schools in our study provided a recent example of how regulation may stimulate more of what it sets out to restrain. The Equity in Athletics Disclosure Act now requires schools to report publicly on the amounts they spend on coaching and other aspects of intercollegiate athletics (data we use extensively in Chapter 11). An entirely unintended consequence of this disclosure was to give knowledgeable athletic directors a weapon to use in pressuring their own schools to spend more on athletics. Since the ADs know their way around these complicated data far better than any school budget officer, an AD can call attention to categories of expenditure in which his or her program is falling behind the competition without noting areas in which it may be ahead. The end result is a "leveraging up" of everyone's spending.

The Rules of Engagement

Regulation of college sports began with debates over the still-being-formulated rules of the games themselves, before moving on to ask who should be allowed to play and under what conditions. Unlike life itself, and certainly unlike what happens in classrooms, sports require precise rules. Baseball mounds are 60 feet and 6 inches from home plate in every park. And although fans sometimes forget that rules are continually being tweaked—3-point shots and 24-second clocks were added to liven up basketball games—agreement on common rules is fundamentally a cooperative and regulatory process. As historian Ronald Smith has noted, the question of whether graduate students were eligible to play football in the 1890s was only the beginning. One group of Princeton players "enrolled" at Columbia long enough to help beat Yale, and 7 Michigan players had no affiliation whatsoever with the University! It was 1905 before the leading schools, led by the Big Ten, ruled that only currently registered undergraduate students could participate. Concern about the state of intercollegiate athletics led to attempts, beginning in the aftermath of Howard Savage's 1929 Carnegie Foundation report, to regulate other aspects of college sports as well.[12]

The history of regulating college sports is important for understanding the degree to which institutions today emphasize athletics in allocating admissions slots and other resources. As we have already noted, rules are inherently double-edged in that while they may seem directed at stopping you from doing certain things (e.g., from paying an athlete above the standard aid package) they also legitimize what you can do and, in fact, set a common target. So, for example, before 1956 athletic scholarships were forbidden. By legalizing them (in the hope of controlling abuses), the NCAA also encouraged their proliferation and, in effect, raised the bar determining what participation at the highest competitive level would require of institutions.

Payment of athletes was one major aspect of the management of athletics programs that, by the 1950s, schools had begun to take an active interest in regulating. Before 1956, paying for an athlete's tuition on the basis of the student's athletic ability rather than financial need was considered breaking the rules but was nevertheless a widespread practice; afterward, it became standard and legitimate. When scholarships were first instituted, athletes were given four-year awards. In the face of lawsuits that made such agreements seem very much like an employee relationship, the rules were changed; in the 1970s, coaches gained the power to "re-up" or rescind scholarships on a year-by-year basis. All such arrangements—seen either as manifestations of the great American dream of opportunity based on merit or as systematic professionalization of amateur sport activity—should be understood as regulation that solidified institutional control of, and involvement in, athletics.

Another great battlefront in the regulatory arena concerned academic standards. By the early 1970s, the efforts to set common standards for the eligibility of athletes had, for the most part, failed. The only academic achievement required for admission, for a scholarship, or for competition (from 1973 to 1986) was the requirement that athletes graduate from high school with a GPA of 2.0 or better.[13] At the 1983 NCAA convention, in response to the efforts of an ad hoc committee of presidents that had sought to bring about reform of athletics through the American Council on Education, new academic requirements were adopted. As of 1986, freshmen were not able to participate in sports unless they had an SAT score of 700 and a 2.0 high school GPA in 11 core courses. (These requirements were both tightened and made more flexible at the 1992 convention with the adoption of Proposition 16.) Debates then took place over whether the more elaborate regulations were improving graduation rates.

In the Ivy League, academic regulation went further. Distressed by the way in which the academic profiles of athletes were drifting further and further from those of their classmates, the Ivy presidents decided to impose formal admissions regulations—to protect themselves from themselves. Recognizing that schools differed in their ability to attract students, and that Harvard, Yale, and Princeton were thought to hold an advantage over the rest of the league in the competition for talented students who were also excellent athletes, the presidents devised an elaborate Academic Index, whereby athletes' admissions credentials were considered in relation to the overall academic profile of students in the school. Thus the allowable "bands" of SAT scores and high school grades for athletes in the High Profile sports of football, men's basketball, and men's hockey varied by school. For example, athletes recruited by Harvard were required to have a higher distribution of SAT scores than athletes recruited by a school with a lower average SAT score (which was permitted to dip deeper into the applicant pool, where greater numbers of athletically talented candidates could be found). This approach was consistent with the original Ivy League objective of fielding athletic teams composed of students who had academic qualifications that made them more or less representative of their classmates.

This Index (discussed at greater length in Chapter 2, where we examine the admissions process and its results) has been found to have pluses and minuses. Despite requiring a great deal of data collection and analysis, and having had to contend with numerous end runs (including, for example, the obvious tactic of balancing high-talent players who had low SAT scores with low-talent players who had exceedingly high scores in order to produce an acceptable mean), the Index has been found to work. But distrust and discontent across schools have by no means disappeared even as the average SAT scores of football, basketball, and hockey players have improved.

By far the most significant regulatory shift in intercollegiate athletics—and perhaps in higher education more generally—was the passing of the Title IX amendment to the 1972 Omnibus Education Act, whereby the Congress of the United States decreed that "No person in the United States shall, on the basis of sex, be excluded from participation in, denied the benefits of, or be subjected to discrimination under any education program or activity receiving Federal financial assistance."[14] The implications of this legislation have played out gradually over the ensuing three decades, but there is no doubt that mandated gender equity has had, and will continue to have, a fundamental impact on every aspect of college sports.[15]

The implications of Title IX are discussed at greater length in Chapters 5–8 and in Chapters 13 and 14. The general point to be emphasized here is that the ever-closer intertwining of the athletic and academic enterprises has left college and university athletic programs—and the institutions themselves—highly susceptible to both self-imposed and externally imposed regulation. And the cycle of regulation continues. Former college wrestler and current U.S. Senator Paul Wellstone, frustrated over the threat to college wrestling programs that now must compete for funding with women's tennis as well as men's football, introduced an amendment to the Higher Education Act in 1998 that would bar institutions from reducing funding or participation levels for a sport without providing a public "statement of justification."[16] If athletic programs were still looked upon as peripheral activities that existed at the fringes of college life, it seems unlikely that either the presidents of these institutions, the Senate, or the Office of Civil Rights would have taken such a powerful interest in them.

Collective Institutionalization: The NCAA and the Conferences

As the rules of the game—and of who could play the game—became clarified and solidified during the course of the century, the question of going back to a less formal, laissez-faire world became ever more irrelevant. Instead, self-interest brought schools together. The umbrella organization that plays by far the most important role in organizing and regulating intercollegiate athletics is of course the National Collegiate Athletic Association (NCAA). Although it was founded in the early years of the 20th century, it was only in the post–World War II period that it became the dominant entity that we know today, having settled firmly into place because colleges and universities made it clear by their actions that they could not trust one another or themselves. The organizational structure of the association has long been dominated by former coaches and athletic directors—precisely the people whose dependence on athletic success was foreseen by the 1929 Carnegie report.

The NCAA was transformed in the postwar period under the leadership of Walter Byers, a skilled negotiator of television contracts who brought entertainment dollars to the NCAA and then redistributed them, in large part, to the participating schools. But beyond his marketing skills, Byers also was a superb strategist, leading the Association in efforts to head off any threat to the jobs and power that it controlled. In 1980, when the promises of the Title IX gender equity legislation were beginning to become a reality, Byers shrewdly provided irresistible incentives to schools to choose the NCAA as the locus of control of women's sports instead of the group that had long sponsored and led the fight for women's college sports, the Association for Intercollegiate Athletics for Women (AIAW). By paying for travel to championship competitions and insurance for schools, Byers provided incentives for women's sports programs to pass through their adolescence under the direction of the NCAA. When a group of college presidents then sought (in 1983, acting through the American Council on Education) to take control of an athletics structure that was perceived to be acting with complete disregard for academic standards, the NCAA formed its own presidents' commission, thereby solidifying its place in determining which rules would be made and how they would be enforced. All of the disputes over gender equity and all of the concern over academic standards encouraged the NCAA to add to its enforcement and watchdog responsibilities.

The NCAA has been described as the fox watching the henhouse of college sports, but the Association's consolidation of power cannot be attributed only to its own ambitions; schools had demonstrated repeatedly that they were unable to protect themselves from themselves and, at the same time, that they had no desire to disband their programs. In response, the NCAA has organized and managed the flow of big money, while orchestrating the cooperation of all segments of higher education. Critics have described it as a powerful cartel that employs 300 people and defends the interests of thousands of coaches and athletic administrators at some 1,041 schools. But, in part through its success in keeping the small Division III colleges and the big-time schools together, the Association has, despite its billion-dollar television contracts, also been able to claim the banner of academic objectives and to retain its not-for-profit status.

The NCAA has also been effective in tweaking regulations to make them even more efficient in ensuring the smooth functioning of the system. For example, in response to rising cost pressures in the early 1990s, the NCAA cut the number of football scholarships that each Division IA school could offer from 95 to 85. The NCAA's role in regulating college sports has also been important in legitimizing and institutionalizing the role of college sports—particularly when backed up by the enormous amount of money generated by the NCAA's multibillion-dollar basketball contract. This money is shared so as to provide not only strong incentives for the big-time programs to compete successfully in the regular season and in the postseason conference, but also incentives for the also-rans and even the small Division III colleges to stay within the fold. The 3.18 percent of the NCAA revenues that is shared among 373 Division III colleges pays for travel to conference championships in all sports and is also used to pay for insurance for athletes and schools.

It would be a mistake, however, to think of the NCAA as the sole organizing element in college sports. Conferences also play important roles as, in effect, companion entities to the NCAA. Historically, conferences grew up as federations within which schools could find a dependable set of competitors with interests that were at least generally aligned with their own. Conferences today serve a variety of purposes: some share revenues, some mutually police each other's admission standards (as we noted in the earlier discussion of the Ivy League's Academic Index), and all enable their schools to compete in at least a reasonably predictable way.

Conferences also have some powers that cannot be exercised by the NCAA. In 1984, a Supreme Court ruling declared that the NCAA could no longer control television football rights for all of college football, a decision that freed individual schools and conferences to negotiate their own arrangements and take home their own profits.[17] This decision set conferences into a scramble to attract football powerhouses that would bring television revenues to the collective: Penn State joined the Big Ten, Florida State was invited to join the Atlantic Coast Conference, and the Southwestern Conference fell apart as Texas and Texas A&M were invited into the Big Eight, and smaller schools like Rice were left to find a new home, after decades in the legendary Southwestern Conference. Individual institutions within conferences are obviously affected by what the conference collective decides. The addition of football powerhouse Florida State to the traditionally basketball-focused Atlantic Coast Conference brought in more revenues, but it also meant that schools like Duke and Wake Forest had to be prepared to either raise their level of commitment to football or risk embarrassment on the field. One problem for the private Division IA institutions in our study is that they are appreciably more selective academically than many of their conference peers. The dilemma that a school like Vanderbilt faces is, as one former Vanderbilt coach put it, wanting "to be Harvard six days a week and Alabama on Saturday."[18]

More than half a century after they invented American college football, the schools of the Ivy League went their own way and became an official conference in 1956—although they had already been a conference in the minds of many for years. It is interesting to note that, despite the widespread collective recognition enjoyed by the eight Ivies (Brown, Columbia, Cornell, Dartmouth, Harvard, Penn, Princeton, and Yale), their only formal connection is through sports, and the only time that their presidents officially convene is to discuss athletic matters at biannual meetings. The league had hesitated to form a conference officially throughout the 1930s and 1940s out of concern that differing academic standards and financial resources within the group would make it hard to share common goals. Finally, with the legalization of athletic scholarships in 1956 (which they opposed), the schools signed the original Ivy principles.[19]

Beginning in the 1970s with the partitioning of the NCAA into divisions, selective colleges and universities had another option. Liberal arts colleges and some universities found refuge in Division III, where no athletic scholarships were allowed. Ten New England small colleges formed the New England Small College Athletic Conference (NESCAC) in 1971. NESCAC provided dependable rivalries among like institutions. They policed themselves, expelling one original member (Union College) when it seemed intent on going in a different and more intense direction than the rest of the conference. Matters became somewhat more complicated in the 1990s when the presidents voted to undertake an "experiment" and to let teams compete in postseason competition, reversing a position that long had been a NESCAC line in the sand. Tasting postseason competition made it very difficult for coaches and students to contemplate going back to their prior position (recall the Williams College lacrosse snapshot in the Prelude). The debate continues to this day as the presidents, by voting to allow only one team from the conference into each postseason competition, try to control the genie they set loose. Some have argued that this movement into postseason competition makes in-season competition more intense than it had been before. Even in a conference praised by the national press as "pure and simple," arms races accelerate when the competitive gates are opened.[20]

SOCIETAL FORCES THAT HAVE SHAPED COLLEGE SPORTS

Understanding how sports in America became institutionalized within colleges and universities, and how regulations have shaped "the rules of engagement," does not tell us as much as we need to know about the large societal forces that have shaped both the incentives and the constraints within which college sports must operate. Although there are surely many ways of attempting to capture the essence of what has happened, we conclude this chapter by focusing on three interconnected forces that underlie many of the developments we have outlined: (1) the growth of the entertainment industry and the commercialization of intercollegiate athletics; (2) the ever-increasing importance of a college degree, the concomitant heightening of competition for admission to the most selective colleges and universities, and changes in admissions philosophies; and (3) the greatly increased specialization of athletic talent from early ages, accompanied by improvements in performance.

The Growth of the Entertainment Industry and the Commercialization of Athletics

In the early 1900s, Ivy League football monopolized the collective imagination of the country and consequently cornered an almost mythical portion of the public's entertainment dollar. For the year ending August 30, 1915, the Yale football team showed expenditures of $95,572.09 and receipts of $194,669.04—a profit of roughly $100,000 (in excess of $1.5 million in 2000 dollars).

The enterprise that brought in almost one-third as much as the school's entire tuition revenue rested on one three-hour ritual—the annual Harvard-Yale football game. At the time of that 1914 game, there were only 29 football games being played nationwide (as opposed to 300 on any given fall Saturday now), and just 14 in the area between Maine and Washington, D.C. There were no professional football games the next day (Sunday) because professional football did not yet exist, and while Lionel Barrymore and Sarah Bernhardt were defining the height of vaudeville, there were no movies, no television, and no radio. Ivy League football dominated the market and, for the moment, all was right in their world. For many years, the local Saturday afternoon game was literally "the only game in town." But, this was to change—dramatically. The rise of sports in the second half of the century coincided with the rise of an entertainment-driven economy. Disneyland was built in 1955—the year that the first cohort of students in our study emerged from college. Disneyland and other theme parks, the music industry, and the world of film, television, and video games constitute an ever-growing sector of the economy, one that attracts and draws upon many of the same passions that sports inspires.[21]

More generally, the extraordinary growth of the entertainment economy has made it much more difficult for college sports programs to compete for attendance. As Figure 1.1 illustrates, Saturday afternoon sports fans have increasingly had to choose between local contests and high-quality transmission of many appealing contests involving the top-rated teams in the country. Consider the same November Saturday afternoon 5½-hour time slot across 38 years. In 1955 viewers could watch 3 hours of sports, with no overlap among programs. By 1979, there were 15½ hours of options, and by 1993 fans could choose from among 43 hours of sports—including 15½ hours of college football alone. Subsequently, "direct TV" has allowed viewers to subscribe to the game of their choice—making the options virtually limitless. Moreover, television producers have worked hard to make their presentations better, in a sense, than reality. Viewers, enjoying the warmth of their living rooms, have become so dependent on features like instant replay that they feel cheated when they attend live games and must actually pay attention to every play, lest they miss the big one.

The financial stake in television revenues of those colleges and universities with big-time programs has become enormous, and, as was noted in the previous section, even those schools with Division III programs share modestly in the revenues generated by the NCAA contract to televise "March madness." The financial aspects of all of these relationships are discussed in Chapter 11, where the costs and revenues of intercollegiate sports played at various levels of competition are analyzed in considerable detail. Perhaps the most obvious point to emphasize here (apart from the fact that billions of dollars are involved) is that the distribution of financial rewards places a tremendous premium on winning, especially in the High Profile sports. Coming in even "second best" can entail large losses, and the financial incentives to be consistently at the top are powerful.[22]

In their book *The Winner-Take-All Society*, Robert Frank and Philip Cook describe how changes in technology have intensified the gap between the winners of any sort of societal contest and the rest of the pack: "As the

Saturday, November 19, 1955

	12:00	12:30	1:00	1:30	2:00	2:30	3:00	3:30	4:00	4:30	5:00	5:30	Hours
Ch 4				Thrills in Sports									1.0
Ch 13									Prs Bx Rev	College Football USC vs. UCLA			2.0
													3.0

Saturday, November 17, 1979

	12:00	12:30	1:00	1:30	2:00	2:30	3:00	3:30	4:00	4:30	5:00	5:30	Hours
Ch 2			College Basketball Duke vs. Kentucky										5.0
Ch 4									Sportsworld (Boxing)				1.5
Ch 7		College Football Ohio State vs. Michigan							College Football Miami vs. Alabama				5.5
Ch 11		High School Football					NFL	NFL			Soccer		3.5
													15.5

Saturday, November 20, 1993

	12:00	12:30	1:00	1:30	2:00	2:30	3:00	3:30	4:00	4:30	5:00	5:30	Hours
CBS								Golf Shark Shootout, 2nd Round, Thousand Oaks, Calif.				NBA	2.5
NBC		NBA											5.0
FOX	Wrestling		American Gladiators	College Football Boston College vs. Notre Dame									2.0
ABC		College Football Ohio State vs. Michigan					College Football						6.0
Ch 8		College Football Big East Game of the Week					College Football						6.0
Ch 58	G. Moeller	Hofstra	Devils	NHL Detroit Red Wings vs. Devils					Wrestling	NFL		Wrestling	1.5
SC													6.0
CNN									Sports				0.5
ESPN	Game Day	W College Basketball Texas Tech vs. Vanderbilt	Tennis ATP World Championship						College Football				6.0
MSG	Tennis Virginia Slims Championships								ATP Tour	TBA	Wrestling	Snapshot	6.0
TNT										Gymnastics			1.5
													43.0

Figure 1.1. Sports Televised (in New York City) during the Harvard-Yale Football Game, 1955, 1979, and 1993

Source: New York Times.

revolution in information processing and transmission continues, there is increasing leverage for the talents of those who occupy top positions and correspondingly less room for others to find a lucrative niche."[23] So, for example, the opportunity to listen to your favorite symphony on digital compact disc as performed by the London Philharmonic mediates your desire to hear the local orchestra play the same piece, and hence lessens the rewards that accrue to the local violinist. In the same way, the college teams that make it big can at least attempt to justify the high costs of competing, and those who lose are left far behind. But the competition for television-transmitted glory is by no means the only intense race for a prize that occurs at selective colleges and universities.

The Increased Competitiveness of College Admissions

As recently as the 1950s, applicant pools at even the strongest colleges and universities were both much smaller and much less diverse. Whereas it once was true that solid applicants from the better-known prep schools and leading public high schools could count on getting into one of the leading colleges and universities, the odds of admission for everyone fell sharply, starting in the mid- to late 1960s, as larger and larger numbers of outstanding candidates sought admission at the strongest schools.[24] Career advancement in our knowledge-based economy has increased the premium that prospective employers, and consequently applicants, place on attending a school with an impressive reputation. Three factors arose simultaneously to change dramatically the terms of the race to the admissions office: new applicants coming from an increasingly national and democratic pool, an improved flow of information that can be used in matching highly qualified applicants with selective schools, and a widely held perception that advantages accrue to those who attend a school that is highly ranked in national polls. In choosing recent classes, Swarthmore offered places to about 20 percent of its applicants; Wellesley, to about 50 percent; Stanford, to fewer than 15 percent; Columbia, to 17 percent; and the University of Michigan, to roughly 64 percent of all out-of-state applicants—and these daunting percentages include only those who applied, not all the other potential applicants who realistically bowed out of the competition before the application deadline.[25]

As competition for admission increased, and admissions officers sought ways of choosing from a surplus of talented applicants, colleges began to move away from identifying and admitting the "well-rounded" student and instead began to concentrate on enrolling a "well-rounded class" of students who stood out in specific ways. The ramifications of this increase in the competition for admission and this shift in admissions philosophy are discussed at length in Chapters 13 and 14. The point of immediate relevance is that admissions offices became much more interested in candidates who offered distinctive qualifications—who were different in some major respect from the rapidly growing number of well-qualified "ordinary" applicants. The much more active recruitment of both minority students and applicants with unusual promise in particular fields such as mathematics was part of this process, as was the willingness to admit the exceptional musician and the truly outstanding athlete who had specialized talent.

One consequence of this change in the composition of the student body, read alongside the change in the entertainment market already noted, is that the once-cohesive audience that was expected to fill the stadium on Saturday afternoon was fragmented. At selective colleges and universities, the competitive nature of the admissions process was drawing an increasingly active student body committed to a burgeoning array of participatory pursuits. Whether out of pure interest or determined careerism, students who attend Northwestern and Wesleyan and Barnard have been building résumés full of extracurricular activities since junior high school or earlier. Between 1980 and 1996 the number of officially registered student organizations at Yale rose from 140 to 230—including 27 music or singing groups, 11 math or science organizations, 16 drama groups, and 18 publications.[26]

It should come as no surprise then that the ritual significance of the big Saturday football contest, in particular, changed on many (perhaps all) of these campuses. Students became increasingly engaged in a host of participatory activities of their own, and many of them were also intensely committed to academic and research pursuits (spending many Saturday afternoons in the lab or library). Average student attendance at football games at Ivy League universities and coed liberal arts colleges has declined, as has the student share of attendance at places like the University of Michigan.[27] At many coed liberal arts colleges, attendance at intercollegiate events consists of a heavy representation of friends, plus some number of family members and others deeply interested in the particular sport. The growth in popularity of sports like lacrosse, soccer, and volleyball, and the rapid increase in the number of women's teams, has meant that students and others interested in campus sports have a much wider array of spectator options than used to be the case.

From the perspective of the place of the athlete on the campus of a highly selective school, this upsurge in the competitiveness of admissions, combined with the search for "distinctive" candidates, had two principal effects. First, it raised sharply the "opportunity cost" of any admissions decision, including the decision to admit someone who ranked high on a coach's list—because the disappointed student at large who might have been accepted had the athlete not been taken was now much stronger than the corresponding candidate who would have been turned down in the 1950s. Second, it introduced onto the campus a group of athletes who were as specialized in their own ways as the most intensely focused computer scientists.

The Increased Competence (and Specialization) of Precollege Athletic Talent

Sports programs for 18- to 21-year-olds who attend selective colleges and universities do not exist in a vacuum. The changes that we have tracked in college sports must be considered in the context of a sports culture that has grown exponentially. The program grid presented in Figure 1.1, showing our society's apparently limitless appetite for consuming sports on television, tells part of the story. Also relevant is how seriously we have come to take games in general, at younger and younger ages, and the role that the institutionalization of sports has played in this process.

The institutional sanction of sports is clearly seen in high schools, where the image of the jock as big man on campus has intensified, and the distinction between "winners" and "losers"—once a social divide set up by the kids themselves—is now reinforced by institutionally sponsored arrangements such as special meals and other privileges. In the aftermath of the Columbine High School massacre, in which athletes were singled out as targets, the costs and benefits of the high school–sponsored "jock culture" were debated in an online forum set up by the *New York Times:* "You cannot have a high school administration that openly condones an ethic of competitive glory-seeking conquerors," one respondent wrote, "without also creating an underclass of noncompetitive 'losers.'"[28] This is, of course, only one opinion, but as athletics are taken more seriously as an institutional activity, stakes do inevitably rise. "On the village green," George Orwell wrote in 1947, "where you pick up sides and no feeling of local patriotism is involved, it is possible to play simply for the fun and the exercise; but as soon as the question of prestige arises, as soon as you feel that you and some larger unit will be disgraced if you lose, the most savage combative instincts are aroused."[29]

Following (or concurrent with) the institutionalization of college athletics, sports have become more specialized, and athletes (and their parents) have become more serious about play in the formative stages of life. A *New York Times* article tells of parents hiring batting coaches for Little Leaguers (at a rate of $70 per hour).[30] There is a link here that is worth noting. At the same time that sports has become more valued as a part of our culture (with parents quoted in the *Times* article as insisting that they have to hire the high-priced coaches lest their children's self-worth be threatened by striking out), colleges have helped define these cultural attitudes through their actions: a Little League spokesman noted that a large share of those paying for private instruction were girls trying to win college scholarships in softball.

Not surprisingly, standards of performance have improved dramatically. One set of relevant data was presented in the context of athletic performance at the Olympics (Figure 1.2), demonstrating cumulative performance time improvements in track and field and swimming of just over 140 percent. Although we are not concerned directly with Olympic athletes, the achievements of the Olympians are only the tip of the proverbial iceberg. Anyone who watches Little League games, high school tennis championships, soccer competitions, or pickup basketball games (let alone televised contests featuring high school all-stars) cannot help but be aware of the trend—in part because of the much heavier investment in coaching, practice, and training that is now made when children are still very young.

Weissmuller, 15 times over:

In 1924, Johnny Weissmuller was the first Olympian to swim the 100-meter freestyle in under a minute. More than half a century later, Vladimir Salnikov maintained that pace over a distance 15 times that of Weissmuller's, when he set a 1,500-meter freestyle world record in under 15 minutes.[31]

Since everyone has limited time, there is a corresponding tendency to specialize in a sport at an early age, so that a young person can become "really good at something." The changes in the philosophy of college admissions, which put greater emphasis on excellence along at least one noticeable dimension, have played at least a small part in encouraging this tendency. To be sure, there are people who remain capable of excelling in many pursuits at the same time. There is, nonetheless, a risk that society will train what a famous economist, Jacob Viner (in speaking about graduate students), once referred to as "a trufflehound . . . finely trained for a single small purpose and not much good for any other."[32]

It is worth keeping in mind this increased specialization among athletes when considering other findings reported in this book. In particular, specialization relates to the nature of recruiting, with coaches focused heavily on identifying candidates who can fill particular niches on their teams (say, outside linebackers). This process is made easier, of course, by the fact that today so much more is known about the athletic skills of

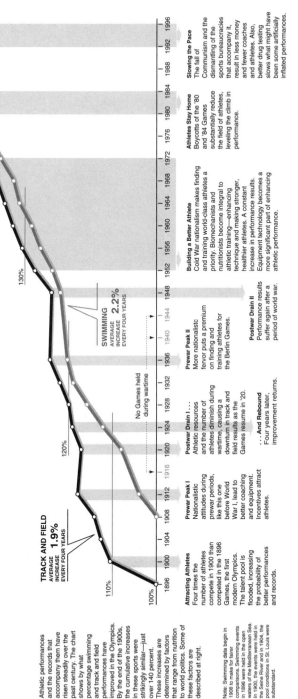

Athletic performances and the records that accompany them have risen steadily over the past century. The chart shows by what percentage swimming and track and field performances have improved in the Olympics. By the end of the 1900s, the cumulative increases in these sports were strikingly similar—just over 140 percent. These increases are determined by factors that range from nutrition to world politics. Some of these factors are described at right.

Note: Swimming data begin in 1908 to make for fairer comparisons. Swimming events in 1896 were held in the open waters of the Mediterranean Sea. In 1900, the events were held in the Seine River and in 1904, the pool conditions in St. Louis were substandard.

TRACK AND FIELD AVERAGE INCREASE **1.9%** EVERY FOUR YEARS

SWIMMING AVERAGE INCREASE **2.2%** EVERY FOUR YEARS

100% 110% 120% 130% 140%

1896 1900 1904 1908 1912 1916 1920 1924 1928 1932 1936 1940 1944 1948 1952 1956 1960 1964 1968 1972 1976 1980 1984 1988 1992 1996

No Games held during wartime

Attracting Athletes
Four times the number of athletes compete in 1900 than competed in the 1896 Games, the first modern Olympics. The talent pool is flooded, increasing the probability of better performances and records.

Prewar Peak I
Nationalistic attitudes during prewar periods, like this one before World War I, lead to better coaching and equipment. Incentives attract athletes.

Postwar Drain I . . .
Athletic resources and the number of athletes diminish during wartime, causing a downturn in track and field results as the Games resume in '20.

. . . And Rebound
Four years later, improvement returns.

Prewar Peak II
More nationalistic fervor puts a premium on finding and training athletes for the Berlin Games.

Postwar Drain II
Performance results suffer again after a period of world war.

Building a Better Athlete
Cold War nationalism makes finding and training world-class athletes a priority. Biomechanists and nutritionists become integral to athletic training—enhancing technique and making stronger, healthier athletes. A constant increase in performance results. Equipment technology becomes a more significant part of enhancing athletic performance.

Athletes Stay Home
Boycotts of the '80 and '84 Games substantially reduce the field of athletes, leveling the climb in performance.

Slowing the Pace
The fall of Communism and the dismantling of the sports bureaucracies that accompany it, result in less money and fewer coaches and athletes. Also, better drug testing slows what might have been some artificially inflated performances.

Figure 1.2. Cumulative Increases in Performance Times in Track and Field and Swimming, 1896–1996
Source: New York Times.

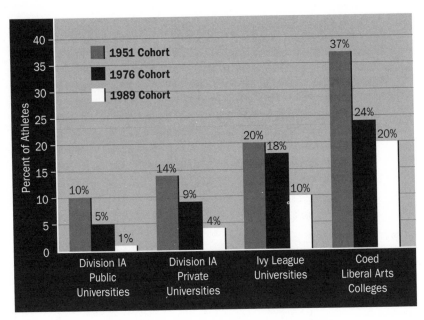

Figure 1.3a. Multi-Sport Athletes as a Percent of All Male Athletes
Source: College and Beyond.

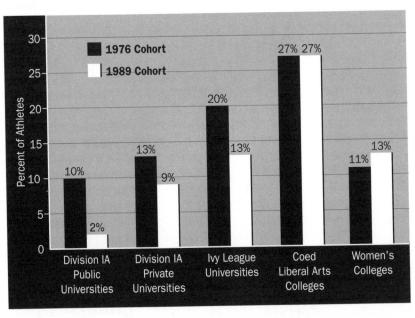

Figure 1.3b. Multi-Sport Athletes as a Percent of All Female Athletes
Source: College and Beyond.

applicants when coaches decide whom to pursue. Increased specialization also translates quite directly into an unmistakable trend away from participation in college in more than one sport. In Figure 1.3a, we show the percentage of all male athletes in each of three cohorts (1951, 1976, and 1989) who played more than one sport in college, with separate figures given for the Division IA programs, the Division IAA (Ivies), and the Division III schools (coed liberal arts colleges). In Figure 1.3b, we present similar data for women, including women enrolled at the women's colleges, in the two most recent cohorts (data for women athletes are unavailable for the '51 cohort).

To begin with the data for the men, a clear story is told by the data at the two ends of the spectrum: in the Division IA public universities, 10 percent of male athletes in the '51 cohort played more than one sport, as compared with 1 percent in the '89 cohort; in the Division III coed liberal arts colleges, the comparable figure falls from 37 percent in the '51 cohort to 20 percent in the '89 cohort. When we compare Figures 1.3a and 1.3b, we see that the women athletes are consistently more likely than their male counterparts to play two or more sports. We also see that women athletes in the Division IA programs and in the Ivy League are following the same trend as the men—that is, the percentage playing two or more sports declined significantly between the '76 and '89 cohorts. The data for women athletes at the Division III colleges (both the coed colleges and the women's colleges), on the other hand, do not show the same effects of specialization—so far.

———————

The changes in college athletics that have occurred over the past half century have been profound. In the 1950s, two very different worlds of college sports existed simultaneously. The big-time programs, while still a "work in progress," were even then increasingly taking on professional overtones. The second approach was much lower key; it was found mainly where sports were seen by students as a part of life that they wanted because they enjoyed playing. As time passed, even the less intensive programs, which were once viewed as ancillary, consumed more and more institutional resources—money, admissions slots, and administration time. This change is fundamental to the questions we explore in the coming chapters for one reason: when we look at athletes from the 1950s, we must realize that they were both products of and participants in a very different ecosystem. The external environment within which colleges and universities live has changed. But the policies of the schools have changed as well. It may be a mistake for the football or lacrosse player of yesterday to look at his counterpart today and assume that the two of them are the same, that their common sport means the same thing to them, or that, despite having donned similar uniforms, they have played the same game.

In the coming chapters, we attempt to gauge in what ways the player in the 1950s and today's more sharply focused recruit are similar and in what ways they differ. It was the eminent social scientist Yogi Berra who once noted the trickiness inherent in tracking systemic changes over time: "The future," he said, "ain't what it used to be."

CHAPTER 2

The Admissions Game: Recruiting Male Athletes and the Implications of Selection

> It's the same for everybody in the conference. If one school can field a "nickel package," we all have to. Here we are with only 400 slots and I'm not just looking for a football player or a linebacker with scores that are respectable, I'm looking for a left outside linebacker who can blitz.
>
> —Tom Parker, director of admissions at Amherst, formerly director of admissions at Williams

IN A PINCH, a strong safety can be converted into a wide receiver. But a coach is presented with an entirely different situation when he has two very good 174-pound wrestlers and no one to step into the circle at 118 pounds. Although the firestorm over wrestling at Princeton began with the pressure to close a university-wide budget gap (and associated concerns over compliance with Title IX), the sport's unusual degree of specialization was an additional problem in the ongoing challenge it presented to an admissions office compelled to choose among a plethora of well-qualified candidates. This chapter describes the numbers of male athletes admitted to academically selective colleges and universities and how those students who play sports differ from their classmates.

At many of the schools in our study, it is not unusual to receive ten applications for every place in the entering class. Every spring, valedictorians with straight A averages, and applicants with stellar SAT scores who may have conducted original laboratory research or made a full-length documentary film, are rejected because there are only so many spots in a class. Because there are so many outstanding candidates, a place in the entering class at Wellesley, UNC–Chapel Hill, or Columbia is a scarce resource. In making these difficult selections, a school places its bets on certain students in the hope that in one way or another each student will contribute to the fulfillment of the institution's mission. It is when decisions are difficult that institutions and individuals demonstrate what really matters to them (as opposed to what they might *say* really matters to them). The admissions process is the key junction in creating not only the student body of the present but also the alumni/ae of the future.

Getting in:

"It's the way we give our children the very best chance for their future," said one Manhattan parent. "The child might be more relaxed if the pressure were off. But try being the only boy in a class of 20 who didn't get into the Harvards of the world. It's not only their future but their self-worth that's in jeopardy."[1]

Although their plight will elicit little sympathy from the applicants who are on the receiving end of the thin or thick envelopes that they send, admissions officers and the administrators and trustees who stand behind them face enormous and conflicting pressures: alumni/ae who want their children, grandchildren, nieces, and grandnephews accepted; the local community, with whom the school can build good rapport by accepting students from nearby secondary schools; and the desire to create a class that benefits from many kinds of diversity—of opinion, social class, race, types of talent, and region of the country and of the world. Meanwhile, amidst the conflicting pressures, institutions set policies and make admissions decisions, knowing that every opportunity granted simultaneously represents many more opportunities lost.

Opportunity costs:

Economics textbooks define the *opportunity cost* of any decision or action as the value of the next best alternative that must be given up (the value of the "sacrificed alternative"). If someone who is working decides to go back to school full time, the costs that he or she faces will be not only the direct outlays for tuition and living expenses but also the opportunity costs of the decision—that is, the money that the individual would have earned while working full time. The tuition rate may be $20,000 a year, but if the person had been earning $30,000 per year, the true "cost" of returning to school is $50,000 per year (assuming that living expenses would have had to be paid in either case). Understanding that every judgment concerning the allocation of a scarce resource has an opportunity cost is central to informed decision making.

RECRUITING ATHLETES

How should we think about the role that athletic talent plays in this competitive admissions environment, where every opportunity granted also represents an opportunity forgone? We begin by describing "the lay of the land"—the numbers of students who play intercollegiate sports and the degree to which their athletic skills contributed to their having been admitted. When we think about college athletics, we usually imagine a football stadium on a fall afternoon—and thus we tend to think that where the stadiums are to be found, there too are the college athletes. At the schools in this study, however, the vast majority of intercollegiate athletes are the less visible swimmers, soccer players, runners, and lacrosse players who populate up to 38 varsity teams at some schools.

> *An important matter of definition.* We are counting as "athletes" all students who received one or more athletic awards—or "letters"—while in college. This is our objective definition of who is an athlete, and the underlying information, which was obtained from institutional records, is more reliable than aggregate data on numbers of "athletes" reported by schools. These aggregate data may involve double-counting—a student who plays two sports may be counted twice, which is not a problem with College and Beyond data—or reflect other inaccuracies. We distinguish these intercollegiate athletes both from students who played intramural or club sports and from those who played no sports at all. Although the great majority of athletes earned varsity letters, some earned freshman awards (especially in years before freshmen were eligible to play varsity sports) and some earned junior varsity awards. The criteria used to determine who received an award may well vary somewhat from sport to sport, school to school, and cohort to cohort. In general, it is best to assume that essentially all students who played on intercollegiate teams through the season received "awards."

Throughout this study, we look at this broad array of athletes through four main lenses:

- *Type of sport.* Since one thing we want to know is how football players differ from golfers in SAT scores and their other attributes when they enter college, we divide male athletes into two broad categories: those who play the High Profile sports of football, basketball, and hockey, and those who play all other sports.[2] In our standard "scorecard" format (used extensively in the scorecards in Appendix A to summarize data), we compare both groups of athletes with all other students, whom we call "students at large." At times, we also distinguish two subsets of students at large: those who played high school sports but did not play sports in college and those who participated extensively in time-intensive extracurricular activities other than athletics.

- *Level of competition.* We group those athletes who played each type of sport according to whether they played in Division IA public universities, Division IA private universities, Division IAA universities (Ivies), Division III coed liberal arts colleges, and, when we come to the data concerning women (beginning in Chapter 6), Division III women's colleges. (The list of all participating institutions, grouped by division, is given in the Preface.)
- *Student "generation" or year of matriculation.* The third lens we use is time, to see whether differences in qualifications and other attributes have changed between the cohorts who entered college in the fall of 1951, the fall of 1976, and the fall of 1989.
- *Gender.* A crucial topic is the growth in the number of women's teams and in the ways in which women athletes do and do not share the attributes of their male counterparts. It is confusing, however, to move back and forth constantly between consideration of men's and women's teams at each stage of the discussion; a clearer picture emerges when we first examine the admission of male athletes and then present a comparative analysis for the women, beginning in Chapter 6.

Numbers of Male Athletes

The percentage of male students in the '89 entering cohort who earned athletic awards ranged from 5 percent at the Division IA public universities and 9 percent at the Division IA private universities to 27 percent at the Ivy League schools and 32 percent at the Division III coed liberal arts colleges (Figure 2.1).[3] Even more recent data from the Equity in Athletics Disclosure Act (EADA) filings show that in 1997–98 the absolute number of men playing intercollegiate sports at an illustrative set of these schools was 209 at Tulane, 305 at Denison, 362 at the University of Michigan, 371 at both Duke and Columbia, 411 at Williams, 460 at Stanford, and 537 at Princeton (Table 2.1). These numbers represent the total number of athletes on campus (from four or five classes) as opposed to the single-year cohorts that we are studying.[4] The six sports that enjoyed varsity status at all eight of these schools were football, basketball, baseball, track, golf, and tennis. Swimming was a varsity sport at all but one school, but then the pattern varies. Ice hockey was offered at three schools; fencing, rowing, and lacrosse at four; wrestling at six; squash, volleyball, and water polo at two; and skiing at only one. Of course, many students at large also play sports at schools where intramural programs and club sports are extremely popular activities. At Denison University, for example, 87 percent of all students compete at either the varsity, club varsity, or intramural level, and the comparable percentage at Notre Dame is 85 percent.

We explore the influence of athletes on campus ethos later in the chapter. But we take note here of a fact that may strike some readers as both surprising and ironic: at many of the schools that emphasize big-time sports, the number of intercollegiate athletes tends to be small in relation to the size of the student body. On the other hand, where there is less emphasis on the highly visible big-time sports, the number of athletes playing on intercollegiate teams is often much larger, certainly in relation to the size of the student body and sometimes in absolute terms as well. At Williams, for example, approximately 40 percent of the undergraduate men play on an intercollegiate team, as contrasted with approximately 3 percent at Michigan. At schools such as Williams, the influence of the athletes on the makeup of the class is likely to be much more consequential than at a very large institution, where the athletes constitute

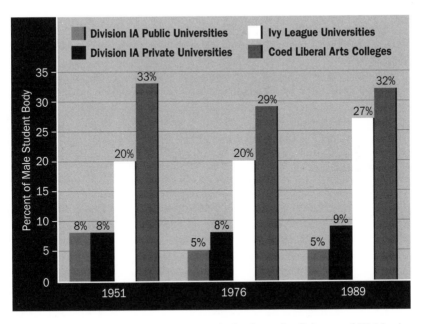

Figure 2.1. Athletes as a Percent of All Male Students (by Cohort and Division)
Source: College and Beyond (see Scorecard 2.1).

TABLE 2.1

Intercollegiate Athletes by Sport, 1997–98 (Selected Schools, Male Only)

	University of Michigan	Stanford	Duke	Tulane	Columbia	Princeton	Denison	Williams
Baseball	42	36	25	34	23	31	30	25
Basketball	16	13	15	18	16	15	22	20
Fencing	—	17	14	—	23	20	—	—
Football	121	98	98	105	70	109	68	75
Golf	22	17	11	13	9	8	13	12
Gymnastics	16	11	—	—	—	—	—	—
Ice hockey	27	—	—	—	—	26	—	25
Lacrosse	—	—	41	—	—	46	46	30
Rowing	—	49	—	—	43	41	—	22
Sailing	—	12	—	—	—	—	—	—
Skiing	—	—	—	—	—	—	—	16
Soccer	—	23	24	—	28	22	28	27
Squash	—	—	—	—	—	19	—	13
Swimming	28	26	20	—	29	30	41	31
Tennis	9	13	11	22	10	12	12	17
Track–cross-country	47	71	93	17	102	106	45	80
Volleyball	—	16	—	—	—	15	—	—
Water polo	—	27	—	—	—	17	—	—
Wrestling	34	31	19	—	18	20	—	18
Total	362	460	371	209	371	537	305	411
As percent of all men	3	14	11	7	14	22	31	40
Number of teams	10	15	11	6	11	16	9	14
Lower Profile athletes	225	349	258	86	286	413	215	316

Source: Equity in Athletics Disclosure Act filings, 1997–98.

only a tiny fraction of the total student body. This is an extremely important point, to which we will return many times.

We see from Figure 2.1 that the overall college athlete percentages have remained consistent over time. The '51 entering cohorts look very much like the '89 cohorts in this regard. These percentages have changed the most in the Ivies, with the athletes increasing from 20 percent of the male student body in both the '51 and '76 cohorts to 27 percent in the '89 cohort (a change due entirely to a marked increase in the relative number of athletes in the Lower Profile sports). Otherwise, the proportions of award-winners in the classes have been remarkably steady over time. One might be tempted to conclude that little has changed, that the presence of athletes in the student body is no different today than it was in the mid-1950s.

But are the athletes playing on intercollegiate teams today really the same as their predecessors in the 1950s? Are today's athletes as representative of their classes as the athletes of the 1950s? Suppose, for example, that in 1951 19 percent of students who had already been accepted to academically selective colleges *ended up* playing sports and earning letters, whereas more recently 19 percent of the class at these same schools was *sought out* to come to the school to play sports; in this case, similar percentages would mask substantial underlying differences. To what extent, if at all, is this example correct? The key questions are both the degree to which athletes are actively recruited and the ways in which they differ from their classmates who do not play college sports—and whether the answers to these questions have changed over time.

We were reminded in the previous chapter that college football has been taken seriously by a broad public since the late 1800s. It would be naïve to believe that the teams that filled stadiums in the early 1950s and prompted the first television contracts were dependent for players on whoever showed up on the first day of school and decided to play. Indeed, the 1929 Carnegie report noted that "the recruiting of American college athletes, be it active or passive, professional or non-professional, has reached the proportions of nationwide commerce."[5] Still, recruiting may have taken on a different meaning in the context of the highly competitive admissions processes of recent years.

Patterns of Recruitment

If you coach at Bates College and know that next year you are going to play Colby College in lacrosse on April 12th, you will want to be sure that there are some good lacrosse players in your student body. Duffy Daugherty, when he was head football coach at Michigan State, is reputed to have said, "Sure, I believe in need-based financial aid. If I need a nose tackle, I get one!" Although there may be a natural process by which players simply show up to play on teams, the coaches and the administrators who oversee college sports programs are not likely to be willing to depend on the luck of the draw. Recruitment can range from paying special attention to a prospective athlete in the application process to providing all-expenses-paid trips to campus for an athlete. Recruitment may play a substantial role in determining a candidate's chance of admission, or it may play only a very minor role.

The number of recruited athletes is directly related to the rules of the game (as stipulated by the NCAA), but in ways that some may find surprising. The presence of athletic scholarships allows Division IA schools to act much more efficiently in admitting football players and (to varying degrees) other athletes than schools without athletic scholarships. The NCAA limits the total number of scholarships in football to 85 and caps the number of first-year awards in football at 25. The traditional admissions process plays less of a role in situations in which big-time sports are considered major investments and in which (within the NCAA guidelines) the coaches are generally able to get the players they want. Ironically, the absence of athletic scholarships at the Ivy League schools and at liberal arts colleges can lead these schools to recruit *larger* numbers of athletes than they really need to fill their rosters. Although the big-time schools may be more willing to accept substantially lower academic qualifications and to pay scholarship money, the apparently more "innocent" levels of play may involve the recruitment of *many more* athletes, and not simply because these schools often field larger numbers of teams. This simple but basic point was, we are told, a revelation when communicated to one board of trustees.

The lack of scholarships in effect requires schools to "over-recruit" in order to guarantee sufficient numbers of goalies, relief pitchers, and long-snappers. In the Ivy League, if your top quarterback chooses to spend the autumn mountain biking in Hanover or becomes dazzled by the lights of Broadway and quits the team, there is no major financial disincentive for him, since financial aid is not contingent on the student's willingness to keep playing. As a consequence, what one of our commentators called "walk-off" attrition is a much more serious concern for coaches at non-scholarship schools than for coaches in big-time programs (although of course they too lose athletes, sometimes because of decisions to embark on professional careers before graduating). So, ironically, the less "serious" Ivy League allots 35 freshman slots a year to football players—which implies a hypothetical total of 140 recruited football players in college at any one time. For Columbia, where there are only 630 undergraduate men in each class, this 35-person limit (which, if the coaches prevail, is almost always reached) ensures that 6 percent of the freshman men will be football players. Hence, even the high proportions of award winners in the Ivy League and at the Division III coed liberal arts colleges shown in Figure 2.1 may well understate the total number who were recruited by these groups of schools.

With these different contexts in mind, we can try to determine the degree to which the percentage of students playing intercollegiate sports reflects the predilections of students who were accepted for other reasons by Swarthmore or Penn or Duke, and to what degree it reveals the number of places in the entering class that were set aside for the purpose of filling rosters.

Recruiting practices in the early 1950s are known only from anecdotal evidence. In general, it appears that good high school football players, in particular, were recruited by a wide variety of schools. One future collegiate star running back from that era recalls having been encouraged by a local alumnus to think about the school that he ended up attending, and also having been contacted by alumni from a number of other schools. One out-of-state school actually sent a representative to visit him at his home (a very rare occurrence in those days). High school coaches often screened approaches from colleges and not infrequently steered players to one school or another. Several athletes from the 1950s with whom we spoke recall their high school coaches as especially trusted advisors and friends. Apart from football, recruiting in even this relatively relaxed mode was uncommon. A tennis player at a Division III coed liberal arts college in the 1950s recalls having taken the initiative in contacting the coach of his sport and having being encouraged to apply and then to come, but that was the extent of it. A one-time captain of the tennis team at another school in our study was, in his words, "definitely" not recruited; he never met his future varsity coach until he was on campus. In this broadly defined group of sports and schools, the application process in the 1950s was generally initiated by the prospective student who had decided, first, that he wanted to go to the school in question and, second, that he wanted to continue playing sports.[6]

In the 1960s, top tier athletes were ever more actively—and nationally—recruited by colleges and universities at all levels of competition. Bob Blackmun at Dartmouth is reported to have begun the first highly organized national recruiting program for football in the Ivy League, and by the late 1960s the "Blackmun system" had spread to other major sports. By the time the '76 cohort entered the schools in this study, there is evidence that recruiting had become much more important, in the High Profile sports especially, but in other sports as well. The most obvious way of gauging whether students were recruited to play sports is simply to ask them. As part of the Cooperative Institutional Research

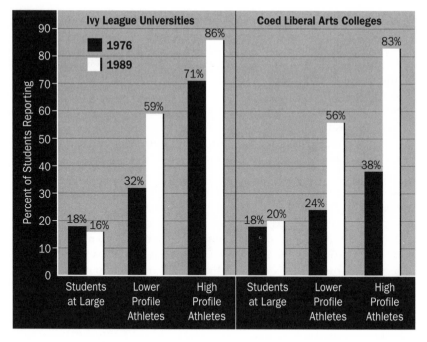

Figure 2.2. Percent of Students Reporting that Being "Recruited" Was a "Very Important" Reason for Choosing This Specific College (by Athlete Status and Cohort, at Ivy League Universities and Coed Liberal Arts Colleges, Male Only)
Source: College and Beyond (see Scorecard 2.2).

program (CIRP) survey that many students answered when enrolled in college in '76 and '89, incoming freshmen were asked to say whether being recruited by a representative of the school played an important role in their choosing to attend that college. These numbers were high for athletes in the '76 entering cohort (Figure 2.2 and Scorecard 2.2)—71 percent for High Profile athletes in the Ivy League and 38 percent for those at the liberal arts colleges, as compared with 18 percent for students at large in both sectors.[7] Even so, these figures are probably underestimates because the CIRP questionnaire did not ask specifically about athletics.

By 1989, the CIRP questionnaire had been changed to add a question about athletic recruitment, and 73 percent of those who earned athletic awards in college now reported that being recruited had played a role in their choosing which college to attend; in contrast, only 13 percent of students at large reported that they had been recruited (sector composite in Scorecard 2.2, bottom panel). The percent-recruited figure is much higher for athletes who played High Profile sports and in fact was 86 percent in the Ivies and 83 percent at the Division III coed liberal arts colleges. Even in the Lower Profile sports, nearly 60 percent of the award winners in the '89 cohort in the Ivies and well over 50 percent of those in the liberal arts colleges said that they had been recruited; the corresponding figures for Lower Profile athletes in the Division IA schools would almost certainly be far higher. These percentages suggest that the days of the "walk-on," especially but not only in the High Profile sports and the big-time programs, may be numbered—if they have not already disappeared. A major consequence of this trend is that coaches have come to play a far more significant role in the admissions process.

The process of athletic recruitment has become highly complex. Coaches play a critically important role by contacting attractive prospects directly and by having their assistants attend competitions, camps, tournaments, and other events to identify promising candidates. Alumni, high school coaches, and others refer high school athletes to coaches and alert the coaches to the presence of promising candidates at particular secondary schools. Prospective college athletes, or their parents, frequently contact coaches directly, in part because such contact may increase the odds of being admitted. (As we show later in this chapter, applicants on a coach's preferred list have a much better chance of surviving the highly competitive admissions process than do other students.) Because pre-collegiate records are now kept so meticulously, coaches of Lower Profile sports, as well as coaches of the High Profile teams, are almost certain to know a great deal about the competitive success of, say, a swimmer, a runner, or a tennis player at the time of the college application process. We are told that on occasion an entirely unheralded player still appears and ends up making a team, but this is a less and less frequent occurrence. Because of the extensive information available on precollegiate athletic achievement, and the natural desire of the prospective athlete to ensure that the coach knows about him or her, the odds that someone unknown to the coach would appear on campus, compete successfully for a spot on a team, and earn a varsity letter are, in the words of one admissions dean, "essentially zero."

The main exception to this generalization, the dean added, is crew. Because so few high schools have rowing programs, the crew teams welcome promising students—sometimes, we are told, going so far as to pick them out of registration lines. "Crew is the last amateur sport," the dean went on to say, in the sense that a student can arrive as a freshman, never having rowed, and conceivably end up as an Olympic rower—although this is far less likely to be true in the specialized sport of "lightweight" crew. In sharp contrast, one tennis coach at a non-scholarship school could remember only three top varsity tennis players on his teams over the past

15 years who had not been recruited. A basketball coach said that, over the past 19 years, he could not think of a single player who had contributed substantially to the success of the team who was unknown to the coaches at the time of admission.

THE ATHLETIC "ADVANTAGE" IN ADMISSIONS

There is, we believe, a more reliable way of measuring the changes that have occurred since 1976 in the emphasis given to athletic recruitment. Instead of asking individual students what factors affected their enrollment decisions (an inevitably subjective and error-prone approach), or asking coaches or even deans of admissions, we can compare the actual admissions probabilities for four groups of students *after controlling for differences in their SAT scores:* a base group of students at large, legacies, minority students from underrepresented groups, and athletes recruited by coaches. This exercise requires having full data on all applicants, not just those who were accepted. Fortunately, thanks to the foresight of a dedicated archivist, we have a complete compilation of such data for one of the non-scholarship schools in our study. This school is representative of that part of the College and Beyond universe in which athletics matters, but where the coach's word is not the last word in admissions.[8]

The story told in Figure 2.3 is dramatic. In the '76 entering cohort, a recruited athlete had a 23 percent better chance of being admitted than a student at large, after adjusting for differences in SAT scores; in that same cohort, legacies had an admissions advantage of 20 percent over non-legacies, and minority students had a 49 percent better chance of being admitted than a white student with comparable SAT scores.[9] In the '89 admissions cohort, the advantage enjoyed by the recruited athlete was modestly higher than it had been in '76 (30 percent versus 23 percent), the legacy advantage was also up slightly, and the admissions advantage of minority students was much lower than it had been in '76—and in fact was now the smallest of the three "advantages." Most striking of all are the results for the '99 cohort: in this group, the recruited athletes had an admissions advantage of *48 percent*—substantially more than the degree of advantage enjoyed by legacies and minority students. Data for one other non-scholarship school for which we have information concerning all applicants in the '89 cohort (including all recruited athletes) allow us to confirm the '89 part of the picture shown in Figure 2.3. At this second school, the admissions advantage enjoyed by recruited athletes in the '89 cohort was even greater than at the first school, and it was much greater than the advantage enjoyed by legacies and minority students. (The marked decline over these three cohorts in the admissions advantage of

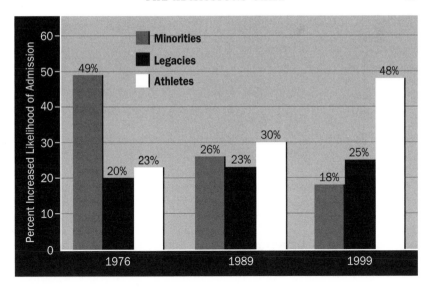

Figure 2.3. Adjusted Admissions Advantage at a Representative Non-Scholarship School, Controlling for Differences in SAT Scores (1976, 1989, and 1999, Male Only)

minority students is presumably due in large part to the continuing improvements in the qualifications of those who apply. In the epilogue to Chapter 3, we say more about similarities and differences in the recruitment of athletes and the enrollment of minority students.)

These data illustrate clearly the special attention given to athletes in today's admissions process. When race is considered as a factor in admissions, emotions run high and lawsuits are filed. And yet black and Hispanic students make up, on average, roughly 10 to 15 percent of the population at these selective schools. Admitting legacies also earns the ire of some who complain that "insider affirmative action" has no place in a democratic country. There are obvious differences in the rationale for giving special attention to members of these three groups, but, at a minimum, looking at them side by side causes us to reflect on the mission of the college or university as it is reflected in the admissions process.

In the case of athletic recruitment, there are two primary justifications. As we noted in Chapter 1, building strong athletic teams by recruiting top performers may be regarded as a good direct investment by the institution. By fueling an enterprise that potentially provides a return through gate revenues, community relations, increased fundraising, and name recognition ("image"), vigorous athletic recruitment may increase the resources available to support other activities. The second principal justification for recruiting athletes is that their athletic talent is considered a proxy for other skills and attributes that serve the institution's core educational mission. This second line of argument assumes that intercollegiate athletes have personal qualities (values, strengths, power) that will distinguish them when the games of sports end and the game of life begins. Keeping in mind these two very different justifications (support of the institution versus being part of the core educational mission) will help us assess the degree to which sports programs are playing the role that they are expected to play at selective colleges and universities.

THE SIGNIFICANCE OF SELECTION

As we noted earlier, opportunity cost is one central concept in social science that must be considered at every step along the way in assessing the investments made by schools in their athletic programs. Distinguishing "selection effects" from "treatment effects" is a second concept of equivalent importance, if the subjects of an experiment are not chosen at random. *If we hope to learn anything about the effect that playing college sports has on those who play, it is essential to take account of the differences between intercollegiate athletes and their classmates that already existed when these students were admitted, and to disentangle, as best one can, these selection effects from the treatment effects that are produced by playing sports at the collegiate level.* Examples abound as to why it is so important to distinguish "selection" effects from "treatment" effects.

"Selection" effects distinguished from "treatment" effects:

The photographs of well-coifed men and women that hang in the windows of many hairdressers' storefronts provide an excellent example of why it is important to recognize differences among subjects at the beginning of an experiment. In every case, the people look beautiful. The message that we as potential customers are receiving from these photographs is "Come in here, and you too will leave looking beautiful." But if, alas, we are far from beautiful when we walk in the door, the chances are that we will not be beautiful when we leave. We may look better—the "treatment" may have a positive effect—but we cannot hope for the outcomes intimated by the alluring photos wherein inputs (beautiful people with great hair) were jumbled together with "treatment" (haircuts).

In educating students, schools seek to have a substantive impact on those who matriculate. To gauge such impact—both within the classroom and also through the other experiences that students have—we need to understand students' academic preparation and other attributes when they entered college. Whether the objective is to prepare students for careers, for informed citizenship, to assume leadership roles, to embody certain values, or simply to develop students' academic capacity, achievement of that objective should be judged in terms of the degree of change that occurred during college. If students were randomly assigned to schools, we could start with freshman year and take up the investigation. But since students—and especially the students who play sports—are far from randomly selected, we need to start by learning as much as we can about their differences at the time they were admitted, so that we can accurately gauge how much of what we see later was already evident from the beginning.

DIFFERENCES IN ACADEMIC QUALIFICATIONS

Setting to one side their athletic prowess, perhaps the most important respect in which athletes are thought to differ from other students is in how well prepared they are academically before entering college. One of the most widely circulated myths about college athletics is the image of the "dumb jock," admitted on the basis of his ability to tackle an opposing running back rather than to do mathematics or to hold forth on literature. To test this myth empirically, we must be much more specific. Is the myth of the less-well-prepared athlete truer at some levels of competition than at others? Have the Ivies and the Division III coed liberal arts colleges escaped the perceived problems of the universities with big-time athletic programs? Is the myth more accurate in recent cohorts than it was in earlier eras? And, finally, are there marked differences in the academic credentials of those who play different types of sports?

'89 Cohort Comparisons

We start out by comparing the SAT scores of those athletes in the '89 entering cohorts who went on to play both the High Profile sports (football, basketball, and hockey) and the Lower Profile sports with the SAT scores of their classmates (students at large). The general pattern is the same in all four sets of schools depicted in Figure 2.4:

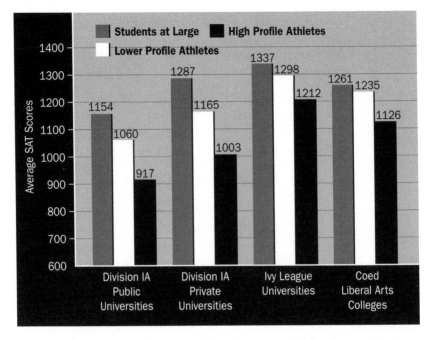

Figure 2.4. Average SAT Scores by Athlete Status and Division (1989 Cohort, Male Only)
   Source: College and Beyond (see Scorecard 2.3).

- The gaps in average SAT scores between students at large and High Profile athletes are very large in every set of schools, and especially at those places that operate big-time programs. The largest gap in scores (284 points) is at the Division IA private universities, and this is hardly surprising. These schools recruit athletes who can play football and basketball at the most demanding level of play while simultaneously attracting some of the most academically outstanding students in the country.
- Consistent with the data presented earlier in the chapter on the presence of a large "advantage" for athletes in general in the admissions process, we find that those playing the Lower Profile sports also had lower average SAT scores than students at large (with the gaps ranging from roughly 100 to 120 points at the Division IA level and from 25 to 40 points in the Division III coed liberal arts colleges and Ivy League schools).

The Growth in the Test Score Gap

How new are these patterns? We have reliable data for the '51 cohort for only the Ivy League and the Division III coed liberal arts colleges. Even in that early year and in these schools with less intensive athletic programs, High Profile athletes had lower SAT scores than did students at large. So, the existence of differences in academic preparation between athletes and other students is not a new phenomenon; it was also present in the 1950s. But the differences were much smaller then. The gaps in SAT scores have grown over time, especially in the High Profile sports: they were larger in the '76 cohort than they were in '51 in both the Ivies and the Division III coed liberal arts colleges; and they were appreciably larger in the '89 cohorts than in the '76 cohorts in the Division IA public universities, the Division IA private universities, and the Division III coed liberal arts colleges (Figure 2.5). Only in the Ivies did the gap in scores between students at large and the athletes playing High Profile sports decline between the '76 and '89 cohorts—and this was an "against-

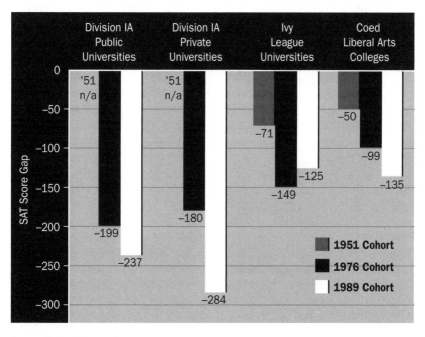

Figure 2.5. High Profile Athlete SAT Divergence from Students at Large (by Cohort and Division, Male Only)
Source: College and Beyond.

the-grain" shift that was a direct result of a league-wide policy decision (discussed in Chapter 1 and later in this chapter).

This pattern should be viewed in the context of the steadily increasing competition for admission to all of these schools. Between 1951 and 1976, a sea change occurred in what admission to a selective college or university meant. "Democratization," the enrollment of women and minorities, greater emphasis on the desirability of attending a school with a strong academic reputation, and the "nationalization" of the application process fundamentally changed the rules of admission—including the academic criteria that helped determine who made it to campus. In the Ivies, the average SAT score of students at large increased by 114 points between 1951 and 1976. By 1976, the private universities that make up the Division IA group had become very strong academically. Stanford, Duke, Northwestern, Notre Dame, Vanderbilt, Tulane, and Rice were recruiting a much more academically talented group of students than they had in earlier days. The average SAT score of students at large was 1215— high by national standards although still 84 points below the average for the Ivies and 13 points below the average for the Division III coed liberal arts colleges. The academic selectivity of the schools in each of these divisions continued to increase between the '76 and '89 cohorts, and it is the ever-higher scores of the students at large that are primarily responsible for the continued widening in the gaps in academic preparation between the students at large and the High Profile athletes, whose absolute SAT scores declined slightly in '76 and '89 (Scorecard 2.3).

Only in the Ivies did the SAT scores of the High Profile athletes rise more rapidly between '76 and '89 than the SAT scores of the students at large (causing the gap in SAT scores to decline from 149 to 125 points over the same interval that it rose by over 100 points in the Division IA private universities and more modestly in the Division IA public universities and the Division III coed liberal arts colleges). The stated goal of the Ivy League since its inception had been to enroll athletes who were "representative" of the student body at large, and, in the early 1980s, it became more and more evident that action was required if these were not to be empty words. After much discussion, the Ivy League presidents decided to regulate the degree to which the academic credentials of athletes could vary from those of their peers at the institution. Acting together, the presidents adopted a measuring rod called the Academic Index, which was plainly responsible for the reduction in the SAT score gap that is so visible in Figure 2.5. In the 13 years between 1976 and 1989, the average SATs of football, basketball, and hockey players in the Ivy League increased from 1150 to 1212—a gain of 62 points.

The experiences of the liberal arts colleges offer an interesting counterpoint. As institutions, they too became appreciably more selective over the course of the 1980s, but the mean score of their football, hockey, and basketball players actually declined by 3 points over this period. So, while the test score gap in the Ivy League had narrowed to 125 points (from 149 in the '76 cohort), it widened in the liberal arts colleges from 99 to 135 points. In the next chapter we answer the obvious question of whether these differences in test score gaps affected the actual academic performance of the athletes versus the performance of their classmates.[10]

The Less Visible Sports

In the 1950s, in both the Ivy League schools and the liberal arts colleges, the average test scores of students who played the Lower Profile sports were only about 20 points lower than the average test scores of their classmates. By the time of the '89 cohort, the situation had changed markedly (Figures 2.6a–d). In fact, now only a small number of Lower Profile teams fell inside the 20 to 30 point range: four in the Ivies, four in the liberal arts colleges, five in the Division IA private universities, and two in the Division IA public universities. The sports that most frequently record average SAT scores that are more or less comparable to the general standard for the school are crew, squash, fencing, golf, and swimming (See Appendix Table B.2.1).[11] What is most surprising is the size of the test score gap that has emerged in a sport like tennis: in 1989, tennis had the second largest gap of *any* sport in the liberal arts colleges (–143 points, second only to football) and gaps of more than 100 points in both the Ivies and the Division IA private universities. None of these gaps is of course nearly as large as those characteristic of basketball and football (which are in the –300-point range in the Division IA private universities), but the gaps in these Lower Profile sports certainly appear to be moving in the same general direction.[12]

A Broader Perspective

At selective colleges and universities, questions of academic preparation have little to do with having enough brainpower to "survive" college. The mean SAT scores of male athletes at the Division III coed liberal arts colleges and Ivy League universities in the study were above the 80th percentile of all male test-takers nationally; the mean scores of athletes at the Division IA private and public universities were above the 70th percentile and the 55th percentile, respectively.[13] The athletes at these selective schools are clearly smart people. Nonetheless, there are differences in pre-collegiate academic preparation between athletes and their class-

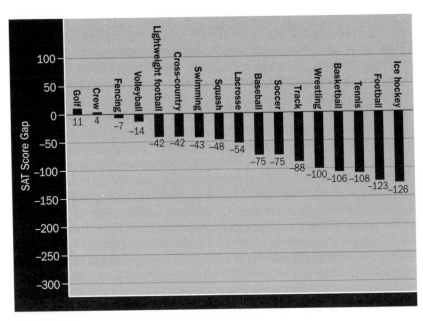

Figure 2.6a. 1989 Ivy League Athlete SAT Divergence from Students at Large
(by Sport, Male Only)
Source: College and Beyond.

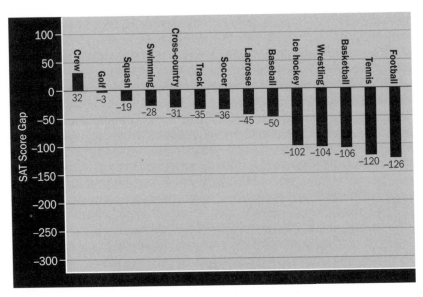

Figure 2.6b. 1989 Division III Athlete SAT Divergence from Students at Large
(by Sport, Male Only)
Source: College and Beyond.

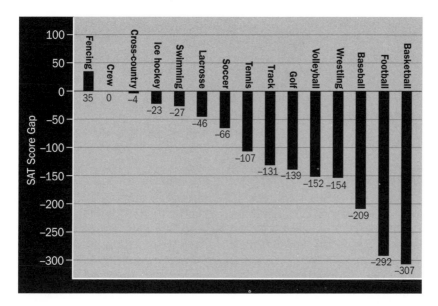

Figure 2.6c. 1989 Division IA Private Athlete SAT Divergence from Students at Large (by Sport, Male Only)
Source: College and Beyond.

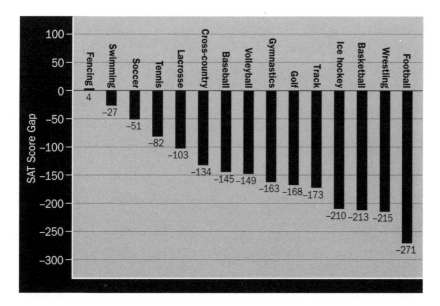

Figure 2.6d. 1989 Division IA Public Athlete SAT Divergence from Students at Large (by Sport, Male Only)
Source: College and Beyond.

mates, and these differences have generally become much more pronounced over time. These patterns of difference in academic preparation are clear *at every level of play and in sports of many kinds, not simply in the
High Profile programs at the Division IA schools.*

DIVERSITY

Athletes differ from their classmates not only in academic preparation
but also in backgrounds, goals, and outlook on the world. One place
where the stated aims of the admissions process at selective schools overlap naturally with the lore of college sports is in the building of a diverse
student body. Colleges and universities that can choose from among a
panoply of valedictorians and high-scoring test-takers have long understood that students learn from one another, and that a monolithic student body makes it harder for students to transcend the limits of the
world that they already know. Moreover, colleges and universities also
have defined their mission, since their earliest days, to include providing
opportunity for social mobility and training those who will provide leadership for all segments of society.

Athletics and Socioeconomic Status

First-generation college-goers are becoming an increasingly rare presence on the campuses of selective colleges. This is testimony both to the
facts of demographic change in America (many more parents are now
college graduates) and to how hard college-educated parents work to
push their offspring upward and onward. The percentage of all C&B students with a father who had a college degree (or an advanced degree)
rose from 46 percent for the '51 cohort to 64 percent and 75 percent in
the '76 and '89 cohorts respectively (Scorecard 2.4).

As the backgrounds of students at large have become more advantaged, students playing the High Profile sports of football, basketball, and
hockey have become a more important source of socioeconomic diversity. In the '89 entering cohort, students playing these sports were far less
likely than their classmates to come from families with fathers who were
college graduates (Figure 2.7). This clear pattern holds at every level of
play, even though it is most pronounced at the Division IA schools.[14]
Coaches and other advocates of athletic recruiting are right in noting that
recruiting those who play High Profile sports helps provide educational
opportunity for those who have been less advantaged.

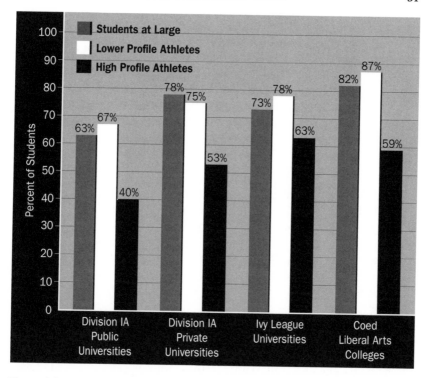

Figure 2.7. Percent of Students with a Father Who Has a Bachelor's Degree or Higher (by Athlete Status and Division, 1989 Cohort, Male Only)
  Source: College and Beyond (see Scorecard 2.4).

The same claim cannot be made, however, on behalf of those athletes who play the Lower Profile sports. If anything, the typical student who plays lacrosse, swims, or plays soccer is somewhat more likely than the student at large—never mind the football player—to have come from an advantaged background (Figure 2.7). The same pattern is found when the educational attainment of mothers is examined and when we compare the numbers of students who attended private secondary schools.

Magnitudes matter, and it is interesting to ask how the percentage of all students attending the various types of schools from different socioeconomic backgrounds would change if there were no recruitment of athletes (or if athletes came from the same backgrounds as all other students). In the '89 cohort, the percentage of all students whose fathers had a B.A. or an advanced degree would not have changed at all at the Division IA public universities or at the Ivies, while at the Division IA private universities and at the Division III coed liberal arts colleges it would have risen 1 percentage point (from 77 to 78 percent and from 81 to 82 percent, respectively). The overall impact of athletes on socioeconomic status is less than one might have expected it to be because of (1) the generally high socioeconomic status of those who play Lower Profile sports and (2) the *relatively* small number of High Profile athletes, especially in the Division IA schools.

The Enrollment of African Americans

One of the myths associated with college sports is that athletics provides a particularly attractive pathway for minority students, and especially black students, to escape from poverty. When a school makes an admissions decision, it not only offers an opportunity to an individual, it also sends a signal to others, including students who have not even applied. Through this signaling effect, the school is saying, in effect, "here is what we value." What message concerning race have schools been sending through their athletics programs, and what have been the direct and indirect effects?

There has been a great deal of debate about the role of sports in this country's minority communities. At one end of the spectrum are those who advocate an emphasis on sports for the sake of the lessons learned on the field—the justification used by those who support midnight basketball programs. A number of coaches, in particular, also argue that without the appeal of intercollegiate athletics many fewer African American students would attend college. The contrary view, espoused by sociologist Harry Edwards and Henry Louis Gates, the chairman of African American Studies at Harvard, is that by excessively celebrating sports and sports heroes we fail to celebrate the success stories, the traits, and the educational values that are more enduring and more widely attainable than the fleeting glory of the slam dunk. But before we debate the effects *for the black community* of athletics as a means of access to higher education, we should examine the record of what degree of racial diversity athletics has brought to selective colleges and universities.

In 1951, fewer than 1 percent of the students enrolled at the schools in this study were reported to be black, and enrollment data at a number of the schools do not show that they had any black students at all (Scorecard 2.5). During these years, athletics provided a limited avenue of access at a very few places, with schools like Michigan and Oberlin enrolling black students who played High Profile sports in higher proportions than they were represented elsewhere on the campus. For the most part, however, African Americans who sought a college degree (regardless of their athletic interests) went mainly to the Historically Black Colleges and Universities.

By 1976, the world had changed. All schools in our study were now actively seeking to admit talented black students, although even with race being taken into account in admissions only 5 percent of all male students were black (the percentage was slightly higher in the Ivies). A much bigger change was evident in the High Profile sports. The overall proportion of football and basketball players coming from the African American community at the scholarship-awarding schools in Division IA was now four to five times their proportion in the student body at large. In the '89 cohort, the percentage of High Profile athletes who were black was higher yet (Figure 2.8). At the scholarship-granting schools, African Americans accounted for nearly 40 percent of all students playing football or basketball. For these students, it seems, the "golden ring" held out to African American high school students who were excellent athletes had been seized, and the campus was more racially diverse as a result. Not everyone, however, saw the picture this way:

Sociologist Harry Edwards on the role of sports in the black community:

Black communities, black families, and black student athletes themselves also have critically vital roles to play in efforts to remedy the disastrous educational consequence of black sports involvement. The undeniable fact is that through its blind belief in sport as an extraordinary route to social and economic salvation, black society has unwittingly become an accessory to, and a major perpetuator of, the rape, or less figuratively put, the disparate exploitation of the black student athlete. We have in effect *set up our own children* for academic victimization and athletic exploitation by our encouragement of, if not insistence upon, the primacy of sports achievement over all else.[15]

Under current admissions policies at a few universities, the athletic director who told us "If it weren't for our programs, you wouldn't see a black face on this campus," is more right than wrong; however, other minority students could presumably assume the places in the class now filled by athletes, especially if given the same resources (recruiting efforts, financial aid, and tutoring). Even at the liberal arts colleges, where there were (and are) no athletic scholarships, the opportunity to play sports was surely one part of the allure that attracted some black students who might otherwise have felt no particular desire to attend college in small rural towns like Gambier, Ohio, or Clinton, New York. And while the Ivy League football and basketball teams continued to have higher proportions of

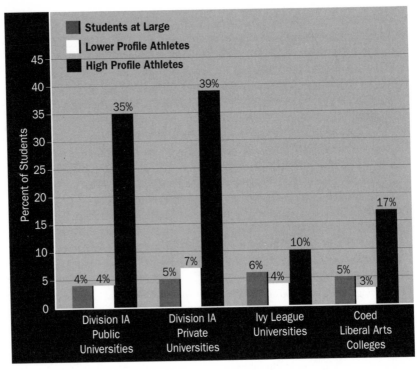

Figure 2.8. African Americans as a Percent of Male Students (by Athlete Status and Division, 1989 Cohort)
  Source: College and Beyond (see Scorecard 2.5).

black players than were present in the overall student populations, the percentage of High Profile athletes who were black was lower (about 10 percent) than in the other sets of schools. This difference may be due to the influence of the Academic Index, which prescribes the SAT bands within which recruited athletes must rank. It has been argued that this internal regulation has limited the ability of the Ivy League schools to recruit talented African American athletes since, for the rest of the admissions pool, SATs are considered as one factor among many in admissions, but without any hard and fast rules about what level of scores is required.

Thus the racial composition of the High Profile sports teams has clearly helped to diversify campuses, and it has sent the message to prospective students that if you are African American you would be particularly welcome at these schools if you have football or basketball talent. The same statement cannot be made, however, for the Lower Profile sports (Figure 2.8), in which the percentage of male athletes who were black was generally in the 3 to 4 percent range. The case for recruiting athletically talented candidates to play these other sports (which account for two-thirds of the athletes on campus) cannot plausibly include reference to racial diversity.

If we conduct the same kind of test that we used earlier to estimate the net effect of athletic recruitment on socioeconomic status, we find that, although athletics helps promote racial diversity, the impact is modest. Focusing for the sake of simplicity on the sector composite, *we find that the percentage of African American males in the '89 cohort would have declined 1 percentage point, falling from 6 percent to 5 percent, if the athletic contribution to racial diversity had been eliminated—assuming that those slots and resources were not devoted to admitting other talented black applicants.*

Differences in Outlook and Goals

Anyone who has taught knows that there is nothing more limiting than a classroom that houses no disagreement. Nothing will further student learning more than a heated debate over the best way of reducing welfare rolls, the reason behind Hamlet's delay in killing Claudius, or the role of glucose in transmitting brain signals. Correspondingly, since college years should be an important period of personal growth, education occurs when lively debates take place in the dorms and the dining halls, as well as in the seminar rooms.

From this perspective, one relevant question is: what sorts of views did athletes and other students already hold when they arrived on campus? Critics of academically selective institutions often complain that these campuses are monolithically liberal, and the CIRP surveys of entering freshmen allow us to investigate this issue. We find that male athletes in the '89 entering cohort were less likely to classify themselves as either Liberal or Far Left than students at large. In the coed liberal arts colleges, for example, 34 percent of the athletes put themselves in this category, as compared with 45 percent of the students at large (Scorecard 2.6).[16] We also find that athletes who played High Profile sports were less likely to classify themselves as liberal than those who played the Lower Profile sports. This finding is in part related to the differences between these two groups of athletes in socioeconomic status that we noted earlier. However, controlling for differences in socioeconomic status has only a modest effect on these differences in outlook. Athletes tend to be less liberal than other students even when we compare only those from similar family backgrounds.

Other questions on the CIRP survey that probe attitudes on specific issues of the day confirm that there are some real differences in the outlooks typical of athletes and other students. To cite just one example, 36 percent of male athletes in the '89 entering cohort agree, or agree strongly, that "the federal government should do more to control the sale of handguns" as compared with 46 percent of students at large. In short, male athletes contribute to the campus scene a somewhat different perspective than most of their classmates. The next question, to which we return in Chapter 3, is whether there is enough interaction between athletes and other students to allow these differences to have the kinds of beneficial educational effects that we would expect them to have.

Evidence of difference is also present when we shift from consideration of broad social and political points of view and ask what goals are most important to students when they enter college. Athletes, and especially those who play the High Profile sports, are much more inclined than students at large to emphasize the importance to them of achieving financial success. When asked about their goals in life, consistently higher percentages of athletes than of students at large say that, for them, it is "very important" or "essential" to "be very well off financially." Although the overall importance attached to financial success varies by type of school, the same pattern holds at every type of institution in our study, from the large Division IA public universities to the small coeducational colleges (Figure 2.9).[17]

It would be natural to expect first-generation college students, or students from families with modest resources, to be more concerned about making money than students from privileged backgrounds, who may simply assume that they will do just fine in the "economic game." One way of correcting for differences in family circumstances is by comparing the goals of athletes and students at large after first grouping students according to the educational attainment of their fathers. The same pattern still exists. For example, among male students at the Division III coed liberal arts colleges whose fathers were not college graduates, 32 percent of the athletes and 23 percent of the students at large said that it was "very important" or "essential" to "be very well off financially"; at the other end of the spectrum, among those whose fathers had earned advanced degrees, 22 percent of the athletes and 16 percent of the students at large checked the "very important" or "essential" to "be very well off financially" response. We will see in subsequent chapters that this strong interest in economic returns affects both choices made in college (of field of study, for example) and later decisions concerning sector of employment and occupation.

The point to emphasize is a simple one, but one that is often overlooked: decisions to admit students in order to achieve a particular objective (filling the rosters of highly competitive intercollegiate teams) have other consequences as well. As one experienced university administrator liked to say,

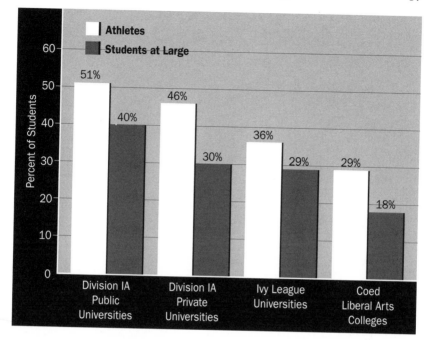

Figure 2.9. Percent of Freshmen Reporting It Is a "Very Important" or "Essential" Goal to "Be Very Well Off Financially" (by Athlete Status and Division, 1989 Cohort, Male Only)
    Source: College and Beyond.

"people come in packages"—that is, one characteristic (athletic prowess) may well correlate with a wide range of other skills, characteristics, values, and goals. Much of the rest of this book is devoted to seeing how this particular "package" translates into differences in how athletes fare as students and in the paths that they choose later in the game of life.[18]

This examination of the recruitment and admission of male athletes has shown, first of all, that athletes make up a far higher percentage of the overall number of male students at both liberal arts colleges such as Denison or Wesleyan and at Ivy League universities than they do at large private and public universities. Thus, contrary to what many may assume, athletes will have a much greater impact on the makeup of the class—and on campus ethos—at the non-scholarship schools in our study than at universities with high-visibility athletic programs such as Michigan, where only 5 percent of the male students are athletes.

Second, the recruitment of athletes has become much more aggressive, professional, and intense. This is true at all levels of competition, including Division III, and in all sports, including the lower-visibility ones such as tennis and swimming. Coaches have come to play a much more important role in the admissions process than they used to play, and there are fewer and fewer "walk-on" athletes.

Third, as admissions has become ever more competitive at these academically selective colleges and universities, the admissions "advantage" enjoyed by athletes has increased markedly. In the case of one school for which we have complete data, the recruited athlete who entered college in 1999 had a 48 percent greater chance of being admitted than the average student at large, after controlling for differences in SAT scores. This admissions advantage has increased steadily over time and is now much greater than the corresponding advantage enjoyed by legacies and minority students.

Fourth, as one would expect, the typical athlete enters college with weaker academic credentials than his classmates. The gaps in SAT scores have grown over time (as the academic credentials of students at large have improved), and they have spread from the big-time programs to the colleges and from the High Profile sports to all sports.

Fifth, although athletes contribute to both the socioeconomic and racial diversity of colleges and universities, these effects are very small (in part because the Lower Profile sports attract relatively few minorities or others from less advantaged backgrounds). For example, we estimate that, if the athletic contribution to racial diversity were eliminated altogether, the overall percentage of male students who were African American would fall by about 1 percentage point.

Sixth, the selection effects associated with athletic recruitment are not limited to differences in academic preparation, racial mix, and socioeconomic background. Athletes also tend to be more conservative than other students and to have an appreciably greater interest in being very well off financially. These differences persist even after we control for associated differences in socioeconomic status.

CHAPTER 3

The College Game:
Academic Outcomes for Men

As WE SAW in the previous chapter, the male students who are admitted to selective colleges and universities and play intercollegiate sports are, increasingly over time, different from other admitted students. Since the 1950s, their test scores have diverged more and more from those of their classmates. Especially in recent years, they have come to campus with different values, interests, and aspirations. They want different things from school and from life.

Recognizing these differences, we next consider what the college careers of these students have been like, off the field. At the big-time schools, an athletic scholarship may provide an opportunity for a free education, but it also entails obligations that could hinder learning. The non-scholarship schools in our study are often held up as exemplars of how the ideal of the scholar-athlete balance can be maintained. Students who play sports there are more likely to enter college as high academic achievers, but they too have different aims and are slightly less well prepared academically than their classmates. Although there is clearly a major difference in circumstances between those athletes who have athletic scholarships and those who do not, competing at the intercollegiate level requries serious commitments by athletes at all of these schools.

Do athletes have different collegiate experiences than their classmates? In this chapter, we first consider trends in graduation rates and grades before looking deeper into the factors that affect academic performance. We conclude by considering the degree to which athletes choose different fields of study than other students, and, more generally, the extent to which they are isolated from, or integrated into, the various academic and social communities that one finds on a campus.

GRADUATION RATES

In response to calls for accountability from both outside and inside the organization, the NCAA began in the mid-1980s to track the graduation rates of athletes and students at large at all Division IA institutions and to make these data public. Though no sanctions are imposed upon schools for having low graduation rates, the very publication of figures showing what percentage of athletes graduated was intended to shame schools into doing a better job of graduating those whom they admit.

It is by no means evident, however, that "the cleansing light of the sun" has been all that effective in this instance. A recent NCAA study found that while the overall graduation rate for Division IA male athletes was 58 percent, "only 41 percent of male basketball players in Division IA graduated [within six years of entry], the lowest rate since 1985 . . . ; and 51 percent of football players graduated, also the lowest since the class entering in 1985."[1] The graduation rates for black athletes are appreciably lower and have likewise declined. It should also be noted that the overall graduation rates for athletes are roughly the same as, and actually slightly higher than, the overall graduation rates for all students—a more encouraging result, but one that must be judged in light of the fact that many athletes receive tutoring and other forms of special support. Moreover, athletes at scholarship-granting institutions do not face the same financial barriers to graduation as other students do.

Graduation rates at the selective schools in our study can be seen to be a world apart (Scorecard 3.1). In the 1989 cohort, graduation rates for athletes at the selective schools dwarfed the national averages and were higher than the graduation rates for students at large at all levels of play, except for the Division IA private universities. This statement holds for the athletes who played football and basketball, as well as for those who played the Lower Profile sports. Clearly, "surviving" college has not been a big issue for athletes at these selective schools. Sports involvement may in fact have provided a stronger incentive to continue in school and a greater degree of stability than many other students experienced.[2]

When we look at longer-term trends, we see that the graduation premium for athletes—that is, the increased likelihood that a college athlete will graduate—has been present all along and has actually diminished over time as other students have been catching up with the athletes. In the '51 entering cohort, the overall graduation rate for athletes was 19 percentage points higher than the overall graduation rate for students at large (82 percent versus 63 percent in the sector composite), whereas in the '89 entering cohort the differential favoring athletes was only 3 percentage points (89 percent versus 86 percent). The narrowing of the differential has occurred because graduation rates for athletes—which have always been high at these selective schools—have increased only modestly, whereas increased selectivity has combined with students' increased focus on claiming a diploma to raise graduation rates for other students dramatically. Of course, noting that the gap in graduation rates has narrowed is hardly a criticism of athletes—what more could they do than graduate at extraordinarily high rates? Instead, this comparison merely acknowledges that what had been a distinct advantage for those who played sports in the earlier years has now become more commonplace.

Part of the explanation for the high graduation rate of athletes at the selective schools is surely that playing a sport—or taking anything seriously in college—helps to keep students on track. Figure 3.1 shows the graduation rates of athletes in High Profile and Lower Profile sports, a group of students whom we were able to identify as having participated intensively in other extracurricular activities, and students at large. Although we did not try to identify all students involved in every kind of extracurricular activity, we were able to identify a group whom we knew to have participated in an active and time-consuming way.[3] Among the musicians, student newspaper editors, actors, leaders of debate societies, and others who make up the extracurricular group, graduation rates are

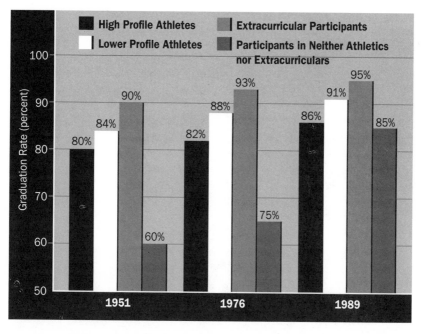

Figure 3.1. Six-Year Graduation Rate (by Athlete/Extracurricular Status and Cohort, Male Only)
    Source: College and Beyond (see Scorecard 3.1).

also much higher than the norm and are even higher than the rates for the athletes. As the figure shows, the extracurricular pool also has been graduating at high rates since the 1950s. Clearly time spent on an activity outside classes does not in any way lessen the chances that a student will earn a degree.

GRADES: ACTUAL AND PREDICTED ACADEMIC PERFORMANCE

Rank-in-Class

Inspection of the grades earned by athletes in recent years conveys an entirely different—and far less favorable—picture of their academic performance. The athletes in the 1989 cohort who played football, basketball, and hockey had average grade point averages (GPAs) that put them, as a group, at the 25th percentile of their class; the athletes who played the Lower Profile sports ranked, on average, at the 40th percentile (Figure 3.2). As the figure shows so clearly, these are by no means the results

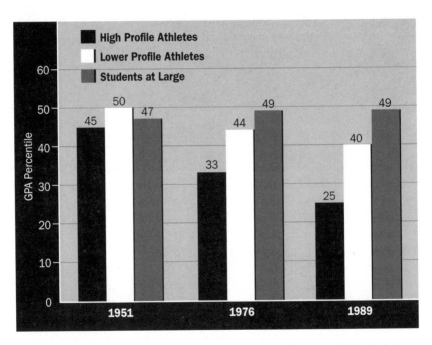

Figure 3.2. Mean GPA Percentile (by Athlete Status and Cohort, Male Only)
Source: College and Beyond (see Scorecard 3.2).

achieved by the athletes who attended these schools in the early 1950s. The football, basketball, and hockey players in the '51 entering cohort had an average class rank that was only slightly below that of students who played no college sports at all, and those who played the Lower Profile sports actually had a *higher* mean class rank.[4]

Averages obscure the extremes of the ranges, which are even more revealing. Among the members of the 1989 entering cohort, 72 percent of the High Profile athletes and 49 percent of the Lower Profile athletes ranked in the bottom third of the class. The comparisons with earlier cohorts (Figure 3.3) show the pronounced shift in this bottom-third share from one cohort to the next. At the other end of the range, we find that only 9 percent of the High Profile athletes in the '89 cohort finished in the top third of their class.

In short, the change over time in the overall academic performance of athletes is dramatic. No one would want to claim that grades are the most important thing in life, but in seeing these marked changes over time, we are reminded that those who remember the scholar-athlete balance of by-

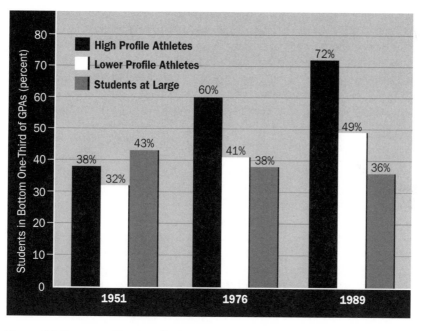

Figure 3.3. Percent of Students with GPA in Bottom One-Third of Class (by Athlete Status and Cohort, Male Only)
   Source: College and Beyond (see Scorecard 3.3).

gone days are recalling a group whose overall academic profile differs dramatically from today's realities.

The patterns across all levels of competition are surprisingly similar (Scorecards 3.2 and 3.3). One of the noteworthy comparisons is between the High Profile athletes in the Division III coed liberal arts colleges and those in the other divisions. The average rank-in-class of the High Profile athletes, which declined sharply at all levels of competition between the '51 and '76 cohorts, declined by a smaller amount over those years at the coed liberal arts colleges. However, by the time of the '89 cohorts, the High Profile athletes at the coed liberal arts colleges were doing no better academically (relative to their classmates) than their counterparts in the Ivy League and the Division I public universities. The respective mean rank-in-class was the 28th percentile at the Division III coed liberal arts colleges, the 29th percentile in the Ivies, and the 27th percentile in the Division IA public universities. We interpret these figures as demonstrating again the degree to which patterns generally associated with the High Profile programs in Division IA universities have spread even to the Division III colleges.

A special word must be said about the situation facing the Division IA private universities, such as Duke, Notre Dame, Stanford, and Vanderbilt. From the standpoint of their relative academic performance (compared with that of their classmates), the High Profile athletes in this set of private universities fared worst of all; their average class rank is at the 18th percentile. As pointed out in the previous chapter, these schools simultaneously attract some of the ablest students in the country and yet must also compete for the very best players with all the other High Profile programs. Given these circumstances, it is perhaps not surprising that over 80 percent of the High Profile athletes in the Division IA private universities ended up in the bottom third of the class (Scorecard 3.3).[5]

We saw in the previous chapter that the Ivy League's Academic Index, which was instituted in the mid-1980s, slowed the decline in SAT scores among Ivy athletes, but we now see (Scorecard 3.2) that the in-college class rank of those same athletes continued to decline. In other words, while the SAT scores of football, basketball, and hockey players in the Ivy League *rose* by over 60 points between 1976 and 1989, and while the SATs of students at large at these schools rose by only 38 points, the mean rank-in-class of Ivy League High Profile athletes continued to *fall*, and an ever larger share of them ended up in the bottom third of the class. In one sense, the Index clearly worked (average SAT scores of athletes rose both absolutely and relative to those of their classmates); but in a larger sense, its effects seem limited (the average rank-in-class of these athletes continued to fall). The decline in rank-in-class among High Profile athletes in the Ivies during a period when their admissions qualifications improved leads us to ask an important question: to what extent are these athletes living up to their academic potential?

Actual Performance versus Predicted Performance

The straight facts are useful in pinpointing who finished where in the class, but a more sophisticated assessment requires looking at outcomes in juxtaposition to what might have been expected in the first place. The first-round draft pick with all the talent in the world but an inability to "deliver" is often labeled an "underperformer." Conversely, a player like former Chicago Bears linebacker Mike Singletary, who was considered too small to make the NFL but who became all-pro, earns the title of "overachiever"—the person with something extra that enables him to get the most out of the tools at his disposal. To evaluate fully the myth of the "dumb jock"—or to ask if athletes today are more or less like their peers in the 1950s—it is not enough to look at grades alone. We need to see if the athletes did better or worse than we might have expected them to do on the basis of the academic preparation that they brought to campus in the first place. The conflicting trends in the Ivy League data between 1976 and 1989 (when athletes' SATs *rose* more than those of their classmates, and yet their relative place in class rankings *fell*) certainly suggest that differences in SAT scores were not the full explanation for differences in academic performance.

Intercollegiate athletes differ from students at large in a number of respects that help to predict academic performance, and multivariate analysis allows us to take account of these differences. We know from companion research that, other things equal, the rank-in-class of students in these academically selective schools tends to be higher if (1) they had relatively high SAT scores on entering college; (2) they majored in the humanities or the social sciences rather than in the sciences and engineering; and (3) they came from families with high socioeconomic status.[6] Taking account of differences between athletes and other students in these respects helps account for the pronounced differences in rank-in-class reported previously, but significant differences remain.

We see in Table 3.1 the *net* effects on rank-in-class of being an athlete, after controlling for the effects of these other factors. Results are presented separately for athletes who played High Profile sports and athletes who played other sports.[7] (There are no results for the '51 entering cohort because we lack sufficient test score data to conduct the same analysis; in any case, there is no gap in academic performance that needs to

TABLE 3.1
Underperformance of Athletes, Controlling for Differences
in SAT Scores, Major, and Socioeconomic Status
(by Athlete Status, Cohort, and Division, Male Only)

	Division IA Public Universities	Division IA Private Universities	Ivy League Universities	Coed Liberal Arts Colleges
1976				
High Profile athletes	3.7	**–5.0**	**–10.1**	–3.5
Lower Profile athletes	2.1	2.5	**–4.5**	**–8.3**
1989				
High Profile athletes	–1.1	**–7.7**	**–10.8**	**–8.8**
Lower Profile athletes	–3.8	**–7.2**	**–6.7**	–3.0

Source: College and Beyond.
Note: **Bold** values are significant at a 90 percent level of confidence.

be explained for that cohort.) In the 1976 cohort, we find a performance gap among the High Profile sports athletes at the Ivies of −10.1 points, which means that the typical football or basketball or hockey player at one of these schools had a rank-in-class that was 10.1 percentile points lower than the rank-in-class of a student at large who had the same SAT scores, majored in the same field, and came from the same family background; the Ivy League athlete in the Lower Profile sports had a performance gap that averaged −4.5 points. The athletes at the coed liberal arts colleges also had performance gaps (−8.3 points for the Lower Profile athletes).

Performance gaps in the Division IA public universities were not statistically significant, but this result has to be interpreted in the context of the relatively small numbers of athletes at these schools, and especially athletes in the High Profile sports, who had SAT scores that overlapped with those of their classmates. To be sure, the High Profile athletes, in particular, did not do at all well academically at these schools (recall Scorecards 3.2 and 3.3), but their performance was consistent with what they might have been expected to do. They came in with appreciably lower test scores than their classmates, and although their grades did not exceed what might have been anticipated, they did not fall short either, relative to what could have been foreseen. In the Division IA private universities, the Ivies and the Division III coed liberal arts colleges, on the other hand, athletes came in with test scores that were high enough to permit comparisons of academic performance with large numbers of other students who did not play sports. In these settings, statistically significant degrees of underperformance are observed on a consistent basis.[8]

By 1989, the phenomenon of athletes underperforming their predicted class rank had spread to all levels of competition in the Lower Profile sports, and it had deepened in the High Profile sports at all levels of play except for the Division IA public universities (where, even more than in the '76 cohort, radically different distributions of SAT scores make statistical comparisons difficult). The widespread nature of the phenomenon can be seen both in the bottom panel of Table 3.1 and in Figure 3.4 (where the shaded areas on both sides of the point estimate, representing one standard error in either direction, show how confident we can be that this finding of underperformance is not a statistical artifact). The results speak for themselves. There is obviously a pervasive problem

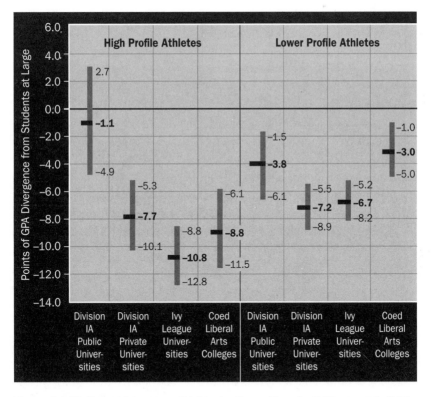

Figure 3.4. Underperformance of Athletes, Controlling for Differences in SAT Scores, Major, and Socioeconomic Status (by Athlete Status and Division, 1989 Cohort, Male Only)

Source: College and Beyond.

that requires an explanation. The test scores (and the other factors included in the regression) predict what students should have been expected to achieve if the college game were all about class rank, if everyone were starting in the same place, and if everyone shared the same goals. But is this the right way of looking at the question?[9]

Roots of Underperformance in High School

As we saw in the previous chapter, college athletes did not become athletes overnight at age 17. Having focused on sports—and having been successful enough to attract the attention of college coaches and admissions officers—future intercollegiate athletes may have had different notions from their fellow high school students of what is most important in school and how they should allocate their time and energy. Is it possible that maximizing one's academic potential—even among those with relatively high test scores—becomes a lower priority before college even begins for those who are succeeding at sports and, in the process, garnering institutional approval from their high school as well as admiration from peers and family?

We were able to test the question of whether the performance gaps that we have identified existed before the future winners of athletic awards entered college—at the time that they were admitted—by using data about other tests (AP exams, subject-specific Achievement Test scores) and high school grades. By adding this additional pre-collegiate information, we are able to ask whether participation in college sports should be blamed" for the underperformance of intercollegiate athletes or whether doing so would be specious, since the differences in performance were there all along.

Adding this other pre-collegiate information does in fact explain away some part of underperformance (compare Table 3.2, which shows how much underperformance is left after we add the additional information, with the results in Table 3.1). The underperformance of High Profile athletes in the '89 cohort at the scholarship schools is reduced substantially. In the Ivy League, the 10.8-point underperformance of players in the High Profile sports is cut to 4.8 points after controlling for differences that were already revealed at the high school level. In the coed liberal arts colleges, underperformance among High Profile athletes drops, but not as much as elsewhere, suggesting that a bigger part of the shift away from academic priorities for these athletes took place in college.

The evidence suggests, then, that high school underperformance (or, more accurately put, high school performance that is less outstanding than that of the students at large who were accepted with comparable

TABLE 3.2
Underperformance of Athletes, Controlling for Pre-Collegiate
Underperformance in Addition to Differences in SAT Scores, Major, and
Socioeconomic Status (by Athletic Status, Cohort, and Division, Male Only)

	Division IA Public Universities	Division IA Private Universities	Ivy League Universities	Coed Liberal Arts Colleges
1976				
High Profile athletes	9	−2.2	**−8.7**	**−4.9**
Lower Profile athletes	4.6	**3.4**	**−4.1**	**−7.7**
1989				
High Profile athletes	1.5	**−4.6**	**−4.8**	**−6.1**
Lower Profile athletes	−0.7	**−6.1**	**−4.1**	−1.3

Source: College and Beyond.

Note: **Bold** values are significant at a 90 percent level of confidence.

SAT scores) accounts for a good deal of overall academic underperformance in college, especially among football, basketball, and hockey players. This makes sense, since colleges have been willing to be more accommodating in looking at the high school transcripts of those students that they recruit for the most visible sports. If those students had already been setting different priorities in high school and seeking their satisfaction by maximizing sports success at some sacrifice of academic success, they were justly rewarded for the choices that they made by the system of athletic recruiting. They read the signs correctly and were treated accordingly.

But we also see that, although differences in academic achievement at the time of admission explain a good part of the performance gap, they do not explain it all. Statistically significant differences in rank-in-class remain after controlling for high school records as well as for standardized test scores and the other predictors in the regression equation. What accounts for the additional impact that participation in college sports has on academic performance, beyond those differences that were already there when the admission decision was made?

Time Commitments

Playing sports today requires a great deal of time. In an effort to account for the possible effects on grades of the fact that athletes are spending more time than many of their peers on an activity other than classwork, we compared the mean rank-in-class of those who played sports with the mean rank-in-class of those who were heavily involved in extracurricular activities. The students who devoted large amounts of time to these other out-of-classroom pursuits constitute a very useful control group. What we found is that those who stayed up late editing the newspaper, played in the orchestra, or participated in student government did not suffer the same academic penalty for their activities as those who played sports; in fact, the "extracurriculars" finished much higher in the class, on average, than students in general (Figure 3.5).

Nor is this result due to pre-college differences in academic aptitude. When we control for differences in SAT scores as well as in field of study and socioeconomic status, we find that the extracurricular participants in both the Ivies and the coed liberal arts colleges *overperform*—that is, they earn *higher* grades than one would have expected them to earn on the basis of the credentials that they brought with them to college.[10] Thus, whereas heavy time commitments to athletics may harm the academic performance of some athletes, the evidence does not suggest that, by itself, time spent away from the library is a generic cause of underperformance.[11]

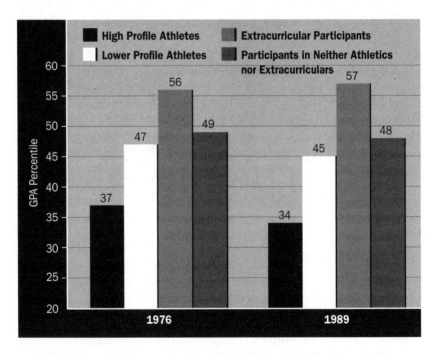

Figure 3.5. Mean GPA Percentile (by Athletic/Extracurricular Status and Cohort, Male Only)
Source: College and Beyond.

The Role of the Faculty and of Coaches

In thinking about what factors (besides time) might affect the academic performance of athletes, it is worth considering their relationships with the adults who have influence over their college "careers"—the faculty members who decide their grades (and presumably influence them in other ways) and the coaches who recruited and guided them. The College and Beyond survey instrument is helpful in that it contained a question asking former students in the '51, '76, and '89 entering cohorts whether there was anyone at college who "took a special interest" in them or in their work, "someone you could turn to for advice or for general support or encouragement." Respondents were then asked whether this person(s) was a faculty member, a coach, or someone else.

The data for the Ivy League, which are the most useful in this context, indicate clearly that big changes in mentoring relationships have occurred since the early 1950s (Figure 3.6). Among the 1951 Ivy League students, athletes (and especially those who played the High Profile sports of football, basketball, and hockey) were *more* likely to cite a faculty member as a mentor than were other students. Almost forty years later, the sit-

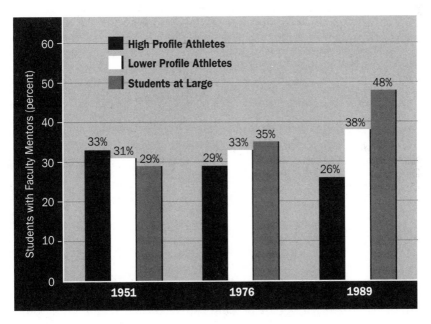

Figure 3.6. Percent of Male Students with Faculty Mentors at Ivy League Universities (by Athlete Status and Cohort)
Source: College and Beyond.

uation was very different: in the '89 cohort, the percentage of athletes playing High Profile sports who reported having a faculty mentor was only about half the comparable percentage for students at large (26 percent versus 48 percent).[12] This pronounced shift is relevant to the issue of academic underperformance because we know, from other research, that students who had close relationships with faculty were more likely than other students to do well academically.[13]

Not surprisingly, many of the athletes reported having coaches as mentors. At the Ivies, 21 percent in the 1951 cohort, 24 percent in the 1976 cohort, and 30 percent in the 1989 cohort reported such a relationship. These coaches spend far more time with students than do most faculty, and many survey respondents volunteered that they had learned important lessons about life from these coaches, many of whom see themselves as teachers first and foremost. At the same time, we also know that the coach-athlete relationship does not always encourage emphasis on academics. Some coaches seem to work not in partnership with aspiring students but more as managers of professional teams. Much of the responsibility for this kind of emphasis rests, of course, with institutions that make clear to coaches that winning games may be the most important thing.

At one school in our study, a student was about to quit a varsity team when her coach said (according to a student newspaper account), "I'm not saying I performed any miracles, but who knows if you would have gotten in on your own? Who knows the effect my backing had on your application? I find myself questioning the integrity of those students who profess their love of a sport and then simply walk away from [it] . . . two years later . . . I feel somewhat used by those students, as if they got what they wanted from me and then walked away."[14] The primary result of an interaction of this kind could only be for the student to question her own academic ability.

There are many, many coaches who work tirelessly to encourage athletes to do well academically and to look ahead to a productive life beyond sports. But as the intensity of athletic competition increases and as the reward system for coaches becomes ever more closely related to the competitive success of their teams, there is an increasing likelihood that some number of coaches will be anything but fully committed advocates of academic achievement.[15] Using the survey responses, we see that those students in the '89 cohort from the Ivy League schools and the coed liberal arts colleges who cited a coach as a mentor faced *additional* rank-in-class penalties of 5 points.[16] We should be careful, however, to avoid oversimplifying the attribution of cause. Coaches can mentor only those students who are open (or eager) to being mentored. These may well be those individuals in the athlete population who chose to make athletics a particularly high priority. One commentator on an early draft of the manuscript noted that the mentor relationships could also have changed over the years because the number of coaches has grown so dramatically. Today, as this person noted, the "coach-student" ratio may be much higher in most schools than the "faculty-student" ratio. This shift, plus the growing difference in incentive structures (with coaches rewarded more for team performance than for student scholarship), could well have affected mentoring relationships.

In thinking about the changing relationships between the student who plays intercollegiate sports and the faculty and coaches on campus, we should also recognize that faculty attitudes toward athletes may themselves have changed significantly. One knowledgeable commentator noted that faculty at his university were much more supportive of athletes and athletics three decades ago (when he was both an outstanding athlete and a serious student) than they are today. He attributes what he calls "the shifting attitudes of the faculty" to (1) the increased number who were educated in other countries with differing athletic traditions (and who therefore have not grown up with American collegiate sports); (2) a greater emphasis on research relative to teaching; and (3) less interest in all aspects of "college life," defined broadly. Other commentators have gone farther and asked bluntly: Do athletes face prejudice in the classroom? Could some part of academic underperformance be the result of professors not taking athletes seriously and assuming that they will not do well in the classroom? This is clearly possible, but the hypothesis is difficult to test. It is worth recalling, however, that we find statistically significant underperformance not only in sports like football and basketball (where athletes are most likely to be visible and known to be athletes) but also in the Lower Profile sports like fencing, crew, and soccer.

Faculty attitudes, and the campus climate in general, may affect the academic performance of athletes in other ways. On one campus, there is an ongoing debate over the time at which evening classes should start. At present, they begin at 7:00 P.M. This is a problem for athletes who have afternoon practice and thus do not have time to shower, eat, and get to class by 7:00. The athletic director regards this situation as both unfair and harmful to academic achievement, and he has been disappointed by what he regards as an entirely unsympathetic attitude on the part of the faculty member who chairs the relevant committee. A second example concerns a Summer Scholar Institute at one school that overlaps with the start of football practice. Incoming football players who would benefit from participating in the Institute (and who may need the program the Institute offers more than almost any other students) are unable to participate without missing the two-a-day practices that are considered very important for the success of the team.

The question of principle underlying these debates is whether, and to what extent, attention should be paid to the particular needs of athletes in organizing and scheduling classes and other academic activities. While compromise may be possible (and sensible) in some situations, the more general point is that the academic settings found at the most selective colleges and universities should be regarded as "givens." They are unlikely to change. As these colleges and universities have become stronger and stronger academically (as all of them have), there is bound to be a growing tension between their academic side and an athletic enterprise that is itself becoming more intensive.

The Culture of Sport

Still broader forces are also at work. As we have seen earlier and as we discuss at greater length later in this chapter, athletes share something of a common culture. It is not surprising that those who flock together—on practice fields and in buses—will develop a common culture, particularly when they start college with similar aspirations and goals. Moreover, when their daily practices tie them to a set of cultural values and attitudes that have been applauded and enjoyed both today and in the past, it is easy to see how these bonds grow tighter.

Directly relevant to the question of academic underperformance is a finding by psychologists Nancy Cantor and Deborah Prentice that athletes tend to disidentify with academics. They conclude that "The culture of athletics is at least in part responsible for students' relatively poor academic performance. . . . Athletic participation somehow exacerbates their academic weaknesses and insecurities."[17] Educational researchers Ernest Pascarella and Patrick Terenzini and their colleagues also find that differences in cognitive development during college "are not explainable by difference between these athletes and other men in their experience of college (i.e., amount studied, credit hours completed, work responsibilities, place of residence, or pattern of course work taken)." They postulate that "the norms of such a subculture [that does not always value academic or intellectual achievement], when combined with the time commitments of participation, might function to isolate football and basketball players from the kinds of interaction with diverse student peers and faculty that enrich the intellectual experience of college."[18]

Field of Study

Graduation rates and grades (rank-in-class) are important academic markers; but so are the fields of study chosen by students. The American college system is highly unusual in the degree of flexibility it allows students in deciding what they will study after they enter college. In most other parts of the world, students enter a certain type of college—a school of law or of the arts or of engineering or business. But American colleges and universities typically offer a broad curriculum, wherein students can wander quite freely. Their primary restriction is that they must choose a major. Hence, whereas a student may enter college thinking that he wants to be a poet, he may well exit as a political scientist—or vice versa. What field a student majors in is important, in part because career paths are often (but not always) built on this concentration.

Examining the percentage of students electing to major in the social sciences is a useful way of highlighting major changes over time in the preferences of athletes versus other students for different academic concentrations (Figures 3.7a and 3.7b and Scorecard 3.6).[19] In the 1951 entering cohort, athletes and other students chose to major in the social sciences in roughly equal percentages. By the time of the 1976 cohort, however, a sharp divide had appeared. Just over one-third of all athletes in the Ivies now majored in the social sciences as contrasted with about one-quarter of students at large; in the Division III coed liberal arts colleges, the movement toward the social sciences was even more pronounced, with nearly half of the High Profile athletes now having chosen the social sciences (versus just over a quarter of male students at large). As the figures illustrate so clearly, this divide then became even more pronounced: in the '89 cohort, the percentage of athletes in the High Profile sports majoring in the social sciences reached 44 percent in the Ivies and 58 percent in the coed liberal arts colleges. The sets of majors that have experienced the biggest loss of athletes are the math-engineering cluster in the Ivies and the humanities in the coed liberal arts colleges (Scorecards 3.4 to 3.7). A sea change has occurred since the 1950s: the athletes in the more recent cohorts—and especially those who play the High Profile sports—are seen to be *very* different from their classmates in the fields of study that they elect.

The increasing preference of athletes for the social sciences is surely due in some part to their greater interest in earning high incomes (see the discussion of goals in Chapter 2), combined with the perception of many people that economics, in particular, is a partial substitute for a business major in colleges and universities that do not have undergraduate offerings in business. Of course, individuals who major in the same field may do so for a variety of reasons. One relevant piece of evidence is what athletes and other students who ended up majoring in economics and political science said when they entered college about their advanced degree aspirations. In the Ivy League, nearly a quarter of the students at large who majored in these two subjects had expressed a desire to earn a Ph.D.; only 5 percent of the athletes in the High Profile sports expressed a similar inclination. The same pattern exists in the coed liberal arts colleges.

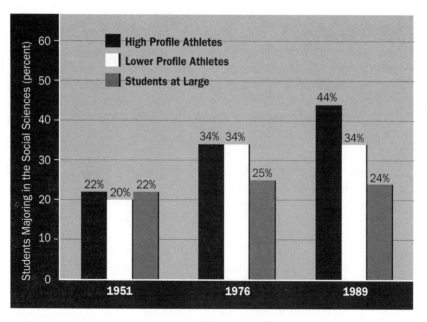

Figure 3.7a. Percent of Male Students Majoring in the Social Sciences at Ivy League Universities (by Athlete Status and Cohort)
Source: College and Beyond (see Scorecard 3.6).

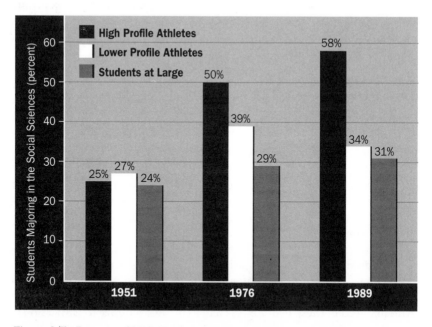

Figure 3.7b. Percent of Male Students Majoring in the Social Sciences at Coed Liberal Arts Colleges (by Athlete Status and Cohort)
Source: College and Beyond (see Scorecard 3.6).

Differences of opinion as to what an economics major ought to be about are revealed by a recent exchange at Yale:

Debate over a proposed finance concentration within economics at Yale:

For Yale's future investment bankers and business moguls, a new major may be on the horizon. . . . "I think it is a great idea and it will make Econ with a concentration in Finance students very strong candidates for leading investment banks and other business firms," Economics Curriculum member Greg Hintz '00 said in an e-mail. . . . "I think it will be useful for those freshmen who already know what they want when they come here," Maxime Ko '99 said.[20]

Yale's economics department has emphasized the study of economic decision-making. By opting for a finance concentration, many Yale economics majors would miss out on welfare, labor, developmental, and public economics, among other fields. . . . Yale should maintain its commitment to the liberal arts education in all disciplines and not just train twenty-something college students for Wall Street. They might be financial whizzes and quant jocks, but they won't be economists.[21]

Needless to say, many students at large are interested in studying economics for very practical, business-oriented reasons, just as there are of course varsity athletes who want to understand rational choice models and general equilibrium theory for purely intellectual reasons. Still, differences in goals are bound eventually to shape the discourse in study groups and classroom conversation. There is also the more general question of the extent to which the high concentration of athletes in certain fields is part of a broader tendency for athletes to live at least something of a life apart from other students on these campuses.

The "bunching" of athletes in certain fields such as political science can affect their academic experience. The popularity of these fields with athletes has contributed to a more general problem: the core social science disciplines such as economics and political science have become greatly oversubscribed on many campuses. The consequence is that faculty in these heavily enrolled fields have less time to spend with individual students, are not able to provide as many detailed comments on papers, and in general may not be able to devote as much attention to their students as they might wish. The parent of one athlete known personally to us was distressed by the lack of attention his son's senior paper had received. But then he noted that this was true for all the students majoring in political science at the school in question. There were just too many of them.

What the parent did not recognize was that the bunching of athletes in these courses was an important source of this problem. The number of faculty mentors available for athletes is also bound to be affected by this bunching phenomenon.

The concentration of athletes in certain majors, and especially athletes in the High Profile sports, is likely to be even more pronounced at Division IA schools. Although our database does not allow us to quantify the extent of such concentrations, there seems to be little doubt about their existence (see note 5, about the bunching of athletes in the urban studies department at the University of Tennessee). Referring to some of the schools in this study, a former university president commented as follows:

> The problem of ensuring that athletes are exposed to the more challenging disciplines is somewhat different in the Division IA schools than in the Ivies, etc. In many large universities there are schools or curricula which informally have become places where you can "store" athletes with a reduced likelihood that they will hurt themselves. At the University of ———, the program in Sports Management was a jock haven. (One insider account of the conduct of the program began with the lecturer's opening question to the class, "Can anyone give me an example of a license?")
>
> At the University of ———, a disproportionate number of athletes gravitated to the "Human Development and Organizational Management" curriculum. Because the curriculum did not have a math or foreign language requirement it was more congenial to less-prepared or hard-pressed athletes. Enrollment in this course of study, incidentally, helped to maintain high graduation rates for athletes.

TEAMING UP: INTEGRATION, ISOLATION, AND PEER EFFECTS

As we noted earlier, Cantor and Prentice have been studying the values, norms, and behavioral patterns of students who play sports at a number of schools like those in our study. They find that those who play sports report forming strong bonds and enjoying powerful friendships and a sense of belonging—in terms of both having a role in campus life and relating to the history of the school. Tradition helps to legitimize the choices that members of that culture then make. Being able to bond in person or over a historical distance with those who went before can provide tremendous security to 18-year-olds trying to figure out who they are. But in their surveys, Cantor and Prentice find that the strong bonds of athletic culture entail costs as well: "Compared with other students, athletes report having grown less as people at college and having spent limited time at cultural events, pursuing new interests, or meeting new people from different backgrounds. . . . Other students who are equally active in extra-curricular pursuits manage to make time for more of the broadening activities."[22]

Playing sports unquestionably brings students together for a common cause, requires sacrifices, and provides a community that will stay to-gether throughout college and often beyond. When asked about how much college contributed to their ability to form friendships, athletes were consistently more likely than any other group to report that college made the highest level of contribution. But, as Cantor and Prentice point out, this bonding can also isolate athletes within their groups and lead to a variety of peer effects, not all of which are positive.

The huge athlete—eating and lifting:

One of the consequences of intense specialization within athletics is that those who play particular positions take on a special set of attributes. One of our commentators recalled the case of an offensive tackle who weighed 300 pounds (about right for his position). As this person described his ed-ucational experience, "all I did was eat and lift." Following that regimen, a person can become very large indeed. This individual felt, as a senior, so in-timidating that he could not, in his words, "have a normal social relation-ship with anyone." Moreover, faculty stereotyped him because he was, again in his words, "such a monster." After this student graduated, he lost over 50 pounds and reappeared in the commentator's office to discuss his career prospects. It was, our commentator said, an "amazing transformation." The former student had now become a regular person again, and he regretted that the demands of his position had caused him to become so gigantic.

Concentrations of Athletes

Legend has it that athletes have not always had to observe the same aca-demic rules of the playing field as other students—having been awarded special favors by teachers in high school, having been passed along from course to course even though they find classroom life uncongenial, and so on. The milder version of this legend—and the one more relevant to the students and the schools in this study—has it that athletes choose (or are placed in) special classes and special majors that enable them to main-tain their eligibility to play and accommodate their practice and travel schedules. There are anecdotes aplenty in support of this allegation at schools with big-time athletic programs, but we have no way of judging their reliability or the frequency of such happenings. Such practices are less likely to be found at the non-scholarship schools.

What we do know is that male athletes at all of the schools in our study, including the coed liberal arts colleges, cluster in certain majors. This is a phenomenon that extends beyond the general tendency, which we noted earlier, for athletes to concentrate in the social sciences and in the more "practical" majors. In college after college, and university after university, we find that athletes in the High Profile sports, in particular, are highly concentrated in certain departments. Without mentioning schools by name, we offer these illustrations (all for the '89 cohort):

- At one Ivy League university, 54 percent of High Profile athletes majored in economics or political science versus 18 percent of male students at large.
- At another Ivy League school, 59 percent of High Profile athletes majored in economics, political science, and history—versus 35 percent of other male students.
- At one of the selective private universities in Division IA, 75 percent of High Profile athletes majored in economics, political science, and psychology—as compared with 19 percent of male students at large.
- At another leading Division IA private university, 66 percent of High Profile athletes majored in history or political science, as compared with 30 percent of male students at large.
- It is perhaps more surprising to learn that similar patterns exist at Division III coed liberal arts colleges—with 60 percent of High Profile athletes in one college majoring in either history or political science and 50 percent at another college majoring in economics alone.

These concentrations have become much more pronounced in recent years than they were even in the 1976 cohort, and it is possible that the explanation goes beyond shared curricular and career interests, relevant as these are. There is presumably some tendency for word-of-mouth referrals to affect decisions about fields of study, for friends to want to stay together, and for other social factors to come into play. These concentrations also encourage peer group effects, including some that are relevant to the issue of academic underperformance.

We also were able to chart the changes in rooming patterns of athletes from freshman to sophomore year at one of the non-scholarship schools in the 1989 cohort. In freshman year, 62 percent of all rooms contained at least one male student who played intercollegiate sports, and in only 17 percent of those rooms with athletes did the fraction of athletes reach 2 out of 3. By sophomore year, the share of the rooms with at least one athlete had fallen to 48 percent, and 34 percent now had a two-thirds concentration or more. The natural tendency for people to want to be with those who are like themselves, and to be with those with whom they share interests, affects life in the dorm as well as in the classroom.

In their more textured study, Cantor and Prentice compared the time that athletes spent with their "primary group" with the time that other students spent with fellow members of performing arts groups, members of social groups, participants in intramural athletics, others involved in campus political groups, and fellow students who shared strong service commitments. The athletes spent an average of 19.3 hours per week with their primary group, as compared with 8.56 hours per week for the performing arts group (the next highest number) and 5 to 8 hours per week for the other groups. They also found that male athletes spent less than 2 hours per week with groups other than their primary group and that the athletes (not surprisingly) reported appreciably greater difficulty than other students in spending time "with new and different people."[23]

Peer Effects

When athletes test their values against those of their peers, attitudes may solidify as the group reinforces them. "Rather than reaching some kind of middling consensus or compromise," Goethals, Winston, and Zimmerman have written, "as often happens with ordinary opinion comparison, people compete to support the [dominant] value at least as much, or a little bit more, than their peers, and thus the group polarizes, and expresses the value more extremely." They go on to note that people make choices to follow others "if the behavior [that they observe] leads to some kind of reward or reinforcement."[24] In high school, highly visible athletes often saw that emphasizing sports over an all-out commitment to academics was rewarded—they saw their teammates before them get accepted to colleges, and they acted accordingly. Is there evidence of similar peer reinforcement effects in college?

In an effort to find out if the academic performance of peers could be used to predict a student's own performance, we tested whether the percentage of an athlete's team that underperformed or overperformed academically had an effect on that student's own rank-in-class. In other words, aside from the general or average class rank "penalty" paid by students who played sports, if 75 percent of a team underperformed, did that impose an additional class rank penalty? What if 50 percent of the team performed less well than would have been predicted?

The findings are clear-cut. In addition to general rank-in-class penalties of 8 points (High Profile sports) and 4.8 points (other sports), substantial additional class rank penalties are paid if large numbers of a student's teammates underperform: 14.4 points if 75 percent of the team (or more) underperforms, 13.6 points if 50 to 75 percent of the team underperforms, and 5.6 points if the concentration of underperformers is between 25 and 50 percent.[25] This may be an actual peer effect (whereby students share values and build identities that jointly reinforce each other's choices about priorities), or it may be that such concentrations reflect the patterns of recruiting for certain teams. For example, if a reward system that devalued maximization of academic performance was well established before students started college, a team consisting of highly recruited players might well show up for their first practice already sharing these well-established behavior patterns. More generally, what we are calling "peer effects" really represents a combination of peer effects and other team-specific effects that may exist. As one commentator noted, what we observe is that there is a kind of "serial correlation" among athletes playing a specific sport at a specific school.

The main conclusions reached in this chapter can be summarized succinctly. Athletes at these academically selective schools graduate in large numbers; thus, whereas graduating is a problem for athletes at many schools, it is not usually a problem at these schools. However, athletes playing all sports at all levels of competition at these schools do much less well, compared with their classmates, when it comes to grades. Disproportionately large numbers of them rank in the bottom third of their classes (as was decidedly not the case in the 1950s). Beyond this, they underperform academically relative to what they might have been expected to do, given their SATs. Another noteworthy trend is that athletes seem "less connected" to faculty members than used to be the case—a consequence, we believe, of both shifts in faculty interests and changes in the intercollegiate programs on these campuses (including changes in the athletes recruited to these schools).

More generally, it appears that a distinct "athletic culture" is appearing in essentially all sports and at all levels of play, including the Division III coed liberal arts colleges. This culture tends to separate athletes from other students and exacerbates the problems of academic performance. As one example, athletes are more and more concentrated in certain fields of study. Athletes at all of these schools, in the Lower Profile sports as well as in the High Profile sports, seem to be heading in their own directions—and in directions that may or may not be consistent with the missions of the colleges and universities that admitted them.

We spoke with one prominent alumnus who linked what he perceived as the current mediocrity of Ivy League athletics (he may have been thinking mainly of the greater national success of Ivy football teams in the mid-

1950s) to what he saw as a larger problem—his feeling that his alma mater is not training the generation of leaders that it prepared in his day. "Today's Ivy colleges are full of hothouse flowers," he told us, "an over-focused and over-prepped generation who may be able to get 1600s on their SATs but will fade and wither long before they could go on to take the place of my classmates who learned how to deal with life."

There may or may not be deep truth in this expression of concern, and in the following chapters we try to shed some light on this question by examining the later careers of those who have "been knocked down and know how to get back up" alongside the careers of those who chose different types of tests for themselves. But whatever the evidence shows about how different groups of students do in the game of life, the pronounced differences that have emerged over the past 40 years in academic performance and choice of field of study are a powerful reminder that the intercollegiate athletes of today differ in important respects from those who played for schools like Columbia, Duke, Penn State, and Swarthmore in the 1950s. Some of today's students at large are surely far more bookish than their predecessors from the 1950s, but today's athletes may differ from their athlete predecessors in even more profound respects. Measured along many of the academic dimensions that are especially relevant to institutions of higher education, the more recently recruited athletes are less and less like their classmates. In some respects, they are as specialized in their talents and interests as the committed writer or student of physics. "Hothouse flowers" can come in all shapes and sizes.

EPILOGUE: ATHLETES AND AFRICAN AMERICAN STUDENTS— SIMILARITIES AND DIFFERENCES IN ACADEMIC UNDERPERFORMANCE

A final topic that merits discussion is the similarities and differences in academic outcomes between athletes and African American students. We know that the two groups (which of course overlap, but only slightly) share an important initial characteristic: both have been recruited actively and have enjoyed an "admissions advantage." Earlier research using the C&B database found that African American students at these academically selective schools exhibited many of the same patterns as the athletes we have been studying.[26]

On average, African Americans (like athletes) came to campus with less impressive pre-collegiate academic credentials than their peers. Then, once on campus, they earned lower grades than their classmates. Moreover, the average rank-in-class of African Americans, like that of the athletes, was lower than the rank that would have been predicted for them on the basis of test scores and high school grades—which is what we mean by "underperformance."

The Shape of the River contains a long discussion of possible explanations for this phenomenon (pp. 78–86), and many of them could pertain to athletes as well as to African Americans:

- In both cases, the roots of underperformance reach back at least into high school; however, the "unobserved" factors working against high academic performance in college by many black students (e.g., poor schools, inadequate counseling, lack of adequate emphasis on academics, relatively limited out-of-school help with academics) are more potent than the similar set of factors affecting highly recruited high school athletes (more of whom come from good schools and more affluent families).

- In both cases, part of the explanation may be found in what social psychologist Claude Steele has called "stereotype vulnerability": the assumption (or collective societal expectation) that a group of students will not do well academically can cause even high achievers to experience performance anxiety. When Steele removed the anxiety in laboratory settings, performance by both black students and women in mathematics was seen to improve dramatically.[27] Although Steele did not conduct similar experiments with athletes, there is certainly a widespread impression on many campuses that athletes (and especially High Profile athletes) are "dumb jocks," and there is no reason to doubt that such stereotyping could have similar negative effects on classroom performance. Here again, however, we would not expect the effect to be as strong for athletes as it is for black students—who are, after all, always highly visible by dint of skin color, unlike many athletes, who may be harder to identify.[28]

- Peer group pressures can also afflict both groups. Anthropologist John Ogbu has suggested that black students sometimes exert pressure on their peers not to "act white" and not to identify with "white" academic values.[29] We saw earlier in this chapter that the athletic culture has its own values and that team-specific effects can harm the academic performance of athletes.

The Shape of the River concluded that more research was needed to understand better the root causes of the academic underperformance of African Americans, that it was a problem that should be confronted directly, and that colleges and universities should be encouraged to follow the lead of those institutions that have already made progress in overcoming it.

Before suggesting that the institutional response should be the same (or different) in the case of athletes, it is useful to step back and consider the similarities and differences in the justifications that have been offered for the special efforts involved in admitting the two groups. Recruiting efforts on behalf of both can be traced to central aspects of the history of higher education that we reviewed in Chapter 1. We have seen that competition for places in the most selective schools has increased dramatically; as a consequence, applicants have felt pressure to differentiate themselves from other candidates for places in the class, and debates (and tensions) have arisen over what factors are appropriate for admissions officers to take into account in choosing among large numbers of well-qualified applicants. At the same time, colleges and universities became much more interested in the conscious pursuit of diversity, measured along many dimensions, including race, socioeconomic status, athletic talent, other unusual gifts, and special backgrounds.

Starting in the 1960s, essentially all selective colleges and universities elected to seek out talented minority candidates for two reasons. First, there has been widespread agreement that achieving greater racial diversity is an important way of enriching the educational environment for *all* students, especially at a time when colleges and universities are committed to preparing students to be effective citizens in an increasingly pluralistic world. As University of Michigan President Lee Bollinger put it: "Diversity is not an optional appendage to a first-rate liberal arts education—it is as much at the core as Shakespeare. For centuries commentators on Shakespeare have remarked on his extraordinary capacity to enter the minds of his characters and accordingly make them real. This is what we strive for through diversity as well."[30]

Second, leaders of these institutions have felt a special obligation to educate larger numbers of minority students who could then be expected to play leadership roles in the mainstream of American life. The goals have been to reduce at least somewhat the unequal distribution of access to opportunity that still exists in our country and to ensure that the most sought-after educational opportunities are available to all segments of society.

These considerations relate directly to the educational mission of these institutions and to the obligation that they have assumed to serve what many regard as pressing needs of the larger society. The contributions of minority students to the educational process on campus and their later life accomplishments indicate that these objectives have been largely achieved, notwithstanding the problem of academic underperformance.

The corresponding justifications for making special efforts in athletic admissions are similar in some ways and different in others. On campus, athletes are valued for contributing to community spirit through their efforts on the playing fields. Although it was clearly possible at one point in time (as the academic success of the 1950s cohort demonstrates) to manage the enterprise in such a way that athletics and academics were complementary, in today's world academic underperformance may be part of the price that must be paid for recruiting and building *winning* teams. We are left with the question of how much of a premium should be assigned to competitive success—a question to which different people will give different answers.

The Shape of the River documents how, later in life, African Americans who attended these colleges and universities have found success in the marketplace and have taken on leadership roles in civic activities in significantly higher proportions than their white classmates. This "giving back" has, to our minds, strengthened the case for making special efforts to admit talented minority candidates. One part of the corresponding justification for making special efforts to admit athletes is that they too have special leadership capacity. While we defer to later chapters (especially Chapters 4, 8, and 9) the question of the uses to which athletes ultimately put their education, the prima facie case for recruiting athletes is, to our way of thinking, less powerfully connected to the educational missions of these institutions than is the case for making special efforts to achieve racial diversity.

CHAPTER 4

Men's Lives after College:
Advanced Study, Jobs, Earnings

HAVING CHARTED what male athletes and male students at large were like when they arrived on campus, and having followed them through college, we are now in a position to investigate how they performed in at least some aspects of "the game of life." Having attended a school like Michigan, Vanderbilt, or Penn gave most of these young people a range of options that many others do not enjoy.

The subsequent choices that these graduates made, including decisions to pursue advanced study and then to follow various career paths, depended of course not only on what—and how—they did in college, but also on the aptitudes, attitudes, and interests that they had when they were entering freshmen. In short, it could be an error to credit (or blame) participation on an intercollegiate team for having "caused" all kinds of later life outcomes; at various points in this chapter we return to the important question of how much of what we observe in later life should be attributed to "selection" (the attributes that athletes brought with them to college) and how much to "treatment" (their experiences playing on teams in college).[1]

GRADUATE AND PROFESSIONAL SCHOOL

Advanced Degree Attainment

By the time they answered our survey in 1997, the 1989 entering cohort had been out of school approximately four years, and already 56 percent of these graduates had either completed an advanced degree or were working toward one. This is an astonishing level of commitment to graduate and professional education, and it reminds us that for many fields an undergraduate degree is no longer viewed as adequate preparation; more generally, as the percentage of the population with a B.A. continues to rise, young people increasingly choose to differentiate themselves by earning advanced degrees. Today, advanced training has become almost a requirement in many fields besides medicine and law, from architecture to social work, in which twenty years ago an undergraduate degree and an apprenticeship sufficed. For many, the MBA has an unquestioned appeal, even though it is not formally required for entrance into the field of business.

Most graduates in the '76 entering cohort have by now had ample time to complete their advanced training. Although both athletes and their former classmates earned large numbers of advanced degrees of all kinds, the athletes were more likely than other graduates to have earned an MBA and less likely to have earned a Ph.D. or an advanced degree in law or medicine. Also, appreciably higher percentages of students at large have taken masters degrees in the humanities and in a wide variety of other fields, such as public policy, public health, urban planning, social work, and architecture. This pattern is highly consistent across types of schools; the only exception is that the athletes at the Division IA public universities were less likely than their classmates to earn advanced degrees of any kind, including business degrees (Figure 4.1).[2] Distinguishing between male athletes who played the High Profile sports and those who played the Lower Profile sports, we find that the same pattern holds, but that those who played football, basketball, and hockey were less likely than Lower Profile athletes to earn advanced degrees, and especially degrees in law and medicine (Scorecards 4.1 to 4.5).

These are not new patterns. Athletes in the '51 cohorts at these schools also were more likely than their classmates to pursue degrees in business and somewhat less likely to pursue Ph.D.s and degrees in law and medicine. The differences in '51 were, however, more muted than those in '76. The data for the younger '89 cohort are harder to interpret since advanced degrees of many kinds, and especially business degrees, are often pursued after an intervening period of employment. Still, the early returns suggest that the broad differences in advanced degree patterns between male athletes and their classmates have continued to widen, especially in the Ivies. For example, 6 percent of the former intercollegiate athletes in the '89 cohort in the Ivy League schools reported that they were studying for a Ph.D., as contrasted with 15 percent of their classmates (Scorecard 4.4).

Aspirations versus Attainments

As already noted, a recurring question in this study is to what extent differences in later life outcomes between athletes and students at large

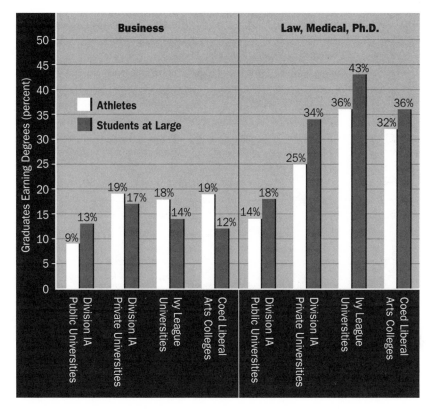

Figure 4.1. Graduates Earning Advanced Degrees (by Athlete Status and Division, 1976 Cohort, Male Only)
  Source: College and Beyond.

reflect the inclinations and aptitudes that the groups brought with them to college rather than the effects of playing sports in college. Comparing advanced degree aspirations at the time students entered college with the advanced degrees they eventually earned is one way of beginning to address this complicated question.

We present the relevant data for the recipients of medical and law degrees in Figure 4.2 (for the Ivies and the Division III coed liberal arts colleges only, because the survey data for aspirations are much more complete for those who attended these schools). Once again, a consistent picture emerges. In the case of medicine, nearly half of all entering freshmen who said that they aspired to earn medical

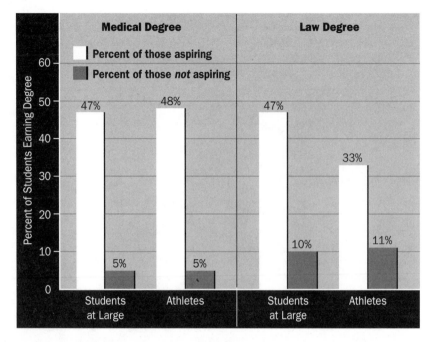

Figure 4.2. Aspiration and Attainment of Medical and Law Degrees at Ivy League Universities and Coed Liberal Arts Colleges (by Athlete Status, 1976 Cohort, Male Only)
   Source: College and Beyond.

degrees went on to earn them; in contrast, only 5 percent of non-aspirants (those who did not state a desire to earn a medical degree) eventually earned an M.D. These percentages are nearly identical for students at large and for athletes. For both of these groups, the odds of earning a medical degree were *ten* times higher for those who said on entry to undergraduate college that this is what they wanted to do than for all other students.

   The connection between aspirations and the attainment of an advanced degree is looser in the field of law, but the general pattern is the same. The main difference between medicine and law is that a larger percentage of students who did *not* aspire to a law degree when they were freshmen in college nonetheless went on to law school and earned a law degree (roughly 10 percent of the group). Also, we see that in this field there is a difference between students at large and athletes in the relationship between aspirations and attainment: among those who said that they aspired to earn a law degree, athletes were less likely than students at large to complete law school. Still, even for the athletes, the odds of earning a law degree were three times higher for aspirants than for non-aspirants—and the odds were nearly five times higher for student-at-large aspirants than for non-aspirants.

In short, we see clear evidence of the predictive power of knowing what people were like, and what they wanted to do, at the time of selection. The aspirations that freshmen had when they began college are an important predictor of the paths that they followed when they graduated from college and pursued advanced degrees, whether or not they were college athletes. The disproportionately large number of athletes who earned MBAs is surely a reflection of the strong interest in business and in being well off financially that these students expressed when they entered college.

There is also anecdotal evidence that athletic status per se sends signals to business schools. At one Top 20 business school, the dean seemed taken aback by our question of whether athletic status played a role in the admissions process. Describing how the school was competing fiercely to lift the academic ranking of its class ever higher, and recognizing that mean GMAT scores count in the national rankings, he initially responded, "No one on our committee even looks at that." But, intrigued by the question, he spoke to his admissions director before calling us back. "It turns out," he said, "that we do, in fact, yield a bit in terms of grades and scores if someone was an athlete. We take it as a sign of energy, stamina, and a goal-oriented approach to life." Steve Christakos, who worked in admissions at Darden, Kellogg, and Wharton, also commented on how and why athletics mattered to him as he reviewed applications:

> I always liked athletes for the same reasons that I liked people who had been in the military: they were confident, team-oriented, and had the interpersonal skills to do well in a corporate environment. Even at business school, where six-person study groups were the rule, these guys knew how to compete together as a team. In a massively oversubscribed admissions process where interviewing 10,000 candidates is simply out of the question, it was definitely a tilt factor that we used as a proxy for the characteristics that we were looking for, because we knew what the employers would be looking for at the other end.

Thus both pre-collegiate aspirations and the fact of having been an athlete play important roles in advanced degree attainment.

JOBS

The 1976 Cohort

There is a broad congruence in the job choices made by the men from the '76 entering cohort who attended these highly selective schools (Figure 4.3). Both the athletes and the students at large were more likely to be executives than to fall into any other job category. Both groups were also heavily represented in professional fields, including law, medicine, research, and finance. Nonetheless, there are some evident differences, which are, in the main, quite consistent with what we would have expected, given the interests and goals that the two groups had when they entered college and the different kinds of investments made by athletes and students at large in advanced study:[3]

- The male athletes were much more likely than the students at large to enter the three "business" fields shown on the left-hand side of the figure: as executives (24 percent) or to work in other capacities in finance (14 percent) or marketing (11 percent).[4] All told, nearly half

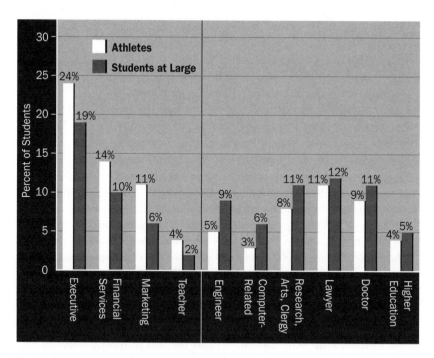

Figure 4.3. Occupations in 1995 (by Athlete Status, 1976 Cohort, Male Only)
Source: College and Beyond.

of the athletes (49 percent) were in one of these three categories, as compared with just over a third of the students at large (35 percent). Athletes were also more likely to be high school teachers, coaches, or administrators than students at large, but only small numbers from both groups chose to work in one capacity or another at the secondary school level (4 percent of the athletes versus 2 percent of the students at large).

- Conversely, the students at large were more likely than the athletes to be engineers and computer scientists, or to be working in the "research, arts, clergy" category (the right-hand side of the figure). They were also more likely to be lawyers, doctors, and academics (or employed in higher education in another capacity).[5] We see once again how closely job choices track earlier decisions concerning undergraduate majors and subsequent pursuit of various types of advanced degrees. We also see again the power of selection, since disproportionately small numbers of athletes declared, on entry to college, an interest in "writing original works" (to cite that single example).

There are some notable differences in the job choices made by athletes who played High Profile sports compared with athletes in the Lower Profile sports. The job profiles for the athletes in the High Profile sports differ more from the profiles for the students at large than do the profiles for the athletes in the Lower Profile sports (athletes in the High Profile sports are even more likely than other athletes to be in business, even less likely to be in the professions, and so on). These differences are especially pronounced among those athletes who were educated in the Ivy League and the Division III coed liberal arts colleges and then became lawyers and doctors. For example, only 8 percent of the athletes in the High Profile sports in the '76 cohort from the Division III coed liberal arts colleges became lawyers, versus 17 percent of the athletes in the Lower Profile sports; in the Ivies, the corresponding percentages are 11 and 19. The same pattern is present for doctors, but the differences are smaller.[6]

Trends

Most of the differences in job choices between athletes and students at large that we see among members of the '76 cohort were smaller in the '51 cohort (if they existed at all then), and they are magnified when we look at the early vocational choices made by members of the more recent '89 cohort. One of the most pronounced shifts is the decreasing share of athletes entering the fields wherein structures are created and technological products designed. Among the members of the '51 cohort, athletes and other students were as likely to enter the fields of engineering and architecture as were other students. As Figure 4.3 illustrates, a gap had opened by the time of '76 cohort, and this gap was wider yet in '89, particularly at the scholarship-granting schools. Even larger gaps are emerging in the fields that focus on computers and information technology. Just 4 percent of the athletes in the '89 cohort were working in these fields, as compared with 12 percent of students at large.

One place athletes have gone in large numbers is into marketing. Athletes who played the High Profile sports have always been somewhat more inclined toward this field, and increasing numbers of them are now selling (20 percent were in marketing in the '89 cohort, as compared with 13 percent in both the '51 and '76 cohorts).[7]

The data also show that, increasingly, the job sector of choice for many College and Beyond graduates—and for former athletes in particular—is financial services. Between the '76 and '89 cohorts, the percentage of men employed in financial services rose from 7 to 14 percent for students at large and from 10 to 17 percent for athletes. The shift has been most pronounced in the Ivy League schools, where 20 percent of students at large and 31 percent of all athletes from the '89 cohort entered these fields (Scorecard 4.6).[8] At the same time that the percentage of athletes in financial services has been rising steeply, the average class rank of this particular group of former athletes has been declining—from the 53rd percentile in the '51 cohort to the 41st percentile in the '76 cohort to the 31st percentile in the '89 cohort (Scorecard 4.7). This drop mirrors the overall decline in average class rank for all male athletes at these schools over this time period (compare Figure 3.2). Interestingly, however, the average class rank of those students at large who entered financial services has risen—from the 45th percentile in the '51 cohort to the 47th percentile in '76 to the 51st percentile in '89.[9] In short, whereas the athletes who entered these fields in the mid-1950s had higher class rank than the other students who ended up in financial services, in more recent years their average class rank is decidedly lower than the average rank of their classmates in this sector.

"Financial services" is, of course, an extremely broad area, and college grades may be much better predictors of success in some kinds of jobs than others within this sector. For example, one reader of our manuscript suggested that former athletes are more likely than other graduates to be found on the "sell side" of the securities business, and that the qualities that bring success in this area may have little to do with whether one got an A or a B in microeconomic theory. More generally, firms may believe that athletes bring "something special" to the financial services sector and that employers should therefore be willing to accept more modest academic credentials from these graduates of the selective schools. Such employers may be seeking personal characteristics for which participation in college sports is thought to serve as a useful proxy.

In addition, athletic involvement undoubtedly affects job placement by exposing participants to networks that are cemented in grinding practice sessions and emotional competitions. Moreover, playing on a team brings together younger students with those from classes ahead of them, thereby constructing a bridge between those who will come back to campus the next year and those who will already be out in the workplace and perhaps even involved in recruiting for their firms.

EARNINGS

Overall Differences in Earnings: Athletes versus Students at Large

For better or worse, the most common scoreboard that people watch to see who is ahead in the game of life is marked in dollar signs. Figure 4.4 demonstrates how male graduates of the C&B schools have fared financially. It is evident that they have done very well indeed, with full-time

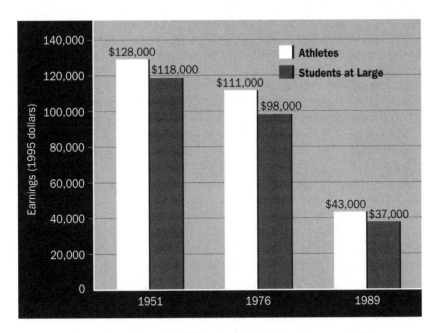

Figure 4.4. Mean Own Earned 1995 Income (by Athlete Status and Cohort, Full-Time Male Workers)
Source: College and Beyond.

workers in the '51 cohort earning roughly $120,000 on average (in 1995) and their younger counterparts in the '76 cohort averaging roughly $100,000 (also in 1995); the corresponding national average for the '76 cohort is approximately $60,000.[10] More relevant for present purposes is the clear evidence that former athletes in both cohorts earned more than their classmates (about 9 percent in the '51 cohort and 13 percent in the '76 cohort). A sizable differential exists in the '89 cohort, too, and these differences are present not only in all three cohorts but also in all four institutional groupings. The pattern is absolutely consistent: *in every one of these 12 pairwise comparisons, the average earned income of the former athletes exceeds that of the students at large* (Scorecard 4.8). The differences are not enormous, but their consistency indicates that they are consequential.

The evidence of consistent earnings differentials favoring athletes is, in at least some respects, a surprising finding. The typical male athlete had lower test scores than his classmates, came from a less affluent family, was slightly more likely to belong to a minority group, and did less well academically in college. And we know from companion research that earnings are influenced by SAT scores, socioeconomic status, racial category, and rank in class.[11] Since athletes were "disadvantaged," as it were, in all four of these respects, the earnings advantage that they enjoy over their classmates is all the more striking.

Factors Responsible for the Earnings Advantage of Athletes: A Preview of the Main Findings

How then do we explain the fact that former athletes end up making more money than most of their classmates? Is their relatively greater financial success due primarily to "treatment effects"—to battles won or lost in the pool, on the court, and on the field, to traits acquired and lessons learned through tough competition at the collegiate level? Is some part of the earnings advantage due to treatment effects of a quite different kind—to friendships formed and connections made? Is the advantage due primarily to "selection effects": to hard-to-measure qualities and attributes that tend to go along with being an athlete, but that were acquired in large part before entering college (discipline, drive, self-confidence, and affability, for example)? Or is the earnings advantage of male athletes influenced heavily by another kind of selection effect—by the greater degree of importance that future college athletes attached to making money when they were still in high school (compared with students at large), and thus by their greater interest in careers in business and in other relatively lucrative callings?

We make no claim to being able to sort out, with precision, the relative impact of the various treatment and selection effects at work here. But our data do point to some straightforward conclusions. To anticipate findings presented in some detail later in the chapter, the main elements of the story line are these:

- A first source of the athletes' earning advantage is their greater presence in the for-profit (and self-employment) sector, where average earnings for everyone are higher than they are in the not-for-profit (and governmental) sector.
- There is no statistically significant earnings advantage for athletes within the not-for-profit sector.
- Within the for-profit sector, the earnings advantage of athletes is concentrated in financial services occupations; it is not an across-the-board phenomenon.

These patterns lead us to believe that the earnings advantages of athletes are, in all likelihood, more attributable to pre-collegiate selection effects than to in-college treatment effects. Experiences gained through playing college sports did translate into higher earnings for some former athletes. However, the highly concentrated "location" of the overall athlete earnings advantage suggests that it is mainly a function of some combination of the vocational interests and values of athletes (which were evident when they entered college), their experiences playing sports before they entered college, and the contribution of their personal traits to marketplace success in fields such as financial services, where such characteristics particularly affect earnings.

This interpretation is supported by the finding that (with one important exception, discussed on pages 104–8) there is no consistent association between the "amount of athletic treatment" received in college and the earnings of athletes. Earnings do not correlate closely with the number of years that athletes competed, nor did playing sports at the most intensive levels of competition confer larger earnings advantages than those found at less intense levels of competition.

The Evidence in More Detail: Financial Rewards of Working in the For-Profit Sector

In both the '51 and '76 cohorts, former athletes were more likely than students at large to work in the for-profit (and self-employment) sector. In the '51 cohort, 75 percent of the athletes and 68 percent of the other students worked in the for-profit sector. In the '76 cohort, both of these percentages were 4 points higher: 79 percent of the athletes and 72 percent of the students at large worked in the for-profit sector (Figure 4.5a).[12] As one would expect, C&B graduates who worked in the for-profit sector earned considerably more than those graduates who worked in either the not-for-profit sector or for government at some level. The difference in average annual earnings between sectors was just under $30,000 in the '51 cohort and just over $40,000 in the '76 cohort (Figure 4.5b).[13]

Thus part of the overall earnings advantage enjoyed by athletes can be attributed quite directly to the presence of relatively large numbers of them in the sector of the economy where average earnings were higher for everyone. This pattern is consistent with the data reported earlier showing that, at the time they were admitted to college, athletes as a group gave a higher rating to financial success as a goal in life than did their classmates (Scorecards 4.9a and 4.9b). Similarly, we have seen that athletes were more interested in business careers than other students and more likely to earn advanced degrees in business. This part of the analysis is all of a piece, and in no way surprising.[14]

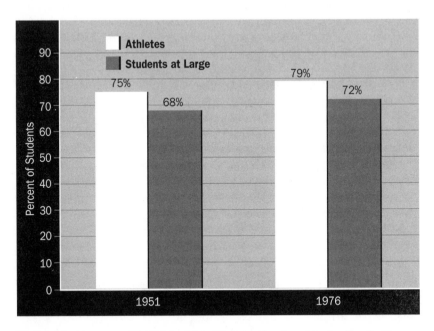

Figure 4.5a. Percent of Full-Time Male Workers Employed in the For-Profit Sector in 1995 (by Athlete Status, 1951 and 1976 Cohorts)
    Source: College and Beyond.

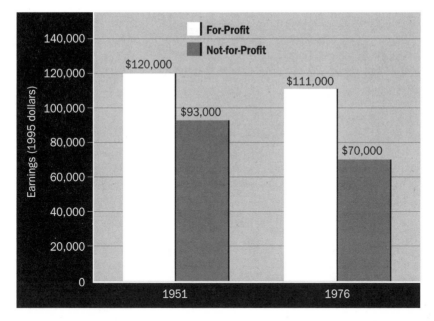

Figure 4.5b. Mean Own Earned 1995 Income (by Sector, 1951 and 1976
Cohorts, Full-Time Male Workers)
Source: College and Beyond.

Locating the Earnings Advantages of Athletes by Sector and Occupation

The second step in "unpacking" the sources of the earnings advantage of
athletes is to compare the earnings of athletes and students at large separately within the for-profit and not-for-profit sectors (focusing on the '76
cohort, where the data are most extensive). Simple tabulations indicate
that athletes enjoyed an earnings advantage of roughly $8,000 in the for-
profit sector and of roughly $1,000 in the not-for-profit sector (Figure
4.6). A somewhat more complex approach using multivariate analysis
confirms that (1) the athletes in the for-profit sector enjoyed a statistically
significant earnings advantage (of roughly $12,000 to $13,000, depending on the specification of the model), and (2) there was no significant
difference in earnings between athletes and other students in the not-for-
profit sector.[15]

The next question is whether, within the for-profit sector, athletes consistently earned more than students at large throughout the sector, or
whether the earnings advantage of athletes is much more pronounced in
some types of work than in others. The results are clear-cut.[16] There is
one—but only one—broad occupational category within which athletes do

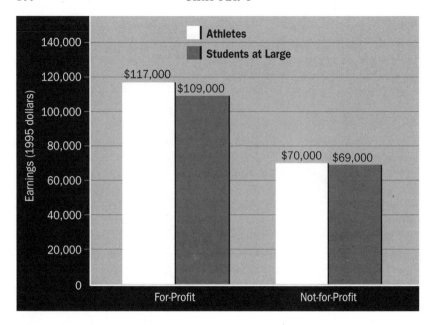

Figure 4.6. Earnings Advantages of Athletes (by Sector, 1976 Cohort, Full-Time Male Workers)

Source: College and Beyond.

much better financially than other students: financial services. Athletes from the '76 cohort who worked in financial services earned an average of $34,000 more than students at large, a difference that easily passes tests of statistical significance. Former athletes also appear to have earned more than other graduates in two or three other for-profit occupational categories (especially "other executives" and "marketing"), but in no case were the differences statistically significant at the 90 percent level of confidence. Although these last differences are not large enough to be statistically significant, we regard them, taken together, as a likely source of some part of the overall earnings advantage enjoyed by athletes.

Also noteworthy are three major occupations within the for-profit/self-employment sector in which there was, for all practical purposes, *no* difference in the average earnings of athletes and other graduates: average earnings of business CEOs, medical doctors, and lawyers for former athletes and other graduates were indistinguishable. CEOs who had been athletes had average earnings of about $1,000 more than CEOs who had not been athletes, as did lawyers who had been athletes; on the other hand, medical doctors who had been athletes averaged about $2,000 less than doctors who had not been athletes.[17]

The key finding, of course, is the powerful association between the fact of having been an athlete and the presence of distinctly above-average earnings in the field of financial services. We suspect that two related processes are at work:

- First, we have observed repeatedly that athletes and students at large differ in more ways than simply their size, strength, or level of hand-eye coordination. They began college with different personal traits, values, and goals, and their college experiences as athletes may have reinforced many of them. It is impossible to say whether playing sports at a young age caused these differences or whether sports appealed to a certain set of individuals who already had these traits. In any event, athletes as a group seem to us to be especially likely to possess characteristics that simultaneously make them not only good rowers and rebounders but also unusually successful in some vocations. One of these characteristics can be thought of as drive—a strong desire to succeed and unswerving determination to reach a goal, whether it be winning the next game or closing a sale. Similarly, athletes tend to be more energetic than the average person, which translates into an ability to work hard over long periods of time—to meet, for example, the workload demands placed on young people by an investment bank in the throes of analyzing a transaction. In addition, athletes are more likely than others to be highly competitive, gregarious, and confident of their ability to work well in groups (on teams). It seems reasonable—although we have no way of proving the proposition—that this set of attributes is especially valuable in financial services.

- Second, it may be that employers in financial services are especially interested in hiring former athletes—in part for the very reasons we have just suggested, and in part because they find that graduates who attended well-known, academically selective schools, and who were also athletes, are especially effective in meeting clients and gaining business for the firm. Thus having been an athlete may increase the chances that a graduate will obtain an entry-level position with a financial services firm and then, in the vernacular, "take it from there." There is, in short, a demand side to this employment equation as well as a supply side.

Presumably the same attributes that lead to marketplace success for athletes in financial services would be expected to benefit them in many (perhaps most) other callings. But if that is true, what explains the *lack* of an earnings advantage for athletes in so many other (almost all other) fields, in both the not-for-profit and the for-profit sectors? Part of the answer may be, as we have already suggested, that athletically related skills and inclinations—which we refer to as the "A-Factor"—simply count for less when one is working in other occupations. Also, as several commentators on an early draft of the manuscript suggested, the positive traits of athletes may be offset (and sometimes even more than offset) by both being less accomplished in other respects (having less of an analytical bent, for example) and having certain less positive attributes sometimes associated with being an athlete. These may include a reluctance at times to step back, think again, and defer a decision, even when that is the wise thing to do; less of a predilection to work for long periods on one's own; or less inclination to stick to an unpopular point of view in the face of pressures to conform. To repeat an injunction from a wise friend that we quoted earlier, people do come in packages, and the package that is optimal in one line of endeavor may not be optimal in others.

More on Precollegiate Differences: Evidence from the Earnings of High-School-Only Athletes

There is another way of testing to some degree the proposition that traits formed earlier in life, and present in large measure when students entered college, do in fact explain part of the earnings advantage that athletes enjoy. Our approach involves searching for a group of people other than college athletes in which athletically related traits might also be found (albeit in a less fully developed form) and seeing if they also achieve at least some part of the athletes' earnings advantage. Fortunately, there is an identifiable subgroup in the '76 cohort, heretofore buried within the larger population of students at large, who meet this criterion—namely, those individuals who played sports in high school but not in college.[18] When we compare the average earnings of these high-school-only athletes with the average earnings of both the remaining students at large (who did not play high school sports) and the college athletes, we see that former high school athletes did indeed benefit from part of the "college athlete effect" without ever having put in a day of college practice (Figure 4.7). The average earnings of the high-school-only athletes exceed the average earnings of the remaining students at large in all four of our sets of schools, and by amounts that range from $5,000 per year in the Ivies up to roughly $10,000 per year in the Division IA private universities. We also see that, with the single exception of those in the Division IA public universities, college athletes earned more than the high-school-only athletes.

The most obvious way of thinking about this pattern is in terms of movement along a scale measuring the intensity with which various groups pursued athletics. Presumably those who continued playing

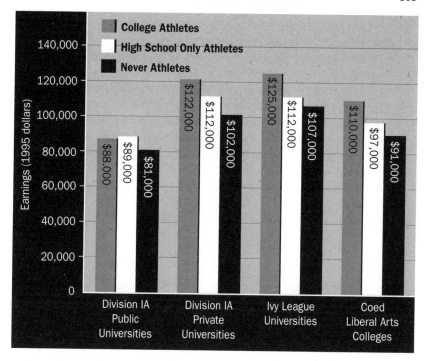

Figure 4.7. Mean Own Earned 1995 Income (by College and High School Athlete Status and Division, 1976 Cohort, Full-Time Male Workers)
Source: College and Beyond.

sports in college were even more imbued with "athletics-related" characteristics—which, to repeat, we see as, on the one hand, traits associated with the athletic culture, such as competitiveness and a highly focused commitment to achieving an objective (winning), and, on the other hand, values and preferences including especially those related to the pursuit of financial goals. Making use of the CIRP survey data described earlier, we next sought to understand more fully the roots of these differences in earnings. What we found is that those students at large who had played high school sports categorized themselves in terms of certain traits (self-perceptions of social self-confidence and leaderships skills) in the fashion of college athletes; on the other hand, they were much less like college athletes and more like their student-at-large peers in their vocational interests and in the degree of importance they attached, as freshmen, to being well off financially (Figure 4.8).[19]

Although high-school-only athletes are seen to have been similar to college athletes on entry to college in ways that may help explain their earn-

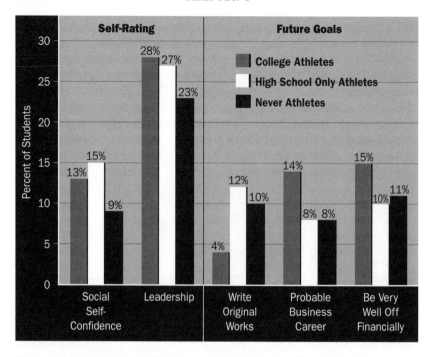

Figure 4.8. Pre-College Self-Ratings and Life Goals (by High School and College Athlete Status, 1976 Cohort, Male Only)
  Source: College and Beyond and CIRP.

ings advantage over the remaining students at large, we must also consider whether the considerable earnings advantage that college athletes enjoy over the high-school-only athletes is due not just to a muted form of "selection" effect but also to an in-college "treatment" effect. That is, perhaps the college athletes earned more than the high-school-only athletes because, by continuing to play competitive sports, they received more of the kinds of on-the-field training in traits such as leadership and discipline that athletics is thought to provide. Fortunately, it is possible to explore these broad types of alternative explanation by examining in more detail the earnings of athletes who played different types of sports and for different periods of time.

Athletes Classified by Years of Play and Type of Sport

We first divide the college athletes from the '76 cohort into subgroups on the basis of how many years they played. Roughly 20 percent of the athletes played (received awards) for four years, and the average earnings of this group exceeded the average earnings of the athletes who received letters in only one, two, or three years by approximately $10,000. In turn, the less-than-four-year athletes had average earnings that were roughly $11,000 higher than the average earnings of the students at large. Thus, like the high-school-only athletes, the less-than-four-year college athletes occupied an intermediate position in the earnings hierarchy, earning more than the students at large, but less than the four-year college athletes.[20] One straightforward interpretation of these results is that those athletes who competed for four years presumably had more of the "A-Factor" (athletically related skills and goals) than students who won letters in fewer years—and thus earned more money. Alternatively, one could argue equally persuasively that the four-year athletes benefited from a longer-term exposure to the educational benefits of intercollegiate athletics and earned more money for this reason.

Looking separately at the High Profile athletes and the Lower Profile athletes is instructive (Figure 4.9). When we make this distinction, we find that the four-year athletes had significantly higher earnings than other athletes *only in the High Profile sports*. Among those on football, basketball,

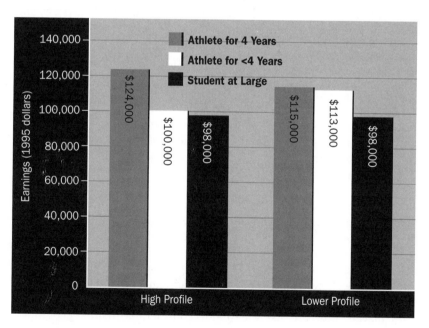

Figure 4.9. Mean Own Earned 1995 Income of Athletes (by Years Played and Sport Profile, 1976 Cohort, Full-Time Male Workers)
  Source: College and Beyond.

and hockey teams, playing for four years increased earnings substantially; members of these teams who played fewer years earned far less, *and in fact there is no statistically significant difference between their earnings and the earnings of the students at large.* The situation is dramatically different— essentially reversed—in the Lower Profile sports, such as rowing, soccer, swimming, baseball, and tennis. All of the athletes who played these sports, however many years they played, had significantly higher earnings than the students at large; but the difference in earnings between those who played for four years and those who spent less time on athletics is negligible (about $2,000) and does not come close to passing any test of statistical significance.[21]

The next obvious question is whether athletes who played only one year earned appreciably less money than those who played two or three years. The answer is unequivocal: there is *no* consistent relationship between years played and earnings for either athletes playing High Profile sports or other athletes (Figure 4.10).[22] This finding has an especially important implication for the athletes playing the High Profile sports: *the higher earnings associated with having played four years is not the result of a steady progression in earnings as more years are played, but rather the result of a kind of final-year step function or "completion bonus."*

But what accounts for this large bonus in the High Profile sports, and why is no comparable bonus paid to those who played four years in the other sports? A colleague suggested one hypothesis: in her words, those athletes in the High Profile sports who "stay with the program" display a persistence and a dedication not evident among the "quitters" who drop out of these programs; moreover, "staying the course" is a quality that the marketplace might well be expected to recognize and reward. There is, however, one obvious problem with this hypothesis: why does it fail altogether to apply to sports other than football, basketball, and hockey? Why are those who "quit" tennis and crew not also penalized?[23]

Pondering this question leads us to suggest a quite different hypothesis that may account for at least some part of the bonus enjoyed by four-year athletes in the High Profile sports. In these sports, it is highly likely that the four-year performers are also the established stars, and that the stars enjoy much more visibility than other players, even in the non-scholarship schools. They are much more likely to be written about in school papers; in the Division IA scholarship schools, many of these individuals are likely to be covered by the regional if not the national press, and many of them will appear on television. At the minimum, wherever they played, they are likely to enjoy considerable name recognition among the graduates of their own school and in some cases may have celebrity status. Such recognition (a "halo" effect) could have considerable value in the marketplace, since graduates and other influential fol-

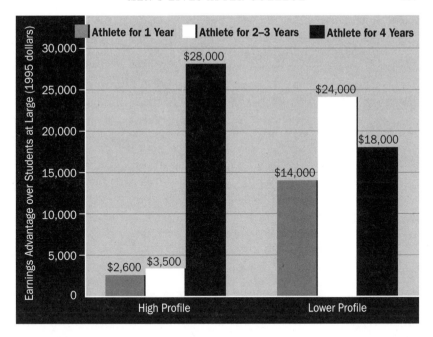

Figure 4.10. Earnings Advantages of Athletes (by Years Played and Sport Profile, 1976 Cohort, Full-Time Male Workers)
Source: College and Beyond.

lowers of the sports programs at these schools would be more likely, one would suppose, to hire such well-known graduates, or at least to recommend them to others. In short, there could be quite a strong credentialing effect associated with being a four-year, high-visibility athlete in a High Profile program. Members of the track, rowing, and fencing teams are much less likely to benefit from any such effect, whether or not they compete for four years.

Many people talk about the role that luck has played in shaping their career path. How many times have we heard someone describe how they were "in the right place at the right time"? Both in the past when career paths were more linear (people often stayed with one firm for their entire careers) and today when frequent job transitions are the norm, career paths do indeed depend upon learning of an opening, knowing the right person, and being able to move when the right opportunity comes up. But surely what seems at first glance like luck (the fortunate intervention of a powerful friend or a good connection) is more accurately perceived as an advantage associated with having been part of a carefully selected pool of people, with the "selection" for inclusion in that pool based in part on where one went to school and what one accomplished in school. High-visibility success as an intercollegiate athlete at an academically selective school (graduation from which implies that the individual exceeds a qualification threshold) surely helps. To be sure, a certain amount of roulette is played at all stages of life (only one out of four former Williams athletes may get a particularly desirable opportunity, and which one is chosen may well be a more or less random event), but the key question is: who is privileged to sit down at the roulette table in the first place? Credentialing and connections also need to be understood in the context of the costs of search, and the value to bankers, law firms, and others of the sorting function performed by graduation from a leading school—and perhaps also by having been a leader on a High Profile football or basketball team.

Comparing the '51 and '76 Cohorts: High Profile and Lower Profile Sports

There is one last finding to be noted, which is based on a comparison not of years played but of the decade in which one played. The data for the '51 cohort are too limited to permit an analysis of the relationship between years played and earnings, but these data do permit a comparison of the respective earnings advantages enjoyed by those in the High Profile and Lower Profile sports in that early cohort. The main finding is easily stated: in the '51 cohort, the earnings advantage enjoyed by the athletes who played football, basketball, and hockey was substantial (about $18,000 more than the average for the students at large in their class). But the Lower Profile male athletes in the '51 cohort had such a small earnings advantage over their student-at-large classmates that the difference fails to pass tests of statistical significance. In sharp contrast, as we have just seen, the situation among the athletes in the '76 cohort is exactly the opposite. It is the athletes in the Lower Profile sports in the '76 cohort who have the largest overall earnings advantage ($16,000), and it is the athletes in the High Profile sports whose average earnings were not far above the average for the students at large (just $8,000, when we lump together those who played four years with those who did not).

This comparison of athletes in cohorts separated by 25 years suggests that, judged in terms of their success in the marketplace, it is the athletes in the Lower Profile sports in the '76 cohort who look very much like the athletes in the High Profile sports in the '51 cohort. This general pattern is consistent with many other data in this study, and especially data on admissions and in-school outcomes, which show, over and over again, that the characteristics associated in the 1950s with football and men's basketball had spread, by the time of the '76 cohort, to almost all other sports. In the '51 cohort, most of the swimmers, golfers, and other athletes in the Lower Profile sports were at their schools for reasons essentially unrelated to their athletic prowess (see the earlier discussion of the lack of recruitment of athletes in these sports in that cohort); they closely resembled their classmates in academic preparation and in essentially all other respects—including, we now see, their earning capacities. In the '76 cohort, on the other hand, the lacrosse players, swimmers, and other Lower Profile athletes were recruited at least as aggressively as athletes in the High Profile sports in the 1950s.

We suspect that the "selection" effects associated with the recruitment process that benefited essentially all athletes in the '76 cohort were present only for the athletes in the High Profile sports in the '51 cohort. Also, for reasons we discuss in more detail in Chapter 13, we suspect that changes in the admissions process over the years have meant that athletes in the High Profile sports in the '76 cohort were in many ways less well prepared to benefit from attending these colleges than were their predecessors in the '51 cohort. The unusually large earnings advantage enjoyed by athletes in the High Profile sports in the '51 cohort may have been due to their having had the benefit of *both* the A-Factor advantages associated with being a recruited athlete and qualifications of other kinds that largely matched those of their classmates.

Two Larger Questions

Having immersed ourselves in all of these numbers and detailed comparisons, it is useful to step back and focus on two larger questions. The first is: how much of the earnings advantage enjoyed by athletes can be attributed to "selection" (who they were when they came to college) and how much to "treatment" (the experiences they had as college athletes)? The evidence leads us to conclude that "selection" deserves the lion's share of the credit for the earnings advantages enjoyed by athletes. The existence of a (muted) selection effect associated with having been a high-school-only athlete is one relevant fact. More compelling, in our view, is the lack of any consistent association between the *amount* of "treatment" received by athletes and their subsequent earnings. In the Lower Profile sports, there would seem to be no basis for coming to any other conclusion, since not even four-year performers earn more than those who earned letters for only one or two years.[24] In the High Profile sports, there are no significant differences in earnings related to years played until one reaches the final, "bonus" stage of an athlete's college career.

The large earnings advantages enjoyed by four-year athletes in the High Profile sports are the strongest counter-evidence, and it is certainly possible that the experience of having been the captain of the football team at any of the schools in this study confers a distinct earnings advantage. It is also possible, however, that (as suggested previously) what is observed here is in some measure a credentialing effect—which is, to be sure, a kind of treatment effect, but not the kind that most people have in mind. The final point has to do with magnitudes. Of all the athletes in the '76 cohort in the database, fewer than 1 in 10 (9 percent) were four-year athletes who played High Profile sports. So even if these students did learn important lessons from their athletic experience that helped them in their subsequent vocations—which could well be the case—there were not that many of them.

The second question has to do with levels of play. It is worth asking whether the earnings advantages associated with college athletics, whether due to selection or to treatment, are greater when the level of play is higher, there are more spectators watching, and the training is more intense. The clearest evidence is visible when we compare earnings advantages across types of institutions, types of sports, and years played (Appendix Table B.4.1). In general, the largest earnings advantages for athletes are found in the Division III coed liberal arts colleges; the smallest earnings advantages for athletes are in the Division IA public universities. The earnings advantage for athletes is almost exactly the same in the Ivies and in the Division IA private universities, even though the level of play is obviously much higher at the Division IA schools.

A slightly more complicated effort to see if the level of play affected the earnings of athletes (on an other-things-equal basis) yielded the same finding: namely, there is no discernible relationship.[25] We conclude that the market-measured benefits of intercollegiate athletics are present to at least as large a degree in the programs offered by the coed liberal arts colleges as in the somewhat more extensive programs offered by the Ivy League schools and in the far more elaborate programs characteristic of the Division IA public and private universities. We also found no earnings advantage (or disadvantage) associated with having played on a winning (or losing) team.

To recapitulate, we find, first, that both the athletes and the students at large who graduated from these colleges and universities went on to earn an abundance of advanced degrees. The main difference is in the predominant fields of study. Athletes were more likely to earn MBAs and students at large were more likely to earn degrees in law and medicine and

Ph.D.s. These characteristic differences in fields studied at the graduate level give every indication of continuing to widen over time.

The kinds of jobs held by athletes and other former graduates are consistent with both these patterns of graduate study and other indicators of interests and aptitudes. Although there is considerable congruence in career paths, there are also some marked differences. Nearly half of all former athletes were in business fields when they were surveyed in 1995, as contrasted with just over a third of the students at large. Financial services has increasingly become the sector of choice for many graduates of these schools, and especially for the athletes. In contrast, 12 percent of the students at large in the 1989 cohort were working in technology fields that rely on computers and information technology, as compared with 4 percent of the athletes.

Athletes benefit from modest but consistently significant earnings advantages over the students at large. One reason is that athletes are more likely to work in the for-profit sector. But there is much more to the story than that. Within the for-profit sector, the earnings advantages of athletes are highly concentrated in financial services, where they earn, on average, $34,000 more than students at large. Equally revealing is the finding that there is no significant difference in the earnings of athletes and students at large in law and medicine, among those who are CEOs of for-profit enterprises, or in any of the fields in the not-for-profit (or governmental) sector. In short, the earnings advantage of athletes is not at all across the board, but is highly concentrated in a set of fields that appears to take full advantage of the special interests and special skills that we associate with having been an athlete (what we have called the A-Factor).

The earnings advantage of athletes is surely due in some degree to both "selection" and "treatment" effects. It would be strange indeed if either were completely absent. But the two need not be given equal weight. The brunt of the evidence suggests to us that selection effects are much more important than treatment effects. We interpret the presence of an earnings advantage for high-school-only athletes (compared with other students at large) as supporting this interpretation. But the most convincing findings are those that show that the earnings of former athletes are not at all related to the amount or intensity of athletic competition that marked their college lives. Specifically, we find that (1) there is no consistent association between years of play and earnings; (2) athletes in the Lower Profile sports earned as much (and often more) than athletes in the High Profile sports; and (3) the athletics advantage in earnings is, if anything, more pronounced at the Division III level of play than at the Division IA level. In short, larger and larger "doses" of athletic treatment (whether measured in terms of more years played, commitment to a High

Profile sport rather than to a Lower Profile sport, or playing at the highest levels of play) do not translate into higher earnings.

The one striking exception to this consistent lack of an association between earnings and the amount of treatment is found in the distinctly above-average earnings of those athletes who competed for four years in High Profile sports. We speculate that the extra "bonus" earned by these athletes (and not others who also competed for four years) may be due to a kind of "credentialing" or "celebrity" effect.

This line of thinking leads to a broader set of conjectures concerning employer interests and networks. It seems to us likely that, just as a degree from a certain type of school signals something to an employer, being an athlete may also open doors—either through serving as a proxy for a set of characteristics that certain employers want or through the activation of networks that create opportunities through presumed familiarity. An employer who wants to hire someone to close deals may look at a varsity letter as a signal of competitiveness—especially if the individual was a highly visible four-year athlete in a High Profile sport. The employer who hires such athletes may well get employees with the desired traits.

In many cases, it is, of course, those who are familiar with the athletic enterprise of the past who are creating the opportunities for the athletes of today. Such an enhanced set of opportunities would not continue to be offered indefinitely, however, based on good feelings alone. As we think ahead, it is worth posing two questions. First, will the more specialized athletes of today and tomorrow have the same breadth and range of abilities as their predecessors (which we believe accounted, at least in part, for the unusually high earnings of athletes from the '51 cohort)? Second, will the skill sets of today's athletes be the skill sets valued most highly in the future? "Will the same marketing, team-oriented, structure-loving, athletic guy of the past," former business school admissions director Steve Christakos asks, "function the same in the nimble dot-com world? I don't know, but it's surely not the same perfect match as that sought by the corporate structures that dominate the investment banking world." One can also ponder the backgrounds of New Economy leaders who attended schools like those in the study; neither Bill Gates (Harvard), Steve Case (Williams), nor Jeff Bezos (Princeton) participated in intercollegiate athletics, and yet the three of them have played key roles in defining the rules of the New Economy.

Yesterday's good feelings and good experiences will continue to generate exceptional opportunities in the future—but only if those who are offered the most highly sought-after jobs can fulfill high expectations.

CHAPTER 5

The Development of Women's Athletic Programs

> Intellectual freedom depends upon material things. . . . And women have always been poor, not for two hundred years merely, but from the beginning of time. Women have had less intellectual freedom than the sons of Athenian slaves.
> —Virginia Woolf, *A Room of One's Own*

ALTHOUGH A NUMBER of the irate Princeton wrestlers observed that wrestling has been an honored pastime since the time of ancient Greece, Virginia Woolf's observation reminds us that not everyone in ancient Greece was allowed to pursue such pastimes. When Princeton tried to drop its wrestling program, one alumnus asked: "Why should an experience like mine be summarily aborted for future hundreds? . . . You have in essence said that the 600 to 800 past wrestling alumni who gave their blood, sweat, and tears to the University are no longer worthy, in future kind, of admittance to the University." The wrestling alumni understood all too well the concept of "opportunity cost," and they were frustrated that their alma mater was willing to sacrifice places for wrestlers in the entering classes of the future in order to achieve other goals. Part of the University's dilemma was that times had changed; admissions slots were becoming progressively more oversubscribed as a flood of talented applicants—including women athletes—entered the competition for places, seeking opportunities of their own.

Woolf and the self-proclaimed "lone gladiator on the mats" remind us that any discussion of the recent history of women's intercollegiate athletics inevitably begins with the allocation of opportunities. For it is a school's past decisions about how many teams to sponsor, how many coaches to hire, and how much weight to give athletic talent in the admissions process that have provided the structure through which myth, like concrete, has slowly flowed and hardened over the years. Men's sports benefited from these types of support for decades, whereas at a number of schools in the study women were not even considered suitable applicants, let alone suitable competitors in sports. That situation has now changed.

In Chapter 1, we reviewed how, over the course of more than a century, men's sports came to be considered an accepted part of what colleges do, not just what students do. This institutionalization led, over time, to the more determined recruiting and admissions efforts documented in Chapter 2, as well as to policies of many other kinds. In this chapter, we begin to trace in more detail how women have come to share some of the opportunities that men's programs have taken for granted for many years. Testimony from respondents to our survey consistently demonstrates that many women enjoy playing sports every bit as much as many men. This was as true in the days when there was little or no institutional support for women's sports as it is today, when opportunities (not to mention the locker rooms, uniforms, and even towels that were sometimes denied women athletes in days now past) are much more readily available.

But to our minds the relevant question is not whether the women who play college sports enjoy the experience and view it positively. With only the occasional exception, the answer is surely an emphatic "yes" for college athletes in general, men and women alike. Instead, we see the central questions for women's sports to be the same as the questions addressed to the male programs: How has women's intercollegiate athletics changed over time? What have women who played sports at selective colleges and universities made of their educational opportunities—both in college and then later in life? How have women's athletic programs affected the colleges and universities that offer them, and especially the educational values that they espouse?

TITLE IX

Many of today's debates about intercollegiate athletics can be traced to Title IX of the 1972 Omnibus Education Act, whereby the Congress of the United States decreed that "no person in the United States shall, on the basis of sex, be excluded from participation in, denied the benefits of, or be subjected to discrimination under any education program or activity receiving Federal financial assistance."[1] As historian Mary Jo Festle has noted, a crucial and conscious change in this legislation came about when Senator Birch Bayh focused the law's charge on the *institutions* receiving federal funding, not the *programs* that receive funds.[2] Although the working out of what exactly the law was to mean in practice was left to the Office for Civil Rights (OCR) within what was then called the Department of Health, Education and Welfare, and although there had been only limited discussion of the subject of college sports in the crafting of the bill, this mandate has generated enormous change in intercollegiate athletics ever since.

Since virtually every school receives federal funding in one form or another (often through research grants but far more often through federally funded student aid loans and work-study programs), Bayh's crucial change in the law applies the government mandate to practically every college and university in the country. As the law has gone through various policy interpretations and court reviews, schools of all shapes and sizes have had to accommodate to its broad charge. This has not been easy, and the latest series of court decisions has left unsettled the conflict between the massive change that has already occurred in women's sports and the even greater change in men's and women's sports that is apparently required to fulfill the charge. It has thus far proven exceedingly difficult for any school with a football program to achieve full compliance—unless the institution is committed to adding an extremely broad array of women's teams and also to restricting the number of teams for men (or to capping the number of men allowed to participate). A key question all along has been how the goal of equal opportunity is to be defined.

Civil rights legislation (unlike a straightforward budgetary appropriation) is broadly phrased and requires interpretation in order to be implemented. This task fell to the OCR, which in 1974 issued a policy interpretation that was amended and reissued in 1979 and again in 1993. Two sets of guidelines delineated the boundaries that would demarcate a level playing field for women. The first defined what schools would have to provide equally:

(1) Whether the selection of sports and levels of competition effectively accommodate the interest and abilities of members of both sexes;
(2) The provision of equipment and supplies;
(3) Scheduling of games and practice time;
(4) Travel and per diem allowance;
(5) Opportunity to receive coaching and academic tutoring;
(6) Assignment and compensation of coaches and tutors;
(7) Provision of locker rooms, practice and competitive facilities;
(8) Provision of medical and training facilities and services;
(9) Provision of housing and dining facilities and services;
(10) Publicity.

The first of these provisions required additional clarification. How could schools know if they were providing "effective accommodation" of women's interests? The OCR set up three possible ways to establish that a school was living by the law:

(1) Whether intercollegiate level participation opportunities for male and female students are provided in numbers substantially proportionate to their respective enrollments; or

(2) Where members of one sex have been and are under-represented among intercollegiate athletes, whether the institution can show a history and continuing practice of program expansion which is demonstrably responsive to the developing interest and abilities of the members of that sex; or

(3) [If numbers (1) or (2) cannot be satisfied,] whether it can be demonstrated that the interests and abilities of the members of that sex have been fully and effectively accommodated by the present program.

The clarifications themselves have led to all sorts of debate: What does "substantially proportionate" mean?[3] What rate of expansion defines a "continuing practice of program expansion"? How can "interests and abilities" be judged? Since it is the actions of individual students and schools that will provide the battleground, the answers to these matters are left to the courts to decide. How do this law and its implications fit into the history of women's opportunities to play?

In the days when Theodore Roosevelt was summoning the coaches and presidents of the Ivy League schools to discuss how to reform football, women were not yet allowed to vote, let alone attend many selective colleges and universities. Historian Frederick Rudolph notes that in 1895 "the faculty of the University of Virginia announced its considered opinion that women students were often physically unsexed by the strain of study."[4] Women have not been welcome on campus *as students* for long enough to build their own myths, let alone to demonstrate conclusively their abiding interest in sports. As we saw in Chapter 1, the building of sports myth requires not only financial support but also the groundswell of enthusiasm that is provided by the media. Grantland Rice and *Sports Illustrated* probably had little enthusiasm for the play days that brought together women from schools like Wellesley, Smith, and Mount Holyoke. Even in the 1970s, when newly created women's teams were enduring second-class facilities and support, the media paid little attention. Merrily Dean Baker (the first director of women's athletics at Princeton and later the athletic director at Michigan State) recalls that in the 1970s she would write and hand-deliver stories of the women's exploits to the *Daily Princetonian,* only to have the paper refuse to print them.[5]

Fans may or may not someday flock to women's field hockey games (though in many parts of the country they are already flocking to women's basketball games), but who is to say that, with a hundred years of history and high levels of institutional support behind them, women's sports might not capture the collective imagination of alumni/ae the way that football games did in the past and, in some cases, still do today?[6] Schools may not believe that they are able to afford the experiment, but—in lieu of supporting the programs in the same way that men's sports have been supported for decades—they can hardly argue that the absence of myth and history can, in and of itself, stand witness to a lack of interest on the part of women in playing sports or to a presumed lack of interest on the part of others in watching.[7]

THE 1950s: THE SILENT GENERATION

The male students who entered college in 1951 experienced an athletics environment that was less intense than today's—and athletes were for the most part much more like their classmates in terms of academic preparation than are their present-day successors. How different was the world of women's sports in the 1950s? Although institutional structures did not encourage women's sports—and some even feared that participation in sports would de-feminize women—women obviously played sports in the 1950s and before. Basketball, tennis, softball, and field hockey were all enjoyed by women in the 1950s (and much earlier), although coaching was often an afterthought.

Paula Welch has written an excellent account of the early history of opportunities for women to play college sports, in which she cites a 1925 warning from the National Association of Secondary Principals that "sooner or later, the spectacle of interscholastic contests among girls gives rise to undesirable and even morbid social influences."[8] Welch notes that competition took the form of play days (on which students would form teams without regard to their schools), sports days (on which schools played against each other but still had shared food and entertainment at the end of the day), or "by remote" (where women from different schools would record a swimming time or an archery result and then compare their performance with that of women at other schools over the telephone). While the male teams were traveling great distances and becoming progressively accepted as a sanctioned part of their institutions' own agendas, women were playing and competing on their own, with nothing like the same kind of institutional approval. Because disparities in opportunity existed throughout society, the women who played sports did not, as a rule, find gender discrimination in athletics to be particularly noteworthy.

A Smith undergraduate in the 1950s:

I think Smith for its time did have wonderful sports. It's just that they weren't intercollegiate. We had very good facilities in terms of playing fields and tennis courts and the gym. . . . I did play sports but it was disappointing because I had come from this high school where we had wonderful athletics and we had all sorts of interscholastic matches with other schools and that was the focus of the athletic program. We got to Smith and there were no intercollegiate athletics at that point. I guess that it was not considered to be important or somehow it just didn't happen and all you had was intramural sports, which were not half as exciting. . . . We were the '50s, we were called the silent generation. We didn't make too many waves when things didn't go our way. We sort of accepted what we were told. . . . The sports then were done for the love of the sport, I think, for the enjoyment factor to a great extent.

THE 1970s: TRAILBLAZERS

Coeducation at selective colleges and universities had a number of partially anticipated or unanticipated consequences that bear directly on intercollegiate athletics. By 1976, some of these consequences were beginning to become apparent. One of the most obvious ramifications of admitting women to Princeton, Yale, Williams, and other schools included in our study is that competitive admissions became even more competitive. Now the most able and best prepared male high school seniors were competing not only against each other for admission to college, but also against the most talented women. At the same time, these schools began adding women's teams and began to consider women's athletic talent in the admissions equation.

A 1976 Northwestern volleyball player:

I think that had some of today's kids had to rough it at some point in their tender years, they might not have that generational entitlement problem. It's an entitlement generation, and I think that it's a lot about not having to really do without or make the best of what you have and that kind of thing. Even my generation, really; I had money. Somebody put me through school and the people the year before me had to pay $20,000 a year to go to Northwestern. So even just right before me, people that I played on the same court with as a freshman, wanted to keep playing even though I took their starting position away and they didn't have the money for scholarships. They didn't have anything; I just respect that what they did led to us getting what we had, and then what we had led to helping people in the future.

Until this time, however, even the institutions that had long accepted women, and had sponsored women's sports since the 1950s or before, were doing so in a decidedly casual manner. To illustrate, Welch's book cites the case of Ellie Daniel, who won three Olympic medals in swimming in 1968 but was not recruited "by a single coach at any university." She ended up attending the University of Pennsylvania, where she competed for the women's team for two years, before taking time off for the next Olympiad and then retiring from swimming because, as she reported, "My father always told me . . . 'Better to leave the party at the middle and to remember it at its best than to wait around.'"[9] Her story—of remarkable talent that played little or no role in her being admitted to college—tells us a great deal about what athletic opportunities were like for women in the days before Title IX.

Differences and Similarities

> It would be a thousand pities if women wrote like men, or lived like men, or looked like men. . . . Ought not education to bring out and fortify the differences rather than the similarities? For we have too much likeness as it is.
> —Woolf, *A Room of One's Own*

> She was trying to get all up in my face, and I just clocked her. I started hammering her.
> —A 1997 Princeton University women's basketball player[10]

It was perhaps inevitable that the development of women's sports programs would generate the conflicts that other advancements in women's rights had produced. The Title IX legislation of 1972 came as somewhat of a mixed blessing to a group of women athletics administrators who were working to develop a model of intercollegiate athletics based not on equality and sameness but on opportunity and difference. To what extent has Title IX provided opportunities for women and what shape have those opportunities taken?

"The athletic model designed and perpetrated by men pervades schools and society," wrote women's sports administrator Jan Felshin in 1974, "and it is, in part, a repellent one. Women cannot, in good conscience, enter a struggle for the prize of brutality, authority, or the exploitation of young athletes."[11] But when Title IX came along, the only way to measure equality was in terms of the coin of the realm—the number of teams, the number of scholarships, the coaches' salaries, the quality of food on the training tables. Faced with continuing discrepancies—practice times in the middle of the night, long bus rides while the men's teams flew, and all-around second-class citizenship—women's sports grew and began to prosper in the only way that it could: in imitation of the male model.

In the 1970s, when the ramifications of Title IX were still unclear, the NCAA's executive director, Walter Byers, realized that there were two possible paths: (1) a clarification of the law that would recognize the unusual place and demands of football and thus mollify the implications of the law, or (2) a future in which women's athletics would occupy a substantial part of the men's intercollegiate athletics empire. Preparing for both possibilities simultaneously, Byers did not allow the ambivalence of women athletic administrators to confuse the issue as he organized the NCAA's determined effort at the end of the 1970s to absorb women's athletic programs.

The Association for Intercollegiate Athletics for Women

The Association for Intercollegiate Athletics for Women (AIAW) was founded in 1971 by a group of women administrators of physical education and intercollegiate athletics. Although it grew up alongside the women's movement of the 1960s and 1970s, the group's roots were in the physical education programs of the 1950s, which had emphasized the value of health and recreation. While the political and social gains of the women's movement helped advance its cause, the AIAW struggled with the question of how to gain the opportunity to pursue its own programs without necessarily taking on all aspects of the male model. Deeming coed teams impractical, the Association had hoped to maintain a "separate but equal" position. "Men's athletics have had a tradition," noted Carole Oglesby, one-time AIAW president, "of overemphasis on excellence to the degree that it becomes an end that justifies any means. But here are women's programs that have been very student-oriented, moderately balanced, but kind of mediocre. I think they can come together."[12]

The organization outlawed athletic scholarships, judging them to be the source of much of the degradation and commercialization of men's sports. But the alternative model showed the strains of different opinions within the group's member institutions; some schools and students felt that, in taking a stand against scholarships, opportunities awarded to men and now available to women in theory (and in law) would be lost. Faced with criticism from within its own ranks, the AIAW relented and in 1973 allowed (while continuing to discourage) the awarding of athletic scholarships. Nevertheless, the AIAW rules sought to create a different model: scholarships were awarded for four years (in contrast to the NCAA policy of year-by-year renewal at coaches' discretion); moreover, in the AIAW, eligibility was based on academic performance rather than athletics, and women were allowed to transfer to other schools without having to sit out a year of competition—both standard rules for the NCAA's men's programs. At the end of seasons, the AIAW staged national championships in which all teams were invited to participate—a practice intended to foster less of a winner-take-all attitude. However, it was inevitable that the terms of the debate would ultimately be framed by the opportunities and structures of men's sports. In the face of the well-funded and well-organized NCAA, the AIAW was simply overmatched.

Sensing that women's athletics, the concomitant federal commitment, and funding levels were here to stay, the NCAA began offering championships in women's sports in 1980—scheduling them to overlap with the AIAW events and paying for teams' travel to the events. Schools were naturally reluctant to pay dues to both organizations. Soon after the 1982 NCAA convention and after failing in a lawsuit against the NCAA, the AIAW—which at its height had overseen 41 national championships in 19 sports and had proffered a model of athletics that emphasized participation rather than winning and pleasing an audience—closed down.[13] As the women's teams came under the control of the NCAA, their own piece of the action became fair game. Sociologists Vivian Acosta and Linda-Jean Carpenter have documented how absorption into the mainstream has resulted in diminished opportunities for women in coaching and athletic administration. They report that in 1972 more than 90 percent of the women's teams had female coaches; by 1998 only 47 percent of the coaches of women's teams were female.[14]

THE 1990s: MAINSTREAM—CLARIFYING THE RULES OF THE GAME

By 1989, the number of women who played intercollegiate athletics at the schools in our study had risen from 9 percent of the class to 11 percent. Moreover, the percentage of the women who did not play college sports but had played in high school *doubled* (Figure 5.1). Recruitment of women athletes who had, like the men, been playing sports their whole lives intensified. Increased opportunities (combined with greater interest on the part of women) changed the pool of applicants and the level of interest among enrolled students. And change continued—although not rapidly enough for many women interested in competing on the same terms as their male classmates.

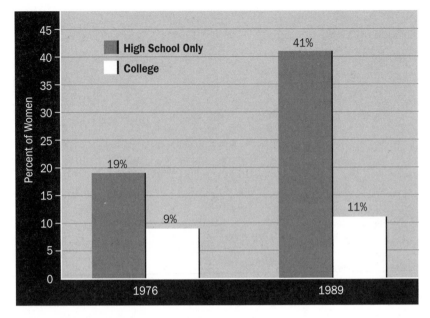

Figure 5.1. Percent of Women Who Played High School and College Sports
(1976 and 1989 Cohorts)
Source: College and Beyond.

An Oberlin field hockey player from the '89 cohort:

Sure it was different. They got the bus, and we had the coach driving the
station wagon. While they had a bathroom on the bus and they had a coach
who could be thinking about the game, we had a coach who was busy driving and finding rest stops to pull into.

In 1992 the Supreme Court ruled that plaintiffs in Title IX suits could
sue institutions for damages (a ruling which made it likely that cases
would end in settlements), leading to a new era of court-moderated
interpretation of the 20-year-old legislation. The delay in formulating
rules as to how Title IX did and did not apply, notes Jeffrey Orleans, current executive director of the Ivy League and one of the framers of the
original OCR guidelines, had confused the public and even called into
question the authority of the act: "A statute that was out of sight was also,
to the public, out of mind."[15] But now, with a means to force colleges and
universities to take action, women had a way to bring gender equity in
sports very much into sight and into mind.

Into the breach—surprisingly enough, considering its exceedingly liberal reputation—stepped Brown University. An Ivy League school with, at the time, more women's sports teams than any school in the country other than Harvard (17 teams, including basketball, crew, cross-country, equestrian, fencing, field hockey, gymnastics, ice hockey, lacrosse, skiing, soccer, softball, squash, swimming and diving, tennis, track and field, and volleyball), Brown had provided opportunities for women to participate long before it was required to do so. Marvin Lazerson and Ursula Wagener have noted that, as early as 1978, Brown had offered twice the number of women's sports as the national average in the mid-1990s.[16]

In 1992, faced with an operating deficit, the Brown administration sought to reduce expenditures by 5 percent in every department. The athletic department elected to demote four sports (men's golf and water polo and women's volleyball and gymnastics) to club status, meaning that they would no longer have the same level of university support. When gymnast Amy Cohen and 12 others sued the University, the administration decided to take a strong stand, refusing to settle out of court. Taking issue with the way in which the OCR rules had been interpreted, with participation rates based on actual participants rather than available roster spots, and asserting that its women's athletics program was "indisputably one of the nation's largest and best,"[17] Brown pursued its case beyond its first loss (and an appeal in the First Circuit Court in 1995) and sought a ruling from the Supreme Court. Joined by an unusual coalition of friends—from the American Council on Education to the College Football Coaches Association—Brown awaited a review of the case that would

> evaluate the merits of the parties' respective positions in their proper context: in the context of Title IX which is not an affirmative action statute, in the context of the ever changing composition of the student body which varies almost daily, in the context of the huge swings in participation on the existing teams from season to season, in the context of the existing athletic program, which Plaintiffs agree is satisfactory in each of its disparate components and which offers nearly 100 participation opportunities for women that are going unfilled, and in the context of the interests and abilities of both men and women.[18]

But in April 1997 the Supreme Court decided not to review the case, meaning not only that Brown had to restore the women's teams to varsity status and abide by the other terms of the original ruling but also that, for the foreseeable future, there would be no final clarification of what constitutes "proportionate" participation. The bottom line for the OCR guidelines, now supported by the First Circuit Court in *Cohen vs. Brown,* is that, when women are not represented proportionately and are interested in playing, schools must yield.[19]

All over the country, schools will continue to wrestle with the ramifications of Title IX. Schools not in compliance—and as of this writing that means virtually all schools—will continue to expand programs. For some schools, this will simply mean buying new uniforms for the women's team because they have bought them for the men. But at other schools, those where scholarship dollars are at stake, substantial sums of money will have to come from somewhere. A complicating factor is that, as women's sports grow, so grow the men's. A recent NCAA gender equity study reports that between 1992 and 1996 average Division IA spending on women's team expenses increased from $263,000 to $640,000; over the same period, spending on men's sports went from $1 million to $2.4 million.[20] Thus, whereas the percentage increase in spending on women's sports was slightly higher than in the men's programs (253 percent versus 232 percent), the absolute dollar gap increased from $786,000 to $1.76 million. Moreover, while the average number of women athletes at Division IA institutions has increased, in 1998 there were still, on average, 119 more male athletes at each of these schools. Corresponding numbers for the Division III colleges tell a similar story. The average college has 16 more women athletes than it did in 1991–92, but it has 67 more male athletes. Similar discrepancies exist in recruiting expenses, coaches' salaries, and (at the Division IA schools) scholarships.[21]

Although one can empathize with the male athletes and coaches who feel that their sports programs now face restrictions, and who in some cases see gender equity as the cause of those restrictions, the major financial discrepancies between spending on men's and women's sports tell their own story.

The success of women at the 1996 Olympics in Atlanta, of the women's NBA, and of the 1999 World Cup soccer team, combined with women's vastly expanded opportunities to play sports, testifies to the manifold ways in which Title IX, directly and indirectly, has helped more women to play and enjoy sports at ever higher levels of competition. One-time University of Pennsylvania basketball star and author John Wideman looks upon the new women's professional basketball league (in which his daughter Jamila plays) with hope: "I see this as a fresh opportunity and I'm optimistic enough to think that something different can happen—not simply because they are women, but because they have the advantage of having seen the mistakes that men have made. We've lost the idea of a game, we've lost the idea of play, we've lost the idea of effort. I hope the women can turn some of this around."[22]

The article goes on to tell of how, on one occasion, Jamila Wideman found herself in a choke hold at the hands of Nancy Lieberman-Cline. Are the women responsible for fulfilling Wideman's (and the AIAW's) dreams—and restoring the notion of play to sport—simply because men have not been able to? Early supporters of women's sports foresaw and sought to resist the temptation to follow the model offered by men's sports. "Must the Women's Rights movement demand for our young girls a share in the things that are wrong in sports today as well as a share in the rights in order fully to prove equality?" asked one AIAW president.[23] Still, the anecdotal evidence suggests that this is exactly what has happened. "We used to get good students who were also good athletes," reported the women's softball coach at Princeton, "Now we get good athletes who are also good students."[24]

In the next three chapters, we attempt to move beyond the anecdote range and examine empirically the extent to which replication of the men's athletic model took place between the 1976 and 1989 entering cohorts (as seen in the admissions process and in academic performance). We also seek to measure the early postcollege results of the experiment that has allowed women to seek a level playing field.

CHAPTER 6

New Players: The Recruitment and Admission of Women Athletes

VIRGINIA WOOLF's plea, in *A Room of One's Own*, for the celebration of difference notwithstanding, the trends in recruiting and admitting women athletes have moved in the same direction as the one we observed among the men. The 1951 cohort serves as a rather different reference point for the women, however, since most women's intercollegiate athletic programs were so undeveloped in that era that it is difficult even to determine, retrospectively, how many women athletes were playing on teams engaged in intercollegiate competition.[1] By the time of the '76 cohort, more intercollegiate competition was occurring, though certainly not on today's scale. Then, by the late 1980s, the broad changes described in the previous chapter are visibly reflected in both enrollment patterns and the admissions process, including the early identification and active recruitment of athletic talent. More impressionistic evidence suggests that these trends in admissions and enrollment were even more pronounced by the late 1990s. The "arrow" has continued to point upward, and we believe that the pace of change has, if anything, quickened.

NUMBERS OF WOMEN ATHLETES

In the 1989 cohort, the percentage of women who were athletes (defined, as in the case of men, as all women students who received one or more letters or other athletic awards for participation on intercollegiate teams while they were in college) ranged from a low of 3 percent of all women students at the large Division IA public universities to a high of 19 percent at the Division III coed liberal arts colleges—with 6 percent at the Division IA private universities, 12 percent at the women's colleges, and 15 percent at the Ivies. These percentages are markedly higher than the corresponding figures for the women in the '76 cohort at the Ivies and the coed colleges, slightly higher than the figures for the '76 cohort at the women's colleges, nearly the same as those for the Division IA private universities, and exactly the same as those for the Division IA public universities (Scorecard 6.1).

TABLE 6.1

Number of 1997–98 Intercollegiate Athletes by Sport (Selected Schools, Female Only)

	University of Michigan	Stanford	Duke	Tulane	Columbia/ Barnard	Princeton	Denison	Williams
Archery	—	—	—	—	34	—	—	—
Basketball	13	16	14	14	13	16	17	15
Fencing	—	14	12	—	20	14	—	—
Field hockey	21	22	20	—	25	24	26	34
Golf	9	8	7	8	—	12	—	—
Gymnastics	15	14	—	—	—	—	—	—
Ice hockey	—	—	—	—	—	19	—	18
Lacrosse	—	24	22	—	27	28	25	25
Rowing	72	40	—	—	23	34	—	27
Sailing	—	—	—	—	—	—	—	—
Skiing	—	—	—	—	—	—	—	16
Soccer	29	24	23	20	24	23	21	21
Softball	19	16	—	—	—	16	15	18
Squash	—	—	—	—	—	15	—	12
Swimming	32	30	16	—	26	42	32	34
Synchronized swimming	—	11	—	—	—	—	—	—
Tennis	11	8	10	12	9	12	12	9
Track–cross-country	61	68	80	29	61	120	59	61
Volleyball	22	15	12	14	12	9	15	14
Water polo	—	23	—	—	—	21	—	—
Total	304	348	216	97	274	405	222	304
As percent of all women	3	10	7	3	6	19	20	32
Number of teams	11	16	10	6	11	15	9	13

Source: Equity in Athletics Disclosure Act filings, 1997–98.

The absolute number of women playing intercollegiate sports varies widely within this universe of institutions, as can be seen from the following 1997–98 figures: 97 at Tulane, around 220 at Duke and Denison, 274 at Columbia/Barnard, about 300 at both Williams College and the University of Michigan, nearly 350 at Stanford, and just over 400 at Princeton (Table 6.1).[2] As the detailed data in the table indicate, almost one-quarter of these women athletes participated in track–cross-country. Women's basketball, soccer, tennis, and volleyball are the other intercollegiate sports offered at all eight of these schools, but typical squad sizes are much smaller. Women's field hockey and swimming are offered at seven of the eight schools; lacrosse is offered at six schools; golf, rowing, and softball at five; fencing at four; and then archery, gymnastics, ice hockey, sailing, skiing, squash, synchronized swimming, and water polo at one or two of the schools in this illustrative subsample of the College and Beyond institutions.

RECRUITMENT AND THE "ATHLETIC ADVANTAGE" FOR WOMEN

The growing importance of recruitment in women's intercollegiate sports was brought home to one of the authors when he was interviewing a job candidate a few years ago. The candidate had just graduated from a school in the study, and when asked what had led her to attend the school in question she replied: "Well, I'm a catcher, and I was recruited to come here to play on the softball team."

The extent of the change in recruitment patterns for women athletes in the Ivies and the Division III coed liberal arts colleges is revealed dramatically in Figure 6.1, which compares the percentages of male and female athletes in '76 and '89 who said that they were recruited to come to their colleges (see also Scorecard 6.2).[3] In 1976, there was considerable recruitment of male athletes, but very few women athletes at any of these schools felt that they had been "recruited" in the sense in which the term is now used. As we saw in the previous chapter, women's sports received rather low-key institutional support in the late 1970s.

A member of the '76 cohort at Yale who played soccer and field hockey:

We didn't get to go to Cornell because it was too far. Of course our men's team would have gone, and now they fly them all over the country. [Still] I thought that we had very good treatment [from the school]. The alumni, I think, were a different story. I still play soccer, and I tell my teenagers that they just don't appreciate what they grew up with. I can still remember alumni walking across our field in the middle of our game. We were wearing uniforms and everything and they thought "oh, isn't that cute." That was before our soccer stadium and everything too. Both teams [soccer and field hockey] started when I was there. Each team just had one coach. Obviously now no team would ever have just one coach. . . . It was a very different approach than today. I think my senior year was the first year that they recruited [for soccer], and people had played their whole lives, you know, from the time they were 6 or 7. Most of us had played for a little bit in high school and then were still able to make the team. . . .

I think that sports is much more serious now but probably because it's a means to an end. A lot of people see it as a means to get into college now. [In 1976] it was just one more activity on the application. I played it because I loved it but it wasn't something that you ever thought, especially as a woman at that time, would make or break your chances of getting into a school.

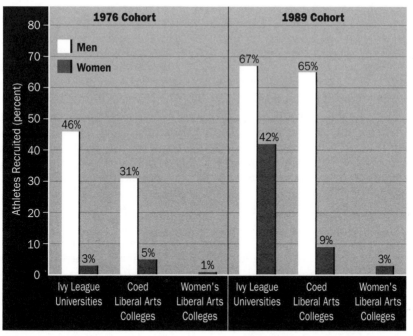

Figure 6.1. Percent of Athletes Reporting That Being "Recruited" Was a "Very Important" Reason for Choosing This Specific College (by Cohort, Gender, and Division)

Source: College and Beyond (see Scorecard 6.2).

The situation was very different in 1989, when over 40 percent of all the women athletes in the Ivies said that they had been recruited (the percentages are even higher at the Division IA universities, but the absolute numbers are too small to justify emphasizing the exact figures). In the coed liberal arts colleges, larger numbers of women athletes felt that having been recruited contributed to their having chosen their college (9 percent, as compared with 5 percent in 1976), but the recruitment of women athletes at the Division III level was obviously still lagging behind recruitment in the Ivies. (In contrast, by 1989 the extent of recruitment of male athletes at the coed liberal arts colleges had essentially caught up with the Ivy League pattern, in spite of different rules concerning off-campus recruiting.) The recruitment of women athletes by the women's colleges, which was almost nonexistent in 1976, was visible (but just barely) in 1989.

The general impression conveyed by Figure 6.1 is that the pattern of recruitment of women athletes is indeed emulating the pattern established for the men who play intercollegiate sports, but it is following with a lag. We suspect strongly that if we had data for the 1999 entering cohort, the recruitment of women athletes at all of the schools in the study, including the women's colleges, would be seen to resemble the recruitment of men much more closely than it did in 1989. Conversations with admissions officers and others at these colleges support this interpretation.

There is a more convincing way to document the changing emphasis given to the recruitment of women athletes. In Figure 6.2, we compare (as we did with the men) the admissions "advantage" enjoyed by women who were minorities, legacies, and identified athletes at a non-scholarship school in our study that was able to provide comprehensive data for all applicants.[4] This figure is so important, and conveys so much information, that we should explain again the approach used in creating figures of this kind. We are comparing here the actual admissions probabilities for four groups of students—a reference group of students at large, legacies, minority students, and athletes identified by coaches—after controlling for differences in their SAT scores.[5]

All three of the targeted groups enjoyed a significant admissions advantage in 1976. The advantage of 15 points enjoyed by the women athletes (which means that they had a 15 percent better chance of being admitted than a student at large with the same SAT scores) is noteworthy in light of the very small number of women in that cohort who related their attendance at college to a direct recruitment experience. The point is that admissions officers could—and apparently did—favor candidates with athletic talent even in the absence of the more overt kinds of recruitment now in vogue. By 1989, a woman who was a recruited athlete had a 26 percent better chance of being admitted than a female student at large, af-

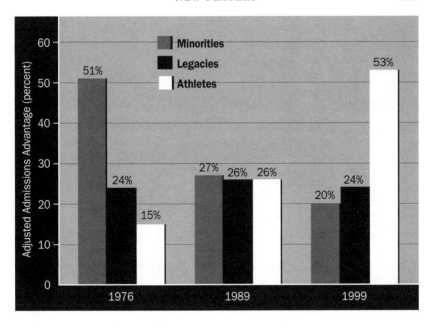

Figure 6.2. Adjusted Admissions Advantage at a Representative Non-Scholarship School, Controlling for Differences in SAT Scores (1976, 1989, and 1999, Female Only)

ter adjusting for differences in SAT scores;[6] women legacies and minorities in the '89 cohort both enjoyed essentially the same admissions advantage as the women athletes. But by far the most striking set of data in this figure are those for the 1999 admissions cohort: in this recent group of applicants, the recruited athletes had an admissions advantage over students at large of *53 percent*—now essentially twice the degree of advantage enjoyed by legacies and minority students.[7]

For the 1989 and 1999 cohorts, the pattern of admissions advantage for women is amazingly similar to the pattern for men. To illustrate the degree of similarity, we have reproduced the figures for both the women and the men in Figure 6.3. In the '89 cohort, the male and female athletes enjoyed admissions advantages of 30 and 33 percent, respectively. The admissions advantages enjoyed by both men and women on the coaches' lists had increased markedly by the time the '99 cohort was admitted, both in terms of their absolute values and in relation to the advantages enjoyed by legacies and minority candidates; moreover, the admissions advantage for women athletes has now surpassed (slightly) the advantage enjoyed by their male counterparts.

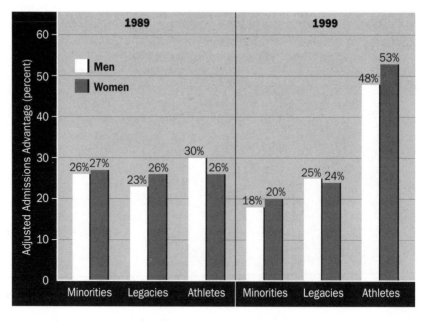

Figure 6.3. Adjusted Admissions Advantages at a Representative Non-Scholarship School, Controlling for Differences in SAT Scores (by Gender, 1989 and 1999)

ACADEMIC QUALIFICATIONS

Since the role of athletics in the admissions process for women who play sports has mimicked the pattern shown by the men, measurable differences in academic preparation should begin to be evident in the data for the 1989 cohort. And this is in fact the case. Between the 1976 and 1989 cohorts, average SATs rose by 40 points for female students at large (in the sector composite shown on Scorecard 6.3), while they fell slightly for women who went on to play intercollegiate sports. As one would suspect, the more that another factor (athletic ability) counts in the admissions equation, the less likely it is that those who rank high on that scale will match the SAT scores of those who do extremely well on the standardized tests.

The consistency of this shift across types of schools is shown in Figure 6.4. With the single exception of the women's colleges, every type of college or university in our study exhibited at least a modest SAT deficit for women athletes in 1976. (The women athletes in this cohort at the women's colleges actually had modestly higher test scores than the stu-

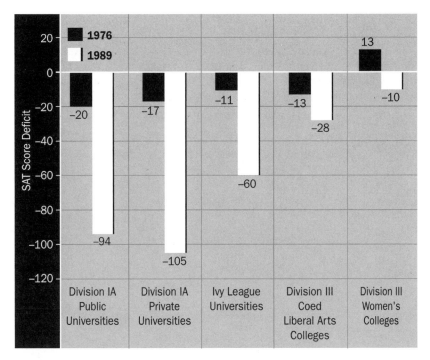

Figure 6.4. Athlete SAT Divergence from Students at Large (by Cohort and Division, Female Only)
Source: College and Beyond.

dents at large.) But in 1989, even the women's colleges reported lower SAT scores for their athletes than for other women students, and at every type of college and university represented in the figure the gap in SAT scores between women athletes and students at large had widened appreciably over this 13-year period. The sizes of the SAT deficits also correlate at least roughly with the different degrees of emphasis placed on athletic recruiting (refer back to Scorecard 6.2); in particular, the women athletes at the Division III colleges (coed and women's) are less likely to have said that they were recruited and, in general, have SAT scores that are closer to those of their fellow students.[8]

We are also able to look at SAT scores separately by sport (see Appendix Table B.6.1). The most consistent pattern that emerges is that women basketball players, especially in the Division IA public and private universities, had SAT scores *far* lower than those of other women students: the gaps are −177 points at the public universities and −240 points at the private universities. In the Ivies, the basketball players had an SAT deficit of –98 points. This pattern is consistent with the movement of women's basketball toward the High Profile sports category, a trend that is now much more pronounced than it was when these data were collected for the '89 cohort. It should also be noted, however, that *some* SAT gap (or deficit) is found in almost every women's sport within almost every type of school (the clearest exceptions are crew and a few other sports in the Division III coed liberal arts colleges). The important point is that the results shown in the text are not driven by admissions concessions confined to a small number of sports.

Entering students bring with them not only SAT scores and other objective measures of their academic performance in high school but also their own perceptions of how talented they are academically. In Figure 6.5 and Scorecard 6.4 we chart the intellectual self-confidence of the women, as compared with the self-confidence of their male classmates. Since we would expect those with higher SAT scores to have more intellectual self-confidence than those with lower scores, we superimpose average SAT scores on the figure. The first story line, demonstrated so powerfully in the figure and consistent with the findings in many other studies, is that women appear to undervalue (or at least to underreport) their intellectual ability relative to men with comparable SAT scores. The second story line is that women athletes are even less likely than other women to express the highest level of intellectual self-confidence (only 13 percent put themselves in the top decile, as compared with 20 percent of all women students at these schools) and that this differential can be explained only partly by the lower SAT scores of the women athletes. The male High Profile athletes, at the other extreme, exhibit *higher* intellectual self-confidence in relation to their test scores than do other students.[9]

Given time, the women athletes may, like the male athletes in the High Profile sports, learn to feel confident—perhaps even overly confident—about their intellectual prowess, rather than understate it. This could well be the case, especially if our culture ends up bestowing upon young girls who play sports the same sort of approbation showered upon young boys who excel at sports. Such support could go a long way in helping women gain the confidence that men derive from sports—the confidence that Virginia Woolf admired when reading something written by a man: "It was so direct, so straightforward after the writing of women. It indicated such freedom of minds, such liberty of person, such confidence in himself. One had a sense of physical well-being in the presence of this well-nourished, well-educated, free mind, which had never been thwarted or opposed, but had had full liberty from birth to stretch itself in whatever way it liked." As of 1989, however, there were no signs

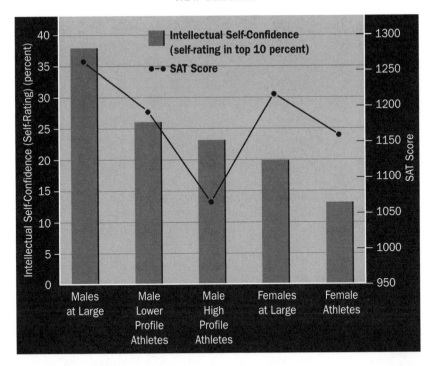

Figure 6.5. Intellectual Self-Confidence and SAT Scores (by Athlete Status and Gender, 1989 Cohort)

Source: College and Beyond (see Scorecard 6.4).

of this happening. In the race to establish a presence in a seminar or in a coed study group, this apparent gap in intellectual self-confidence (undeserved as it appears to be) afflicted women athletes disproportionately.

DIVERSITY

The presence of women has itself represented an enormous increase in diversity at schools that were all male in 1951. By 1989, over half of the population of the schools we are studying was female. Now that women are equal partners in gaining access to the world of selective colleges and universities that was once male-dominated, are women athletes also adding to the racial and socioeconomic diversity of the female campus population?

Racial Diversity

Contrary to some popular impressions, more aggressive recruitment of women athletes is not bringing disproportionately larger numbers of African American women to campuses (as it is in the case of the male athletes in the High Profile sports). Only in the Division IA private universities has the presence of women athletes increased the relative number of African American women. In every other set of schools, the share of African American women playing intercollegiate sports is much lower—even half the corresponding percentage of African American women in the student-at-large category (Figure 6.6). Moreover, the percentage of African American women playing sports at these schools, relative to the overall percentage of African American women enrolled, was, if anything, lower in '89 than in '76 (Scorecard 6.5). The explanation presumably lies in the increased number of women's teams, many of which are in traditionally "white" sports such as golf and fencing. There is of course no women's equivalent to football, and sports such as basketball and track

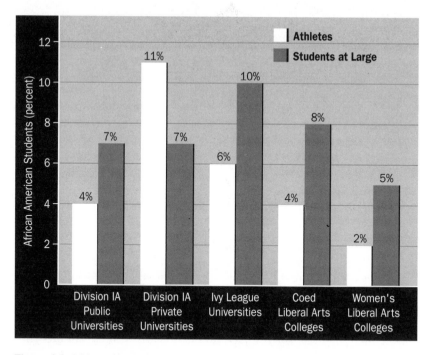

Figure 6.6. African Americans as a Percent of All Female Students (by Athlete Status and Division, 1989 Cohort)
Source: College and Beyond (see Scorecard 6.5).

(which traditionally have been more likely to include minority participants) were already in place in 1976. In any event, the pressure to increase athletic opportunities for women, driven in large part by Title IX,
cannot be said to have encouraged a greater degree of racial diversity.

Socioeconomic Backgrounds

In 1976, opportunities for girls in secondary school (and for even younger
girls) to play many sports were often limited either to those who could develop such interests through clubs or to those who attended private
schools or upscale high schools that could afford to provide such opportunities. Thus it is not surprising that women who played sports were more
likely than other women to come from private schools and to be children
of parents who were college graduates (see Scorecards 6.6 to 6.8). Overall, 28 percent of women athletes in the '76 cohort attended private
schools, as compared with 21 percent of all women students attending the
colleges in our study; 80 percent of the fathers of the women athletes (and
60 percent of the mothers) had B.A.s, as compared with 73 percent of the
fathers of other women students (and 55 percent of the mothers).

By 1989, this had changed, as girls were now playing sports in a much
wider array of secondary schools across the country. Thus the "prep
school advantage" that is evident in the 1976 cohort had largely disappeared by 1989, when the women athletes and other women students
were, for all intents and purposes, equally likely to have parents with college degrees; by 1989, women athletes were actually slightly more likely
to come from public schools than were their classmates. Athletics, for
women, has ceased to be an activity with leisure class overtones, and if
present trends continue we can expect women's athletics to make at least
a modest contribution to socioeconomic diversity (if not to racial diversity) on the campus in future years.

Attitudes and Goals

We recall that the male athletes demonstrated a pattern of shared values,
many of which could be considered more conservative than those held
by their male classmates. Are these same views shared by women athletes?
In some respects they are, but with at least one interesting difference.

Most relevant are the responses of the women to the direct question of
how they classify themselves politically (Scorecards 6.9a and 6.9b). In
both the '76 and '89 cohorts, women athletes were less likely than other
women to put themselves in the "liberal" or "far left" categories: 37 percent of the women athletes versus 47 percent of the other women in '76,

and 39 percent of the athletes versus 46 percent of their classmates in '89. Conversely, more women athletes than other women considered themselves "conservative" or "far right." This is true of women in both the '76 and '89 cohorts, but here we also see a shift over time: whereas women athletes in the '76 cohort were only slightly more likely than other women to classify themselves as conservatives (15 percent versus 13 percent), this gap was considerably larger in the '89 cohort (21 percent of the women athletes classified themselves as conservatives versus 15 percent of the other women).

In this regard, as in so many others, the degree of recruitment matters. The differences in political views between women athletes and other women were much more pronounced in the schools where women were more intensively recruited. For example, in the Division IA private universities, 38 percent of women athletes in the '89 cohort rate themselves as conservative versus 23 percent of students at large (Scorecard 6.9b). In interpreting these CIRP survey data by type of school, we must remember that cell sizes are smaller at the Division IA universities than elsewhere; still, the general pattern seems established, especially when we compare the Ivies with both the coed liberal arts colleges and the women's colleges. Women athletes are significantly more conservative than other women in the Ivies, whereas the differences in political orientation at both the coed liberal arts colleges and the women's colleges are negligible.

Thus it appears as if both male and female athletes (especially recruited athletes) hold political-social views that differ somewhat from those espoused by male and female students at large. But this congruence between men and women who play sports in college disappears when we investigate the importance they attach to making money. Whereas a disproportionate share of male athletes (as compared with other male students) entered college rating the goal "to be very well off financially" as "essential" or "very important" (refer back to Figure 2.9), there is no such difference between women who were and were not athletes (Figure 6.7). Women students who attended the schools included in this study are consistently less inclined that their male peers to aspire to be very well off financially. Those women who played sports at the scholarship-granting schools are only slightly more likely than the students at large to count this as an essential goal, and at the non-scholarship schools there is a clear tendency for women athletes to be less likely to aspire to be very well off financially. In short, the typical woman athlete has not yet assumed the male athlete's view of the goals of the game of life. If this trend continues at the non-scholarship schools, it may be worth pondering what the consequences will be for women who share the politically conservative attitudes of the male athletic culture, but not the concomitant ambition to maximize their earnings potential.

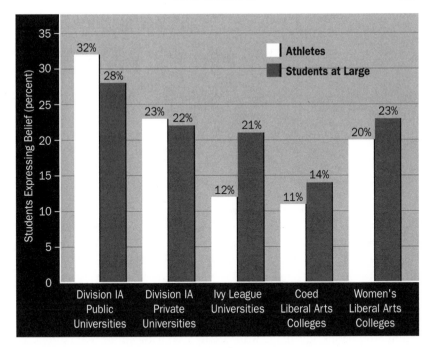

Figure 6.7. Percent of Freshmen Reporting It Is a "Very Important" or "Essential" Goal to "Be Very Well Off Financially" (by Athlete Status and Division, 1989 Cohort)
Source: College and Beyond.

Though there is clearly at least one important difference in attitudes between the women and men who are serious about college sports, women athletes, and especially those who were recruited, appear to be, in the words of former Northwestern University President Arnold Weber, "following the men down the primrose path." By 1989, the institutions that were recruiting women athletes with the same intensity with which they were recruiting men had largely succeeded in replicating the male model. How thorough will this imitation of the men's model become in the context of continuing efforts to achieve gender equity? We have some evidence that, in the decade since the 1989 cohort was admitted, emulation has continued to occur. As we saw at the coeducational school for which we have complete admissions data for 1999 as well as for 1989, the admissions advantage for women athletes has become very large, and it has even exceeded (slightly) the advantage enjoyed by the male athletes. Testimony from admissions officers confirms that recruitment of women athletes has become more and more intense, and that the same kinds of special consideration are given to both groups of athletes in the admissions process.

At the women's colleges, where gender equity has never been an issue (for obvious reasons), the imitation of the men's athletic model had not truly begun in 1989. The mean SAT score of the women who played sports at Barnard, Bryn Mawr, Smith, and Wellesley was essentially the same (only 10 points lower) than the mean SAT score of their student-at-large peers. But even though there were no internal institutional pressures to achieve equity with men, external pressures brought about by national trends were unmistakable. "All of a sudden in the early '90s," one athletics administrator at a women's college told us, "we looked up and were going 0–11 or 2–13 in a lot of sports." Whereas the coeducational colleges against whom they competed had geared up their women's programs to keep pace with their men's teams, the seeming insularity from Title IX of women's colleges had allowed them to lag behind. Recent data, however, tell a different story. Having been given access to 1999 admissions data for one of the women's colleges in the study, we learned that recruited athletes in that college's '99 cohort enjoyed a 26-percentage-point admissions advantage when compared with students at large. This level of admissions advantage was comparable to that for underrepresented minorities (30-point advantage) and appreciably higher than for legacies (16 percentage points). Current trends suggest that in another ten years the admissions picture at the women's colleges may well resemble even more closely the picture at the other schools in our study.

In earlier chapters, we have seen the ways in which differences in academic preparation, backgrounds, and goals have played out in college and then over the course of the lives of the male students. How being recruited to college to play intercollegiate sports will affect women's lives is far harder to judge, since the "experiment" is so recent. It is also important to recognize that changes in educational and career opportunities for high-achieving women have by no means reached a steady state. For example, a great deal of debate surrounds the question of whether women are now able to choose their paths—and to play the game of life—by the same rules as men or whether women are now merely free to pile career opportunities and the attendant pressures on top of the old expectations associated with home and family responsibilities. These are questions that can be addressed more knowledgeably after we examine, in the next chapter, the academic outcomes achieved by women in college (including their choices of field of study) and then, in Chapter 8, the post-college experiences of women who did and did not play college sports.

CHAPTER 7

Women Athletes in College

IN THE PREVIOUS CHAPTER we saw that there have been marked changes, between the 1976 and 1989 cohorts, in the academic and non-academic profiles of the freshmen women who went on to play college sports. Women who played sports in 1989 began to exhibit more—but by no means all—of the characteristics of the men who played college sports: they had lower SAT scores than their classmates, had different perceptions of their own abilities (especially intellectual self-confidence), and shared some of the men's more conservative political and social views, though they did not have the same sense of college as a path to large economic rewards. In this chapter we examine how the women from these two generations fared academically in college.

Even with all the debate over the consequences of Title IX, the experiment of more aggressive development of women's college sports is still young; nevertheless, enough time has passed for us to begin to discern the consequences of the changes that are still unfolding. Have the increased opportunities for women to compete in athletics transplanted the culture of male sports to the women athletes (including effects on academic performance and choices of field of study) or have women who play college sports formulated an alternative model?

GRADUATION RATES

Patterns of graduation rates are very similar for women and men: women athletes attending these schools have graduated at very high rates in both the '76 and '89 cohorts, and at higher rates than their classmates (Figure 7.1). The athlete's "advantage" in graduation rates has narrowed for the women as it has for the men, but this narrowing of the gap, in both instances, is due to the improvement in the graduation rates of students at large between 1976 and 1989. Women who participated in other time-intensive extracurricular activities were (as was the case with the men) even more likely to graduate than women athletes. The story line here is the same for the women as for the men: athletes and other students heavily engaged in organized activities of one kind or another are more likely to graduate than students at large, who may be more

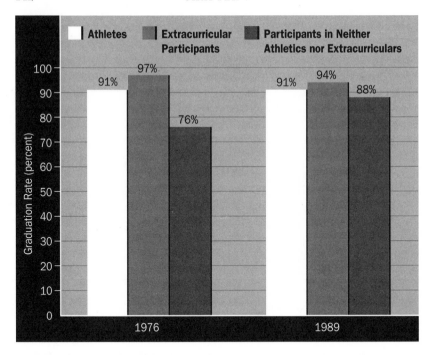

Figure 7.1. Six-Year Graduation Rate (by Athlete/Extracurricular Status and Cohort, Female Only)
    Source: College and Beyond.

prone to living semi-isolated existences on campus. In these selective schools, women athletes (like the men who play college sports) are clearly capable of completing academic programs—and they do so in very large numbers.[1]

GRADES

Rank-in-Class

One of the themes of this study is that, over time, women athletes have taken on many of the patterns of behavior demonstrated earlier by male athletes. Nowhere is this proposition more evident than in the recent history of academic achievement, as measured by rank-in-class (Figure 7.2). As in the case of the men, above-average graduation rates for women athletes are not the result of above-average records of academic achievement. In the '89 cohort, women athletes as a group ranked in the 46th

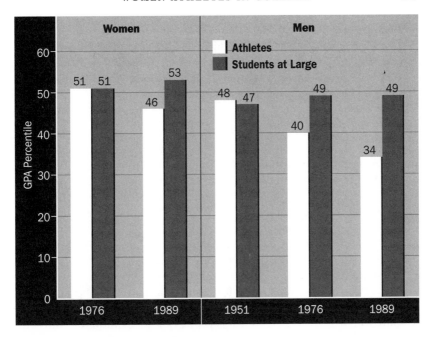

Figure 7.2. Mean GPA Percentile (by Athlete Status, Cohort, and Gender)
   Source: College and Beyond (see Scorecard 7.1).

percentile of their class, as compared with women students at large, whose average GPA put them in the 53rd percentile. This grade point gap is a recent development. The average GPA of the '76 cohort of women athletes was precisely the same as the average GPA of their women class-mates—both stood at the 51st percentile.

A member of the '76 cohort at the University of Pennsylvania, now an astrophysicist, had these recollections:

I played sports all the time growing up and basketball was my favorite. I played softball, I ran track, I played volleyball, and I played flag football. There weren't a lot of sports for girls in those days. [But] I hadn't planned on going out for sports when I went to college. I played in the intramural basketball leagues and I think I was the high scorer in the men's medium intensity league or something like that, so I got recruited and played on the team the last two years. The coach came and found me. I really liked my basketball experience, it helped everything, and my grades went up. Academics were definitely number 1; I studied astrophysics. If you couldn't make a practice because of a lab or something that was OK. I think the priorities were straight. I very much felt that other women that played sports had the same priorities. The years I was on the team, the team GPA was Dean's List.

The academic equivalence between athletes and other students that we observe for the women in the '76 cohort was also found among the men in the '51 cohort. Recruitment of male athletes was low key in 1951, and male athletes were very much like their peers in most important respects; similarly, as we saw in the previous chapter, recruitment of women athletes was still relatively low key in '76, though by then the recruitment of male athletes was taken much more seriously. By 1989, the recruitment of women athletes had begun to approximate the pattern for the men in '76 (at least in most sets of schools), and we find that the grade point gap between the athletes and the students at large for women in '89 (10 points) is as large as the gap was for male athletes in '76 (9 points) (see Scorecard 3.2).[2] The data on the admissions advantage enjoyed by women athletes in the '99 entering cohort that we examined in the previous chapter certainly suggest that this pattern, with its consistent lag, may continue to roll forward (compare the left- and right-hand sides of Figure 7.2). Will the women athletes in the '99 cohort exhibit a grade point gap as large as the 15-point gap recorded by the male athletes in '89? No one can know how these women will do in the classroom, but it would be optimistic to assume that the tendency to follow the male pattern will not continue to play out in their class rank.

The emerging difference in academic performance between women athletes and other women students has not occurred uniformly across schools playing at different levels. The overall grade point gap that is seen in the '89 cohort but not in the '76 cohort is concentrated in those divisions or conferences that were most strongly committed to recruiting women athletes—that is, the Division IA public and private universities and the Ivy League schools (Scorecard 7.1). There is only a modest GPA gap in the Division III coed liberal arts colleges and no gap at all in the women's colleges. Again, this pattern of differences in GPA gaps by level of play mirrors almost exactly differences in recruitment activity at the time the '89 cohort was enrolled.

Another way of looking at academic performance, and at differences by type of school, is to examine the percentages of women athletes and of other women students who finished in the bottom third of the class. In the '76 cohort, the women athletes were actually less likely than their female classmates to rank in the bottom third of their class on graduation

(30 percent of the women athletes were in the bottom third versus 33 percent of other women in the sector composite). By 1989 this had changed drastically: 39 percent of women athletes finished in the bottom third of their class as opposed to 29 percent of other women students. This 10-point differential for the women in 1989 mirrors almost precisely the pattern for the men in 1976 (when 49 percent of male athletes finished in the bottom third, as compared with 38 percent of male students at large).

Equally noteworthy are the differences by type of school. In the '89 cohort, women athletes at the Division IA public and private universities, and in the Ivies, were much more likely than other women students to finish in the bottom third—at the Division IA private universities, nearly half (48 percent) of women athletes finished in the bottom third of the class, as compared with 29 percent of the other women; in the Ivies, 41 percent of the women athletes were in the bottom third, versus 27 percent of other women (Figure 7.3). The differential was smaller in the Division III coed liberal arts colleges and nonexistent in the women's col-

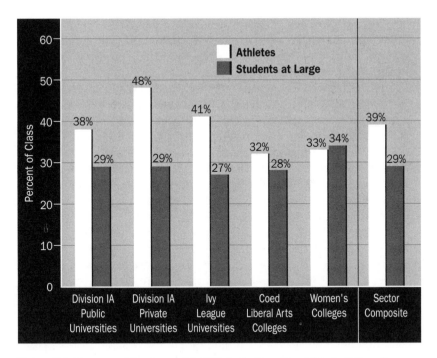

Figure 7.3. Percent of Students with GPA in Bottom One-Third of Class (by Athlete Status and Division, 1989 Cohort, Female Only)
Source: College and Beyond.

leges. We know that athletes in the women's colleges entered college with essentially the same SAT scores as their classmates, something that cannot be said of the women athletes in the other institutional clusters (compare Figure 6.4). But does this fact alone explain the differences in academic performance?

More generally, how much of the dramatic turnaround for women athletes between the '76 and '89 cohorts (from having been 3 percentage points *less* likely to finish in the bottom third of the class to 10 percentage points *more* likely to finish there) is due simply to differences in academic potential known to everyone when they entered college? Or, as in the case of the men, have different priorities and attitudes, peer group effects, extensive time commitments, and the values of an "athletic culture" also come to affect the academic performance of women athletes? To ask this key question more precisely, did women athletes in the '89 cohort underperform academically after we control for SAT scores, race, socioeconomic status, and field of study?

Actual Performance versus Predicted Performance

In the case of the '76 cohort, whatever differences in pre-collegiate academic preparation there might have been between the women athletes and their female classmates, there was no evidence of systematic academic underperformance in college. In this key respect (as in others), the women athletes in the '76 cohort were "at the same place" as the men in the '51 cohort who played intercollegiate sports.

By 1989, the situation had changed markedly. The lower rank-in-class of the women athletes, and the higher proportion who finished in the bottom third of the class, cannot be explained merely in terms of their lower SAT scores on entry. Nor does taking account of racial mix, family socioeconomic status, or the fields in which students chose to major cause differences in rank-in-class to go away. Women athletes who were like their female classmates in SAT scores and all of these other respects were nonetheless likely to earn lower grades. This pattern of academic underperformance is evident to some degree within every type of school in our study except the women's colleges; it is most pronounced in the Ivies and then in the coed liberal arts colleges.[3]

In Figure 7.4 the black bars indicate the "point estimate" of the degree of academic underperformance by women athletes at each type of school while the shaded areas provide some sense of the reliability of the point estimates. Thus we see that female athletes in the Ivies had an average rank-in-class 8.6 percentile points below that of other women students who had comparable SAT scores, socioeconomic status, fields of study,

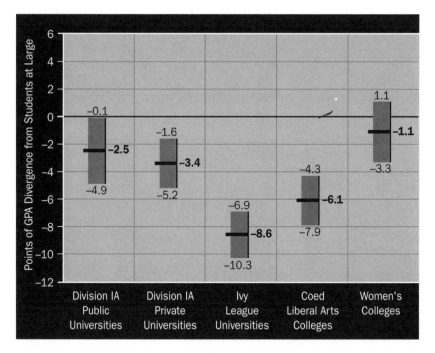

Figure 7.4. Underperformance of Athletes, Controlling for Differences in SAT, Race, Socioeconomic Status, and Major (by Division, 1989 Cohort, Female Only)

Source: College and Beyond.

and race/ethnicity; the relatively small "reach" of the shaded areas on both sides of this point estimate (which represent one standard error in either direction) shows how confident we can be that this finding of underperformance is not a statistical artifact. Women's colleges occupy the other end of the spectrum. While the point estimate for athletes at these colleges is also negative (−1.1), we see from the shaded areas that the true value of the estimate could quite easily have been positive; there is no statistically significant evidence of underperformance at these schools. There is some evidence of underperformance at the Division IA public and private universities, but it is more muted than in the Ivies and coed liberal arts colleges. As we saw in Figure 7.3, nearly half of all women athletes at the Division IA private universities finished in the bottom third of the class, and so one might have expected to find strong indications of underperformance there. But it is necessary to remember that the SAT scores of women athletes at scholarship schools with big-time athletic programs for men and women are so much lower than the scores for students at large (over 100 points lower, on average) that the *predicted* rank-in-class of those athletes is very low to begin with; thus there is relatively little room for actual grades to fall below the predicted level.

The women athletes with higher SAT scores who entered the Ivies and coed liberal arts colleges had more "opportunity" to underperform, and the significant degree of underperformance that in fact is found for the '89 women who attended these schools is noteworthy. It is noteworthy not only when considered solely on its own terms, but also when set alongside the results for the '89 men who attended these schools (compare Table 3.1 and Figure 3.4). In this respect at least, the women athletes appear to have caught up with their male counterparts—a dubious distinction! The fairest comparison is presumably with the men who played the Lower Profile sports, and we find that the degree of under-performance recorded for the women athletes is essentially the same as the degree of underperformance recorded for these male athletes in the Ivies, more pronounced than the male athletes at the coed liberal arts colleges (−8.6 points for the women in the Ivies versus −6.7 points for their male classmates who played Lower Profile sports, and −6.1 points for the women in the coed liberal arts colleges versus −3 points for their male classmates in the Lower Profile sports). Moreover, the underperformance exhibited by the women athletes at these schools is only modestly less pronounced than the underperformance by the men who played the High Profile sports (−10.8 points in the Ivies and −8.8 points in the coed liberal arts colleges).

The next question to ask for the women athletes is the same one that we posed earlier for the men: to what extent can their underperformance be explained by other aspects of their pre-college academic preparation? The answer, again, parallels the answer for the men: roughly one-third of the rank-in-class penalty associated with being an athlete is removed when we also take account of differences in high school grades, quality of high school attended, and the results of Achievement Tests (Figure 7.5).[4] At any given level of SAT score, the women athletes were earning lower grades in high school and, in general, were less well prepared academically than their women classmates on these dimensions as well as in terms of SAT scores—and there were predictable consequences in terms of their academic performance in college.

For the women athletes in the '89 cohort, as for the male athletes, it appears that an early focus on athletic accomplishment was achieved at some cost in terms of academic preparation. We are unable to determine the extent to which this pattern is due to different priorities in the allocation of time, different interests, or different expectations and assumptions about how well it was necessary to do in high school in order to gain admission to a selective college or university (or, for that matter, to what

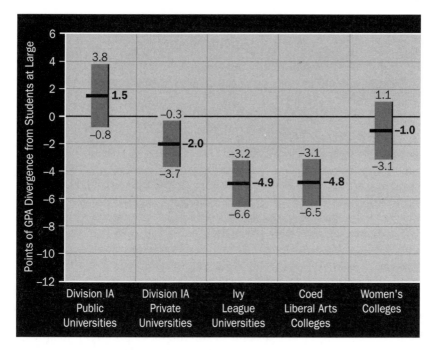

Figure 7.5. Underperformance of Athletes, Controlling for Additional Pre-
Collegiate Academic Variables in Addition to Differences in SAT, Race,
Socioeconomic Status, and Major (by Division, 1989 Cohort, Female Only)
  Source: College and Beyond.

extent the pattern is due to differences in the weight that the admissions
offices placed on academic preparation by athletes and other students in
making admissions decisions). But the results, in terms of differences in
pre-collegiate academic preparation, are clear enough. In effect, these
women athletes, like their male counterparts, have been performing less
well academically than classmates with comparable SAT scores before
they were admitted to college.

Even more important is the finding that, especially among the women
athletes in the Ivies and in the coed liberal arts colleges, evidence of
significant academic underperformance *in college* remains after taking account of pre-collegiate harbingers of what was to come. Here again we find
that the remaining underperformance by the women athletes exceeded
the underperformance by the men who played the Lower Profile sports at
these same schools (−4.9 for the women athletes in the Ivies versus −4.1
for the men athletes in the Lower Profile sports, and −4.8 for the women
athletes at the coed liberal arts colleges versus −1.3 [not statistically signifi-
cant] for the men athletes in the Lower Profile sports at these schools). It

seems that whatever combination of peer effects, "jock culture," and different priorities and incentives has led male athletes to underachieve academically has now been replicated within women's sports, where underperformance appears to be at least as widespread.

It is of course possible that the heavy time commitments now associated with many women's sports are also at least partially responsible for the grade point penalty paid by women athletes. As one way of testing this proposition, we examined the academic records of women students who had been involved in time-intensive extracurricular activities in college outside the athletics arena. Once again, the findings are clear-cut: there is no evidence of academic undeperformance among women with major commitments to such activities as editing school papers, playing in orchestras, and running the student government. On the contrary, women identified as highly active participants in extracurricular activities were, if anything, likely to *over*perform academically—that is, to earn higher grades than one would have predicted on the basis of their SAT scores, race, and socioeconomic status.[5] Of course, time pressures in intercollegiate athletics may be both greater than those characteristic of many extracurricular activities and less under the control of the individual, and we have no doubt that these time pressures take their toll in some instances. But there is no reason to believe that they are the full explanation for the academic underperformance that has become so commonplace among women athletes.

FIELD OF STUDY

Gender Gaps

Earlier research on a subset of schools in the College and Beyond database found that between 1951 and 1976 there was an appreciable narrowing in the field of study gender gap, with women shifting in relatively large numbers out of traditional women's subjects and into fields once populated much more heavily than they are today by men. However, the gender gap was by no means closed entirely, and surprisingly little further narrowing occurred between the '76 and '89 cohorts.[6]

A Denison field hockey player in the '51 cohort explains her perception of her academic options:

Women were not valued in colleges at all. The guys were expected to do something but the women weren't. So the classes were very sex-biased. One member there was a big core program at Denison; probably over half of our courses were core. I took this economics course and I went up and got my A paper and the professor said, "Gee, it's too bad you are a girl or you could major in economics." I just answered, "I know it." In the '70s I became quite an activist in the women's movement but I went right along with it back then.

Even when rather pronounced differences in math and verbal aptitude are taken into account, men and women continue to show different preferences in the fields of study in which they elect to major. The extent to which these different preferences reflect an accumulation of messages that women have been "sent" about their abilities, or differences in what women and men anticipate from their careers and their lives, remains unclear. Whatever the reasons, even among those with comparable levels of math and verbal preparation, women will be more likely to major in psychology, whereas men are more likely to choose economics; women will, in general, choose biology and the life sciences, whereas men will choose math, physics, or engineering. To illustrate, when we look only at students in the '89 cohort who had math SAT scores above 750, we find that about 18 percent of the men in this category majored in the humanities versus 25 percent of the women; conversely, about 25 percent of the men with these scores majored in engineering versus 15 percent of the women.[7] We are reminded that after the most obvious barriers that might bar women from following the same career options as men (barriers on entering certain professions, say) are removed, women continue to make different choices than men, both in the fields they study and in the career paths they follow.

What happens, then, when a subgroup of women is recruited to college at least partially on the basis of their interest and demonstrated excellence in an activity that has long been considered male territory—the arena of competitive sport? We recall that increasingly specialized recruiting of male athletes has led to increasingly clear patterns of choice and accomplishment (both in college and afterward). If the sports culture is built on a set of common characteristics that are not themselves determined by gender (competition, determination, teamwork, and such), it would be important to know if recruited women athletes have begun to act more like male athletes, or whether they have distilled their own version of what highly competitive women athletes value. Choice of major provides one lens through which to address this broad question.

Majors Chosen by Women Athletes and Other Women:
The Case of the Humanities

Perhaps the clearest evidence indicating that there is a relationship between participation in athletics and choice of major is found in simple
tabulations showing the relative numbers of women athletes and of other
women in the '89 cohort who elected to major in the humanities. In making these comparisons, it is instructive to look separately at each type of
school in the study (Figure 7.6). The most obvious pattern is found in the
scholarship schools, where women athletes were recruited most assidu-
ously (and are presumably most likely to be truly committed athletes, perhaps first and foremost). The humanities attracted far smaller percentages of these women athletes than of other women students. In the Ivies
and in the coed liberal arts colleges, women athletes were also less likely
to major in the humanities than were other women students, but the differences are smaller. Once again, the women's colleges occupy a field of

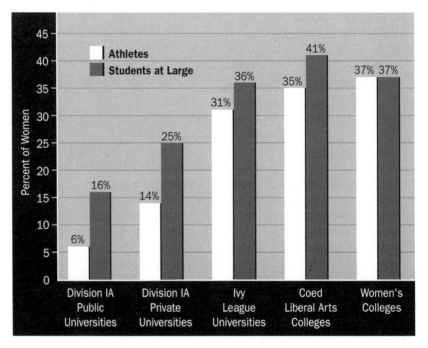

Figure 7.6. Percent of Female Students Majoring in the Humanities (by Athlete
Status and Division, 1989 Cohort)
   Source: College and Beyond (see Scorecard 7.2).

their own, in that athletes and other women were equally likely to choose a humanities field as their major.

Looking back at the '76 cohort, we find consistently smaller differences between women athletes and other women students in their preference for the humanities. Moreover, we do not believe it is coincidental that these differences between women athletes and other women widened far more in the schools that were the most active recruiters of women athletes: the Division IA public and private universities and the Ivies. In the Division IA public and private universities, the percentage of women athletes majoring in the humanities dropped sharply between the '76 and '89 cohorts at the same time that the percentage of other women students choosing these fields increased (see Scorecard 7.2 and, for corresponding data on men, Scorecard 3.5).

The Sciences—and Intellectual Self-Confidence

A lingering imbalance between men and women (without reference, for the moment, to anyone's participation in athletics) is found in the proportions of each who pursue majors—and potentially careers—in the natural sciences, mathematics, and engineering. Whether this difference is due to personal preferences or to an unconscious tracking of women away from these fields that occurs as early as elementary school, women continue to be underrepresented in the sciences and in engineering. These fields are, for women, realms of both opportunity and struggle. Nationwide about 17 percent of women who earn a bachelor's degree do so in the natural sciences, math, or engineering, compared with 24 percent of their male peers.[8] Although it is well beyond the scope of this study to examine the roots of this continuing gender gap, we are able to look at the patterns for women who played sports at this set of selective schools to see if the women who have played sports have gained any ground in leveling the playing field in science.

In the '76 cohort, 20 percent of women athletes majored in the natural sciences, math, or engineering, as compared with 16 percent of other women. By the '89 cohort, however, this difference had disappeared entirely: 18 percent of women athletes and 18 percent of other women majored in one of these scientifically oriented fields. (Overall, in the '89 cohort, 28 percent of the men at these schools, but only 17 percent of the male athletes, majored in natural science, math, or engineering; see Scorecards 7.3 and 7.4, as well as 3.4 and 3.7.)

In the previous chapter, we noted that women who played sports reported lower levels of self-confidence in their intellectual capacities than their female peers and that these other women in turn reported lower levels of intellectual self-confidence than any of the male groups, whether or not they played college sports. However, when we examine the majors chosen by those women who *did* begin college with the highest level of intellectual self-confidence, we find that the women who played sports majored in the natural sciences in disproportionately high numbers (Figure 7.7).[9] Thus, although appreciably lower proportions of the women athletes entered college with this high level of self-confidence, those who did—in 1989—were strongly represented in some of the most challenging fields, in which women were long underrepresented. This intriguing finding, read in conjunction with the evidence that the overall level of intellectual self-confidence among women who play intercollegiate sports has decreased over time (as they were increasingly selected on the basis of their athletic talent), indicates that these institutions may be missing an opportunity to prepare larger numbers of women for careers in science. If this is a reasonable objective, the goal should be to at-

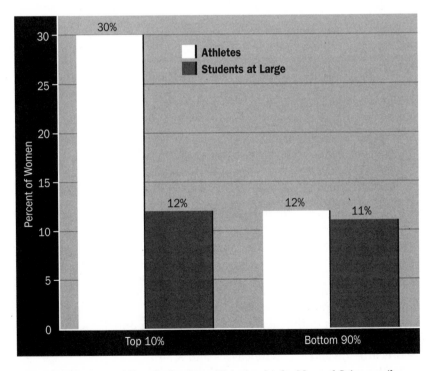

Figure 7.7. Percent of Female Students Majoring in the Natural Sciences (by Athlete Status and Self-Ranking of Intellectual Self-Confidence, 1989 Cohort)
     Source: College and Beyond.

tract women students who have *both* the attributes of the 1976 athletes and also considerable intellectual self-confidence.

Women Athletes and the Social Sciences

We end this chapter by describing the picture in the social sciences, which is more complex, in part because psychology (favored disproportionately by women as a major) and economics (favored disproportionately by men) are both located here.[10] When we look specifically at psychology, we find that in the '89 cohort women athletes were appreciably more likely to major in this field than other women; in the '76 cohort, on the other hand, there was no such pattern. Within the social sciences more generally, we do *not* see, among the women, the monumental increase that was so notable among the male athletes in the popularity of these fields, which are often seen as launching pads to financial success (compare Scorecards 7.5 and 3.6).

———————

The most important conclusion to be drawn from examination of the academic outcomes of women athletes is that, increasingly over time, they have come to replicate the patterns found among the men who played college sports. Both women and men who attended these selective schools had high graduation rates, whether or not they participated in intercollegiate athletics. Neither group of athletes did nearly as well academically, however, as their classmates, and gaps in academic performance, as measured by rank-in-class, appear to be widening.

Whereas the women athletes in the '76 entering cohort did as well academically as other women, this situation had changed by the time of the '89 cohort. The grade point penalty associated with being a woman athlete in the '89 cohort was almost exactly the same as the penalty paid by the male athletes in the '76 cohort (although only half as large as the 15-point rank-in-class penalty paid by male athletes in the '89 cohort). The increasingly intense recruitment of women athletes (and the increased admissions advantage they enjoyed in the '99 cohort), combined with the consistent association between the degree of recruitment and academic performance penalties, lead us to speculate that the gap in grades between women athletes and other women may well have continued to widen in more recent years.

In many ways, the most troubling finding for the women athletes is that their weaker academic performance (relative to other women students) cannot be attributed solely to differences in pre-collegiate preparation or other characteristics. Like the male athletes, the women who played college sports earned lower grades than one would have predicted on the basis of their SATs and other pre-collegiate factors. In fact, the degree of underperformance was roughly the same for the women athletes in the '89 cohort as for the men (with the women athletes at the women's colleges an exception to this generalization).

Gender is a stronger predictor of field of study than whether or not one was an athlete. But we do find that women athletes in the '89 cohort—and especially those who attended types of schools where recruitment was most in evidence—were somewhat less likely than women students in general to major in the humanities. There is no difference between athletes and other women in their tendency to major in the math, science, or engineering area; women athletes in the '89 cohort were, however, more likely than other women to major in psychology. One difference between women athletes and men athletes is that the women who played sports have not flooded into the other social sciences at anything like the rate of the male athletes. This difference between the men and women athletes in choice of field of study is consistent with the lower priority that women athletes assigned to being very well off financially when they entered college (Chapter 6).

The main story line of the chapter—the falloff over time in the academic performance of women athletes, following (albeit with a lag) the experience of the men who play college sports—is surely a reflection in part of the recruitment process and the criteria used by schools in choosing among applicants. But we suspect it is also a reflection, at least in part, of the interests and motivations of those who were recruited athletes— women like the recent graduate who explained her presence at a particular school by saying, "Well, I'm a catcher. . . ."

CHAPTER 8

Women's Lives after College: Advanced Study, Family, Jobs, Earnings

IN CHAPTER 4, we reflected upon the preferences and career choices of male athletes in the world after college. The data were clear in showing how strongly the post-college paths followed by these former athletes were tied to their interests and personal attributes at the time that they entered college. The norms of the male athlete culture were quite consistent: those who played sports (at all levels and across all three generations) were more likely than other students to look for—and to find—business careers and high earnings. Above all, they were thoroughly competitive, and had been so from the day they arrived on campus. The game of life, for these men, was defined in large part by these rules. The other male graduates, considered collectively, pursued a broader array of "games," with harder-to-quantify definitions of winning.

For the high-achieving women who attended these selective colleges and universities, the choice of games has been appreciably more complex. The game of life for women is more complicated because, simply put, women continue to bear more household and family obligations than men. This is true generally throughout the country: research shows that even working women in America still assume more of the responsibility for childcare and other housework.[1] It is also true among the high-achieving women who attended the selective colleges and universities in our study. If the game of life for men is defined primarily in terms of the career paths they elect to follow, the women must make these same choices while also deciding whether to work full-time, part-time, or not at all, especially during the years when many of them are having children. Of course, some men with children also end up spending appreciable time out of the workforce, but over 90 percent of men from the 1976 cohort were working full-time when, at about age 38, they were surveyed as part of the College and Beyond study. In contrast, fewer than 60 percent of the women graduates were working full-time.

Moreover, even those women working full-time placed a much higher priority on having a flexible work schedule. Of all women in the '76 cohort who were working full-time, 56 percent selected "flexible schedule" as a "very important" characteristic of a job; 42 percent of the men working full-time gave flexibility an equally high rating (and this is a higher percentage than many observers might have expected to see). If we focus on women and men with children, the gender gap in the importance attached to flexible work schedules widens—to 64 percent for women compared with 43 percent for men—and it is only among the women that the presence of children makes an appreciable difference. Among women working part-time, 85 percent cite flexibility as very important in choosing a job. While men's identities are strongly wrapped up in the career path that they follow (and while the importance they attach to having flexible schedules changes hardly at all when they have children), women in their late thirties are far more likely to think in terms of the work-life balance—a "game" that is unquestionably more complicated to play.

In this chapter we examine how women who played sports have managed this balance, by presenting data about the advanced degrees they have obtained, the careers they have chosen, and how they have fared alongside their male competitors and other women in the marketplace. We will also see, at various points in the chapter, that women's outlooks on the world (as captured crudely by their self-reported political preferences) have had an impact on the paths that they followed after college.

It is important to remember that college sports opportunities for women remain a new experiment, without the accumulated traditions and layers of cultural weight that surround men's sports. Women have been enjoying athletics in various formats for decades, but the institutional sanction that has blessed men's sports for more than a century is still a recent phenomenon for women. We have seen in previous chapters how rapidly women's sports has changed. Looked at from the perspective of later life outcomes, one relevant question is whether the justifications for competitive intercollegiate sports programs are (or should be) the same for women as they are for men.

There is little doubt that the Princeton wrestlers had an eminently clear set of impressions about what sports did for men. Have women held the same views? Not always, some say. Women who completed the C&B survey, and especially those from the '76 cohort, often extolled the pure pleasure of playing sports: "Sports then were done for the love of the sport, I think, for the enjoyment factor." "What I find about athletics in general . . . is that when I do it, it makes me happy."[2]

Citing data from a 1984 survey, athletics researcher Wendy Olson observed: "Women participate in sports for different reasons than men do. Fifty-four percent of the women cited improved health as their reason for participation in sport; fourteen percent cited stress reduction; eight percent cited friendship and sociability; eight percent cited competition; and only one percent cited winning."[3] More recently, Donna Lopiano, the executive director of the Women's Sports Foundation, defended Title IX by first citing evidence of health benefits related to athletics before citing marketplace considerations: "In an economic environment where the quality of our children's lives will be dependent on two-income families, women cannot be less prepared for the highly competitive workplace than men."[4] An overriding question is whether these different assumptions, values, and expectations about sports—combined in many cases with different obligations at home and different opportunities in the working world—have led to different choices and different outcomes after graduation. Put another way, it is clear that the post-college paths followed by women in general differ in many ways from those followed by men; this chapter examines to what extent, if at all, these patterns vary depending on whether or not a woman played intercollegiate sports in college.

GRADUATE AND PROFESSIONAL SCHOOL

Decisions about further study, marriage, family, and work are of course interconnected, and there is no one right order to follow in trying to sort them out. Increasingly, however, especially for women who attend the C&B schools, graduate study is an extremely important option. Among the members of the '76 cohort, 60 percent of all women earned advanced degrees, and women who were athletes were appreciably *more* likely to earn advanced degrees than their female classmates (Figure 8.1).

This was not at all the pattern for the male athletes in the '76 cohort, who were consistently *less* likely than other men to earn advanced degrees in all fields except business (compare Figure 4.1). But then it is also true that large numbers of the male athletes in the '76 cohort were recruited for their athletic skills, had significantly lower SAT scores, went on to do less well academically than other students, and even had a lower average rank-in-class than their male classmates with the same SAT scores (that is, they underperformed academically). Given these differences, it is hardly surprising that the '76 male athletes were less likely to earn advanced degrees than other men in their classes.

In sharp contrast, women athletes in '76 were very much like other women students at that time; very few of them reported having been recruited, they too had high SATs, and their average rank-in-class was precisely the same as the average rank-in-class of the other women. Thus we might have expected the women athletes to earn advanced degrees in essentially the same proportions as the other women in their colleges. What is surprising is that the '76 women athletes consistently did *more* than just meet the norm set by their classmates. In every group of schools in our study, from the Division IA public universities to the women's colleges, the women athletes in the '76 cohort were more likely than other women

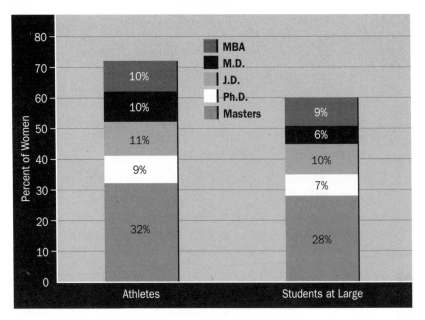

Figure 8.1. Graduates Earning Advanced Degrees (by Athlete Status, 1976
Cohort, Female Only)
   Source: College and Beyond.

to earn Ph.D.s or advanced degrees in law or medicine. Especially in the
Division IA private universities and in the Ivies, the differences in advanced degree attainment between the athletes and the other women students are very large: in the Division IA private universities, for example,
35 percent of the women athletes earned one of these prestigious advanced degrees as compared with 23 percent of other women, and in the
Ivies the corresponding figures are 45 percent for women athletes and 34
percent for other women. In the case of MBAs, the picture is more mixed,
with women athletes from some sets of schools (the Division IA private
universities and the women's and coed liberal arts colleges) more likely
to earn business degrees and women athletes from other sets of schools
less likely to do so (Figure 8.2).

   What accounts for the clear tendency for women athletes to earn more
advanced degrees than other women? Our best guess is that the women
athletes in the '76 cohort—who were so much like other women in their
pre-collegiate academic preparation, in the fields in which they majored,
and in their aspirations—had higher levels of what we described in Chapter 4 as the "A-Factor." Although the database allows us to track differences between athletes and other women along many observable dimen-

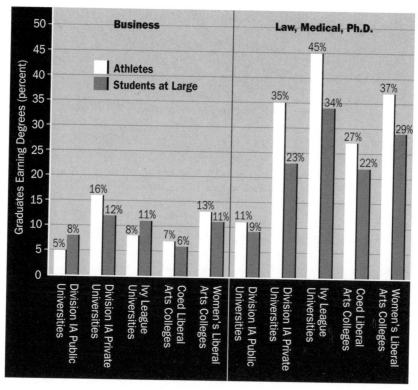

Figure 8.2. Graduates Earning Advanced Degrees (by Athlete Status and Division, 1976 Cohort, Female Only)
Source: College and Beyond.

sions (test scores, socioeconomic status, majors, and grades, for example), other, less easily observed, traits also play important roles in the choices that people make and the lives that they lead. The traits making up the A-Factor are those generally believed to be present in disproportionate degrees among athletes (competitiveness and focus, for example). For women in the late 1970s, going to graduate or professional school was an ambitious undertaking, as the gender balance in such programs was nowhere near what it is today. If women athletes were, on average, unusually energetic and determined, they might well have chosen to invest more substantially than most other women in intense pursuit of advanced degrees. While not referring specifically to women athletes, sociologist Cynthia Epstein explains the general motivation for women to pursue advanced study this way: "Women began to look at the professional schools, where they could attain a defined status—lawyer,

doctor, scientist—and avoid the amorphous situation faced by generations of college graduates whose studies in the liberal arts had opened
the way only to becoming secretaries and assistants."[5]

Investing in further education surely allows women to compete more
effectively in the career game than they could if they have only a bachelor's degree. Advanced training of certain kinds may be especially valuable for a woman who contemplates moving in and out of the labor market at some point in her life, or varying the time she spends in the
workplace, depending on family and home responsibilities. More generally, the A-Factor (as reflected in part in a heightened inclination to seek
and attain advanced training), when combined with the ability to manage time effectively ("playing basketball taught me how to focus my time
well"), may have helped female athletes to counter perceived barriers to
career advancement.[6]

Obtaining advanced training can be a drawn-out process, and former
undergraduates may not choose to begin graduate study in fields such as
business until after they have had some experience in the workplace. For
these reasons, advanced degrees sought or attained by members of the
'89 cohort should be considered a work in progress; it is difficult to compare patterns of graduate study among these students (who would have
graduated only a few years before they participated in the C&B survey)
with the degrees attained over a much longer period by those in the '76
cohort. But it is possible to use the data for the '89 cohort to compare
athletes with other women who were members of the same cohort.

When we make this comparison we find that, by the time of the '89
cohort, graduate school patterns for female athletes had fallen back into
line with the advanced degree patterns of their female peers (Figure 8.3).
By the late 1980s, greatly intensified recruiting of women athletes had led
to lower levels of academic preparation and lower levels of performance
in college, and thus it is not surprising that these women athletes had lost
their advanced degree "edge." In fact, we might have expected women
athletes from the '89 cohort to be less inclined to pursue advanced degrees than their more academically accomplished classmates. The fact
that the advanced degree advantage for athletes had *only* disappeared is
quite possibly due to counterbalancing forces: their energy and drive as
athletes may have compensated for their less accomplished academic
achievements.[7]

It is interesting to note that, at the coed liberal arts colleges and the
women's colleges, women athletes in the '89 cohort continued to be
more likely to have earned an advanced degree, or to be enrolled in graduate or professional school, at the time of the survey (an advantage of
roughly 5 percentage points). We recall that the academic differences between athletes and other women at these colleges were modest (and prac-

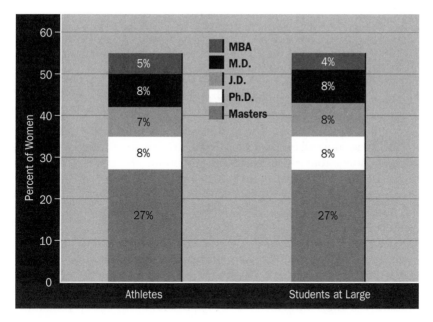

Figure 8.3. Graduates Earning Advanced Degrees (by Athlete Status, 1989 Cohort, Female Only)
   Source: College and Beyond.

tically nonexistent at the women's colleges). Time will tell if these institutions have subsequently "caught up" with the Ivies and the Division IA schools, where 1989 athletes lag their peers in pursuing advanced study.

The 13-year trend line between the '76 and '89 cohorts implies that we should anticipate further changes in these patterns, should imitation of the male model of athletic culture become more firmly entrenched in women's sports. The limited data that we have for members of the '99 cohort, which show even larger gaps in SAT scores between women athletes and other women students, suggest that the advanced degree attainments of the '76 women athletes (like those of the '51 men) may become less and less relevant predictors of the realities that lie ahead.

MARRIAGE, CHILDREN, AND LABOR FORCE ATTACHMENT

There is one respect in which there is absolutely no difference between women who were athletes and those who were not: in both the '76 and '89 cohorts, the percentage of those married is exactly the same for the two groups (79 percent in the '76 cohort and 39 percent among the

younger women in the '89 cohort).[8] Women athletes from the '76 cohort are, however, somewhat less likely than other women to have had
children (60 percent of women athletes had children versus 67 percent
of other women who attended the C&B schools).

An obvious next question is to what extent demographic differences
between men and women generally, and between women who were and
were not athletes, have been reflected in their decisions about what sort
of commitment to make to the workplace. Women athletes from the '76
cohort were more likely than their female classmates to be working full-
time, a pattern that is consistent with the notion that the typical athlete
from the '76 cohort had higher levels of the A-Factor than the typical
student at large. The greater inclination of athletes to work full-time is
present among both women with children and women without children
(Figure 8.4).[9]

Of course it is by no means only women athletes who display unusually
high levels of drive and who have particularly well-honed time management skills. The traits that we have loosely grouped under the heading of
the A-Factor are also likely to be found among other subgroups of
women. One way to test the broader applicability of the proposition that

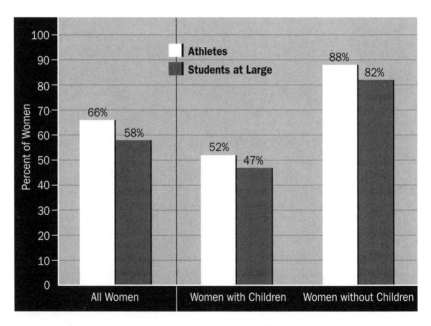

Figure 8.4. Percent of Female Graduates Working Full-Time with and without
Children (by Athlete Status, 1976 Cohort)
   Source: College and Beyond.

the A-Factor matters is by examining the labor force attachment of women in the '76 cohort who were active in time-intensive extracurricular activities other than athletics. The percentage of these "extracurriculars" working full-time turns out to be almost exactly the same as the percentage of the athletes—67 percent versus 66 percent—and both of these percentages are appreciably higher than the comparable percentage among other former women students (58 percent).[10] Highly focused and highly competitive students also excel in a range of activities, including, without question, academics.

Intel kids:

A recent story in the *New York Times Magazine* describes well the life in Midwood High School in Brooklyn of "Intel kids," who are chosen because of their academic aptitude and are then given special opportunities to do research. One of these students, Alice Warren-Gregory, is quoted as saying: "I think it's really good to have something like Intel, because it gives you focus. . . . Right now is a really good time to work hard at something."[11]

If we were able to single out the "Intel kids" as another subgroup, we suspect strongly that they would show the same kinds of work ethic and, as we see later in the chapter, earnings advantages as the athletes—maybe even more so in the "brainiac" age described in the article.

Decisions about work-life balance are of course made on the basis of many considerations, including not only the training and other capacities of the individual but also the kinds of job opportunities available and the financial circumstances of the household.[12] In addition, the values of individuals surely affect what they choose to do. Although the survey data available to us lack the nuanced measures of attitudes that would be needed to address properly the role of values in this complicated equation, it is clear that, when they entered college, equally small percentages of athletes and other women in the '76 cohort (7 percent of each group) agreed with the statement "The activities of married women are best confined to home and family."

Other data presented in Chapter 6 indicate, however, that by the fall of 1989 women athletes were more politically conservative than their 1976 predecessors when they entered college, and more conservative than other women in the '89 cohort. Moreover, once women are out of school, values associated with political preferences can be seen as playing an increasing role in defining the choices that they make. Although men's political views may also correlate with one set of goals or another, almost all men work full-time whatever their views of the world. Among the 1976 women, on the other hand, pre-collegiate political preferences play a definite role in predicting what sorts of lives they will lead after college (Figure 8.5): the tendency of women from the '76 cohort to work full-time (or, at the other end of the spectrum, not to work at all) correlates with where they placed themselves on the liberal-conservative scale when they entered college.[13]

Even more interesting is the fact that this liberal-conservative dichotomy appears to be much more strongly associated with the workplace decisions of women athletes than with those made by other women. Among athletes, 65 percent of the liberals and 42 percent of the conservatives work full-time (a gap of 23 percentage points); among other women, 62 percent of the liberals and 54 percent of the conservatives work full-time (a gap of just 8 percentage points).[14] Since political outlooks sometimes are associated with different views of opportunities for men and women, these gaps may play out differently for women athletes than for the men.

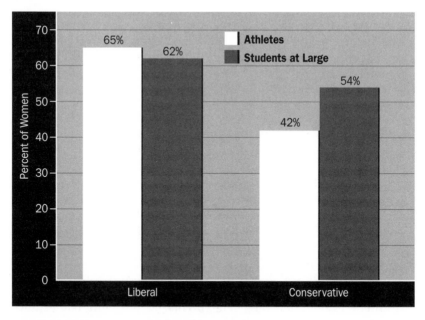

Figure 8.5. Percent of Female Graduates Working Full-Time (by Athlete Status and Pre-College Political Orientation, 1976 Cohort)
    Source: College and Beyond.

CHOOSING JOBS

Attitudes and Inclinations

Whether or not they have children, women who choose careers in professions once dominated by men will spend time "playing the men's game." Working full-time or part-time in business, law, medicine, architecture, or research, women will find themselves competing for contracts, clients, and promotions with men whose goals and responsibilities are generally more clear-cut. Are those women who played sports in college better prepared for this competition? Two somewhat conflicting strands emerge from an examination of attitudes and interests:[15]

- *Competitiveness:* Like the men, women athletes from both the '76 and '89 cohorts are decidedly more likely than other women to emphasize the importance of competition in life after college (Figure 8.6). And, again like the men, women who played sports in 1989 entered college classifying themselves as unusually competitive people.[16]
- *Interest in business and in making money:* In sharp contradiction to the pattern found for the men, women athletes in the '76 cohort were, if anything, *less* inclined than other women students to pursue business careers and to assign a high priority to being well off financially.[17]

In asking how these attitudes and inclinations have been translated into marketplace outcomes, it is necessary to begin by acknowledging one bottom-line fact known to everyone: in general, women earn less money than men. We examine the earnings of women athletes and other women in detail later in the chapter, but we highlight here this ongoing source of frustration for many women who are working every bit as hard as their male peers, since it must be kept in mind as we consider, next, the choices of occupations and sectors of employment made by women.

The disparity in male-female earnings has stimulated an enormous amount of debate among scholars seeking its cause. Some argue that the differences are due entirely or predominantly to barriers, prejudices, and discriminatory practices on the part of employers and society. Others argue that the gaps are driven predominantly by what are sometimes described as supply-side factors: differences in preferences between men and women, different job choices, and differences in attachment and long-term commitment to career paths by women (which affect seniority and opportunities for advancement). More nuanced thinkers realize that there can be a mix of forces at play; for example, what may be seen by some as an ingrained difference between men and women (degree of interest in mathematics, for example) might well prove to be a set of attitudes that

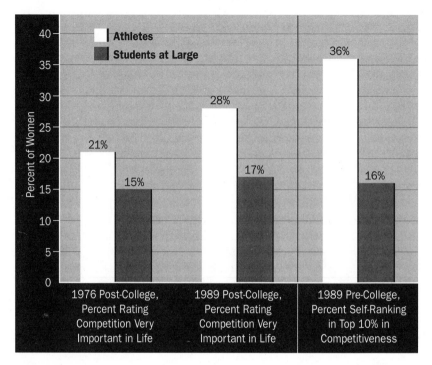

Figure 8.6. Competition before and after College (by Athlete Status and Cohort, Female Only)
Source: College and Beyond.

are socialized into girls at a young age. Also, as our colleague Harriet Zuckerman has pointed out, restricted opportunities are likely to lead women not to seek the same objectives as men; demand-side and supply-side considerations interact. In any event, neither this chapter nor this book is the place to resolve this extremely complex debate. Our goal is more limited: to examine the jobs that women athletes and other women from the '76 cohort actually held at the time of the C&B survey and to compare these "revealed preferences" (conditioned as they have been by market forces) with those of the men from the same cohort.

Job Patterns

The job patterns of the women athletes and the other women from the '76 cohort are interesting in and of themselves, and they are even more interesting when compared with the occupational destinations of the

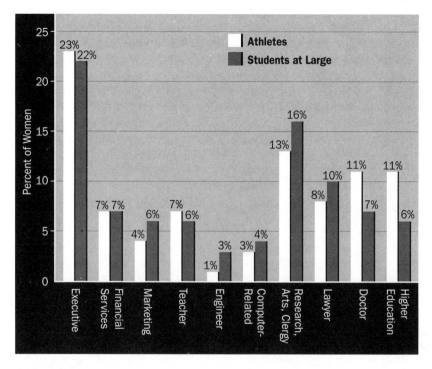

Figure 8.7. Occupations in 1995 (by Athlete Status, 1976 Cohort, Female Only)
Source: College and Beyond.

men in the same cohort (we are looking only at full-time workers). Figure 8.7 shows the numbers of women athletes and other women in the same occupational categories presented earlier for the men; then, to facilitate comparisons, Figure 8.8 shows the *differences* (percentages of athletes in each occupational category minus percentages of students at large) for both women and men.

Looking first at the middle part of Figure 8.8, we see that both female and male athletes are somewhat less likely than students at large to be found in engineering; computer-related fields; research-arts-clergy; and law. Conversely, high school teaching (and coaching) attract slightly more male and female athletes than they do students at large.

But the patterns for the women also differ in striking respects from those for the men:

- The left-hand side of Figure 8.8 shows that the highly disproportionate interest of male athletes in the main "business" categories is entirely absent when we look at the job choices made by the women

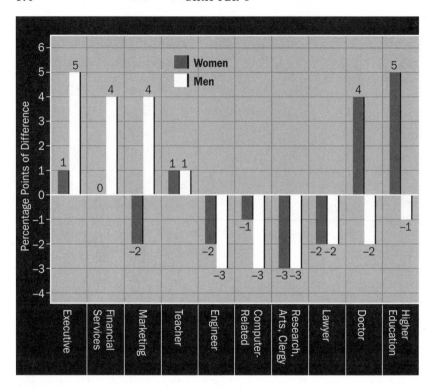

Figure 8.8. Occupational Differences: 1995 Occupations as Percent of Athletes minus Percent of Students at Large (by Gender, 1976 Cohort)
  Source: College and Beyond.

athletes. Whereas male athletes were far more likely than other men to be executives or to be working in financial services or marketing (the percentage of male athletes in these three categories exceeds the percentage of other men by 5, 4, and 4 percentage points, or by a total of 13 percentage points), the percentage of female athletes in these same categories is, taken together, slightly *below* the percentage of other women. Thus far, at any rate, this "business" manifestation of the male athletic culture has not appeared among the women athletes.

• The fields of medicine and higher education (including not only faculty members but also coaches and administrators), which are shown on the far right-hand side of Figure 8.8, are the two alternative areas in which women athletes from the '76 cohort have chosen to "specialize"—in the sense of being significantly over-represented in these fields, relative to other women. The percentage of women athletes in these two broad areas exceeds that of other women by a total of 9 percentage points; in contrast, the percentage of male athletes in these two areas is 3 points below the percentage for all men.

How are we to interpret the divergent career paths followed by the male and female athletes? We can only speculate. High-achieving women, we know from other research, are generally more interested in the health sciences than are men, and it is possible that so many women athletes became doctors in part because the general interest of women in the health fields is even stronger in their case. Both male and female athletes are thought to be somewhat more gregarious than people in general and are therefore especially likely to pursue careers in which there are many opportunities to interact with others (and, conversely, to be less inclined to pursue more solitary occupations such as that of writer). Our conjecture is that this tendency manifests itself differently for at least some number of men and women. In the case of male athletes, this attribute, when combined with an above-average interest in making money, could well encourage participation in "people-oriented" business fields such as marketing and financial services. In the case of the female athletes, who are somewhat less focused on financial rewards, teaching and coaching may loom larger as attractive career options. We must also remember that, when the women in the '76 cohort entered the workplace, business careers were much less open to women than they are today.

These interests and job patterns are consistent with the sectors in which women athletes and other women have been most likely to work. And, again, there is a clear contrast between women and men. Whereas male athletes were more likely than other men to work in the for-profit sector or to be self-employed (79 percent in these sectors for athletes versus 72 percent for other students), women athletes are found disproportionately in the not-for-profit and governmental sectors. Of all women athletes from the '76 cohort who were working full-time, only 53 percent were in the for-profit (or self-employment) sector, as compared with 60 percent of the women students at large (Figure 8.9). By the time of the '89 cohort, however, this difference had narrowed to such an extent that it was no longer statistically significant.

Women Working Part-Time

Understanding the complexities of the lives of women working part-time is beyond the scope of this project, since an analysis of the interaction of

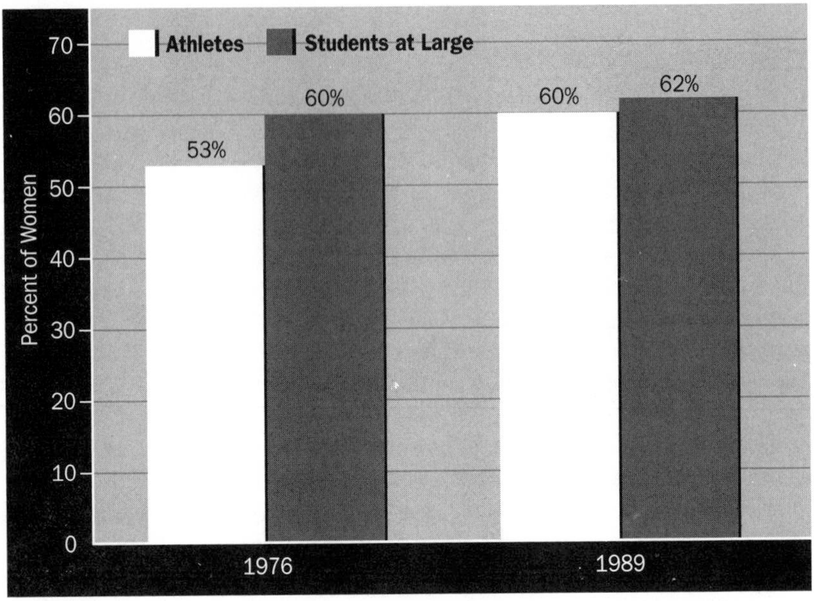

Figure 8.9. Percent of Full-Time Female Workers Employed in the For-Profit Sector in 1995 (by Athlete Status, 1976 and 1989 Cohorts)
Source: College and Beyond.

career paths, family decisions, levels of "at-home" responsibility, and other factors that influence the decision to work part-time rather than full-time or not at all would require a book of its own. And yet, if there were factors that led the former athletes to balance work and life differently than other women, we wondered whether these factors or traits would show up among those who were keeping one foot—but only one—in the working world. Among the mothers who were working part-time, evidence supports the proposition that women from the '76 cohort who played sports exhibit unusually high levels of drive and energy. When asked about the importance of high responsibility, promotion opportunities, and intellectual challenge, the athletes who were working part-time gave answers that were more like those of the women working full-time than those of their peers. Put another way, while making the same work-life decisions as other women who chose to work part-time, the former athletes were decidedly more intent upon getting the same advantages in a job as the women working full-time who (either by choice or by necessity) had more at stake in thinking about their careers.[18]

EARNINGS

Earnings Comparisons: Athletes and Other Women in the '76 Cohort

The women athletes in the '76 cohort working full-time had higher average earnings than their peers. Overall, their earnings advantage was about $7,000 (left-hand side of Figure 8.10). Only in the Division IA private universities did the women athletes fail to earn more than the other women; in every other set of schools included in the study, earnings of women athletes in this cohort exceeded the earnings of other women (restricting the comparison to women who worked full-time), and the differences in favor of the women athletes are especially pronounced in the Division III women's colleges and in the Ivies (top panel of Score-card 8.1).

The overall earnings advantage enjoyed by women athletes in the '76 cohort is modestly smaller than the earnings advantage enjoyed by men athletes in the same cohort: the $7,000 advantage for the women athletes compares with $13,000 for their male counterparts, and the correspon-

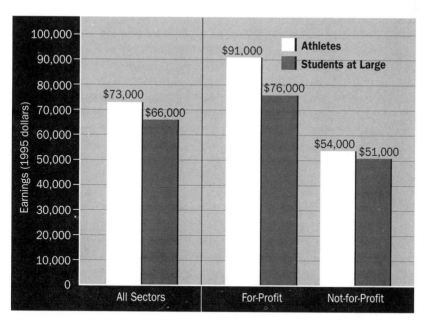

Figure 8.10. Mean Own Earned 1995 Income (by Athlete Status and Sector, 1976 Cohort, Full-Time Female Workers)
Source: College and Beyond.

ding advantages expressed in percentage terms are 11 percent for the women athletes and 13 percent for the men who played college sports (compare Figures 8.10 and 4.4). A key question is whether the factors accounting for the success of the '76 women athletes in the job market are the same as the factors accounting for the even greater success of the male athletes.

Differences Associated with Sector of Employment and Occupation

One major difference has to do with sector of employment. The earnings of male athletes were higher in part because they were much more likely than other male graduates to work in the for-profit (and self-employment) sector; in contrast, we have just seen that women athletes were appreciably less likely than other women to work in this higher-paying sector. Women athletes in the '76 cohort earned more than other women in spite of being disproportionately represented in the lower-paying of the two broad sectors. In fact, *once we hold sector of employment constant, the earnings premium enjoyed by women athletes in the '76 cohort is considerably higher, not lower, than the premium enjoyed by male athletes.*

Those women athletes who did work in the for-profit sector (slightly more than half of all those working full-time) earned substantially more than their women classmates: an average of $91,000 versus $76,000, or a 20 percent premium (right-hand side of Figure 8.10). This is a far greater earnings advantage within the for-profit sector than the 7 percent premium enjoyed by the male athletes who worked in this sector. Whereas the male athletes who worked in the not-for-profit sector had no earnings advantage at all, women athletes from the '76 cohort who worked in the not-for-profit (and government) sector earned a modest premium of 6 percent.

As a next step in the process of attempting to understand the factors responsible for these patterns, it is useful to replicate another part of the analysis carried out for the men and locate the earnings advantage of the women athletes within the for-profit sector. In the case of the men, we found that the athlete's advantage was not at all broadly distributed but rather was highly concentrated in one specific set of occupations, namely those within financial services. We now find that women athletes working in financial services also enjoyed a very large earnings advantage, and that their earnings advantage was *even greater* than the earnings advantage of male athletes ($43,000 for the women versus $34,000 for the men). However, unlike the case of the men, women athletes in several other business-type occupations (CEOs and marketing) also earned significantly more than women graduates in general. In the professions

of law and medicine, on the other hand, there were no significant differences in earnings between athletes and other graduates, either for men
or for women.[19]

In interpreting these patterns, it is important to emphasize again that
opportunities in business were much more limited for women than for
men at the time the members of the '76 cohort were deciding on their
career plans and entering the labor market. We suspect, without being
able to offer proof, that the exceptional financial success of the women
athletes of this generation—who were, we should remember, more than
equivalent to other women graduates in academic achievement in college
and after college—was due in large part to the drive, energy, and competitiveness associated with being a college athlete. In addition, as one commentator has suggested, women athletes from the 1970s may have been
unusually good at working collaboratively (virtues always in favor, but perhaps even more in favor then than now); and these "good-collaboration"
qualities may have been especially prized in the marketplace at a time
when women were beginning to make their marks in what had been
largely male-dominated fields.[20]

In short, the most straightforward interpretation of these findings is
that in the '76 cohort, before women athletes were heavily recruited, they
were very much like other women students in their skills and interests *except* that they may well have had more of those traits that we tend to associate with being an athlete. In addition, we saw earlier in the chapter
that the women athletes in this cohort earned more advanced degrees
than other women students. It was these characteristics, we believe, that
led to the earnings advantages enjoyed by the women athletes in the '76
cohort.[21] This explanation is even more persuasive for the women than
for the men, it seems to us, in part because the earnings advantage of the
women athletes in this cohort appears to have been more broadly based
than the earnings advantage of their male counterparts.

Changes over Time: Women Athletes in the '89 Cohort

Are the earnings profiles different for '89 women athletes? The direct answer to this question is, yes, the earnings advantage enjoyed by women
athletes in the '76 cohort is absent when we look at the '89 cohort.
Women athletes in the '89 cohort who were working full-time had average earnings in 1997 (the year of the C&B survey for this cohort) of
$29,000. The average earnings of the other women in the '89 cohort were
also $29,000 (Scorecard 8.1). When the comparison is restricted to
women who worked full-time in the for-profit sector, we find that women
athletes earned an average of $30,300, as compared with $31,600 for

other women (Scorecard 8.2). More generally, there is no statistically significant difference in average earnings between athletes and other women from this cohort within each type of school. This non-pattern in the '89 cohort is just as consistent as the presence of an earnings advantage for athletes in the '76 cohort (top panels of Scorecards 8.1 and 8.2). To be sure, many of the members of this cohort were still in graduate school or were just beginning their careers when they were surveyed, and so it would be a mistake to make too much of this finding of no significant difference. An earnings advantage for women athletes in the '89 cohort could of course develop as the years pass. However, the same caveats obviously apply to the earnings data for the men in the '89 cohort, and the male athletes from this cohort do enjoy a significant earnings advantage over their male classmates (compare Figure 4.4).

In short, the earnings achievements of the women athletes in the '89 cohort are decidedly less noteworthy than the earnings achievements of the women athletes in the '76 cohort. This comparison takes on obvious significance when we recall the dramatic changes in women's sports that have occurred between the '76 and '89 cohorts. First, women athletes in 1989 were much more actively recruited for their athletic talent than were women athletes in 1976; second, women athletes entered college in 1989 with weaker academic credentials than women athletes in 1976; third, between 1976 and 1989, women athletes went from being *less* likely to finish in the bottom third of the class to being appreciably *more* likely to finish there—a result due only in part to their weaker academic credentials on admission, since we also observed the same kind of academic underperformance among the women athletes that we observed for the men. And earlier in this chapter we saw that the women athletes in the '89 cohort were no longer more likely than their women classmates to earn advanced degrees.

Most of these same changes affected men athletes earlier, and in many respects the women athletes in the '89 cohort resemble the male athletes in the '76 cohort. But the male athletes in both the '76 and '89 cohorts enjoyed an earnings advantage over their male classmates, whereas the women athletes in the '89 cohort had lost this earnings advantage. There is at least one clear difference between the female and male athletes in the '89 cohort that may help us understand what is going on. Whereas an extremely high percentage of the male athletes in the '89 cohort said, when entering college, that it was "essential" or "very important" to them to "be very well off financially" (42 percent of the male college athletes, as compared with 30 percent of the high-school-only athletes and 25 percent of the men who did not play sports in either high school or college), there is no such disparity among the women athletes and the other women. In fact, in the '89 cohort, women athletes were appreciably less interested in being well off financially than were their women classmates (Figure 8.11).

Those women who did pursue business careers undoubtedly benefited in some measure from the same networking advantages that helped male athletes, as illustrated by the anecdote on page 178, related by a former Wesleyan intercollegiate athlete who actually found a job network through a club sport. But such networks need time to become pervasive, and they depend not only on the type of word-of-mouth connection that the Wesleyan student found but also on active and established recruiting on the hiring side. In Chapter 4, we noted how intergenerational expectations ("I played baseball in the '60s and I want to hire people like me") are likely to be a part of the enhanced opportunity set presented to male athletes in financial services. Over time, the women athletes who have been successful in the workplace may seek to establish networks in the same way that the men have done. It is also possible that the greater acceptance and prominence of women's sports programs may eventually come to represent a wide cultural weave that connects the workplace and the playing field. For the time being, however, such networks do not ap-

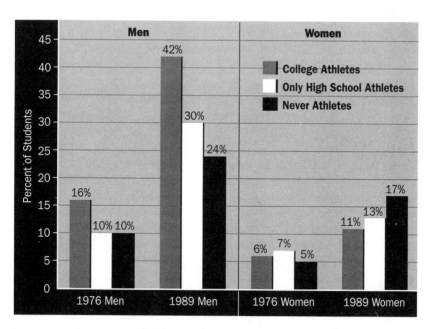

Figure 8.11. Percent of Students Reporting as Freshman That an "Essential" Goal Is to "Be Very Well Off Financially" (by Athlete Status, Cohort, and Gender, Ivy League Universities and Coed Liberal Arts Colleges)
Source: College and Beyond.

pear to be strong enough, or pervasive enough, to outweigh the factors shaping earnings prospects for all women at these selective schools—including, of course, their level of academic achievement.

One 1989 Wesleyan intercollegiate athlete explains how she ended up at J. P. Morgan:

A very good friend of mine from my rugby team was a few years older than me and was working at J. P. Morgan and said that she really thought I would enjoy the training program that she went through and the experiences she was having. So I looked into it and figured maybe I'll interview, and I got the job. I took no econ or math in college. I thought it would be exciting to try to do something new that I really didn't know much about and I said "Why not?" Looking back, I realize how lucky I was.

Years of Play, Intensity of Competition, and Earnings

On one important point, the findings for the women athletes reinforce a conclusion reached earlier for the men. There is no evidence that earnings for women athletes are enhanced by larger "doses" of athletic training in college:

- First, for the women athletes there is no consistent association of any kind between years of play and earnings (Figure 8.12). This figure resembles closely the parallel figure for men from the '76 cohort who played the Lower Profile sports, which is the most relevant comparison (see right-hand side of Figure 4.10). There is only one noteworthy difference: in the case of the women athletes, those who won awards all four years they were in college enjoyed *less* of an earnings premium (over students at large) than did either those who played for one year only or those who played for two or three years.[22]
- Second, for the women athletes as well as for the men who played college sports in the '76 cohort, there is no association between earnings advantages and the level of play. In fact, the Division IA private universities are the only group of schools at which women athletes enjoyed *no* earnings advantage; conversely, the highest earnings advantage accorded college athletes is found in the women's colleges (Scorecard 8.1). Moreover, women athletes in the '89 cohort—when competition was generally more intense in all divisions—had no statistically significant earnings advantage over their classmates.

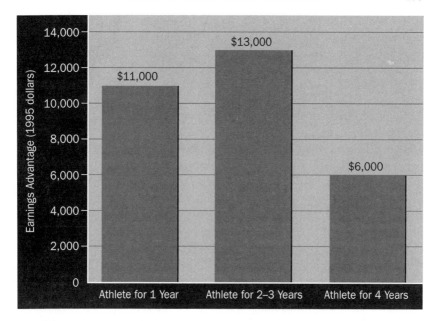

Figure 8.12. Earnings Advantages of Athletes by Years Played (1976 Cohort, Full-Time Female Workers)
Source: College and Beyond.

These consistent results support the proposition that it is primarily the attributes that women athletes bring with them to college that enhance their subsequent earnings. In the language used in Chapter 4, "selection" seems more powerful than "treatment."[23]

The C&B data have given us an opportunity to check in on one generation of women at a point in their lives when they were likely to be wrestling with the question of how to balance the amalgamation of pressures in the workplace and the home. Studying the experiences of this '76 cohort, who were approximately 38 years old when they answered the C&B survey in 1995–96, allows us to see how the athletes of that generation, underfunded and often unappreciated as they were as athletes, have fared in life. In Chapter 6 we saw that these women were very similar to their peers at the time of their admission to college. In Chapter 7 we saw that their academic performance did not fall off because of their athletic participation. What do their postcollege experiences tell us about the paths they have followed after graduation?

We began this section of the book by asking whether flourishing women's sports programs would offer a different—a less specialized and professionalized—model of sports. With the active intervention of forces as varied as the women's movement, the NCAA, and the federal government, women's sports have moved away from an alternative approach and toward a replication of the men's model. One major benefit that many of the male athletes are gaining from their model (higher earnings) is something that the female athletes in the '76 cohort were already enjoying. Given enough resources and time for the women's athletic experiment to develop fully, their adoption of the men's system might reproduce the men's athletic culture in its entirety. What would this mean for the women?

We can identify two possible scenarios (and no doubt there are many others). In the first, a sports culture based on the men's could, in the fullness of time, bring women all of the men's rewards—increased self-confidence, the applause of growing numbers of fans, and post-college networks that support them as they move from the playing fields to the trading desks. Women who play sports could, with ever-increasing focus and determination, build upon and magnify the rewards that we have already seen accrue to the 1976 women athletes. If women who played sports in the fairly casual and improvised state of the late 1970s were more likely to pursue advanced study, enjoy higher earnings, and be eager to take on greater challenges, one could posit a world in which intensified sports programs would bestow even more of these opportunities on the women who were more intensely recruited.

The second scenario is that the game of life will never be quite the same for women who play sports. Under this reading, as under the first one, women will continue to seek and to attain opportunities to play sports seriously, and they will enjoy doing so in the same way that men do; in these respects, the male model of athletic culture will be replicated. But because of the way that society is structured, many women athletes will be unlikely to have the same set of career opportunities (and outcomes) as their male counterparts. In this regard, it is important to remember that some elements of the male sports culture, with its generally conservative values, emphasize different roles for women than a model that is focused strongly on work outside the home. The women athletes, in absorbing such a model, could win the battle for equal access to athletic opportunity but lose the larger war for equal pay and a wider range of career opportunities. Right now, it is impossible to say which of these radically different scenarios will play out—the two readings can only be assessed when the experiment has had time to run its full course.

In the preceding three chapters, we were, however, able to make some initial comparisons between the 1976 women athletes and their 1989 successors. The admissions qualifications of the 1989 women athletes were substantially lower than those of their female peers. Like the male athletes, the 1989 female athletes were performing less well academically and less well than would have been predicted. In effect, very talented field hockey players took the places in the '89 entering class of other women who might have benefited in different ways from the academic and non-academic opportunities that these selective colleges and universities offer. Early indications of the post-college experiences of the '89 cohort of women athletes suggest that, when they follow the men's model, they may not only fail to receive benefits that are equivalent to those enjoyed by the men but in fact fail to garner all of the advantages enjoyed by women athletes in earlier days.

Grades matter for everyone, and probably even more so for women when they compete in the marketplace. Opportunity structures also matter, but they only develop over long periods of time, and it may be some years (if ever) before having turned a double play in softball opens the same the doors as having participated in a memorable goal-line stand. Ironically, there may turn out to be a disjuncture between increases in the "quality" (or "seriousness" or "professionalism") of women's sports programs and the longer-term quest for the proverbial level playing field.

CHAPTER 9

Leadership

In sports, you learn about teamwork and getting
along with others; you learn that you get out of
something as much as you're willing to put in, and
that success takes hard work and dedication.
Sports also teach the importance of responsibility. . . . For the vast majority of people that participate in sports, sports help them grow as individuals and prepare for life.
                    —Morgan Wootten, Basketball Coach,
                    DeMatha Catholic High School (1995)[1]

Results of in-depth analyses of moral reasoning in
sport have shown that athletes have a tendency to
shrug off moral decisions as not their responsibility and that they also exhibit a self-serving bias
when judging what violent behavior is appropriate.
                    —Andrew Miracle and Roger Rees,
                    Lessons of the Locker Room (1994)[2]

IN THE DATA presented thus far, we have not attempted to address some
of the most common, and rarely questioned, myths about sports that go
beyond the grades students receive or the amount of money that they
eventually earn. Our title, *The Game of Life,* alludes to the ways in which
life in society can be seen as structured like a game—with a starting line
and a finish line, intermediary goals, and externally imposed rules (laws)
that define what sort of play is acceptable.

Some people argue that competitive sports are an excellent training
ground for life. The current speaker of the U.S. House of Representatives, Dennis Hastert, on being inducted into the Hall of Outstanding
Americans at the National Wrestling Hall of Fame, attributed much of his
success to lessons learned as a wrestler and as a coach: "A lot of what I do
as speaker of the House is just old coaching philosophy. You learn you
don't win overnight, it takes a long time to build success and you have to
pull people together and you have to work as a team."[3] Others argue that
sports foster values that, when carried "outside the lines," may indeed

serve an individual well in the game of life—but perhaps at a societal cost. "Trained to sacrifice body and soul for the team," writes one critic of the lessons that sports teach, "taught to depersonalize opponents, schooled in the art of aggression, willing to dutifully follow coach's rules, orders, and schedules without question—what boss wouldn't like to employ a team of ex-athletes?"[4]

The images we see in the newspapers and on television are wildly contrasting. Sports stars are seen devoting time and energy to United Way campaigns and hospital visits. At the same time, as several commentators on our manuscript noted, those who would extol the character-building values of athletics must address the impression that college athletes are more likely than other students to become discipline cases on campus. And of course there are the occasional widely publicized cases of violent behavior. Anecdotes will not resolve this debate: Bill Bradley was an athlete at Princeton, but so was Lyle Menendez.

Although there is a considerable literature on the broad subject of education and character, we know no direct way of testing the proposition that playing sports in college is an especially effective way of developing this much-prized but elusive attribute.[5] Putting to one side the extreme cases such as Bradley and Menendez, it is difficult to know not only whether sports build character, but what constitutes "good character" in the first place. In the end, judgments about character are, except at the extreme ends of the spectrum, best left to the eye of the beholder. There are, however, related questions that are more amenable to analysis. On the tail of the question of whether organized sports build character comes the question of whether participating in college sports trains one to be a leader—a contention that was heard frequently during the Princeton wrestling controversy. In this chapter, we examine the leadership roles that athletes and other former students take on, and we consider what sort of leadership they are providing.

PERCEPTIONS OF LEADERSHIP

Is there a factual basis for associating athletic prowess with leadership? We begin, not with objective facts about leadership roles, but rather with the views that the athletes and other students have of their own leadership ability. Future intercollegiate athletes, when they were still in high school, were more likely than future students at large to rate themselves highly in terms of leadership. This pattern holds for men in both the 1976 and 1989 cohorts and for women in the 1989 cohort (Figure 9.1 and Scorecard 9.1).

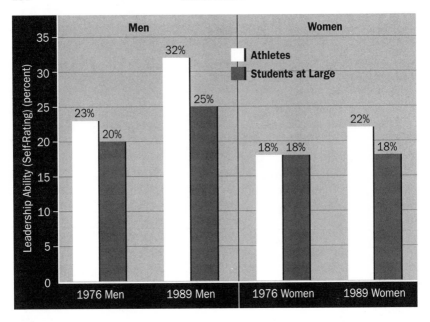

Figure 9.1. Percent of Freshman Rating Themselves in the Top 10 Percent
of Peers on "Leadership Ability" (by Athlete Status and Gender, 1976 and
1989 Cohorts)
    Source: College and Beyond (see Scorecard 9.1).

The only exception to the pattern is the women athletes in the '76 cohort, and it is probably not a coincidence that these women athletes were
much less intensively recruited than either the male athletes in the same
cohort or the women athletes in the '89 cohort. Athletic recruiting has
become more intense over time for both men and women, and the highest self-rating of leadership shown in the figure is for male athletes in the
'89 cohort. In short, high leadership self-ratings appear to correlate with
how intensively future college athletes were recruited, and further evidence in support of this proposition is found when we look separately at
the men in the '89 cohort who played the High Profile sports. For instance, in the Ivy League 55 percent of the '89 male athletes who played
High Profile sports rated themselves in the top 10 percent in terms of
leadership as compared with 34 percent of the male athletes in the other
sports and 29 percent of the male students at large. This pattern is replicated almost precisely in the Division IA private universities, but it is
much less pronounced in the coed liberal arts colleges.[6]

There is no clear answer to the question of what explains this relationship between athletic intensity and self-ratings of leadership ability.
It seems implausible that the ability to run faster or to jump higher is it-

self a predictor of leadership. But college athletes, when in high school, may have been more likely than other high school athletes (never mind other students) to be a team captain and to serve in other roles that connote leadership. It is also possible that the early accomplishments of highly recruited athletes (receiving all-city or all-state honors, and so on) led these students to feel good about themselves and thus to give themselves high leadership ratings. Whatever the cause of high levels of self-perception of leadership, the result is entirely consistent with other findings in the book about the importance of differences between college athletes and other groups of students at the time of admission; college athletes believed they had above-average leadership capacity when they first arrived on campus.

The association between participation in athletics and attitudes toward leadership persists well beyond college and, if anything, is even stronger and more consistent in the post-college C&B survey data. Former athletes were much more likely than their classmates to report that "leadership" had been "very important" (rated a 5 on a 1–5 scale) in their life since college (Figure 9.2). Moreover, the relationship between athletics and

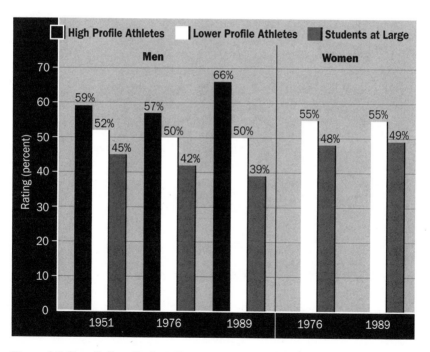

Figure 9.2. Post-College Rating: "Leadership" Has Been "Important" in Life since College (by Athlete Status, Cohort, and Gender)
    Source: College and Beyond.

the importance attached to leadership is somewhat stronger among the men than among the women, clearly stronger among the High Profile male athletes than among the other male athletes, and especially strong among the men in the '89 cohort. All of these patterns suggest that the intensity of a person's athletic involvement, and of the degree to which he or she was recruited, correlates with the emphasis that that person placed on leadership. Greatest importance is placed on leadership within male High Profile athlete categories (i.e., those who play football say leadership is more important than men or women who swim) and within types of schools that compete at the highest levels of play (among athletes at Michigan and Notre Dame versus those at Hamilton or Bryn Mawr). Whatever defines leadership—in the eye of the beholder—it is clear that the more seriously sports are taken, the greater is the importance attached to "leadership" in life.[7]

ASPECTS OF LEADERSHIP

Thinking that leadership is important and being a leader may or may not be the same thing. Moving from self-ratings and self-pronouncements to the realm of the actual exercise of leadership presents problems of definition that we cannot resolve in any fully satisfactory way. There are innumerable aspects and styles of leadership and no agreed-upon set of criteria for establishing whether a given person is or is not a leader. One aspect of leading is having the vision to see beyond the moment—the idea that the present situation of a group, a company, or a country is not ideal and that there is some goal toward which the group should be moving. Other aspects of leadership can include autonomy, courage, the ability to visualize solutions beyond the present array of options, the ability to identify talent, and the ability to motivate. Leadership can also be thought of as being essentially creative—not simply carrying out orders but innovating. The creative aspect of leadership must, however, be combined with the instrumental skills needed to achieve results. Public speaking, self-confidence, and the ability to convince others are necessary tools, as is the ability to know one's own limits, to learn from setbacks, to delegate, and to exercise good judgment. Finally, following Max Weber in *The Theory of Social and Economic Organization,* it is important to realize that leadership is not necessarily a characteristic of an individual that is transferable from one setting to another; rather it inheres in the specific relationship between a leader and his or her followers. Throughout this chapter, we try to distinguish between leadership measured as some form of self-confidence and as specific roles played within a defined context such as the workplace or a civic activity.

Leadership and Public Service

Traditionally, leadership is thought to be easiest to identify in political life and in the military. From the realm of political leadership, we think of Winston Churchill, Golda Meir, and Nelson Mandela; from the military, George Patton, Douglas MacArthur, and Colin Powell. Part of the reason that we can see leadership clearly in these realms is obvious: leadership shines in crisis and war, and a national or international platform allows leaders to lead, and to do so in a public way. Because of overall sample sizes, too few of the C&B graduates from our cohorts entered the military or are known to have been elected to high political office to permit us to compare the roles played by athletes and other students in these most visible arenas.

There may be merit in thinking more broadly about leadership as it is expressed through active involvement in public affairs. When we simply count individuals who worked for a governmental entity at any level, we find no pronounced differences between athletes and other graduates. Male athletes in both the '51 and '76 cohorts were slightly less likely than their classmates to be working in the governmental sector, and women athletes in the '76 cohort were somewhat more likely to be employed there.[8] But of course aggregate data of this kind fail to distinguish between those who provided leadership in some genuine sense and those who worked in mundane capacities.

It is somewhat more revealing to examine the public service career choices made by those who earned Ph.D.s and high-prestige professional degrees (M.D.s, J.D.s, and MBAs), whose training would presumably provide access to a wider array of leadership opportunities in any sector than are available to many of those with a bachelor's or a master's degree. When we narrow the comparison in this way, the differences between athletes and other students widen. Among the 1951 men, 13 percent of those male students at large holding these advanced degrees were employed by the government, as compared with 8 percent of the athletes; among the 1976 men, 14 percent of the students at large holding these degrees and 10 percent of the athletes were working in government; among the 1976 women, the governmental sector employed 17 percent of the students at large holding these advanced degrees and 15 percent of the athletes. These data can be interpreted in two diametrically opposite ways: as indicating that more of the students at large with impressive post-college academic credentials "took shelter" in the less frantic world of government employment or that more of them were willing to put their advanced training to use in public service. At the minimum, it seems fair to conclude that, when public service is defined in this broad way, athletes are no more likely than others to be contributing their talents.

Workplace Leadership

The academically selective schools included in this study take under-standable pride in the leadership provided by their graduates in other major sectors of society, including of course the private sector. When the former students who participated in the C&B surveys were assessing the importance of leadership in their lives, large numbers of them must surely have had in mind their roles as leaders in the workplace.

The C&B surveys identify explicitly those individuals who, as chief ex-ecutive officers, were most clearly exercising leadership in one realm or another. The odds that someone would become a CEO were similar for athletes and the other graduates of these schools. Among the men in the '51 cohort, 9 percent of the athletes and 8 percent of students at large became CEOs; in the '76 cohort, 4 percent of the athletes and 4 percent of the students at large had risen to the top. Among women athletes, 3 percent of the '76 cohort were top executives, as opposed to 2 percent of the female students at large. (We assume that higher numbers of this cohort will take up leadership positions later in their careers—at the time of the C&B survey, they were approximately 38 years old.)

A next obvious question is how the market has valued the contributions of the CEOs who worked in the for-profit sector (Figure 9.3). Among the male CEOs from the '51 cohort, the athletes earned, on average, slightly more than the students at large (in the sector composite, $183,000 ver-sus $179,000 which is not a statistically significant difference). Within the '76 cohort, the pattern is quite different; here the former athlete who had already become a CEO earned, on average, $22,000 *less* than the typ-ical CEO who had not played college sports. This pattern is entirely con-sistent and exists within every type of school.[9] Why did the male athlete CEOs in the '76 cohort earn less relative to other men holding CEO po-sitions, when this was not true for their predecessors in '51? The '76 male athletes who played sports were, as discussed in previous chapters, much more intensively recruited as athletes, and whatever their athletically related strong points, they may lack some of the other qualities (breadth of view, and so on) that helped the athletes of an earlier day develop lead-ership that was rewarded in the marketplace.

We cannot make the same kinds of comparisons for women in the '76 cohort because there are just too few who both had been intercollegiate athletes and were already CEOs of for-profit companies. We can point out, however, that among *all* women executives (not just the CEOs) from the '76 cohort, there is no consistent difference in average earnings between the former athletes and the students at large—$91,000 versus $90,000 in the sector composite.[10]

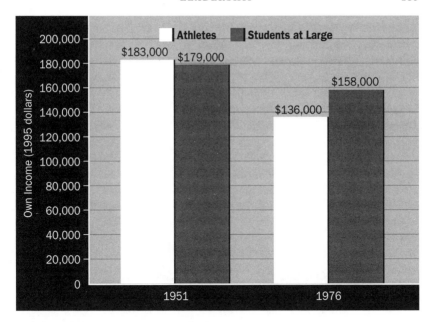

Figure 9.3. Mean 1995 Earned Income of For-Profit CEOs (by Athlete Status, 1951 and 1976 Cohorts, Full-Time Male Workers)
  Source: College and Beyond.

Earnings as a Proxy for Leadership

We are interested, of course, in workplace leadership that is expressed in many ways, and not just by being a CEO. In the absence of direct indicators of who does and does not provide "leadership" in other roles and in various professions and occupations, we are driven back to treating earnings as a crude proxy for how individuals are viewed within the fields they have chosen. Although it is obviously a highly imperfect measure, there is presumably some correlation between, for example, the earnings of private sector lawyers and their stature in their field. And we would expect earnings to be a still better proxy for leadership in more hierarchical sectors such as business, where compensation often (though not always) is correlated with executive responsibility.

Looked at in this way, the earnings data analyzed in such detail in Chapters 4 and 8 shed at least some light on the leadership question. There was, as the reader will recall, a considerable "earnings advantage" enjoyed by male athletes in both the '51 and '76 cohorts and by female athletes in the '76 cohort, *but it proved to be an advantage that was highly concentrated in certain classes of jobs.* Specifically,

TABLE 9.1

Earnings Advantages in 1995 of Athletes by Occupation (thousands of dollars)
(by Cohort and Gender, Full-Time For-Profit Workers)

	1951 Men	1976 Men	1976 Women
CEOs	**22**	0	**47**
Other executives	8	**27**	−5
Financial services	−11	**36**	**43**
Lawyers	10	1	2
Doctors	3	−5	17

Note: **Bold** values are significant at the .10 level.

- On an "other things equal" basis, athletes who were executives, broadly defined, earned modestly more than students at large who became executives (although the differences rarely pass tests of statistical significance); especially in the '76 cohort, both male and female athletes who worked in financial services earned much more than classmates who were students at large.
- On the other hand, athletes who were lawyers or doctors, or who were employed in other fields, such as teaching and research, earned essentially the same amount of money as their similarly situated classmates.

Earnings advantages conferred on athletes are summarized for selected occupational categories in Table 9.1; those athlete earnings advantages that are statistically significant are shown in boldface.[11]

What explains these divergent patterns? As we suggested in Chapters 4 and 8, our conjecture is that the attributes often associated with being an athlete (competitiveness, energy, single-minded pursuit of goals, gregariousness, and ability to work in teams) are especially likely to be rewarded in enterprises that often depend on building relationships and that closely monitor the achievement of financial targets and goals. Financial services, consulting, and CEO positions would seem to meet these criteria. But these same athlete type attributes may offer few advantages (and perhaps even some disadvantages) in careers that emphasize critical thinking, autonomy, and the capacity to know when not to seek a "win" at all costs (for example, knowing when it is prudent to settle a case rather than litigate indefinitely or when to avoid pushing ahead with a risky surgical procedure). Similarly, the scientist and the researcher must often be satisfied with following a sometimes lonely course. Finally, recalling the role that opportunity structures can play in creating networks upon which former athletes can draw, one can surmise that in addition to traits that are particularly helpful to those athletes in financial services, lingering effects of familiar bonds may help in career advancement as well.

Another question is why the '76 male athletes enjoy no discernible earnings advantage in CEO positions even though they do make more money in finance, consulting, and "other executive" jobs (although this latter difference is not statistically significant). One highly accomplished former athlete from the same generation as the '76 cohort (who now serves as a CEO) suggested that perhaps the contacts and connections available to male athletes, and especially to those in High Profile sports, help get them good jobs which pay well, and that their energy, drive, and so on then take them some distance up the ladder in these desirable positions. But, when it comes to success as a CEO, none of that may count for much. His argument is that, at the CEO level, strategic thinking and other kinds of "smarts," above and beyond energy and drive, determine how well one does.

Civic Leadership

America has a long tradition—and an important role in the world today—in stressing the value of volunteerism. The ideas of "giving something back," of "helping others because you should," of not relying solely on the marketplace or on government to solve large social problems, are all part of the American character. No discussion of leadership would be complete, therefore, without an accounting of the contributions made by the graduates of the C&B schools, athletes and others, as volunteers within a society that depends heavily on this form of leadership.

Civic Leadership by Type of Activity

When we examine patterns of civic (volunteer) leadership among one-time C&B students, we find that there are more similarities than differences between the former athletes and the other former students (Table 9.2). Both groups are very active as volunteers, and there is no easy way of giving an overall prize for civic contribution to one group or the other. But there are some differences. Former athletes are slightly less likely to be leaders of arts or culture organizations and slightly more likely to be leaders of alumni/ae activities or to be leading youth organizations (such as Little League, youth soccer, or the Boy Scouts).

Before looking in more detail at these two areas where athletes are especially prone to be leaders, it is worth noting that, despite somewhat higher incomes, former athletes are providing volunteer leadership at es-

TABLE 9.2
Leadership of Civic Activities
(by Athlete Status, Cohort, and Gender) (percent)

	1951 Men		1976 Men		1976 Women	
	Athletes	Students at Large	Athletes	Students at Large	Athletes	Students at Large
Alumni/ae activities	8	5	5	4	4	3
Arts activities	7	8	3	5	5	7
Community activities	8	7	4	6	7	7
Educational activities	6	4	5	4	10	11
Political activities	7	5	4	4	3	3
Professional activities	18	15	9	11	10	8
Religious activities	14	16	13	11	10	15
Social activities	8	8	5	4	6	5
Sports activities	6	3	15	8	10	3
Youth activities	6	5	21	14	12	11

sentially the same rates as other graduates in most not-for-profit areas. In general, earning more money serves as a statistically significant predictor of whether one will be a leader of a civic activity, and from this perspective a finding of "no difference" in civic contributions between athletes and others is mildly surprising. We have no way of knowing if former athletes are being more or less generous to good causes than their less affluent classmates, but our data do disprove any notion that former athletes are appreciably more likely than other graduates to be leading civic activities of all kinds. They appear to be very much like their classmates in their overall tendency to be leaders of schools, religious groups, community associations, civil rights groups, museums, libraries, and soup kitchens.

In contrast, one of the most noteworthy conclusions reached in a previous study of differences related to race was that black graduates at the C&B schools from both the '76 and '89 cohorts were much more likely than their white classmates to take on leadership positions within virtually every type of civic endeavor.[12] This difference is a crucial one when we reflect on the justifications often heard for giving consideration to race or to athletic prowess in the admissions process. At the end of Chapter 3, we noted the different aims of recruiting minority students and recruiting athletes. The data presented here provide one basis for comparing the benefits that accrue to society at large from these two admissions efforts; we conclude that while African Americans who attend these schools are decidedly more likely to take on leadership roles in a wide range of civic activities than their white classmates, the same cannot be said of former athletes whose admission was justified, at least in part, on their leadership potential.

In searching for potential board members and other volunteer leaders, not-for-profit organizations often take a special interest in CEOs. Such individuals may be able to contribute in a wide variety of ways: through their own practical experience in guiding organizations, through their generosity, and through knowledge of other potential funding sources. CEOs may also have an unusually strong sense of obligation to contribute outside their own organizations, an active interest in education and community service, and a desire to set a good example for others who work for them. For all of these reasons, we would expect to find disproportionately large numbers of CEOs providing civic leadership, and this is exactly what the data show (Appendix Table B.9.1). CEOs are often *twice* as likely as all C&B graduates to be playing leadership roles in not-for-profit entities of many kinds, and this pattern is very much the same for both former athletes and other CEOs. One difference is that the athlete-CEOs are especially likely to be found among the ranks of alumni/ae leaders, a finding to which we will return later in this chapter.

Leadership of Youth Groups

Among both the '76 and '89 cohorts, former male athletes are, as we have seen, *twice* as likely as their classmates to be leaders of youth groups. (Interestingly, this pattern is not found among the women, for whom there is no difference between athletes and others in leadership of youth groups.) The examples listed in the survey for this sort of activity were "Little League coaching, scouting, etc." It is not surprising that those who had taken sports seriously throughout their own youth and young adulthood would play an active role in fostering such activities among the next generation. Since these former college athletes might be imparting a variety of lessons to their young charges, we thought that it might be interesting to look at how highly they ranked "competition" in terms of its importance in life, as well as how highly they ranked "working collaboratively with others" (data drawn from another part of the C&B survey). Among these "soccer dads" we found that competition is much more important in their minds than it is for the other youth leaders who did not play sports in college: among the 1976 male former athletes who led these activities, 42 percent gave "competition" the highest ranking (5, on a 1–5 scale) when asked to rate its importance in life since college, whereas only 26 percent of the other graduates who led youth groups checked this box (Scorecard 9.2). Moreover, they were consistently more likely than the student-at-large leaders of youth activities to rate competition as more important in their lives than working collaboratively with others.[13]

There has been considerable discussion in recent years of the intensity of Little League sports; the following account is just one example: "Jay George . . . , whose son Jason, 12, plays on the Washington Little Caps team, had to summon a referee to remove some parents from the opposing team who were overheard telling their kids, 'If you're going to get a penalty, really hurt someone.'"[14] Anecdotal evidence suggests that it is the *failed* athletes rather than those who had a satisfying athletic career who are most likely to put undue pressure on their kids to win at all costs, and it would certainly not be fair to place responsibility for crazed Little League parents on the shoulders of former C&B athletes. At the same time, it is important to recognize that intensification of athletics is occurring throughout the system, across genders, and at every level of play, and to ask why. It seems logical to suppose that former athletes who participated in college programs that involved high levels of specialization and rigorous training regimes could be inclined to push young people to achieve excellence in a goal-oriented environment.

Determining when a high-intensity drive for excellence in athletics goes too far is well beyond the scope of our study. But it is helpful to be aware that those who played sports in college are more likely to volunteer as coaches, to feel that competitiveness is very important in their lives, and to believe that competitiveness is more important than collaboration (all findings from the C&B surveys noted earlier). Children are not born with an inalterable sense of what the game of life is about, and the roles played by these youth leaders remind us that parents and schoolteachers are not the only ones defining the rules of the game.

Alumni/ae Leaders

Preparing enthusiastic alumni/ae—those who will serve their alma mater as trustees, class officers, and committed advocates—is often cited as one of the fruits of institutional investment in athletics. As we can see from Figure 9.4, this objective has been achieved, for male and female athletes in general, and particularly those who are CEOs.

In the epilogue to this chapter, we present data showing how the College and Beyond alumni/ae, including alumni/ae leaders, viewed their college's current priorities, as well as what they thought the priorities should be. Not surprisingly, the priorities of the athlete-alumni/ae leaders differ somewhat from the priorities of others (Figure 9.5, for men in the '76 cohort). Athletes who became alumni/ae leaders believe that athletics should occupy a much higher place among the school's priorities

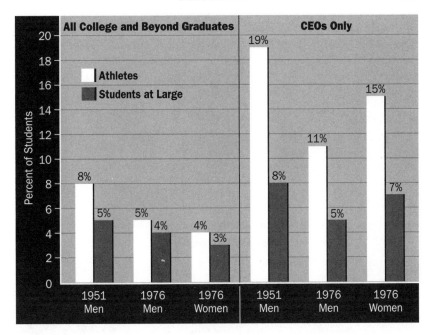

Figure 9.4. Leadership in Alumni/ae Activities, Students at Large and CEOs (by Athlete Status, Cohort, and Gender)
    Source: College and Beyond.

than they currently do, and they differ with both the other alumni/ae leaders and the alumni/ae more generally on this question. These ath-lete-alumni/ae leaders also are more strongly in favor of increasing the emphasis placed on other extracurricular activities than are the other groups. At the same time, they would prefer to see less emphasis placed on the liberal arts and on intellectual freedom than would other leaders and other alumni/ae (a group which, of course, includes other athletes).

When we examine the views of athlete alumni/ae leaders of an earlier generation (male athletes in the '51 cohort) we find the same patterns of priorities as shown above for the '76 cohort, but with less intensity. Also, the women athlete alumnae leaders from the '76 cohort state very similar views—more like those of the men in '76 than of the men in '51 (Appendix Table B.9.2). Once again, we see that at least some of the norms and values of the athletic culture are shared—across generations, institutional types, and gender lines. (It is of course possible, and probably even likely, that when women answered the survey question concerning intercollegiate athletics they had in mind the degree of emphasis that the school was plac-ing on *women's* sports, but we have no way of testing this hypothesis.)

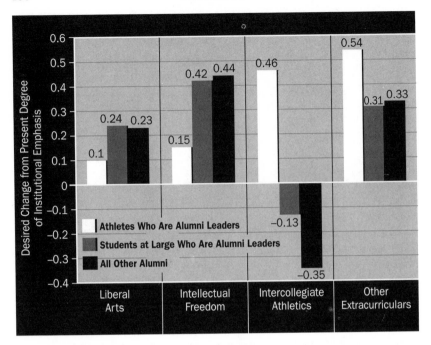

Figure 9.5. Institutional Priorities of Athlete Alumni Leaders, Student-at-Large Alumni Leaders, and All Other Alumni (as Desired Emphasis minus Perceived Current Emphasis, 1976 Cohort, Male Only)
Source: College and Beyond.

It is also revealing to compare the views of athlete alumni/ae leaders with the views of "athletes at large." Focusing on the attitudes of the men in the '76 cohort toward intercollegiate athletics, we find that the athlete alumni/ae leaders feel much more strongly about increasing the emphasis on athletics *than do the rest of the former athletes.* This pattern holds consistently across types of institutions, but it is most pronounced in the Ivy League (Figure 9.6).

Considering the divergence between the views of former athletes who play leadership roles and those of the rest of the alumni/ae body (even the athlete alumni/ae), it is worth pausing to consider the impact that this subgroup can have. The trustees of a school are a constituency that a president can ignore only at extreme peril. One president of a selective university commented on how the voices reflected in Figure 9.6 can have a powerful effect on policy:

Because trustees of Ivy and Ivy-like schools tend to be alumni of the schools—as is frequently not the case with the public institutions—they are more vis-

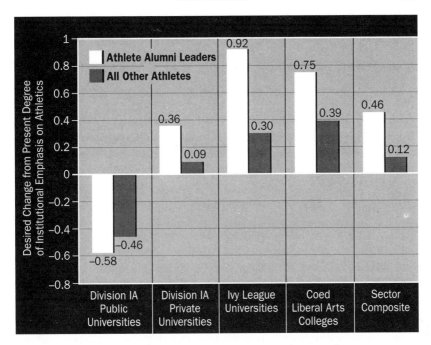

Figure 9.6. Institutional Priorities: Intercollegiate Athletics, by Alumni Leader Classification (as Desired Emphasis minus Perceived Current Emphasis, 1976 Cohort, Male Only)
Source: College and Beyond.

cerally engaged in the successes and failures of their athletic programs. The sports programs at such schools are also smaller, less publicized, more closely controlled, therefore more vulnerable to "inside" influences than Big Ten programs. A small number of trustees can carry a great deal of weight, partly because of their generous contributions to one or two athletic teams. This problem can be quite troublesome because it takes place well behind the scenes and is unlikely to be detected by the public, or even on campus.

––––––––––

What then have we learned about alumni/ae leadership in the context of college athletics? First, we have seen that those who play college sports feel that leadership is important in their lives and have felt this way since before college. Yet, surprisingly, this greater inclination toward leadership is not reflected very clearly in any measures of actual leadership that we can identify. This is one of the two main conclusions of the chapter.

Overall, C&B graduates who were athletes (and who went on to earn advanced degrees) seem slightly less likely than other C&B graduates to work in public affairs. Former athletes are no more likely than other C&B graduates to provide leadership in the marketplace via service as CEOs. There is indirect evidence, using earnings as a proxy for leadership, that former athletes contribute more "extra" leadership in the marketplace broadly defined (at below-CEO levels) than do other former students at large working in the for-profit sector. But this "extra" leadership is found primarily in the finance-consulting area. In the professions of law and medicine, and in occupational categories such as teaching and research, there are no observable differences between athletes and other former students. Similarly, athletes and students at large display quite similar patterns of civic leadership, with the exceptions of leadership of youth organizations and alumni/ae groups.

It is not clear to us what accounts for this disjunction between the subjective importance attached to leadership by athletes and the actual pattern of leadership that is displayed. Perhaps part of the explanation is as simple as the tendency for any group to believe certain "mantras." One such mantra is that athletics teaches leadership. Reiteration of such beliefs may outrun their translation into actual conduct. At least partial support for this interpretation is provided by cross-tabulations which show that former athletes are more likely than students at large to assign a high degree of importance to leadership even in occupational categories such as law and medicine in which there is no evidence that the former athletes are doing better, or providing more leadership, than others. For example, among '76 male lawyers, 43 percent of the former athletes and 36 percent of the students at large assigned a high rating to the importance of leadership; the corresponding figures are almost identical among doctors, with 44 percent of the athletes and 38 percent of the students at large assigning a high rating to leadership.

A second major conclusion is that in those civic areas where athletes do contribute an extra measure of leadership, they bring a distinctive set of values. This is clearly the case in the field of alumni/ae affairs. As trustees and active alumni/ae, former athletes want to define the priorities and hence, the mission, of their school somewhat differently from their peers, and even from their fellow athletes who are not serving in volunteer leadership capacities. We have also seen how athlete alumni/ae are likely to volunteer in disproportionate numbers for youth activities—coaching Little League or youth soccer, leading boy scout troops, and the like.

As a result of these views having been put into practice, reward structures shift. In admissions, the weight of demonstrated athletic talent in the competition for places in the class has increased over time (as we have seen in Chapters 2 and 6). Signals are sent—to potential students, secondary schools, parents, and anyone else who is watching. Over time, the world gets the message that these academically selective institutions see this kind of high-level athletic performance as a vital part of education. It may be that those who were present at an earlier stage in the cycle—who enjoyed sports in the 1950s, when settings were very different from the ones that they have helped to produce today—think that the world has not changed, perhaps because a 6–4 won-lost record in 1955 looks from the outside a great deal like a 6–4 won-lost record from 1995. The process by which the aims of the athletics enterprise are slowly but steadily altered must be seen as quite unanticipated and unintentional. Sociologist Robert K. Merton, upon reviewing these findings, emphasized that this is an excellent example of something that has happened without any malicious intent: "These are unanticipated consequences. They are not planned or 'conspiratorial' as naïve theorists promptly conclude *must* be the case when consequences turn out to be individually or collectively consistent with someone's perceived self-interest. The chains of consequences may be self-generating or self-perpetuating or self-realizing, but they are not simply manipulative or conspiratorial."

It is easy to see how the cycle could have begun with a group of people who loved sports and saw these programs as entirely beneficial and certainly not harmful. But because of the culture that binds sports with a set of non-sports values, turning up the dial "imports" something stronger. The coaches and soccer dads pass along to children the rules of "the game of life" by which they themselves have lived and which the colleges that they attended have sanctioned. The process then moves forward. Those former athletes who take on leadership roles as alumni/ae press their schools to do still more in intercollegiate athletes, and the spiral takes another turn. And so, after a few generations, that which is sought (athletically driven and focused young initiates) is present in increasing numbers with an intensified set of the values that were associated with sports in an earlier day. At the end of the book, we provide a framework for evaluating what has taken place. Here our objective is only to note the self-reinforcing nature of the rather complex engine that is running.

EPILOGUE: HOW THE ALUMNI/AE VIEW ATHLETICS

As those former students who attended the C&B schools go off and live their own individual lives, they also become the collective body known as "the alumni/ae." This body, although usually absent from campus, is rarely absent from the minds of decision makers on campus. In the next chapter, we examine their role as donors—how much they contribute financially to their schools. But first we present an overall picture of how they view the institutions that they attended.

Although this epilogue presents data on retrospective views of all kinds, we are especially interested in one myth, which is among the oldest and most difficult to examine of those that swirl around college sports: the notion that the alumni/ae pressure their schools to put ever greater emphasis on intercollegiate athletics. This question has been difficult to answer analytically because, when administrators take the pulse of alumni/ae, they usually do so at reunions or club gatherings. These are settings in which self-selected alumni/ae congregate, and it is sometimes the case that those with the loudest voices push to the front of the crowd. It is against this backdrop that the exceptionally high response rates attained in the C&B survey are of unusual value. They permit us, for the first time, to hear the views of a broad and deep cross section of *all* the alumni/ae—and to gain at least a somewhat better sense of how they really feel about sports.

Former students were asked what level of emphasis they felt their schools currently place on intercollegiate athletics, along with a range of other activities and programs (undergraduate teaching, residential life, and other institutional priorities). They were then asked to indicate what they thought the level of emphasis *should* be. Using these data, we are able to see for the first time whether or not different generations of students perceive the role of athletics in the same way, how they rank these programs alongside other institutional priorities, and whether they want their schools to place more, less, or about the same emphasis on athletics. If policy decisions are to reflect, at least to some degree, the concerns of alumni/ae, understanding their views is essential.

Systematic data from the C&B survey have distinct advantages over more impressionistic attempts to understand the views of "the alumni/ae." First, because the survey went to 60,000 alumni/ae from the entering classes of 1951, 1976, and 1989, the results can be seen as at least roughly representative of the views of the majority of the living alumni/ae of these institutions. Moreover, unlike many other alumni/ae surveys that gain only a 30 or 40 percent response rate, C&B responses were received from more than 75 percent of the alumni/ae: this unusually high response rate gives us confidence that we heard not only from those people who were particularly pleased with life or had strong feelings that were biased in one direction or another, but from a true cross section of the former students.

The pattern that emerges is consistent with what one might have expected to find in some respects and surprising in others. In Figure 9.7, we see which institutional priorities these alumni/ae would like to see re-

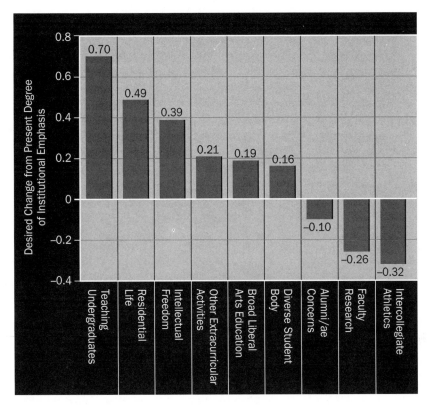

Figure 9.7. Institutional Priorities (as Desired Emphasis minus Perceived
Current Emphasis)
Source: College and Beyond.

ceive more emphasis and which they would like to see given less emphasis. (To illustrate the derivation of the numbers shown: if, on a 5-point
scale, an alum believes that an activity should receive an emphasis of 5,
but also believes that it currently receives an emphasis of 4, his score for
the item in question would be +1.0.) The scores shown in the figure combine (and average) the views of men and women from all three cohorts;
they include the views of both former college athletes and students at
large. What comes across clearly is that the alumni/ae "vote" for placing
less emphasis, not more emphasis, on intercollegiate athletics.

Faculty research is the only other activity that receives a substantial negative score. This is, at least for us, much less surprising than the even
larger negative score received by athletics. Anyone who has talked to

undergraduates, especially undergraduates at a research university, knows that most of them feel strongly that professors are there to be their teachers and that time spent on research distracts the faculty from teaching (as it sometimes does, but certainly not always).[15] Many alumni/ae clearly feel that the undergraduate teaching function is where the focus of the institution should be, and this strongly held view is reflected directly in the highly positive value of +0.7 shown for "teaching undergraduates." This is where most undergraduate alumni/ae definitely want more emphasis to be placed.

In the nonacademic sphere, it is revealing to compare the scores received by intercollegiate athletics and by "other extracurricular activities": whereas intercollegiate athletics gets a score of –0.32, "other extracurricular activities" gets a score of +0.21. Former students also want more emphasis placed on "residential life," which receives the second-highest positive score on the figure, +0.49.

The negative score received by intercollegiate athletics is surprisingly consistent across the generations included in the survey. The overall composite score of –0.32 shown in Figure 9.7 is an amalgam of –0.25 for the members of the '51 cohort, –0.31 for the '76 cohort, and –0.33 for the '89 cohort. Although these data show some evidence of greater support for athletics among the older graduates, even they are inclined, on balance, to want less emphasis placed on athletics.

More differences are apparent when we compare types of schools, which we do in Figure 9.8 for the members of the '76 cohort. We see a stronger desire for de-emphasis of athletics among the graduates of the Division IA public universities (–0.98) and Division IA private universities (–0.46) than among graduates of the Ivies (–0.19) and the coed liberal arts colleges (–0.15). The women's colleges are the one set of schools at which the general opinion favors greater emphasis on intercollegiate athletics.[16]

Further insight into these differences is obtained when we look separately at the priorities identified by those alumni/ae who are former intercollegiate athletes and by their classmates. Not surprisingly, we find (Figure 9.9) that the former athletes at every type of school are more inclined than students at large to favor placing more emphasis on athletic programs.

Of course, the simple arithmetic of this exercise guarantees that the students at large will be less inclined to believe that more emphasis should be given to athletics than are all students (a group that includes the former athletes). A comparison of Figures 9.8 and 9.9 shows that this difference is particularly pronounced at the Ivy League schools and at the Division III coed liberal arts colleges. In fact, the negative score for intercollegiate athletics is nearly twice as high among the students at

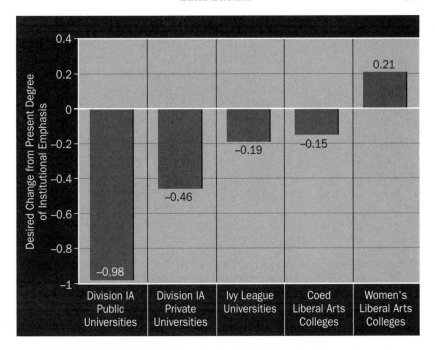

Figure 9.8. Intercollegiate Athletics as an Institutional Priority (as Desired Emphasis minus Perceived Current Emphasis, by Division, 1976 Cohort, Male and Female Combined)

Source: College and Beyond.

large at these schools as it is among all students (–0.19 for all former students versus –0.32 among students at large in the Ivy League, and –0.15 for all students versus –0.27 among students at large in the coed liberal arts colleges). In contrast, the two measures are essentially the same at the Division IA public universities. The main part of the explanation has to do simply with relative numbers: at the Division IA public universities, the athletes are few in number relative to the size of the overall undergraduate population, whereas at the Ivies and the coed liberal arts colleges the former intercollegiate athletes may represent as much as a quarter or even a third of all graduates. This serves as a reminder of what we have noted elsewhere in the book: the impact of sports programs at places like these may not be as visible on national television, but it can, nevertheless, end up being more consequential.

All of these expressions of opinion are of course directed at the athletic programs of these schools as they existed when the survey was administered (1995 and 1996 for the '51 and '76 cohorts and 1997 for the '89

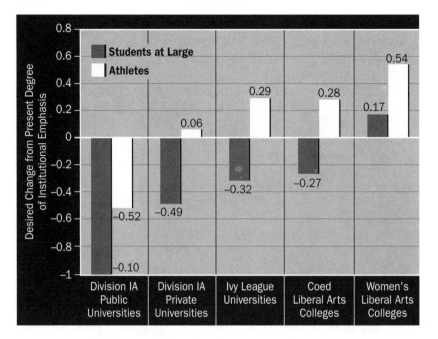

Figure 9.9. Intercollegiate Athletics as an Institutional Priority (as Desired Emphasis minus Perceived Current Emphasis, by Athlete Status, 1976 Cohort, Male and Female Combined)
Source: College and Beyond.

cohort), and there is no way of knowing whether these graduates would have expressed the same views about the emphasis given to athletics during the years when they were in college. In addition, we know that a number of respondents—although a minority—call for more emphasis, and it may be that this minority is more vocal than the majority who either are content with the status quo or would prefer less emphasis.

We emphatically do not believe in basing policy decisions on surveys of opinion. Still, in thinking about the state of intercollegiate athletics today, and where these programs may be heading, it is worth knowing that there is no groundswell of opinion from the alumni/ae of these schools in favor of assigning a high priority to intercollegiate athletics. These data suggest that most graduates of these schools would support well-thought-out modifications of athletic programs that retained—or enhanced—the values of the athletic experience.

CHAPTER 10

Giving Back

> When I go out to raise money for Stanford and
> talk to former athletes, I tend to hear things like,
> "I gave my knee to Stanford—that's all you're
> getting from me."
>
> —Stanford University athletic
> director Ted Leland

As we saw in the preceding chapter, there is a factual basis for the myth that former college athletes are likely to be active alumni/ae, working on committees, coordinating class activities, and serving as trustees. We also learned that, as one might have expected, alumni/ae leaders who were college athletes have distinctive views as to how much emphasis their schools should place on the curricular mission of the school as well as on athletics and other extracurricular activities. Recognizing that the reality of the budget is central to achieving whatever agenda an institution chooses to pursue, we turn now to an examination of the direct dollar contributions that athletes and other alumni/ae make to their schools. We know of no one who would question the growing importance of private giving to the health and future prospects of colleges and universities, public and private. While the educational mission of these schools is central, they also must be financially strong in order to achieve any of their educational goals.

Those schools that have built and sustained good relationships with their graduates have benefited greatly; annual giving, targeted gifts, and capital campaigns are of critical importance in providing the resources that colleges and universities need to fulfill their missions. Unlike institutions of higher education throughout the rest of the world that are for the most part government supported, the leading U.S. colleges and universities have always been highly dependent upon the generosity of their alumni/ae. At the same time, colleges and universities are aware that their aggressive pursuit of private donations has to be balanced by an awareness of the potential dangers of leaning too far in any one direction for the sake of a check.

It is with this balance in mind that we turn to two of the most powerful myths that circulate around college sports. The first of these is that former athletes, having become financial winners in the game of life and having had the privilege of representing their school in competition, are disproportionately generous toward their alma mater; the second is that winning sports programs encourage alumni/ae in general to give more money. Understanding how sports programs affect alumni/ae giving is an important part of understanding how these programs contribute to, or detract from, the fulfillment of the school's mission.

Using data provided by 18 of the colleges and universities that participated in the College and Beyond study, we are able to answer at least some of the most obvious questions linking intercollegiate athletics to giving.[1] In the first part of the chapter we examine how the willingness to give depends on whether an individual was or was not an award-winning athlete, on the level of play (Division IA, the Ivies, and Division III), and on the type of sport played (High Profile sports such as football and basketball versus other sports). We then examine the amounts that people gave and test the argument that giving to athletics reduces the amount given for other purposes. The characteristics and attitudes of those who are particularly generous (whom we refer to as the "big givers") are considered next; key questions are how many of the most generous donors are athletes and whether the big givers favor putting more or less emphasis on athletics. At the end of the chapter we examine the broader effects of a school's won-lost record on the giving behavior of alumni/ae.

GENERAL GIVING (PARTICIPATION) RATES

Male Athletes Compared with Other Male Alumni

A major theme of this discussion is that there are pronounced differences in the relationship between participation in athletics and giving behavior among those who went to college in different eras—differences in both giving rates (which is what we focus on in this section) and amounts given.[2] Differences in these relationships have emerged between institutions competing at different levels of play (especially between the Division IA private universities and the Division III coed liberal arts colleges) and between athletes who played the High Profile sports and athletes who participated in other sports.

The early 1950s provide a useful benchmark. As we recall from Chapters 2 and 3, the men who played sports in those days were very similar to their peers: their SATs were, on average, only 36 points lower (as opposed to the 118-point gap in 1989); their grades were much like those of their classmates; and they were *less* likely than their classmates to finish in the bottom third of their class. Many of them played a year of fresh-

men sports before going on to other activities, or to enjoy the other aspects of college life. Former male athletes of this generation, at both the
Ivy League schools and the Division III coed liberal arts colleges, were
somewhat *more* likely than all other male alumni to make unrestricted
gifts; at the Division IA private universities such as Duke and Northwestern, the percentages of the 1951 entering cohorts making gifts for general purposes were essentially the same for athletes and others (Scorecard 10.1, top panel).[3]

Athletes who attended these schools in the late 1970s were about as
likely as former students at large to make gifts for general purposes, and
athletes who attended the coed liberal arts colleges were even more
likely than their classmates to be givers. The marked exception to this
generalization is the High Profile athletes in the big-time programs—that
is, the male football, basketball, and hockey players at the Division IA
private universities, where the giving rate for these former athletes was
just 29 percent, as compared with 49 percent for former students at large
(Scorecard 10.1, middle panel). This reluctance to support general educational programs is even more pronounced among those younger
High Profile athletes from the Division IA private universities who entered college in the fall of 1989; only 18 percent of this group of men
made gifts for general purposes, as compared with 47 percent of former
students at large. (By focusing on comparisons between athletes and students at large *within the same cohorts,* we reduce considerably the problems inherent in making comparisons across cohorts that are at different stages of their life cycles.)

Stanford University athletic director Ted Leland reports that he is not
surprised that the data fail to show numerous financial commitments
from former High Profile athletes (see epigraph at the beginning of the
chapter).[4] A similar intergenerational shift in the relationship between
having played sports and giving behavior is found in the coed liberal arts
colleges, although in much more muted form. The '89 High Profile athletes who attended the coed liberal arts colleges, although still frequent
supporters of their schools, are now (unlike their predecessors in the '51
and '76 cohorts) *less* likely to give for general purposes than the athletes
who played sports such as tennis and soccer or the students-at-large. Only
in the Ivy League schools have High Profile athletes continued to give for
general purposes at roughly the same rate as their classmates (Scorecard
10.1, bottom panel).

We believe these data tell two simple but consequential stories. First,
the fact that former athletes have generally been so supportive of the
broad educational purposes of the schools they attended is reassuring. It
is also, in our view, indicative of the way in which organized athletics (like
other activities we discuss later in this chapter) can bond students to their

schools. As we saw in Chapter 4, male athletes frequently follow career paths that "convert" their B.A. degrees into high-paying careers, and we see now that some of this money is indeed returning to the schools.

The second, and much less encouraging, story describes the changing nature of some of these relationships, and especially the apparent weakening of the ties that bind athletes (at least those in the High Profile sports) to their schools. The overall giving rate among male High Profile athletes in the '51 cohort was 8 percentage points *higher* than the rate for students at large; in the '89 cohort, their giving rate was 12 points *lower* (Figure 10.1). The football and basketball players of an earlier day, including those who played for Division IA schools in the early 1950s, apparently continue to identify closely with their schools in much the same way that their classmates do. They were less isolated from the mainstream of college life than were the athletes of subsequent generations, who—at the scholarship-granting Division IA schools, in particular, thanks to such practices as housing athletes in separate dorms—may well have been more inclined to consider themselves a "group apart."[5]

It is important to remember that the football and basketball stars of the 1950s were more likely to be regarded as "big men on campus" and

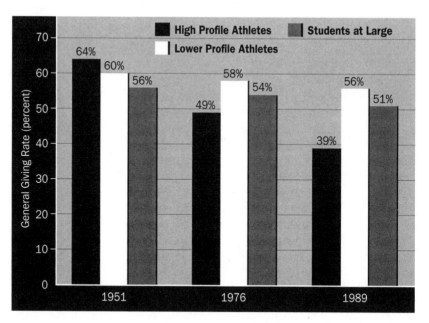

Figure 10.1. General Giving Rates (by Athlete Status and Cohort, Male Only)
Source: College and Beyond (see Scorecard 10.1).

as leaders *of their classes* (not just of their teams) than were their counterparts in more recent years. The increasing professionalization of college athletics means, we suspect, that in those situations in which such professionalization is most advanced, the focus of college life for these athletes is more on the team—and even on the individual athlete—than on the college.[6] We have been told, for example, that recruits in basketball and football are very conscious of who may be ahead of them at their position, and coaches report that a student's potential playing time often plays a major role in his or her choice of a school or a subsequent decision to transfer.

Feeling "used":

Former athletes are probably less likely to "give back" to the university after graduation because increasingly they feel that they were "used" when they were engaged in intercollegiate competition. The bald expression of this sentiment is, "The university makes lots of money on our back but won't pay us a dime." Hence the recurrent demand that athletes receive direct monetary compensation in addition to the prescribed scholarship package.

> —Arnold Weber, president emeritus of Northwestern University
> and also a former president of the University of Colorado

Even within the Division III coed liberal arts colleges, the growth in intensity within the High Profile sports, especially football, may have led to increased separation of athletes from the rest of the school, which in turn may have diminished, to some degree, the bonding effect that athletics in general promotes. On these smaller campuses—where a freshman class is typically made up of 300 to 500 students—the widening gulf between the academic preparations, attitudes, and interests of a subgroup of athletes and those of the student body at large may be even *more* likely to polarize a campus. A recurring theme in our research has been that the Division III schools tend to follow practices and patterns established in the other levels, albeit with a lag.

The bottom line is clear: the curve breaks at the extreme end of the college sports spectrum at these selective institutions where athletic scholarships combined with professional aspirations lead to disidentification by at least some athletes. The tale of the scholarship athlete who gave his knee and plans to give little else warns us of one possible outcome of the trend toward increasing athletic intensity.

Giving Patterns of Women Athletes

Overall, giving rates were essentially the same for men and women graduates of the schools for which we have data (Scorecard 10.2). We also see evidence of the positive effects of participation in athletics on giving among the women in the coeducational colleges and, even more powerfully, in the women's colleges—where the giving rates of the women who were athletes are *far* higher than those among their classmates. We should recall that, as with the men from the '51 cohort, these findings reflect the outcomes in settings where women who played sports were very similar to their peers in school, and, if anything, were higher achievers afterward.

Extracurricular Participants (Men Only)

To provide another point of reference, we examined the giving patterns of former students who participated in highly time-intensive extracurricular activities, such as editing student newspapers, playing in orchestras, and leading student government organizations.[7] We saw in earlier chapters that this group provides a useful control group for looking at whether time devoted to another activity besides academic work could account for the depressed academic performance of college athletes. The pattern of giving by these alumni/ae with strong commitments to extracurricular activities is very consistent across cohorts and types of schools: they are more likely to be donors than are other graduates (Scorecard 10.3). Clearly extracurricular activities serve a similar function in building loyalty and affection for the school that sports programs do.[8]

There is, however, a major difference between the giving rates for the high-intensity extracurricular participants and for the athletes: in sharp contrast to the findings for athletes, the positive association between extracurricular participation and giving rates does *not* decline as we move from the '51 cohort to the '76 and '89 cohorts; the positive association is as pronounced in the most recent cohorts as in the earlier cohorts (Figure 10.2). Two possible explanations are that students who are strongly interested in extracurriculars today are similar in key respects to their predecessors of 40 years ago, and that the role of extracurricular activities on campus may have changed relatively little over these decades. In both of these respects, athletics has changed much more: the athletes are more intensely recruited and less representative of their classes than they used to be, and intercollegiate athletic competition has become much more all-consuming.

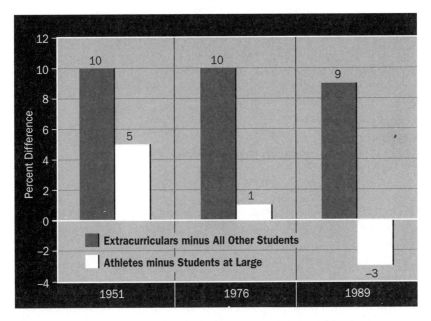

Figure 10.2. Increased Likelihood of Giving for Participants in Athletics and
Other Extracurricular Activities (by Cohort, Male Only)
   Source: College and Beyond.

Academic High-Achievers

We also grouped the graduates of these schools by their level of academic
achievement. Here again, giving rates form a clear pattern (Scorecard
10.4). We find, with almost no exceptions by cohort or type of school, that
the graduates who finished in the top third of their class were more likely
to be donors than the graduates in the middle third, who in turn were
more likely to be donors than the graduates in the bottom third.[9] Graduates who did well academically evidently formed strong identifications
with their colleges and universities, perhaps through close ties with faculty members and their departments. This kind of bonding is most likely
to occur in the more intimate settings of the small coed liberal arts colleges, and, in fact, it is at those schools that the positive relationship between class rank and giving is strongest.[10]

   Although it is true that, as some people regularly point out, there is always going to be a bottom third of the class, this group of students may
not be as contented, or as supportive of the college in the future, as is
sometimes assumed. As more of the men and women who play sports end

up in the bottom third of their classes over time, this relationship could affect the inclination of athletes to support their schools. Athletes who played sports in the 1950s finished higher in their classes than their more recent counterparts, and this "double bonding" (as a result of both athletic associations and positive experiences as students) may help to explain why they are today *more* likely than their classmates to be donors.

ATHLETIC GIVING RATES

Among Male Graduates

Overall, about 5 percent of all male graduates of these colleges made a gift directed specifically to an athletics program. This percentage is roughly constant across all three cohorts (Scorecard 10.5). The former athletes, naturally, were more likely to give to athletics than were other graduates. Even among the athletes, however, the percentage making gifts to athletic programs is far lower than the percentage making gifts for general educational purposes (as a rule, under 20 percent gave to athletics, whereas roughly 50 percent or more gave to general purposes).

Perhaps the most striking statistics are those for the High Profile athletes in the '89 cohort who went to the Division IA private universities. Only 10 percent of these recent graduates made an athletic gift during the five-year period we are studying, as compared with 28 percent of their predecessors in the '51 cohort. These intergenerational differences are of course due in part to very different capacities to give (life cycle effects). What is noteworthy, however, is that this drop-off in athletic giving rates mirrors the drop-off in general giving rates for this same group of former High Profile athletes (whereas there is no corresponding drop-off in general giving rates among students at large). It cannot be said that the recent participants in these big-time sports programs have simply shifted allegiance from the school to their own sports program; rather, we see a general decline in allegiance.

The Ivies and the coed liberal arts colleges present contrasting patterns. In the Ivies, gift giving for athletic purposes is much more pronounced among the '51 and '76 cohorts than among the '89 cohort (but here, in sharp contrast to the Division IA private universities, the drop-off in athletic giving rates is far greater than the modest decline in general giving rates). Among the coed liberal arts colleges, we see a distinct movement toward *increased* willingness to make athletic gifts among the more recent graduates. Very, very few members of the '51 cohort at coed liberal arts colleges made athletic gifts (3 percent overall and only 5 percent of the former athletes), whereas 11 percent of the former athletes in the '89 cohort made an athletic gift. In many instances, coed liberal arts colleges did not solicit gifts in support of athletic programs until relatively recently. We interpret these data as a further indication that the athletic programs at the coed liberal arts colleges are gradually mimicking the programs in the higher-intensity divisions.

Among Women Graduates

Women graduates in general are much less likely to make targeted gifts to athletics than are their male counterparts, and only 2 to 3 percent of women graduates in the '76 and '89 cohorts made such gifts (Scorecard 10.6). As in the case of the men, women graduates who played sports are of course more inclined to give for athletics than are those who had other interests. More interesting is the fact that, among women in the '89 cohort in the Ivy League schools, the percentage of former women athletes who made gifts for athletics was almost identical with the percentages among the Lower Profile male athletes at the Ivy League schools and the coed liberal arts colleges. As they have taken on more of the characteristics that differentiate male athletes from their classmates (lower test scores, lower grades, more politically conservative attitudes), the women who play sports have also mirrored their male counterparts' attachment to the programs that helped bring them to their campuses in the first place.

SIZES OF GIFTS AND COMPETITION FOR GIFTS

Average Sizes of Gifts

The relatively small number of graduates of the coed liberal arts colleges, men and women, who gave to athletics also made very modest gifts (averaging around $20 to $25 per year for the men and about $15 per year for the women).[11] In the Ivies, too, gifts to athletics were modest, ranging from a high of $185 per year among the male contributors in the '51 cohort to $26 per year among the female contributors in the '89 cohort. The typical gift to athletics made by both men and women in the Division IA private universities was appreciably larger. The male donors in the '51 cohort who gave to athletics made gifts that averaged over $800 per year, and the donors among the High Profile athletes gave an average of more than $1,700 per year. In the '76 cohort, too, the athletic donors at the Division IA private universities are somewhat more generous than those at the other groups of schools, a pattern that does not extend, however, into the '89 cohort (Scorecard 10.7).

In general, donors who gave for general purposes made appreciably larger gifts than donors who gave specifically to athletics. The male contributors in the '51 cohort are, not surprisingly, the most generous group, and their average annual gift for general purposes was nearly $750 (with gifts by those who attended the coed liberal arts colleges averaging almost $1,000 per year). In the '76 cohort as well, the average gift to general purposes was larger than the average gift to athletics, and here it is possible to make a direct comparison between male and female contributors. The men tend to make larger gifts, but the male-female difference is far smaller than much of the mythology of fundraising would lead us to expect—the average gift by a woman graduate was roughly 60 to 70 percent of the average gift by a male counterpart. The average gift for general purposes made by an athlete tended to be quite similar in size to the average gift made by other graduates (Scorecards 10.8 and 10.9).

Since athletics is but one relatively modest part of the entire educational enterprise, it is hardly surprising that the average gift to athletics is smaller than the average gift for all other purposes. The modest size of the average gift for athletics may also reflect a sense that many donors think a show of support is what is appropriate. Relevant too are the uses to which athletic gifts are put. Within the Ivies and the coed liberal arts colleges, "friends" groups have traditionally raised money for athletics primarily to pay for such "extras" as spring trips for the baseball team, team banquets, and "fly-in" visits by recruits (a pattern which, however, may be changing, as we note in the next chapter). To date, individuals have not been expected to make huge gifts for such purposes. At the Division IA level, gifts from "friends" may serve similar purposes, but in these settings large gifts may also entitle the donor to special seating and other perquisites, which in turn may help explain why the average athletic gift is larger at these institutions. According to one survey of 56 bigtime athletic programs, 95 percent (or 53 schools) used donations to athletics to determine "seat location or eligibility to purchase tickets for football games."[12]

Competition for Gifts

We are able to provide new evidence pertinent to one hotly debated proposition, even though we are not in a position to render a definitive judgment. The question at issue is whether gifts to athletics are likely to cannibalize gifts that otherwise would go to the library, scholarships, or the general fund. There is certainly no indication in the data we have collected that private giving to athletics today is so substantial (in either the number of donors or the size of the average gift) that it is likely to detract

in any substantial way from fundraising for broader educational purposes. This is not to deny that there are situations in which a donor has
decided how much in total he or she can give to the institution and then
prorated the total between athletics and general purposes. We have been
told of instances in which a strong appeal from a newly successful coach
led a donor to cut back on what the donor had intended to do for the
university at large. We suspect, however, that such situations are rare and
their effects minimal.

There is some empirical evidence in support of this conclusion. A careful analysis of the giving patterns and other characteristics of male donors
in both the '51 and '76 entering cohorts fails to show any general tendency for those who gave to athletics to give less in support of the general purposes of their schools. On the contrary, in both the Ivies and the
coed liberal arts colleges, the relationship between giving to athletics and
the amount given for general purposes is positive, not negative, on an
"other things equal" basis. (There is also a positive relationship, albeit a
somewhat weaker one, among the men in the '51 cohort in the Division
IA private universities, although not among those in the '76 cohort.) The
strongest association is in the '51 cohort in the Ivy League schools, where
donors who gave to athletics also gave, on average, $1,487 more to gen-
eral purposes than did their fellow donors who gave nothing to athletics
but were comparable to them in household income and other respects.[13]

We do not interpret this result, which easily passes all tests of statistical
significance, as implying that people gave more to general purposes *because* they gave to athletics: correlation is not causation. In this group of
1950s graduates, we think this strong positive association means that
graduates who are atypically generous in helping to meet the general
needs of the institution are also atypically generous to specific causes (in
this case, athletics). Giving to athletics may well have served as a proxy for
general enthusiasm or generous intentions, and the same positive association between the amount of support provided for general purposes
and gifts to athletics might have been obtained had we included a measure of giving to any other specific purpose, such as the library.

It would be comforting if there were reasons to be confident that the
apparent lack of serious competition for funding between athletic programs and the other purposes of the institution would continue into the
future. Unfortunately, we do not think such confidence would be warranted. At colleges and universities of all kinds, coaches and heads of
friends groups feel increasing pressure to raise more and more money
for their particular sports, and they are likely to become ever more determined fundraisers. Moreover, the intergenerational shifts in patterns
of giving shown in this chapter suggest that younger graduates who are
strongly interested in athletics may prove less inclined than their prede-

cessors in the 1950s to be equally enthusiastic supporters of the broader purposes of the college.[14]

THE BIG GIVERS

Their Overall Importance

Total giving to the colleges and universities in this study is highly concentrated among a small percentage of the alumni/ae. In the case of the male members of the '51 cohort, three-quarters of all dollars contributed for general purposes came from 5 percent of the graduates (the group that we refer to as the big givers). The bottom 80 percent of the graduates, ranked according to amounts given, contributed only 6.6 percent of the total amount of gifts received. In the '76 cohort, nearly two-thirds of all dollars came from the top 5 percent of donors. Although we would expect giving to be especially highly concentrated in the older classes, where there is the greatest capacity to make large gifts, even in the '89 cohort half of all dollars came from the most generous 5 percent of the cohort (Figure 10.3).[15]

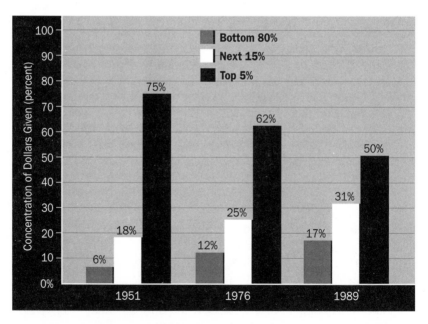

Figure 10.3. Concentration of Total Gifts Given by the Top 5 Percent, Next 15 Percent, and Bottom 80 Percent of Male Graduates
  Source: College and Beyond.

Profiles of the Big Givers

The top 5 percent of all male donors in the '51 cohort contains disproportionately large numbers of athletes, legacies, academic high achievers, and individuals with very high family incomes (Figure 10.4). The big
givers among the male members of the '76 and '89 cohorts had similar
characteristics, but with one notable exception: former athletes no
longer appear in disproportionate numbers. In these more recent cohorts, the athletes are distributed among the big givers, the other givers,
and the non-givers in roughly equal numbers.[16]

Even more interesting is the relationship between membership in the
big givers group and the donor's attitudes toward intercollegiate athletics. The patterns are clear-cut:

• Among the men, big givers as a group are somewhat more inclined
  to want to reduce emphasis on athletics than to increase it. This is

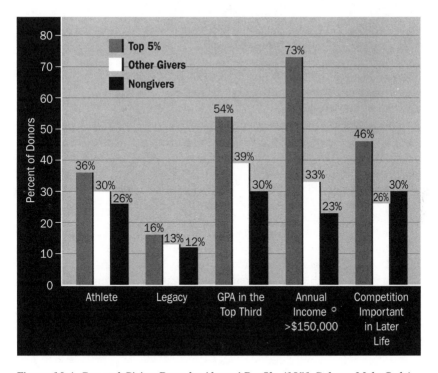

Figure 10.4. General Giving Rates by Alumni Profile (1951 Cohort, Male Only)
  Source: College and Beyond.

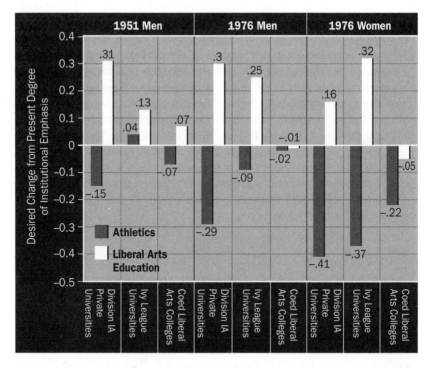

Figure 10.5. Views of Athletics and of Broad Liberal Arts Education among the
Top 5 Percent of Donors (by Cohort, Division, and Gender)
  Source: College and Beyond.

particularly true of the men in the Division IA private universities
and of the 1976 graduates of the Ivy League schools (Figure 10.5).
• Among the women, big givers are even more likely to favor placing
  less emphasis on athletics than to favor more emphasis.
• Figure 10.5 also shows (for comparative purposes) the desired emphasis on the liberal arts, and there is a clear inverse relation between
  these bars and those showing attitudes toward athletics. That is, in
  those sets of schools in which big givers favor putting less emphasis
  on athletics, the big givers also favor putting more emphasis on the
  liberal arts. (The small size of the bars for the coed liberal arts colleges has to be interpreted in light of how high the perceived
  emphasis on the liberal arts already is at these schools; there is very
  little room for increasing it.)
• When we examine the attitudes of big givers in a broader context
  (see Figure 10.6, which shows data for men in the '76 cohorts at all

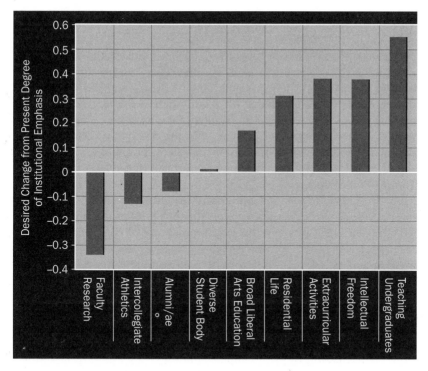

Figure 10.6. Institutional Priorities of the Top 5 Percent of Donors (1976 Cohort, Male Only)
Source: College and Beyond.

types of schools), we see that only faculty research is viewed more negatively than intercollegiate athletics. The contrast between the weakly negative attitudes toward athletics and the strongly positive attitudes toward other extracurricular activities is particularly interesting.

These data do not suggest that institutional decisions about the role to accord intercollegiate athletics should be considered hostage to the attitudes of the most substantial donors, although any given institution may well feel pressure from a handful of generous and vocal graduates. But before coming to any strong conclusion on this key proposition, we must examine the last channel by which intercollegiate athletic programs, if successful competitively, may affect the generosity of alumni/ae: do winning teams instill a pride in the school that translates into more and larger gifts across the board?

WINNING AND GIVING[17]

The first and simplest aspect of this question about the impact of competitive success on giving is team specific. Does playing on a winning team (or, conversely, being a member of a losing team) affect giving, and especially giving to athletics? It would not be surprising if athletes on winning teams proved to be more likely than athletes on losing teams to give money in support of athletics, but the data fail to show any such pattern. In fact, athletes on losing teams were, if anything, more likely to make gifts in support of athletics than those who played on winning teams.

The broader and far more important question is whether the overall competitive record of a school affects the giving of its alumni/ae. When the question is put this way, the relevant measure of competitive success is the won-lost record of the school *in the years when we observe giving behavior,* not in the years when particular graduates attended college. Supplemental records added to the database have made it possible to examine year-by-year winning and giving records and track what happened to giving behavior when won-lost records improved or worsened. These data make it possible to estimate the effect on giving of having a winning football team and to provide separate estimates for type of school (the Division IA private universities, the Ivies, and the Division III coed liberal arts colleges), for men and women, and for former athletes versus students at large.[18] The study is based on 10 years of data detailing the year-by-year relationship between winning and giving for the members of the '76 entering cohort at 15 of the C&B schools.[19]

Broad Patterns

First, contrary to much of the mythology about winning and giving, the study finds no relationship of any kind between won-lost records in football and general giving rates at either the Division IA private universities that operate big-time programs or the Ivies. The association between winning football teams and general giving (participation) rates for the Division III coed liberal arts colleges, on the other hand, is positive and statistically significant. In general, at these colleges an increase in the winning percentage of 0.5 (moving from a 50–50 record to an unbeaten season) is associated with an increase of about 2.5 percentage points in the share of the class making a gift during any given year. Fielding winning football teams at any level—the Division IA schools, the Ivies, or the colleges—has no discernible effect on overall rates of gifts targeted specifically to athletics.[20] Good feelings no doubt abound, but they are not translated into additional donations in any consistent manner.

A parallel analysis that focuses not on participation rates but on the amounts given reveals only one significant, and somewhat puzzling, result. Improvements in Division IA football performance on a par with moving from a 50-50 record to an unbeaten season are associated with an average *decline* of about $135 per person in general giving per year, with no offsetting increase in athletic contributions.

Differences in Giving Behavior between Former Athletes and Students at Large

To understand the behavioral patterns underlying these overall findings, it is necessary to look separately at the giving behavior of those donors who were (and were not) intercollegiate athletes as undergraduates. With regard to general giving rates,

- *There is no statistically significant association between football won-lost records and the general giving rates for any group of donors who did not play college sports ("students at large" in our terminology).* This conclusion holds for men and women alike, and it holds regardless of the NCAA division in which their school competed. The important point is that the positive relationship between winning and giving rates found in the aggregate data for Division III coed liberal arts colleges does not appear among the students at large who attended these schools.
- As one might have expected, the giving behavior of former athletes turns out to be more sensitive to the athletic fortunes of their schools—*but primarily at the Division III schools.* This conclusion does not hold at the Division IA level of competition. However, positive and statistically significant relationships between won-lost records and general giving rates are found among athletes who competed in the Division III schools and in the Ivy League.

This unmistakable pattern may well surprise many readers, as it surprised us. On reflection, we suspect that the former athletes at the Division III coed liberal arts colleges identify more strongly with their school than do former athletes from other types of institutions. Data reported earlier in the chapter also lead us to suspect that these alums are more inclined to respond to athletic success by making donations than are the former athletes who participated in the big-time programs at the Division IA schools and the men who played sports in the Ivy League. Two key considerations are central to understanding this phenomenon among the athlete alumni/ae of the coed liberal arts colleges:

- First, intercollegiate athletes make up higher proportions of the student bodies of the Division III coed liberal arts colleges than of the student bodies at either the Ivies or the Division IA schools. For example, in the '89 cohort, an average of 32 percent of the male graduates of the coed liberal arts colleges played on an intercollegiate team, as compared with averages of 27 percent in the Ivies and 9 percent in the Division IA universities; the percentages for the women exhibit this same pattern. Recalling the overall relationship between winning and giving at the Division III coed liberal arts colleges that was noted earlier, we now see that *it is the former athletes who drive these results*. Their giving behavior has a strong impact because of the combination of their greater sensitivity to won-lost records and their larger presence in the student bodies of these colleges.

- Second, it is important to recall that the '76 women who played sports were not markedly different from their classmates at the time of admission and were subsequently as successful academically as their classmates in college. And while the '76 male athletes at the Division III coed liberal arts colleges were displaying some of the differences from their peers that were found elsewhere, only 31 percent reported that being recruited was an important or a very important reason for their choosing that college (as opposed to 46 percent of the Ivy athletes in 1976 and 59 percent of the Division III college athletes in 1989).

In other words, those who played intercollegiate sports during the late 1970s at the coed liberal arts colleges are numerous enough to have an impact on the overall giving rates of their colleges, and they, alone among the former athletes in this cohort, are affected in their giving behavior by whether or not their team wins the big game. But whether these trends among the Division III athletes of yesteryear will continue depends on how athletic programs evolve at this level of competition. Whereas the High Profile athletes at the Division III coed liberal arts colleges in the '76 cohort were more likely to be donors than students at large (69 percent versus 63 percent), High Profile athletes at these colleges in the '89 cohort were *less* likely to be donors (54 percent versus 60 percent).[21]

The disaggregated relationships between won-lost records and the levels (or amounts) of giving also contain some surprises. One particularly noteworthy finding is that improving won-lost records *depress* general giving levels among students at large at Division IA schools; the coefficient is significant and far from trivial in size. We can only speculate as to the meaning of this pattern. Some graduates may assume (erroneously, in almost all instances, as we will demonstrate in the next chapter) that winning football teams generate so much revenue that they have no need to make as large a gift as they would have otherwise. We know from the C&B surveys that students in general at these schools believe that intercollegiate athletics is, if anything, overemphasized (see the epilogue to Chapter 9), and it is possible that a better won-lost record by the football team feeds this impression, leading to resentment and reduced giving. A related possibility is that some students at large may have taken genuine pride in the fact that their school was *not* an athletic power and may interpret greater success on the field as an indication that values have changed and that their school is not the same place that they attended. Whatever the underlying explanation, it is the behavior of these students at large that is driving the negative coefficient for the amount of giving at the Division IA schools.

Winning also has a negative impact on the amount of general giving among the male *athletes* who attended Division IA schools. This result is related, we suspect, to the fact that whereas winning has no impact on the average amount given to athletics by students at large, it has a clearly positive effect on the size of athletic gifts made by former athletes from Division IA schools (men and women alike) and by former male athletes at Ivy League schools. The combination of these positive effects of winning on the size of athletic gifts and the negative effects on the size of general gifts is consistent with the view that some shifting of funds is occurring. That is, the reduced level of *general* giving by former Division IA athletes may be explained, at least in part, by their increased support of athletics. This finding is specific to these athletes at these schools and runs counter to the more general finding reported earlier—that giving to athletics does not, as a rule, come at the expense of general giving.

Implications of the Winning-Giving Analysis

One conclusion stands out: in assessing the arguments for and against the large investments in intercollegiate athletics generally thought to be necessary to produce winning teams in the most competitive settings, there is no evidence to suggest that "paybacks" will come in the form of enhanced generosity by alumni/ae. Indeed, one of the more striking findings derived from this year-by-year analysis is that at the most intensive level of play (NCAA Division IA), winning appears to have had, if anything, a modest *negative* effect on the overall amount of alumni/ae giving. The evidence suggests that the majority of the former students at these schools who were not themselves intercollegiate athletes may give less, not more, when the football team does better. And the graduates who were intercollegiate athletes as undergraduates show some tendency to substitute larger athletic gifts for general gifts when the won-lost record improves.

This analysis does not, of course, take account of gifts from local boosters and corporate sponsors. We would expect winning in big-time programs to lead to greater revenue from these sources. In addition, success in big-time athletics may well have a positive reputational or "advertising" effect among the general public that encourages more potential students to apply for admission and to enroll. Some evidence of the existence of such a relationship has been found, but it is less clear that the effect is very large or that it leads to any marked improvement in the quality of future entering classes.[22] And then there is the unavoidable question of whether whatever gains are achieved can be used to justify the very large expenditures needed to bring about big-time success.

An even more interesting story line, in at least some respects, is the very different picture that emerges from the winning and giving patterns at the Division III coed liberal arts colleges. From the perspective of the frequency of alumni/ae donations, winning actually turns out to be *more* important at these schools than at the institutions with much higher profile athletic programs. This initially surprising result is really not so surprising when one thinks of both the institutional bonding effect of athletics (which is likely to be especially strong in these schools, leading many students who play sports to feel a closer identity to their schools than they would otherwise) and the relatively large number of undergraduates who play intercollegiate sports at the leading coed liberal arts colleges.

We interpret the positive relationship between winning and giving in the coed liberal arts colleges, for the members of the '76 cohort, as evidence that successful athletic programs may well have encouraged more of the former athletes who attended these schools to contribute. At the same time, it would be a mistake to exaggerate the financial consequences of this finding. Taking into account both participation rates and the sizes of average gifts, even a quite dramatic decline in the fortunes of the football team at a Division III coed liberal arts college should not be expected to lead to an appreciable reduction in the amount of giving by former athletes. Of course, it is one thing to recognize that winning matters and quite another to define the contours of the playing field. If the Division III colleges were to decide, *collectively,* to put less emphasis on recruiting athletes, there is no reason to believe that the winning percentages for any school would necessarily change. A principal implication, then, of this finding that winning matters for the Division III schools is that "unilateral disarmament" is a risky strategy.

There could also be another implication of this set of findings for the Division III coed liberal arts colleges. The recruited athlete of today is the alumnus or alumna of tomorrow. If this large group of potential donors regards the won-lost record of tomorrow's team as very important, then the ability to accept the realities of up and down seasons, to resist the temptation to confer more advantages on athletes (either in admissions or in the building of facilities), and to continue to keep the big picture of the institutional mission in mind will become an ever more difficult challenge for liberal arts college presidents and trustees. The pressures to continue to win may be great.

Since Chapter 2, we have seen that those who play college sports have had different expectations from the time that they entered college, different priorities in the classroom, and different views as alumni/ae of what the priorities of the college should be. We have also seen that the degree of these differences is increasing over time. In the epilogue to the previous chapter we saw that, among those who are most involved with the college as alumni/ae, those who played sports have a different agenda for their school. In this chapter we have seen how playing sports has indeed bonded students to the college—through an association of tradition and martial honors—and that the schools in the study have for the most part benefited, through contributions, from these passions. The data presented in this chapter indicate that this loyalty can run out—as exemplified by the way that High Profile athletes in big-time programs feel that they have given more than they have gotten. Finally, it is also clear that at the places where athletics is deemed generally to be the most carefree, winning has greater consequences for alumni/ae because of the sheer numbers of them who are bonded to the school via sports.

We introduced this book by arguing that intercollegiate athletic programs can be justified either for their role as part of the core educational mission of a college (as "the sweatiest of the liberal arts"), for their role in building community spirit, or as an investment that provides financial support for the core educational mission. Thus far we have seen how the profiles of athletes have changed over time, how they have articulated their reasons for attending a selective college or university, and the uses to which they have put their education in the world. In this chapter we have examined the factors that lead them to give back and the role that a winning football program plays in determining their generosity toward their schools.

The proverbial bottom line is that the inclination of athletes to be more generous than other graduates—which is demonstrated most clearly by the giving patterns of the athletes in the '51 cohort—is dissipating over time. Increasing professionalization of college sports has reduced the degree of athletes' identification with their schools. Looking ahead, colleges and universities may want to recognize that the big givers of today and tomorrow are more interested in priorities other than athletics, and that the athletes are—sadly, from our perspective—becoming less committed to the general purposes of these places than other high-achieving students (such as those who spend significant amounts of time on other extracurricular activities or who are the highest-ranking students). The direction of change is all too clear, and it encompasses women's athletics as well as the men's programs.

CHAPTER 11

The Financial Equation:
Expenditures and Revenues

> At the heart of the arms race are a series of assumptions that are simply false. But in the superpowers, on the national media, those fundamentals are rarely questioned.
> —Alva Myrdal, *The Game of Disarmament*

> No university generates a large enough surplus to justify the capital expenditures necessary to field a football team.
> —Roger Noll, "The Business of College Sports and the High Cost of Winning"

IT IS ALMOST impossible to have an extended conversation with an athletics director of a program operating at *any* level of play without hearing the metaphor of an arms race invoked. At the beginning of the book, we saw the pressure that a Division IA university like Northwestern faces to upgrade facilities, not only to keep pace in training for its teams but also to avoid losing the battle to attract coaches and recruits—men and women alike. Although Division III coed liberal arts colleges can hardly be expected to provide the same facilities as the big-time programs, they feel the same kinds of pressure in their own orbits: if Wesleyan gets a new pool, Trinity needs a new pool. How much does this "off the field" competition—which of course extends well beyond the provision of facilities—really cost? That is the key question that we address in this chapter.

More specifically, our objective is to provide a clearer factual framework for understanding (1) how much money is spent on intercollegiate athletics programs by colleges and universities operating within different divisions of the NCAA, as well as the factors that drive the level of expenditures; and (2) the main sources of revenue, how they have changed over time, and what the proverbial "bottom line" really looks like for schools that operate in different divisions and that enjoy different degrees of competitive success.

The announcement that the Knight Commission on Intercollegiate Athletics would reconvene in the fall of 2000 focused heavily on what William Friday, co-chairman of the commission, referred to as "the power of money."[1] Not surprisingly, many books on big-time athletics are focused heavily on financial matters and especially on the hotly debated question of whether big-time sports programs contribute dollars to other activities or are a net drain on the institution's resources.[2] If sports programs were to produce net profits, they could be seen as providing direct financial support for the institution's educational mission, in the same way that a museum gift shop provides revenue that supports the museum's core mission of preserving and presenting great works of art. (It is actually a bit more complicated than that, in that even if a super-successful athletics program has positive net revenues in a given year, the extra dollars may stay on the athletics side of the financial "wall" that is in place at some universities, such as the University of Michigan; it may be that there is no way in which the English department can benefit. On the other hand, it is also necessary to recognize that the net revenues generated by big-time sports at places like UNC–Chapel Hill, Michigan, or Penn State can—and often do—provide the resources that will pay for the costs of intercollegiate programs in sports such as soccer that otherwise might have had to turn to the university proper for support.) The much more common situation for the schools in our study is one in which intercollegiate athletic programs are a source of financial drain, and here more weight must be given to the questions examined in earlier chapters—whether the programs themselves are justified by their place in the core educational mission. In that case, they may lose money (in the same way that the library "loses" money) but still may play a part in furthering the educational mission of the institution.

The financing of college sports also matters for two other reasons that are just as important as direct dollar costs. First, budgetary pressures, and the responses to them, can affect the character of the athletic enterprise profoundly. For example, the decision by the Ivy League presidents in 1971 to make freshmen eligible for varsity competition in "individual" sports—a decision with educational and other ramifications—was driven largely, though by no means entirely, by the need to contain the rising costs of athletic programs; fielding separate freshmen teams was expensive.[3] Second, efforts to control the *net* costs of intercollegiate athletics by raising more money from corporate sponsors, friends groups, and the like can create major issues of governance and control, as well as raise questions about the values that schools want to communicate to their students, their faculty, and the broader public. In short, debates "about money" are almost never just about money—in athletics or in anything else.

Is the free swoosh free?

Having migrated from scoreboards to players uniforms, the emblems of Nike, Reebok, and Adidas have become omnipresent in many college sports programs. Nike has provided either in-kind supplies—sneakers and warm-up suits—or cold hard cash to cash-starved athletics departments. However, just as technology or pharmaceutical firms will want research results to justify their investments in academic research, so too, notes Duke law professor John Weistart, will the sneaker company seeking exposure: "What happens when three members of the track team tape over the shoe company's logo to protest the low wages paid to the workers who sew the firm's shoes in Malaysia? Of course, no company paying several million dollars to promoters of its product is going to leave such a contingency unaddressed."[4]

Very few funding sources come with no strings attached, as the recent disputes between Nike and schools such as Brown University and the University of Michigan illustrate (see Chapter 1).

THE COSTS OF COMPETING

The colleges and universities in this study reported total expenditures on intercollegiate athletics in FY 1997–98 ranging from a high of over $47 million at the University of Michigan to about $1.2 million at Kenyon and Wesleyan.[5] The seemingly endless profusion of figures for individual institutions can be numbing, but fortunately there are enough similarities between types of intercollegiate programs to permit us to group most of the College and Beyond institutions into five categories:[6]

- *Division IA "Plus" universities.* The four Division IA universities in our database that have the most ambitious intercollegiate programs and spend the most money on them (University of Michigan, Penn State, Notre Dame, and Stanford).
- *Division IA "Standard" universities.* The four other Division IA universities in our database that also have big-time programs but that generally enroll somewhat fewer athletes and spend somewhat less money on intercollegiate sports (Duke, Northwestern, Vanderbilt, and Tulane).
- *Ivy League universities.* The four Ivy League schools in the database (Columbia, University of Pennsylvania, Princeton, and Yale).

- *Coed liberal arts colleges.* The seven coeducational liberal arts colleges in the database (Denison, Kenyon, Hamilton, Oberlin, Swarthmore, Wesleyan, and Williams).
- *Division III universities.* The three universities in the database that have chosen to operate Division III programs (Washington University, Emory, and Tufts).

The financial obligations associated with participation in big-time sports are revealed in striking fashion by the tremendous differences in total expenditures between the Division IA universities, on the one hand, and the Division IAA Ivy League universities and the Division III colleges and universities, on the other (Figure 11.1). The four Division IA "Plus" universities inhabit a universe of their own, with total annual expenditures for intercollegiate athletics that average $38 million.[7] The Division IA universities that we have labeled Division IA "Standard" had total expenditures averaging $21 million, with three of the four (Duke, Northwestern, and Vanderbilt) in the $20 to $24 million range (Tulane spent $15.6 million).[8] The Division IAA Ivies had average total expenditures of

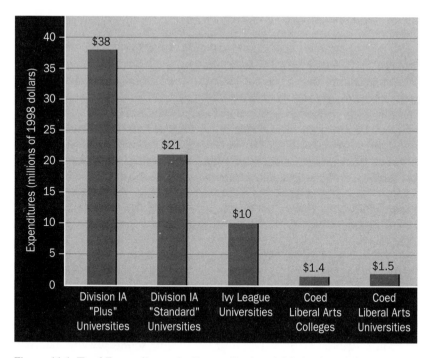

Figure 11.1. Total Expenditures for Intercollegiate Athletics by Division
Source: Equity in Athletics Disclosure Act filings, 1997–98.

roughly $10 million per year, or just about half the outlays of the Division IA "Standard" programs. The Division III coed liberal arts colleges offer a dramatic contrast to all of their brethren: they report total expenditures on intercollegiate athletics in the $1.2 to $1.7 million range.[9]

In seeking to understand these extremely wide disparities, it is useful to distinguish among three main drivers of expenditures on intercollegiate athletics. The first and by far the most important is the *level of play:* joining Division IA means recruiting scholarship athletes and providing the coaching, facilities, and other forms of support necessary to field teams that can compete at a high level.[10] The second key factor is the degree of *aspiration to competitive success within the level:* within any given division, some schools will set more ambitious goals for themselves than will others—for example, the University of Michigan has different aspirations than Miami University of Ohio, although both are Division IA schools; similarly, in Division III, Williams College has different athletic aspirations than Oberlin. Third is *breadth of the intercollegiate program:* more teams and more players obviously mean higher costs, other things being equal.[11]

But before examining total expenditures in relation to these three drivers, we should recognize how difficult it is to find a useful way of calibrating total expenditures on athletics. For reasons explained in detail in endnote 11 and at other places in the chapter, efforts to compare total expenditures by relating them to the number of participating athletes, the total enrollment of a school, or its overall budget all suffer from serious limitations. Toward the end of the chapter, we compare net operating costs of intercollegiate athletics by division (level of play). Such comparisons can be interpreted meaningfully, however, only after we have considered the dominating impact of football and men's basketball programs.

Levels of Competition and High Expectations: The Special Cases of Football and Men's Basketball

Football and men's basketball are such dominant features of the athletics landscape that they must be examined separately (and their expenditures have to be subtracted from total expenditures so that outlays on other men's and women's teams can be calibrated properly). By any reckoning, football is an especially expensive sport. In FY 1998, the four Division IA "Plus" schools in our study reported spending between $8.3 million (Stanford) and $13.2 million (Penn State) on football. Michigan and Notre Dame spent almost $9 million each. Thus, the average outlay on football in FY 1998 was $9.7 million for the IA "Plus" schools (Figure 11.2). The average amount spent on football was $6.1 million for the Di-

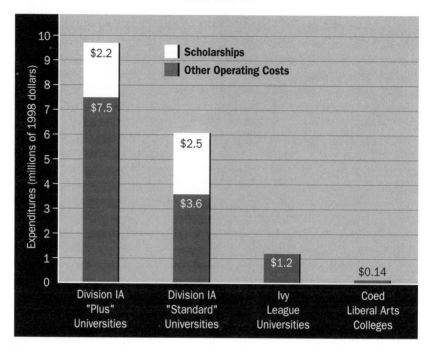

Figure 11.2. Direct Expenditures on Football by Division
Source: Equity in Athletics Disclosure Act filings, 1997–98 (see Scorecard 11.1).

vision IA "Standard" schools (ranging from a low of $4.4 million at Duke to a high of $7.5 million at Vanderbilt). The four Ivies spent much less (an average of about $1,200,000), and the Division III schools less yet (an average of about $140,000). Men's basketball, while also expensive relative to many other sports, is much less expensive than football. Expenditures for men's basketball averaged $1.7 to $1.8 million in FY 1998 at the Division IA schools, about $350,000 in the Ivies, and roughly $50,000 in the Division III coed liberal arts colleges.

The *relative* weight of football and men's basketball in the athletic budget also varies markedly by level of play (Scorecard 11.1). At both Division IA "Plus" and Division IA "Standard" schools, football alone accounted for roughly 45 percent of all expenditures assigned to specific sports on the Equity in Athletics Disclosure Act (EADA) forms, and for 26 to 29 percent of total expenditures on athletics. Adding in men's basketball brings the share of all team-specific athletic expenditures assigned directly to these two High Profile sports to well over 50 percent. At the other end of the spectrum, the Division III coed liberal arts colleges devote less than one-fifth of their team-specific expenditures to football and men's basketball. Although the Ivies spend much more on athletics in general than do the Division III schools, it is noteworthy that they place the same *relative* emphasis on football and men's basketball (judged by dollars spent) as the Division III institutions; overall, football and men's basketball are directly responsible for about 13 percent of the total athletic budget in both the Ivies and the Division III schools.

It is evident that the entry fee for participation in both big-time football and men's basketball is far from trivial. The $1.7 to $1.8 million that Division IA schools in the study spent on men's basketball is more money than an athletically committed coed liberal arts college like Williams spent on its entire intercollegiate athletic program! And the outlays on big-time football are three to four times greater than those on men's basketball. None of these figures, it should be emphasized, includes any of the large amount of money in the athletic budgets that supported what we call "general infrastructure." This is important to note, because it is reasonable to assume that these central costs (administration, marketing, the ticket office) contain costs that are more likely to be related to football and men's basketball than to the Lower Profile sports. Nor do these figures include capital costs. (Later in the chapter, we attempt to penetrate the "black box" that contains the general infrastructure costs and comment on capital costs.) The very substantial entry fees associated with competing at the Division IA level might be expected to give pause to schools contemplating "upgrading" their programs, and especially their football programs.[12]

Although there is a rough consistency in the amounts spent on these high-visibility programs by all the schools in each category, there are also revealing differences. These differences can be thought of, at least in part, as reflecting what one observer has called "the high cost of winning" in big-time collegiate sports.[13] It is no coincidence that the four Division IA schools that spend the most on athletics are more successful competitively, year after year, than the four other Division IA universities in our database. Nor is it a coincidence that Notre Dame spends appreciably less on its men's basketball program, relative to other Division IA "Plus" schools, than it does on its football program; in recent years, Notre Dame has not been a power in men's basketball. Another revealing case is Duke, which is known for its basketball teams but not for its football prowess. Duke reports having spent "only" $4.4 million on football in 1998 (well below the amounts spent by other Division IA schools in our database), but over $1.8 million on its enormously successful men's basketball program. Georgetown is another school known for its basketball program, and it too spent over $1.8 million on basketball in 1998.

This very clear pattern conveys numerous lessons. One is that a school with big-time aspirations and a real chance to reach national championship status in one of the High Profile sports has to be prepared to "spend money to make money." Recruiting the most talented secondary school students is notoriously competitive, and candidates choosing among leading programs of course expect excellent (and well-paid) coaches, first-rate facilities, no skimping on travel and other operating costs, and strong publicity and marketing efforts. Competitive success also has direct effects on postseason costs as well as postseason revenues, as the following box demonstrates. However, although spending money may be a necessary condition for sustained competitive success, it is by no means a sufficient condition. As we will see later in the chapter, only a very small number of schools that are committed to large outlays in these sports actually end up collecting revenues that can be said to justify the expenditures. We are reminded of an insightful comment made by a physics professor who had just rejected a stupendously high salary offer from a university seeking to "buy" academic success in physics: "Excellence can't be bought," he said, "but it has to be paid for."[14]

Hidden costs of competitive success:

When Northwestern beat Notre Dame early in their miracle 1995 season, there were still some empty seats in Dyche stadium the next week. Later in the season, however, games were selling out. "Ten thousand extra fans in the seats," President Henry Bienen noted, "is worth a lot. So is the hype which increased merchandising fees from $40,000 to $400,000 as people flocked to buy everything purple, including noodles, comic books and countless sweatshirts." But the same financial arrangements that had kept Northwestern's nose above the financial surface in the lean 0–11 years—such as the Big Ten revenue sharing agreement by which Rose Bowl proceeds are for the most part split among the schools in the conference—dampened the benefits of the boom years as well. When Northwestern went to the Rose Bowl for the first time since 1942, the $1 million provided by the Rose Bowl for costs incurred was a financial wash: the school paid for the travel costs of 521 players, coaches, trainers, cheerleaders, and band members. "How could I not take the band after so many endless gray days stalwartly showing the flag on drizzling Saturday afternoons?" Bienen asked.

Major Components of Expenditures on Football and Men's Basketball

Inspection of the main components of expenditures on football and men's basketball provides insight into both the relative costs of different types of expenditure and the different philosophies of intercollegiate athletics that lie beneath the major differences in expenditures by NCAA division.

Athletic scholarships. The financial consequences of choosing one level of play rather than another are seen most vividly through dollars spent on athletic scholarships, or, in NCAA language, "athletically related student aid" (defined as "aid awarded a student that requires the student to participate in an intercollegiate athletics program").[15] In Division IA football, 85 scholarships can be awarded, and the annual cost is likely to exceed $2 million. (Scorecard 11.2 contains rough estimates of the major components of expenditures on football and men's basketball, by division.)[16] Squad size is of course smaller in men's basketball; no more than 12 scholarships can be awarded, and the cost is therefore in the $300,000 range.[17]

Under league and Division III rules, neither the Ivies nor any of the Division III schools provide athletic scholarships. They would thereby appear to be spared the attendant financial consequences. This is a bit of an overstatement, however, since some of these schools provide "merit aid," and, although all Division III presidents sign a pledge that aid will not be awarded on the basis of athletic talent, other characteristics that may be a proxy for athletic talent (leadership, determination, contributing to team spirit) can be considered in determining how much aid an applicant is offered. Moreover, athletic recruiting can affect the financial aid bill at schools that provide only need-based aid. Football and basketball players are somewhat more likely than students at large to come from families of modest means (see Chapter 2), and thus they may receive relatively large financial aid awards. The 1998–99 decision by some of the Ivy League schools to improve financial aid packages for students from families with relatively low incomes by replacing the loan component of their financial aid packages with grants means that, in effect, athletes from poor families attending these schools receive nearly as much financial aid as those receiving athletic scholarships at Division IA schools; moreover, the Ivy League students do not have to keep playing intercollegiate sports to retain their aid. At still other schools, recruited athletes may be offered a more favorable mix of grant and loan aid than other students from similar family backgrounds (a practice sometimes called "preferential packaging").[18]

For all of these reasons, the differential "net" cost to Division IA schools of offering athletic scholarships may be somewhat less than the apparent cost. The key question is how much financial aid would have been given to "replacement" students had there been no athletic scholarships, since financial aid is also a major budgetary category outside athletics. Administrators at Duke have estimated that the University would spend roughly one-third as much on financial aid for the same number of students if athletic scholarships were abolished. More generally, the true cost to the school of providing athletic scholarships also depends on whether using athletic scholarships to recruit athletes in fact displaces other potential students who might have paid tuition or, alternatively, simply helps the school achieve its enrollment target. Although most of the academically selective colleges and universities in this study have a surfeit of well-qualified applicants, recruiting athletes at some schools may help fill classes and dorm rooms with tuition-paying students. These important caveats notwithstanding, there is no denying that most schools that provide athletic scholarships are undertaking significantly greater financial obligations than they would incur otherwise.

Coaching costs. Expenditures on coaching also differ markedly among the Division IA universities (many of which spend, in football alone, far more than $1 million on coaching salaries, without considering employee benefits), the Ivies (where estimated coaching salaries in football are on the order of $400,000), and the Division III coed liberal arts colleges (which may spend $100,000 or less on football coaching). A big-time Division IA university may have a dozen full-time coaches dedicated solely to the football program. In the Ivies, the number of full-time football coaches is likely to be half this number, and in some Division III coed liberal arts colleges, not even the head coach of football is assigned full-time to the program. There are of course also marked variations in salaries across divisions, not all of which are captured in the rough figures shown on the scorecard.[19] The *Chronicle of Higher Education* survey of salaries at colleges and universities often lists the salary of the basketball coach or football coach as the second highest salary at the university—or, in the case of Duke, as higher than that of the president. Costs in basketball are lower than in football, but the general pattern is the same (see bottom panel of Scorecard 11.2).

These differences in staffing arrangements reflect radically different philosophies. Whereas many coaches in the Ivy League schools, as in Division IA, are hired to devote full time to a particular sport, coaches in Division III schools are often given other assignments—to help coach another sport, to teach physical education classes, or to handle an administrative assignment. At Denison University, for example, every coach has multiple duties—not even the head coach of football devotes all of his time to that assignment.

Recruiting costs. This "multitasking" philosophy of staffing not only has a major impact on coaching expenses, it also affects recruiting and every other aspect of intercollegiate athletics. Full-time coaches are obviously able to spend more time recruiting—and are expected to do so—than are coaches who have other duties in the off-season. Recruiting expenses at the Division III schools, where coaches generally are prohibited from recruiting off campus, are so modest as to nearly escape detection on our scorecard. At the Division IA schools, on the other hand, direct recruiting costs in football can reach or exceed a quarter million dollars.[20]

Perhaps the most noteworthy aspect of the data on recruiting costs is the difference between the Ivies and the Division III schools: neither provides athletic scholarships, but the coaches in the Ivy League obviously devote a great deal more time and money to recruiting than do the coaches in Division III programs. The reported difference between direct outlays for football recruiting (of, say, $70,000 in the Ivies versus $5,000 in the Division III coed liberal arts colleges) indicates that there is a real difference in the emphasis given to recruiting, but it does not reflect fully the magnitude of the difference; the reported recruiting expenses do not include any allocation of the salaries of coaches and others engaged in the recruiting process.

Operating costs and "other" expenses. The remaining expenditures assigned directly to football and men's basketball consist of a combination of "operating costs" and "other." The easiest piece of this amalgam to understand is "operating expenses," as narrowly defined on the EADA forms (Table 4) to include "transportation, lodging and meals, officials, uniforms and equipment for both home and away contests." Again the level of competition drives these costs: at Division IA football programs, direct operating expenses are in the $700,000 range, as contrasted with $100,000 in the Ivy League and $30,000 at the Division III colleges. (But even at coed liberal arts colleges playing in Division III, football has much higher operating expenses than other sports, especially if an effort is made to upgrade the program, as the following box demonstrates.)

Buses to birdies—operating expenses at a coed liberal arts college:

"We've been playing football with under 40 student athletes," [Swarthmore athletic director Robert] Williams said, "If this [program upgrade] is successful, we'll have 65 to 70 athletes. That will mean more equipment, more beds, more food. Instead of one bus, we'll need a bus and a van. It doesn't just stop." The school has allocated $20,000 for a new look in uniforms and equipment—a sore point to other campus teams. Xaing Lan Zhou, 21, an

> engineering major who plays on the badminton team, complains about the struggle to get money for birdies.[21]

The divisional differences in expenditures in the amorphous category labeled "Football—other" are huge, and they are an important part of the story that explains why the Division IA programs spend so much more money on football than do the Ivies—and why the Ivies, in turn, spend so much more than do the Division III coed liberal arts colleges. Although it is the highly visible athletic scholarships and the salaries of the best-known big-time coaches that often attract attention when journalists ponder the size of athletic budgets, it is the "Football—other" expenditures (estimated at over $3 million in Division IA) that are most important in elevating the level of costs in these football programs. What is in the "Football—other" category? We were given access to detailed data for three Division IA programs, and the four largest components appear to be (1) postseason expenses, including travel and other expenses not only of varsity teams but also of bands and cheerleaders, university officials, and key trustees, regents, and alumni/ae; (2) salaries of individuals other than coaches who are part of the football program—equipment managers, film and video personnel, clerical staff, recruiting assistants, and student help; (3) fringe benefits of the coaches (usually excluded from the salary line) as well as all of these other individuals; and (4) the staffing and other costs of managing a large stadium for home games.

The key point is that there are major recurring expenses associated with running a big-time program that do not fit neatly within the established EADA categories. Making comparisons across all three divisions shows that the Ivies occupy an intermediate position between the Division IA schools and the Division III programs. The Ivies are much closer in their absolute dollar expenditures on "Football—other" to the Division III programs, but, relatively speaking, just as far above Division III as Division IA is above the Ivies. The general principle seems to be that once a school assembles a staff of full-time coaches dedicated to an expensive and complicated sport like football, the costs of running and managing the enterprise grow more than in proportion to the direct costs of coaching and equipping teams.

General Infrastructure Costs

Even more consequential than the sport-specific "other costs" of the kind we have just been discussing are those infrastructure costs that are not normally associated with any one sport (general administration, sports information offices, marketing, business management, support services of all kinds, some facilities costs, fundraising, and so on). These are the costs that create the large gaps between the direct expenditures reported for individual teams on the EADA forms and the total costs of intercollegiate athletics reported on these same forms. It is readily apparent that both the absolute and relative costs of infrastructure are vastly greater at higher levels of play, and, within divisions, are higher the more successful the school is in big-time athletic competition (Scorecard 11.3). At the Division IA "Plus" schools, these costs average more than $16 million, or 44 percent of total expenditures. General infrastructure costs are roughly half as large (in dollars) at the Division IA "Standard" universities and constitute 36 percent of total expenditures. At the other end of the spectrum, general infrastructure costs at the Division III level average about $400,000, or 29 percent of total expenditures. The data for the Ivies are less complete, but again they appear to occupy an intermediate position.[22]

This distinct pattern reflects in part the management and marketing requirements associated with overseeing programs that have important business elements and that generate substantial revenues. The pure salary component of such infrastructure costs is considerable, with personnel devoting time to tasks such as oversight of large facilities, development and alumni/ae relations, sports information and media relations, management of the ticket office, marketing, management of the business office and information technology unit, and compliance. There are of course hefty expense budgets associated with almost all of these salary lines. In addition, large amounts of money are spent on providing student academic support (over $600,000 in one situation), athletic medicine, and strength and conditioning programs. Some schools also include debt service, allowances for depreciation, and even (in a few situations) certain direct capital outlays.

Although it is true that the infrastructure funded by these outlays benefits a wide range of athletic programs, it is surely the case that—at least in Division IA but probably also to some extent in the Ivy League—football, in particular, consumes a disproportionate share of these resources. Georgetown is a most useful point of reference, because it has a big-time basketball program but does not play Division IA football; general infrastructure costs at Georgetown were $3.4 million, as compared with an average of $11 to $12 million for the schools in our Division IA "Plus" and Division IA "Standard" categories (see Appendix Table B.11.1).

Further inspection of the data for individual schools collected in Appendix Table B.11.1 reminds us also of the "high costs of winning." It is surely no coincidence that teams with the most successful football programs have by far the largest infrastructure costs (e.g., Michigan). Thus the figures presented earlier expressing football expenditures as a fraction of total expenditures grossly understate the true proportions. If we were to assume (probably rather conservatively) that football and men's basketball together account for 60 percent of general infrastructure costs, roughly 50 to 60 percent of all expenditures on intercollegiate athletics at Division IA schools can be attributed to these two High Profile sports.

Since infrastructure costs are notoriously difficult to reduce, they also create substantial pressures to maintain revenue streams that will support them. The implications for recruiting, coaching, and, yes, winning, are obvious—a key point to which we will return when we look at the revenues generated by football and basketball.

The World beyond Football and Men's Basketball: The Overall Breadth of Intercollegiate Programs for Men and Women

There are notable differences among schools in the numbers of teams and athletes, with the Ivy League schools fielding the most teams and having the largest numbers of athletes engaged in intercollegiate competition (Scorecard 11.4).[23] Among the Division IA schools in our study for whom we have reliable data, Tulane and Vanderbilt field the fewest varsity teams (14) while Stanford supports 31.[24] Sports offered at Stanford but not at Vanderbilt include fencing, field hockey, gymnastics, rowing, sailing, softball, swimming and diving, volleyball, water polo, and wrestling. Schools in the Northeast are less likely to offer all of the "California sports" found at Stanford, but instead are likely to have ice hockey and squash teams. Several of the coed liberal arts colleges also support large numbers of teams, and Tufts, a Division III university, is tied with Yale for the largest number of participants on intercollegiate teams (967).[25]

One reason for looking in such detail at football and men's basketball was to "clear the tracks" for an analysis of expenditures on the Lower Profile sports played by both men and women students. Their costs are far from trivial, ranging from total annual direct outlays averaging $10 million per school in the Division IA "Plus" category, to an average of $5.7 million per school in Division IA "Standard," to averages of $3.5 million per school in the Ivies and just over $800,000 among the Division III coed liberal arts colleges. The large difference in outlays on these Lower Profile sports between the Division IA "Plus" and the Division IA "Standard" schools is almost entirely explainable in terms of differences in the breadth of athletic offerings (with the Division IA "Plus" schools fielding an average of 23 Lower Profile teams as compared with an average of 14 in the Division IA "Standard" category). The Ivy League schools, on the other hand, field twice as many teams as we find in the Division IA "Standard" schools but spend only about 60 percent as much money on them.

Clearly there are large differences in average spending per team (Figure 11.3), with the two groups of Division IA schools spending an average of more than $400,000 on each Lower Profile team, as compared with averages of $126,000 in the Ivy League and $42,000 in the Division III coed liberal arts colleges (Scorecard 11.5). These large differences demonstrate once again—this time outside the arena of big-time football and men's basketball—the financial impact of the chosen level of play. The Division IA schools spend nearly *ten times* as much per team (and per athlete) as the Division III colleges, and the Ivies spend *three times* as much per team as the Division III schools.

Moreover, this pattern is quite consistent when we make comparisons on a sport-by-sport basis, for both men's and women's teams. The leading exception to this rule is women's basketball, which is on the way to becoming a big-time sport and shows a more pronounced set of differences in outlays by division. The Division IA universities spend an average of about $1 million per year on their women's basketball teams,

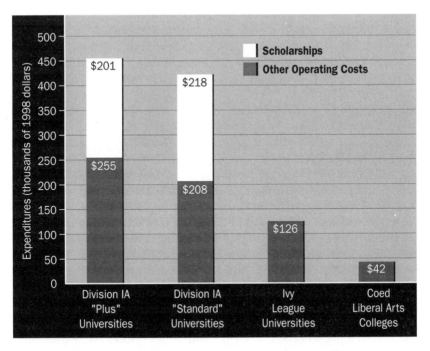

Figure 11.3. Direct Expenditures on Average Lower Profile Team by Division
Source: Equity in Athletics Disclosure Act filings, 1997–98 (see Scorecard 11.5).

whereas the Ivies spend approximately $225,000, and the Division III coed liberal arts colleges about $40,000.[26]

The most interesting comparisons involve the other Lower Profile sports. We were able to collect detailed expenditure data for representative schools in each division for field hockey, tennis (men's and women's), swimming (men's and women's), men's soccer, and men's lacrosse. The similarities in expenditures within divisions are pronounced, especially below the Division IA level. At the Division IA level, the average outlay per sport for the set of sports enumerated above was in the range of $300,000 to $375,000 per year. In the Ivy League, the average outlay was in the $110,000 to $135,000 range, and in Division III it was consistently in the $30,000 to $50,000 range. Men's lacrosse is a relatively expensive sport and tennis (for both men and women) is relatively inexpensive, but the variations by sport are not large.

The differences by division, on the other hand, are striking. They are driven, first, by the large number of athletic scholarships given to athletes playing Lower Profile sports in Division IA, and especially by the scholarships given to women athletes in an effort to balance out the heavy spending on football scholarships for men. Of course, many of the men playing Lower Profile sports at these schools also receive athletically related student aid. We estimate that about half the difference between the Ivies and the Division IA schools in expenditures on Lower Profile sports is due to the awarding of athletic scholarships (with the other half due to a combination of factors listed later in the chapter). This use of athletic scholarships is a clear example of "contagion" effects. Patterns established in big-time sports at Division IA schools spread more or less inexorably to other sports.

We see this same phenomenon, albeit in slightly muted form, in staffing arrangements, which are the second main determinant of divisional differences in outlays in the Lower Profile sports. In this regard, the Ivies have much more in common with the Division IA schools than they do with the coed liberal arts colleges that compete in Division III. In both the Division IA schools and the Ivy League, the common pattern is for the head coaches of most Lower Profile sports to be assigned full time to their sports. This is the reason why coaching costs, as best we can estimate them, differ less than one might have expected as one moves across the divide between Division IA and the Ivies: for example, we estimate that coaching costs (excluding benefits) in field hockey range from a high of $128,000 at one Division IA school to a low of $60,000 at one of the Ivies, with the figures for all of the other schools for which we have data in the $62,000 to $72,000 range; in sharp contrast, coaching outlays for field hockey in the Division III schools for which we have comparable data are around $20,000. Almost identical patterns exist in tennis.

As was noted in our earlier discussion of football and men's basketball, the Division III schools continue to expect most of their coaches to perform a variety of coaching, teaching, and administrative tasks, and the cost savings are both direct and indirect. A very few highly successful Ivy League teams are also coached by individuals who have a variety of duties (an example is Al Carlson, who is head coach of golf and associate director of athletics at Columbia), but the trend is clearly in the direction of more and more single-minded dedication to a particular sport. The only other part-time head coach at Columbia coaches archery.

The presence of full-time coaches makes possible aggressive off-campus recruiting and greater commitments to off-season conditioning and preparation of athletes than would otherwise be feasible. Other expenses of all kinds (especially for equipment and travel, as well as recruiting trips and visits) rise accordingly, and this is why the Ivies spend nearly three times as much per Lower Profile sport as the Division III coed liberal arts colleges. Even when we correct for the fact that there tend to be somewhat more athletes per team in the Ivies than in Division III, we find that total expenditures per Lower Profile athlete in the Ivies are appreciably greater than in Division III—roughly $4,000 in the Ivies versus $1,500 in Division III (bottom line of Scorecard 11.5). Of course, the Ivies regularly compete with Division IA schools for national championships in sports such as lacrosse, crew, and field hockey, and so this level of expenditure is not really surprising when seen in the context of ambitions for success at the highest levels of play. And, if the Ivies are going to compete for coaches and the best athletes with their Division IA counterparts, they are naturally going to feel the pressure to offer reasonably comparable programs (with the exception of athletic scholarships), including similar schedules, travel, and facilities.[27]

Coaches—the costs of commitment and "turf wars":

In February 1997, Yale hired Marisa Didio, the field hockey coach who had left Division IA Northwestern after making the Final Four: "Within the support system that existed, I did not feel that I could take that [Northwestern] team any further. . . . Yale has made a change in commitment with this hire to bring the program, within a time frame, to another level." At the time that Didio was hired, the Harvard coach explained one aspect of the competitive disadvantage that Yale had been facing: "Certainly, a higher level of field hockey is played on Astroturf. Princeton got turf two years ago and that turned their program around. Turf helps in recruiting and in developing team skills. It makes a huge difference."

Raising the stakes: first-class travel?

We had a kid who came to Princeton on an unofficial visit as a junior. He was great, liked the school and all that. That fall, some big-time basketball schools chased him. He came to visit us after that and wanted to know if we traveled first class. We couldn't stand him anymore, and he went somewhere else. If you want to get into the rat race, you've got to be a rat.

—Pete Carill, former head basketball coach at Princeton

REVENUE PAYBACKS AND THE BOTTOM LINE

The most successful big-time sports programs are enormously appealing to a wide audience, as we are reminded each fall when network television cameras pan the more than 110,000 spectators at a Michigan football game and then again when "March Madness" and the excitement of being in "the big dance" captivate basketball audiences nationwide. This mass-entertainment appeal of big-time sports is one justification for the large sums of money spent on the leading intercollegiate athletic programs. As many commentators have observed, the most highly successful football and men's basketball programs more than pay for themselves, at least on a current cost basis. Economist Roger Noll is correct in referring to these programs as "profit centers."[28] What is much less obvious is how many football and basketball programs are in fact profitable, just how profitable even the most successful ones are when all costs are considered, and how the profits that are generated compare with the costs of the remaining parts of the intercollegiate sports programs.

These questions are devilishly difficult to answer. The data collected on the EADA forms are much more useful guides to the degree of participation in intercollegiate athletics and to the direct costs of fielding teams than to the revenue side of the equation. In previous studies of finances conducted by the NCAA and others, institutional subventions (i.e., general funds) are often lumped together with revenues obtained from outside sources; as a result, the grand totals in the revenue columns on the EADA forms are meaningless for many schools. When we compare the total revenues and total expenses on the EADA form for Duke, for example, we find that revenues exceed expenses by more than $2 million; yet we know from discussions with officials at Duke that this apparent "profit" conveys a false picture of the true situation. Duke provides the athletic department with a subvention from its general funds in the $4 to

$5 million range.[29] Columbia University provides an even more extreme example, in that its total revenues are shown on the EADA form to exceed $7 million as compared with total reported expenses of under $6 million; yet we know from other information on the form that the sports programs at Columbia generated under half a million dollars in revenues. To cite a Division III example, Denison University generates almost no earned income from athletics and yet shows total revenues of $1.5 million—almost all of which reflects University subventions.

The NCAA reports that combine revenues and expenses are of some help (especially since they now try to subtract institutional support from total revenues). But these compilations are also of limited value for another reason: both revenue and expense figures are expressed as averages for large numbers of somewhat disparate institutions. There are also vexing accounting issues, which is why we put words like "profit" and "deficit" in quotation marks and sometimes use the qualifying phrase "as conventionally reported."[30]

Finally, it is dangerous to rely on budgeted figures. Often overly rosy revenue projections are used to justify expenditures. Faced with pressures from faculty or other claimants on scarce resources, a president may agree, for example, to limit the athletics subvention to $X million. A budget will then be constructed with revenue projections that are consistent with this agreement. Later, when results are disappointing, there are always quasi-plausible explanations, and the cycle may simply repeat itself. Retrospective reports of actual financial results are more reliable.

All of these problems and caveats notwithstanding, the most recent NCAA report informs us that in 1997 fewer than half of the Division IA programs (43 percent) reported "profits," and that the average "deficit" reported at the other programs was $2.8 million. The reported average deficits for Division IAA and Division II (with football) were $2.0 and $0.9 million, respectively; no figures are shown for "profits" in these divisions, presumably because they were either rare or nonexistent.[31] In the case of Division III programs, the NCAA presents essentially no data on revenues because, in the words of the report, "Division III revenues are not significant."[32] The essential point, buttressed by other data in the NCAA reports, is that a relatively small number of universities generate significant amounts of net income (as conventionally reported), almost all of which comes from highly successful football and men's basketball programs. The great majority of Division IA and Division II schools, and all Division III schools, subsidize their intercollegiate athletic programs out of general funds—as of course they subsidize essentially every activity, in and out of the classroom, that they sponsor.[33]

Four Case Studies

The most useful way of "unpacking" the revenue side of the financing equation is by looking closely at four specific athletic programs: those at Michigan, Duke, Princeton, and Williams. Each of these schools has supplied detailed data that allow us to understand the true situation much more accurately than would have been possible if we had had to rely on the usual published reports and summaries. This set of institutions provides a good set of reference points for another reason: each is an exemplar of athletic success within the domain it has chosen to occupy: Michigan in Division IA "Plus," Duke in Division IA "Standard," Princeton in the Ivy League, and Williams in Division III. Thus examining these four athletic programs allows us to describe what it appears possible to achieve financially through intercollegiate athletics *if a school has the competitive success of a Michigan in all sports, a Duke in men's basketball, and a Princeton or a Williams in the broad array of sports in which they compete at their own levels.*[34]

Judged by both amounts and sources of revenue, the four schools appear to inhabit different planets (Scorecard 11.6 and Appendix Table B.11.2). The University of Michigan's athletic program generated more than $50 million in revenue—more than half the size of the entire operating budget of Williams College! More relevant is the comparison with athletic revenues at Duke, which were roughly $15 million. And Duke's $15 million of revenues from athletics in turn dominates the approximately $3 million in revenue generated by all athletic programs at Princeton, never mind the $150,000 of revenue attributable to athletics at Williams.

The revenue potential of a consistently successful Division IA football powerhouse is evident. Michigan earned over $16 million in football gate receipts alone, whereas gate receipts at Duke, which is not known for its football program, were just one-eighth this amount, or $2 million. In men's basketball, where both Michigan and Duke have enjoyed great success, the gate receipts are closely comparable ($2 million and $1.9 million, respectively), and it is evident that not even the most outstanding basketball programs have the revenue-generating capacity of one of the country's absolutely top football programs—a conclusion that is only strengthened when we consider postseason revenues from bowl games along with regular season receipts. Taken together, regular season and postseason competition in all sports yielded $30 million at Michigan and just about $10 million at Duke.[35] And when we look at the reference data for the "average" NCAA Division IA school, we find that it is Duke that is typical in this regard—at the average NCAA Division IA school, regular season and postseason competition contributed $10 million. Michigan is the outlier.

Another major source of revenue at Michigan is sponsorship, signage, and licensing fees ($8 million); Duke earned roughly $1 million in licensing fees, but at Duke this income is not credited to the athletic department (and thus appears in brackets in Scorecard 11.6 and Appendix Table B.11.2). Fundraising for athletics was highly productive at both of these competitively successful Division IA schools: friends (boosters) groups contributed over $7 million at Michigan and nearly $4 million at Duke.

Looking now at the Ivy League and Division III programs, we see that regular season and postseason revenues together amounted to only about $1 million at Princeton and were negligible at Williams.[36]Although the Ivies, unlike the Division III schools, also generate some revenue from advertising, the revenue source that has become very important to their athletic programs is contributions from friends groups (which, in the Ivy League, although not at big-time schools, are composed overwhelmingly of alumni). At Princeton in 1998–99, about $1.8 million in donated revenues was used to cover intercollegiate athletic costs of various kinds. Traditionally, the Division III schools have been less aggressive in seeking sport-specific donations (see the discussion of athletic giving in Chapter 10), and in 1997–98 Williams received a total of only $100,000 from this source, most of which was given in support of its crew program.

One overriding impression conveyed by these data is the importance of television and postseason revenue generated by the big-time High Profile sports. Michigan garnered over $9 million from these sources and Duke earned over $5 million. The large sponsorship-signage-licensing revenue stream at Michigan is tied directly to its athletic success—as is, in no small degree, the ability of Michigan's athletic department to raise large sums of money from its fans. One of the major inducements to donors is privileged access to good seats and other perks, which have value precisely because of the success of the teams. Prowess on the field and on the court obviously makes a tremendous difference. Consistent competitive success fills large stadiums and qualifies teams for lucrative postseason bowl games and tournaments. Television networks and bowl sponsors of course want to feature well-known, well-publicized teams. As we saw earlier, the cost of winning is high; but, in ideal circumstances, so too are the financial rewards.

What, then, can be said about the proverbial bottom line? At a handful of athletic powerhouses, the headlines proclaiming the financial power of big-time programs have relevance. If we continue to ignore, at least for the moment, both the need to allocate to athletics some part of university-wide overhead costs and the very large capital costs of facilities, football and men's basketball at some of these athletically elite schools can generate enough revenue to cover the operating costs of all the teams fielded by the university and also the large infrastructure costs associated with running a highly successful operation—with, in 1997–98 at Michigan, about $3 million left over. But, as we saw at the beginning of this book, there has been a marked downturn in the financial fortunes of the University of Michigan's athletic program since FY 1997–98. Sudden changes in volatile revenues streams can make balancing a budget quite a feat, even for schools with winning teams. The pendulum can swing quickly.

Revenue volatility: winning and television exposure:

The budget director for Stanford's athletics program recounted how, only one game into the 1996 season, Stanford was upset by Oregon State, leading ABC to decide to substitute the USC-UCLA game for the season-ending Berkeley-Stanford game. Stanford roared back to have an outstanding 7–2 season, but, since the network needed to determine its logistics far in advance, the early season loss led to an irrevocable change in plans. USC and UCLA, rather than Berkeley and Stanford, each received $150,000 in television revenues.

No positive "bottom line" result obtains at most Division IA schools. Even at Duke, with its highly successful basketball program, the athletic department as a whole did not make a "profit": as noted earlier, the university provided a subvention from general funds of roughly $5 million, and the NCAA data for the average Division IA program suggest that subventions are common. Although we lack the detailed data needed to provide similarly reliable estimates for the other Division IA "Standard" schools in our study, perusal of the figures available on the EADA forms suggests that Northwestern, Vanderbilt, and Tulane may have contributed anywhere from $6 million to $12 million in general funds to their intercollegiate athletic programs.[37] In short, there is a large warning flag in these data: the inescapably large expenditures needed to pursue the rewards of winning will be recouped *only if teams are highly successful.* And, as even the University of Michigan and Stanford have learned, the volatility of some major sources of revenue can cause unpleasant surprises when the books are closed on the fiscal year.

Assessing the implications of a subvention on the order of the $5 million provided at Duke is not easy, since presumably some substantial sum would have been spent on intercollegiate sports even if Duke did not play big-time basketball. We do know that the subvention provided by Duke is roughly equal to the direct costs of the Lower Profile sports that the University funds. Thus it does not appear that High Profile sports can be counted on to defray any appreciable part of the costs of the Lower Profile sports. It appears that the High Profile sports at Northwestern, Vanderbilt, and Tulane are even less likely to help cover the costs of these other sports. It must also be remembered that playing Division IA football and basketball inevitably increases the pressure to provide athletic scholarships and, in general, to spend more money on Lower Profile sports.

The situation in the Ivy League schools is less ambiguous in that these schools do not have either the very large costs of Division IA play or the revenue-generating potential that goes with opting to compete at that level. We estimate, conservatively, that the general funds subventions for intercollegiate athletics in the Ivies are in the $5 to $8 million range. In one sense, then, the Ivies appear to have "bottom lines" similar to those of Division IA schools like Duke and Northwestern. Before making too much of this similarity, however, we must take account of numbers of teams and athletes supported, and to look as well at other benchmarks against which to judge the size of athletic subventions.

Capital Costs and Overhead

But first more needs to be said about capital costs and unallocated overhead expenditures. Williams College provides a useful example of the degree to which reported expenditures on intercollegiate athletics at schools in *all* divisions, from Division IA through Division III, understate the full costs of supporting these programs. At first blush, Williams appears to provide an extensive athletics program at a modest net cost. Subtracting the minimal amount of revenue generated by athletics ($152,000) from total expenditures ($1,682,000) implies a net recurring cost of just over $1.5 million.

Digging deeper reveals a different picture. The "global accounting" concepts developed by Gordon Winston, a professor of economics and former provost at Williams, lead, first of all, to the allocation of roughly $420,000 of central institutional costs (a share of the president's salary, a share of admissions office expenses, and so on) to intercollegiate athletics. This adjustment raises net costs to roughly $2 million.

It is capital costs, however, that change the picture dramatically. Professor Winston and his colleagues at Williams have estimated the replacement costs of athletic facilities at Williams (on a building-by-building basis) to be $46.5 million; to this sum, they add the estimated value of related land and athletics equipment ($3.2 million), to obtain a total capital cost of roughly $50 million. They then assume that half of this cost should be assigned to intercollegiate athletics and half to physical education, intramurals, and the like. The final step in the analysis is to assume a depreciation rate of 2.5 percent per year and an opportunity cost of capital of 8.5 percent per year—all very conservative assumptions. The final result is an estimated capital cost for intercollegiate athletics alone of about $2.7 million per year. *The true cost of intercollegiate athletics at Williams, then, is on the order of $4.7 million per year, not the $1.5 million of more easily measured direct costs.* These costs supported over 700 intercollegiate athletes at Williams; even so, the true cost per athlete was over $6,500 a year.[38]

We are unable to make equally precise calculations for other schools, and we know that Williams has an unusually impressive array of athletic facilities for a Division III coed liberal arts college. It would be surprising, however, if a similar mode of analysis yielded capital costs of less than, say, $10 million per year at a school such as Princeton (where a new football stadium alone cost $45 million and the entire athletic plant is valued at roughly $200 million) and perhaps twice that amount at a Duke or a Northwestern. We assume that the University of Michigan, with its huge athletic complex, lives in a capital cost stratosphere of its own. What can be said with confidence is that taking account of the imbedded capital costs of athletic facilities would surely reverse any appearance of financial "profit" associated with even the most successful big-time program. Intercollegiate athletics is a highly capital-intensive activity, and it is foolish to talk (and act) as if these costs did not exist.[39] Economist Roger Noll concluded that "no university generates a large enough surplus to justify the capital expenditures necessary to field a football team."[40]

Capital costs of football:

The fate of the old Sugar Bowl—the former Tulane football stadium—provides a real-life illustration of the opportunity cost of capital. In the 1970s, the city of New Orleans was planning the construction of the Superdome—one of the country's first domed stadiums. At the same time, the football stadium where Tulane was playing its home games was in need of serious repair. The University decided to abandon the stadium for the Superdome, and in return it received a highly favorable lease for playing its home games in the new facility. Since budgets were tight, the administration resisted spending the $2 million required to demolish the stadium. When it finally decided to so do, in 1975, it suddenly found itself with a huge side benefit—access to enormously valuable land on its urban campus where there had been no room to expand. On the site of the old stadium, Tulane built a new law school facility. This episode illustrates how capital tied up in facilities is capital not being employed for other purposes: in lieu of a stadium, Tulane gained a campus for its law school. Had it built a new stadium, some large sum of money (perhaps $20 million at the time) would have come out of unrestricted funds. To track the implications of this road not taken, we estimate that the compound return of the average university endowment from 1975 to 2000 has been approximately 10 percent. In other words, the $20 million that remained in the endowment is worth approximately $216 million in 2000 (less, of course, the amount paid in rent to the Superdome over the years).

Net Operating Costs in Perspective

One way of gaining some perspective is by expressing the current net costs of intercollegiate athletics on a per-athlete basis. As we saw earlier in the chapter, some athletic programs serve the interests of far more students than do others. Dividing total expenditures on athletics by the number of participants makes little sense because of the need to take account of revenue generated by sports such as football and basketball. It is instructive, however, to divide the *net* costs of intercollegiate athletics by the number of intercollegiate athletes who, as participants, are the most direct beneficiaries of these general funds outlays. The results of a very crude exercise of this kind (which ignores both capital costs and unallocated central administrative costs) are shown in Scorecard 11.7 and summed up by the white bars in Figure 11.4.

The zero that we have entered for the Division IA "Plus" schools reflects the assumption that a very small number of the most elite programs succeed in covering at least the direct costs of all intercollegiate programs out of athletically derived revenues (an assumption that certainly does not hold even in all of these situations). The other sets of schools in our study are alike in that none of them can make this claim, but they differ among themselves in all other respects. Whereas the overall net costs of intercollegiate athletics may be roughly the same in the Division IA "Standard" schools and in the Ivies, the average number of athletes is almost twice as large in the Ivies (850 versus 422); thus the net cost *per athlete* is just over $9,000 in the Ivies but nearly $18,000 in the Division IA "Standard" programs included in our study. Duke is a clear exception to this pattern because it has both somewhat lower net costs and appreciably more intercollegiate athletes than the other Division IA "Standard" programs; as a result, the estimated net cost per athlete at Duke of $8,500 is very similar to the net cost per athlete in the Ivies. The more favorable financial picture at Duke reflects its success in holding down the costs of football and the fact that its men's basketball program does so well com-

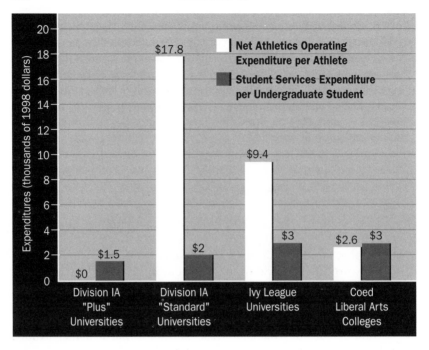

Figure 11.4. Net Athletics Operating Expenditure per Athlete versus Student Services Expenditure per Student
Source: Equity in Athletics Disclosure Act filings, 1997–98, and Integrated Postsecondary Education Data System filings, 1997–98.

petitively. In short, the high cost of being a Division IA school can be moderated somewhat by targeting one's aspirations on basketball and being a consistent winner—which it is certainly not easy to do! It is noteworthy that both the Division III colleges in our study and the Division III universities are estimated to have net costs of roughly $2,500 per athlete—or *less than one-third* of the estimated costs in the Ivy League. Moving up the ladder, from Division III to Division IAA (the Ivies) to Division IA, can obviously be a very expensive proposition.

One way of confirming that this pattern is tied directly to the levels at which schools choose to compete in sports is by examining differences across NCAA divisions in some other category. For this purpose, we have chosen expenditures per student on all student services. These costs turn out to be remarkably similar across divisions, ranging from a low of $1,500 in the large Division IA "Plus" schools, to $2,000 in the Division IA "Standard" schools, to roughly $3,000 in the Ivies, the Division III schools, and the Division III universities (last line of Scorecard 11.7).[41] When we now compare the net expenditures on athletics per participant (the white bars in Figure 11.4) with the more or less comparable expenditures on student services per student (the gray bars in Figure 11.4), we see that the two kinds of costs are roughly comparable at the Division III coed liberal arts colleges; the athletics costs per participant are three times higher in the Ivies and nearly nine times higher at the Division IA "Standard" schools; and only in the case of the small number of Division IA "Plus" schools are the net operating costs of athletics per athlete estimated to be lower than the student services costs per student.

These comparisons neglect all capital costs of both athletics and student services, and they also ignore the fact that students who are athletes also benefit from general student services. To obtain an additional set of reference points, we asked some schools to provide data on the costs of club sports, intramural programs, and other types of student activities. The scattered bits of information available show a surprisingly consistent picture. Expenditures on club sports and intramurals (added together) ranged from $160,000 at one Division III college to $260,000 at several Division IA universities that were able to provide data. Outlays for orchestras and other student groups proved impossible to sort out with any precision, but we were able to obtain a list of such activities at one Ivy League university that together cost $322,000. For this amount, the university supported bands, an orchestra, dramatic and debate organizations, student government, ethnic organizations, and everything from the Anti-Gravity Society to the Chinese Calligraphy Association. These data confirm the simple but important point that intercollegiate competition entails an entirely different level of financial commitment than either the less formal club and intramural sports or the full range of extracurricular activities.

Trends

No one would—or should—ever believe that athletics exists in some "steady state." As the brief historical overview in Chapter 1 illustrates, the dramatic changes that have occurred over the past century have been the product of deep-rooted social forces, including changing uses of leisure time, technological revolutions (especially television), major decisions concerning the organization and oversight of intercollegiate athletics, and government antitrust rulings. Such "big picture" changes are sure to continue, but they are, by their nature, hard to anticipate.

All we can hope to do is note a few general trends. The NCAA's own summary data suggest that the number of Division IA programs "in deficit" (by NCAA accounting, excluding institutional support as well as capital costs) has risen from 49 percent of all programs in 1993 to 52 percent in 1995 to 56 percent in 1997; the size of the average deficit of those said to be "in deficit" has also risen from $2.1 million in 1993 to $2.8 million in 1997.[42] Overall, costs and revenues appear to be growing at annual rates in the neighborhood of 7 to 9 percent per year. Especially interesting is the fact that the NCAA category labeled "*highest* revenue growth" has gone up faster than the category labeled "*average* revenue growth." Taken together, these bits and pieces of information imply that the differences in financial outcomes between the *most* successful programs and all others are widening.[43]

Simply getting to a bowl game may no longer serve to put a program into the "most successful" category. A New Year's Day story circulated by the Associated Press was titled "Plenty of Tradition, Empty Seats for the Orange Bowl."[44] The story went on to discuss the change in fortunes of the Orange Bowl game. The lack of a sellout and the expectation that there would be numerous "no-shows"—even though the game featured two perennial football powerhouses—might have been attributable in part, the story suggested, to declining national interest that is in turn related to the move toward a single major bowl game (pitting the teams ranked number one and number two in the country). In the words of one coach, "It seems like there's one major bowl, and there's all the others." Increasingly, it appears that "the winners" break even and the rest of the contenders incur rising deficits in what must seem to some to be a debilitating struggle to enter the winner's circle. It seems that no one has devised a way of preventing the financial commitments associated with intercollegiate athletics from continuing to grow, and probably to grow even faster than other categories of institutional expense.

A related set of facts concerns changes in the relative importance of different sources of revenue. We have rearranged the NCAA data to group together related sources of revenue for Division IA programs, and we find a clear pattern (Figure 11.5 and Appendix Table B.11.3). Revenue from regular season football and basketball games has declined from 54 percent of all revenues in 1993 to 51 percent in 1995 to 46 percent in 1997.[45] Over the same period, postseason revenues (including conference distributions) have risen from 14 percent of all revenues in 1993 to 17 percent in 1997, and sponsorship-signage-donor revenues have risen from 18 percent of all revenue in 1993 to 21 percent in 1997.

The sources of revenue that are most volatile have become bigger components of total revenue. Thus, at the same time that winning has had larger and larger financial consequences, the downside risks (due to the growing dependence on more volatile sources of revenue associated with winning bowl games and conference championships) have also become greater. Expenditures are notoriously difficult to reduce, since no

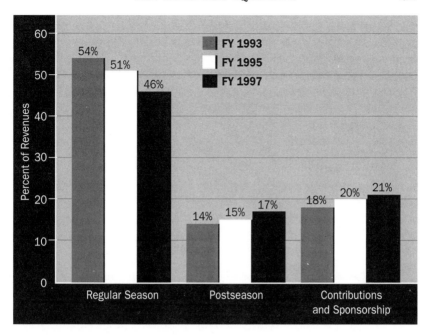

Figure 11.5. Relative Sources of Revenues, NCAA Division IA (by Year)
  Source: Daniel L. Fulks, *Revenues and Expenses of Divisions I and II Intercollegiate Athletics Programs: Financial Trends and Relationships* (Indianapolis, Ind.: National Collegiate Athletic Association, 1993, 1995, and 1997).

one ever wants to give up anything, and it is therefore easy to see why even athletic directors at schools with highly successful programs have reason to be concerned about their continued financial stability.

The increasing importance at many schools of athletically related fundraising provokes a host of questions all its own. Several commentators have questioned whether it is appropriate to credit the athletic department with all of the revenue raised from friends groups and booster organizations, on the theory that some of this money must surely have been raised at the expense of contributions to general funds.[46] It is also argued, as the converse to this proposition, that a major financial benefit of intercollegiate athletics is that it stimulates alumni/ae giving, especially if High Profile teams compile winning records. Yet we saw in the previous chapter that there is no evidence that variations in the won-lost records of either the Division IA or Ivy League schools have any beneficial effect on alumni/ae giving. Moreover, the survey results summarized there provide no indication that either donors in general or the biggest donors are obsessed with success in intercollegiate athletics. This is not to deny that an overt decision to de-emphasize athletics could have repercussions—a risk that schools generally choose to avoid.

One senior administrator has expressed serious worries about, in his words, "pushing unacceptable amounts of athletics budgets onto the annual fundraising of friends groups." Greater and greater reliance on off-budget support provided by friends groups is widespread, and it is a direct consequence of internal budgetary pressures. These pressures in turn stem from the rising costs of competing successfully in both women's and men's athletics, combined with the need inside the institution to prevent the intercollegiate athletics budget from rising faster than, say, budgeted outlays for academic programs. But such an approach entails real risks for the institution, including how to maintain institutional control over teams that are more and more independent in terms of who pays the bills. It is also sobering to recognize that the financial pressures observed in recent years have come at a time of general prosperity for the country and for most colleges and universities, including especially those that have substantial endowments. It is hard to know what internal pressures would be generated, or how they would be handled, if another period of hard times were to be experienced. One can only suppose that the pressures to find off-budget support for athletic programs would increase even more dramatically than they already have.

> A for-profit board has an obligation to *get out* of a
> bad business while a nonprofit board may have an
> obligation to *stay in,* if it is to be true to its mission.
> —John C. Whitehead, former
> under secretary of state

The emphasis on athletics as an integral part of the educational program (and, in the minds of some, the myth of "athletics as a classroom for character") has become so institutionalized that we began our study by exploring in considerable detail the "student experience" side of the athletic ledger. Now, in this chapter, we have concluded the empirical part of our research by examining the myth with which many others might have started: that college sports is an effective money-making machine. It is extremely difficult to conclude that college sports is, by any normal definition, a good business. From the coed liberal arts colleges and the Ivy League universities, where athletics are not expected to break even, to the big-time schools, where the prospect of a postseason payoff is more likely to be the justification for heavy investment, instances of true profitability are exceedingly rare—in fact, probably nonexistent if capital costs are counted. The mantra of the need to "spend money to make money" can be used to justify a great deal of spending, without leading an institution to any destination other than a deeper financial hole.

While revenues rise and fall with the competitive fortunes of the teams and even with trends in fashions (such as the popularity of college sweatshirts), expenditures are far more predictable: they just keep going up. They go up because of expanding programs, scheduling commitments, and competition to have and maintain the best facilities and coaches. *Whatever the other benefits of athletic programs are, or are perceived to be, the pursuit of net revenues is very difficult to accept as a justification.* As a money-making venture, athletics is a bad business. Nonetheless, as John Whitehead's epigraph at the beginning of this section notes, a bad business may be something that a nonprofit college or university should choose to stay in; this is clearly the rationale many non-scholarship schools (and some scholarship schools as well) give for their extensive commitments to athletics. In the concluding chapters of this study, we return to the touchstone that must guide nonprofit enterprises. The appropriate "bottom line" question is how well intercollegiate athletic programs serve an institution's core mission.

CHAPTER 12

Key Empirical Findings

It seemed both possible and just to secure a wide
expression of opinion from past players, and from
those most competent through their connection
with schools and colleges to judge as to the effect
of the game.
—Introduction, Walter Camp Commission on
Brutality in Football, 1896[1]

WE BEGIN the concluding chapters of this book by highlighting our key
empirical findings—which constitute the factual bedrock of the study. We
have used the extensive institutional records of the 30 academically selective institutions in the study to learn about the pre-collegiate preparation of athletes and other students in the 1951, 1976, and 1989 entering
cohorts and their subsequent performance in college. We have also followed the approach suggested more than a century ago by the Walter
Camp Commission on College Football and analyzed the experiences
and views of both former athletes and other students who attended these
schools. In seeking to move the debate over intercollegiate athletics beyond highly charged assertions and strongly held opinions, we use this
chapter to summarize the principal empirical findings that we believe deserve the attention of all those who share an interest in understanding
what has been happening over the course of the past half century.

Then, in Chapter 13, we step back and take stock: we interpret the overall patterns that link these findings in the context of the educational values that these colleges and universities are chartered to serve. Finally, in
Chapter 14, we suggest some approaches that might enhance the capacity of college sports to complement the educational values of colleges and
universities.

SCALE: NUMBERS OF ATHLETES AND
ATHLETIC RECRUITMENT

1. *Athletes competing on intercollegiate teams constitute a sizable share of the
undergraduate student population at many selective colleges and universities,
and especially at coed liberal arts colleges and Ivy League universities.* In 1989,

intercollegiate athletes accounted for nearly one-third of the men and approximately one-fifth of the women who entered the coed liberal arts colleges participating in this study; male and female athletes accounted for much smaller percentages of the entering classes in the Division IA scholarship schools, which of course have far larger enrollments; the Ivies are intermediate in the relative number of athletes enrolled, with approximately one-quarter of the men and 15 percent of the women playing on intercollegiate teams. Some of the much larger Division IA schools, public and private, enrolled a smaller absolute number of athletes than either the more athletically oriented coed liberal arts colleges or the Ivies—primarily because a number of the Division IA schools sponsor fewer teams.[2]

2. *The relative number of male athletes in a class has not changed dramatically over the past 40 years, but athletes in recent classes have been far more intensely recruited than used to be the case.* This statement holds for the coed liberal arts colleges as well as the universities. In 1989, roughly 90 percent of the men who played the High Profile sports of football, basketball, and hockey said that they had been recruited (the range was from 97 percent in the Division IA public universities to 83 percent in the Division III coed liberal arts colleges), and roughly two-thirds of the men who competed in other sports such as tennis, soccer, and swimming said that they too had been recruited. In the '76 cohort, these percentages were much lower; there were many more "walk-ons" in 1976 than in 1989, and there were surely fewer still in the most recent entering classes.

3. *Only tiny numbers of women athletes in the '76 entering cohort reported having been recruited, but that situation had changed markedly by the time of the '89 entering cohort; recruitment of women athletes at these schools has moved rapidly in the direction of the men's model.* Roughly half of the women in the '89 cohort who played intercollegiate sports in the Ivies and the Division IA universities reported that having been recruited by the athletic department played a significant role in their having chosen the schools they attended. The comparable percentages in the coed colleges and the women's colleges were much lower in '89, but women athletes at those schools are now also being actively recruited.

ADMISSIONS ADVANTAGES, ACADEMIC QUALIFICATIONS, AND OTHER "SELECTION" EFFECTS

1. *Athletes who are recruited, and who end up on the carefully winnowed lists of desired candidates submitted by coaches to the admissions office, now enjoy a very substantial statistical "advantage" in the admissions process—a much*

greater advantage than that enjoyed by other targeted groups such as under-represented minority students, alumni children, and other legacies; this state-ment is true for both male and female athletes. At a representative non-schol-arship school for which we have complete data on all applicants, recruited male athletes applying for admission to the '99 entering cohort had a 48 percent greater chance of being admitted than did male stu-dents at large, after taking differences in SAT scores into account; the cor-responding admissions advantage enjoyed by recruited women athletes in '99 was 53 percent. The admissions advantages enjoyed by minority students and legacies were in the range of 18 to 24 percent.

2. *The admissions advantage enjoyed by men and women athletes at this school, which there is reason to believe is reasonably typical of schools of its type, was much greater in '99 than in '89, and it was greater in '89 than in '76.* The trend—the directional signal—is unmistakably clear.

3. *One obvious consequence of assigning such a high priority to admitting re-cruited athletes is that they enter these colleges and universities with consider-ably lower SAT scores than their classmates.* This pattern holds for both men and women athletes and is highly consistent by type of school. The SAT "deficit" is most pronounced for men and women who play sports at the Division IA schools, least pronounced for women at the liberal arts col-leges (especially the women's colleges), and middling at the Ivies. Among the men at every type of school, the SAT deficits are largest for those who play the High Profile sports of football, basketball, and hockey.

4. *Admitted athletes differ from their classmates in other ways too, and there is evidence of an "athlete culture."* In addition to having weaker academic qualifications, athletes who went on to play on intercollegiate teams were clearly different in other ways at the time they entered college. They were decidedly more competitive than students at large. The male athletes were also more interested than students at large in pursuing business ca-reers and in achieving financial success (this was not true, however, of the women athletes); athletes placed considerably less emphasis on the goals of making original contributions to science or the arts. The differences between athletes and their classmates along many of these dimensions have widened with the passage of time. In addition, athletes who compete in the Lower Profile sports (such as track, swimming, lacrosse, and ten-nis) had begun, by the time of the '89 cohort, to share more of the at-tributes of the athlete culture that earlier were found mostly among the High Profile athletes. Similarly, whereas women athletes in the '76 cohort were largely indistinguishable from their classmates in most respects, by the time of the '89 cohort women who played sports had more and more in common with the male athletes (for example, entering college with both lower standardized test scores and more politically conservative views than other women students).

5. *Contrary to much popular mythology, recruitment of athletes has no marked effect on either the socioeconomic composition of these schools or on their racial diversity.* Male athletes (especially those who play High Profile sports at the Division IA schools) are more likely than students at large to come from modest socioeconomic backgrounds and to be African Americans. Nonetheless, elimination of the athletic contribution to racial diversity in the '89 cohort would have caused the percentage of African American men enrolled at these schools to decline by just 1 percentage point—an estimate obtained by recalculating the percentage of African American students who would have been enrolled had the racial mix of athletes been the same as the racial mix of students at large.[3] There would even be an opposite effect among the women, since the share of African American women playing college sports is much lower—often half the corresponding percentage—of African American women students at large. Moreover, until very recently, women athletes were more likely than other women students to come from privileged backgrounds. Those men who play Lower Profile sports continue to come from more advantaged backgrounds than either the other athletes or the rest of their male classmates.

GRADUATION RATES, UNDERPERFORMANCE IN THE CLASSROOM, AND CHOICE OF MAJOR

1. *Despite their lower SATs, athletes who attended the selective schools included in this study, along with their classmates who participated in other time-intensive extracurricular activities, graduated at very high rates.* The national problem of low graduation rates—which has attracted the attention of both the NCAA and the public—does not afflict most athletes or other students who attend these schools.

2. *When we examine grades (rank-in-class), an entirely different picture emerges: the academic standing of athletes, relative to that of their classmates, has deteriorated markedly in recent years.* Whereas male athletes in the '51 cohort were slightly more likely than other students to be in the top third of their class, only 16 percent of those in the '89 cohort finished in the top third, and 58 percent finished in the bottom third. Women athletes in the '76 cohort did as well academically as other women, but women athletes in the '89 cohort were more likely than other women to be in the bottom third of the class. This pattern is especially pronounced in those sets of schools where women athletes were highly recruited; the women's colleges are alone in showing no gap at all in academic per-

formance between women athletes and other women students in the '89 cohort.

3. *Only part of this decline in the academic performance of athletes can be attributed to their lower levels of aptitude or preparation at the time they began college; they consistently underperform academically even after we control for differences in standardized test scores and other variables.* Academic underperformance among athletes is a pervasive phenomenon. In the '89 cohort, it is found among both male and female athletes and among those who played all types of sports (not just among the men who played football, basketball, and hockey); it is more pronounced within the Ivy League and the coed liberal arts colleges than it is within the Division IA schools.

4. *Academic underperformance in college has roots in high school academic performance, in the priority assigned by athletes to academics, and in the "culture of sport."* The degree of underperformance varies not only with precollege academic indicators, but also with how many other athletes who played on the same teams underperformed (possible peer effects) and whether athletes cited a coach as a principal mentor. The "culture of sport" interpretation of this pattern is supported by evidence showing that students who were active in other time-intensive extracurricular activities *overperformed* academically, relative to their SAT scores and other predictors.

5. *Male athletes have become highly concentrated in certain fields of study, especially the social sciences, and female athletes have started to show different patterns of majors as well.* At one Ivy League university, 54 percent of all High Profile athletes majored in economics or political science as compared with 18 percent of male students at large. When considered in the light of differences in career and financial goals, many of the choices of field of study by male athletes seem to be driven by a desire for something akin to a business major. More generally, this evidence on academic concentrations is consistent with other data on rooming patterns in suggesting a greatly increased tendency for athletes to band together. In the 1950s, male athletes were much more broadly distributed across fields of study and, in general, were more like their classmates in all respects.

ADVANCED DEGREES, CAREERS, AND EARNINGS

1. *Women athletes in the '76 cohort (but not in the '89 cohort) were more likely than their peers to earn advanced degrees of every kind; this was not true of the men, however.* Male athletes were more likely than other male students to earn no advanced degree and also more likely to earn MBAs; they were less likely to earn Ph.D.s. Differences between athletes and other students in advanced degree attainment must be seen in context: all students who attended these selective schools, athletes and others, were far more likely to earn advanced degrees than were most graduates of four-year colleges.

2. *Consistent with patterns of advanced degree attainment, male athletes are more likely than other men in their classes to have chosen jobs in business and finance and less likely to have become scientists, engineers, academics, or doctors or lawyers.* These differences were smaller in the '51 cohort than in the '76 cohort (to the extent they existed at all in the 1950s), and they are magnified when we look at the early vocational choices made by the members of the '89 cohort. High Profile athletes have always been somewhat more interested in careers in marketing than either other athletes or students at large, and this vocational preference appears to have intensified in the most recent cohort. Athletes in the '89 cohort were appreciably *less* likely than their classmates to work in computer science and other technologically driven fields.

3. *Male athletes consistently earned more money than their classmates.* The average earnings of former athletes exceed the average earnings of students at large in the '51, '76, and '89 cohorts. This pattern is also found in every type of school, ranging from the coed liberal arts colleges to the Division IA public universities. These consistent differences are on the order of 10 percent.

4. *The earnings advantage of male athletes is attributable to both pre-college differences and post-college choices.* Athletes are more likely than students at large to work in the for-profit and self-employment sectors; moreover, within the for-profit sector, the earnings advantage of athletes is highly concentrated in financial services occupations. There is no significant difference in the average earnings of athletes and of students at large in law and medicine, among those who are CEOs of for-profit enterprises, or in any of the fields within the not-for-profit and governmental sectors. Thus the earnings advantage of male athletes is not an across-the-board phenomenon, and its location in financial services suggests that it is mainly a function of some combination of (a) the vocational interests of male athletes; (b) the special advantages of athlete-alumni networks in fields such as financial services; and (c) the special contribution to marketplace success in these fields of personal traits often associated with being an athlete (such as a high level of competitiveness, discipline, focus on achieving well-defined goals, and ability to take direction and work in teams).

5. *In general, the earnings of male athletes are not associated with how many years they played sports in college.* This lack of any association leads us to believe that the earnings advantages enjoyed by athletes are related more to who they were, what they had already learned, and what they wanted when they entered college than to the amount of further "training" ("treatment") that they received by playing college sports. One clear exception to this pattern is that the small number of High Profile athletes who played for four years earned appreciably more than their teammates—a finding that we suspect indicates the presence of a kind of "credentialing" or "celebrity" effect. Those male athletes who earned letters for four years in the High Profile sports are likely to be the visible stars, who are most likely to have been known by alumni and who may then have had especially good opportunities to enter high-paying occupations in fields where connections are often especially useful.

6. *Intensity of the level of play does not translate into superior later life outcomes for male athletes, as measured by earnings.* On the contrary, the earnings advantage enjoyed by athletes is smallest among those who played at the Division IA public universities and, if anything, larger for the men who played at the Division III level in coed liberal arts colleges than for those who participated in more elaborate programs in the Ivies or in the Division IA private universities. Also, there is no relation between the won-lost record of the team on which a student played and how much that student earned later in life.

7. *Women athletes in the '76 cohort were more likely than their female peers to be working full-time, to be either doctors or academics (unlike the male athletes, who were disproportionately found in business fields), and, like the men who played sports, to enjoy a sizable earnings advantage over their women classmates; moreover, within the for-profit sector, the relative earnings advantage of the '76 women athletes is even larger than the earnings advantage of their male counterparts.* These patterns reflect both the high overall academic achievements of these '76 women athletes (who were only rarely recruited as athletes and met the same admissions requirements as all other women students) and the atypically high levels of drive and ambition often associated with playing college sports. In many respects, these '76 women athletes resemble the men who played sports in the 1950s.

8. *In contrast, women athletes in the '89 cohort are no more likely than other women to have earned, or to be earning, advanced degrees, and they do not enjoy any earnings advantages over their peers.* These women are of course at very early stages in their post-college lives, and much may change over time. But the '89 women athletes differ from their predecessors in having been more actively recruited as athletes, in having entered with weaker academic profiles, and in having subsequently underperformed academically. The experiences to date of the '76 women athletes may be poor predictors of what latter-day women athletes will go on to do.

9. *There is no evidence that earnings for women athletes are enhanced by larger "doses" of athletic training in college.* There is no consistent association of any kind between years of play and earnings; nor is there any association between the earnings advantages enjoyed by women athletes and the intensity of the level of play. In fact, the Division IA private universities are the only group of schools at which women athletes enjoyed *no* earnings advantage; conversely, the highest earnings advantage accorded college athletes in the '76 cohort is found in the women's colleges.

LEADERSHIP

1. *Athletes were more likely than other students to rate themselves highly as leaders before college began and were also more likely to say, after college, that leadership had played an important role in their lives; yet, surprisingly, neither this greater inclination to provide leadership, nor this stronger expression of its importance, is associated with evidence of having actually provided more leadership.* Athletes and their classmates seem about on a par in this regard. Athletes were no more likely than other students to become CEOs, to earn top salaries in professional fields like law and medicine (where earnings may serve as a proxy for leadership), or to be leaders in most civic activities.

2. *Athletes are leaders in exceptionally large numbers in two specific arenas— alumni/ae activities and youth groups (men only)—and having been a college athlete appears to have measurable effects on the priorities that these leaders emphasize.* This is clearest in the case of alumni/ae leadership. Former athletes who now serve as trustees and in other leadership capacities are more likely to favor increasing the emphasis their school places on intercollegiate athletics than are other alumni leaders, alumni at large, or even other alumni who played sports in college.

3. *In the aggregate, alumni/ae from all three eras and from all types of institutions want their schools to place less, not more, emphasis on intercollegiate athletics than the schools do at present.* When asked about their schools' institutional priorities, the alumni/ae consistently wanted more emphasis placed on undergraduate teaching, residential life, and extracurricular activities—but not on intercollegiate atheletics. Former athletes, on the other hand, favor placing more emphasis on intercollegiate athletics.

GIVING BACK TO THE COLLEGE OR UNIVERSITY

1. *In common with high academic achievers and students who were heavily involved in extracurricular activities, former athletes have generally had above-average general giving rates.* All three of these groups have "bonded" more closely with their schools than have most students, in part because they may feel that they had unusually successful and enjoyable experiences as undergraduates. Such feelings of attachment may be the primary reason why these groups have been so supportive of the broad educational purposes of their institutions.

2. *The High Profile athletes at the Division IA schools are a revealing exception to this pattern: they are* much *less likely than others to be contributors.* The main reason, we suspect, is that these High Profile athletes are more likely to be focused on their athletic pursuits and may see themselves as a group apart from the larger academic community (and may even disidentify with it). General giving rates among High Profile athletes have declined over time, relative to the giving rates of others, at both the Division IA private universities and the coed liberal arts colleges (although not in the Ivies)—a finding that may reflect what appears to be a growing separation of athletes on many campuses from the rest of the campus community. Striking evidence in support of this interpretation is provided by the *lack* of any decline in general giving rates on the part of either the academic high achievers or the students active in extracurricular activities.

3. *The data flatly contradict one of the strongest myths about college athletics—namely, that winning teams, and especially winning football teams, have a large, positive impact on giving rates.* Winning football teams do not inspire increased giving on the part of alumni/ae at Division IA private universities or Ivy League schools. Surprisingly, it is only at the coed liberal arts colleges, where teams generally receive less recognition, that winning is associated with increased alumni/ae giving, a finding that can be attributed mainly to the exceptionally large number of former athletes found among the alumni/ae of these schools.

THE FINANCIAL EQUATION: COSTS AND REVENUES ASSOCIATED WITH INTERCOLLEGIATE SPORTS

1. *Expenditures on intercollegiate athletics, excluding capital costs, vary tremendously depending on the level of play at which the institution competes.* Total expenditures, excluding capital costs, reach the $50 million level at

a university such as the University of Michigan, which offers a wide range of highly competitive big-time programs; $20 to $25 million at a more "standard" Division IA university; $10 million at an Ivy League university; and $1.5 million at a coed liberal arts college.

   2. *Level of play has a surprisingly large effect on expenditures on sports such as tennis, swimming, and field hockey, as well as on football and basketball.* Direct annual expenditures on one of these Lower Profile sports may range from $350,000 at a Division IA university, to $125,000 in the Ivy League, to $40,000 at a coed liberal arts college. Thus the budgetary consequences of choosing one level of competition over another are considerable.

   3. *Revenues from athletics, including gate receipts and television and bowl revenues, can offset most, and sometimes all, of the costs of big-time programs if (and only if) teams are consistently successful; even in these settings, most schools lose money, and it is unlikely that any school comes close to covering its full costs if proper allowances are made for the capital-intensive nature of athletics.* We estimate that the overall *net costs* of an intercollegiate sports program, exclusive of capital costs, may range from zero for the most competitively successful big-time programs, to $7 to $8 million at both the "standard" Division IA private universities and the Ivies, to $1.5 million at a coed liberal arts college. Net spending ranges from $2,500 per intercollegiate athlete per year at a coed liberal arts college, to $9,000 per year at an Ivy League school, to $18,000 per year at a "standard" Division IA private university.

   4. *Athletic budgets, seen on a "net" basis, should be regarded as expenditures by the institution that must be justified in terms of the contribution they do or do not make to the core educational mission of the school.* In only the rarest case can athletic expenditures be justified as an "investment" that will somehow benefit the institution's bottom line. Moreover, the increasing volatility of athletic revenues (at those schools where revenues from sponsorships and licensing are consequential) means that the financial risk factor associated with big-time programs cannot be ignored.

CHAPTER 13

Taking Stock

The defects of American college athletics are two: commercialism, and a negligent attitude toward the educational opportunity for which the college exists.

—1929 Carnegie Commission Report[1]

THE FINDINGS OF this study demonstrate that the twin concerns expressed by the Carnegie Commission in 1929 have by no means gone away in the intervening years; on the contrary, both have become even more worrying. But before saying more about modern-day manifestations of these concerns, it is essential to recall that the authors of the Carnegie study also recognized the positive contributions of college sports. "Such qualities as loyalty, self-reliance, modesty, cooperation, self-sacrifice, courage, and, above all, honesty," the report emphasized, "can be more readily and directly cultivated through the activities and habits of the playing field than in almost any other phase of college life."[2] We agree, and we would add that college sports can be very important in bolstering community spirit on a campus. In pursuing these eminently worthwhile goals, colleges and universities have made ever larger investments in talented athletes and in institutionalizing intercollegiate sports programs.

Much of this study has focused on spillover effects—the unintended by-products of the building of ambitious athletic programs under what are clearly admirable banners. In this chapter we seek first to summarize the major changes that have taken place and then to reflect upon the dynamics that have produced—and continue to fuel—the intense competition to excel in intercollegiate athletics at all levels of play.

A major unifying theme of this study is that an ever larger divide has opened up between two worlds. One is an ever more intense athletics enterprise—with an emphasis on specialized athletic talent, more commercialization, and a set of norms and values that can be seen as constituting a culture of sports. The other is the core teaching-research function of selective colleges and universities, with its own increasing specialization, a charge to promote educational values such as learning for its own sake, and a strong sense of obligation to provide educational opportunity to those who will make the most of it—all in a time when the good of the society is increasingly dependent on the effective development and deployment of intellectual capital. This widening athletic-academic divide—its pervasiveness and subtlety—is the core of this book's message.

THE CHANGING FACE OF COLLEGE SPORTS

Rationing Educational Opportunity

Today, as in the 1920s, many of those who play college sports enjoy the experience and benefit from it. But supporting the extensive intercollegiate programs that exist today also entails substantial costs, and the most important may not be the readily apparent dollar outlays required to field teams, build facilities, and (in the case of the Division IA schools) provide athletic scholarships. One of the most valuable resources that the leading colleges and universities must ration is the limited number of places in each entering class. For the most academically selective schools, admissions is a zero-sum game: the more athletes who are recruited, the less room there is for other students.

Recruiting athletes for up to 40 intercollegiate teams at colleges and universities that are vastly oversubscribed by talented applicants has major opportunity costs—especially at the smaller Ivy League universities and the coed liberal arts colleges. In this crucial respect, the consequences of athletic recruitment are far more serious for these schools than for large universities with big-time programs. In the words of a former president of a distinguished public university, "Yes, it was embarrassing when there was a scandal of one kind or another, but the number of athletes was so small relative to the size of the student body that whatever they did or didn't do in the classroom or on the campus didn't really affect the place as a whole." *Athletics is a much more serious business, in terms of its direct impact on admissions and the composition and ethos of the student body, at an Ivy League school or a coed liberal arts college than it is at a Division IA university.* This basic point is often overlooked. Highly publicized incidents at big-time schools get all the press—and they are very important for what they say to both campus communities and a broad public about the values of the institution—but the issues of direct educational consequence flowing from the recruitment of large numbers of athletes are much more serious at the schools where athletes constitute anywhere from 15 to 35 percent of the student body.

Unlike some situations in big-time sports, in which coaches and players are literally at each other's throats, highly visible athletes are arrested for beating up their girlfriends, or self-important boosters contribute to the exploitation of athletes without any thought for their well-being, there are no villains associated with this part of the story. In writing about the implications of athletic recruitment for the rationing of educational opportunity, we most emphatically do not mean to suggest that the athletes who are admitted are bad people, that they will not benefit from attending these schools, or that attending one of these institutions will fail to help them achieve their personal goals. The more difficult, and more relevant, question is whether admitting other students in their place might not have done even more to fulfill the educational mission of the school.

The greatly increased competition for places in the leading schools makes this question far more important today than it used to be. In 1929, when the Carnegie report warned about how athletics might represent a threat to educational opportunity, the Commission members could not have known how scarce and valued those opportunities would become over the course of the century. One factor in the increasingly competitive college admissions process is that, over the past fifty years, new players have been allowed into the game—as women, minority students, and individuals from all socioeconomic classes have been encouraged to seek places where previously they may not have been welcome. Moreover, as our society has moved increasingly toward a knowledge-driven economy, the pressure to obtain the best possible education and to obtain credentials that will open the right doors has become ever more intense. Many students could further their individual goals by attending great universities like the University of North Carolina at Chapel Hill and Columbia, or colleges like Wellesley and Williams, but only so many can attend each year. These schools provide a flexible pool of opportunity that can be utilized in many ways. In addition to the educational advantages that they offer are reputational advantages and the connections that one makes by attending these schools. Having a degree from a leading college or university is helpful in getting a job on Wall Street, getting into graduate school, or making connections in the art world. Deciding who should have such opportunities is extremely challenging, and the outcomes of the admissions process reveal a great deal about how a college or university truly sees—and pursues—its mission.

Taking Full Advantage of Academic Opportunities

Faculty often remark that the most discouraging aspect of teaching is encountering a student who just does not seem to care, who has to be cajoled into thinking about the reading, who is obviously bored in class, or who resists rewriting a paper that is passable but not very good. Such students are failing to take full advantage of the educational opportunities that these colleges and universities are there to provide.

Uninspired students come in all sizes and shapes, and no one would suggest that athletes are uniformly different from other students in this regard. But the evidence presented in this book does demonstrate a consistent tendency for athletes to do less well academically than their classmates—and, even more troubling, a consistent tendency for athletes to underperform academically not just relative to other students, but relative to how they themselves might have been expected to perform.[3] *These tendencies have become more pronounced over time and all-pervasive: academic underperformance is now found among women athletes as well as men, among those who play the Lower Profile sports as well as those on football and basketball teams, and among athletes playing at the Division III level of competition as well as those playing in bowl games and competing for national championships.*

If we take seriously the notion that students should take full advantage of what are very scarce educational opportunities, evidence of high graduation rates should not end the conversation. It is not good enough, we believe, just to get by. Respect for core academic values and the educational mission of these schools requires more than that. Otherwise, colleges and universities are failing to put their most valuable resources— their faculty and their academic offerings—to their highest and best use. In the telling words of the Carnegie report of 1929, they are displaying "a negligent attitude toward the educational opportunity for which the college exists." They are not focused on fulfilling their educational missions.

Rationing Athletic Opportunity

Everyone agrees that opportunities to play on teams can be beneficial (and fun!) for the participants, and in earlier days many college students played several sports, sometimes even learned to play sports they had not played before, and were able to enjoy the satisfaction of dramatically improving their skills. One of the many ironies of the ever increasing intensification of college sports, even at the Division III level, is that many of those who might arguably have benefited the most from college athletics now have little or no chance of being on a team. Standards of performance have risen so dramatically, specialization has become so important, and youngsters hone their skills at such a young age that there is less and less opportunity for the true "walk-on" or late-developing athlete to participate. As recruiting intensifies and incoming athletes become more and more proficient, the benefits of playing on college teams are bestowed increasingly on those who are already "trained up."

Concurrently, intercollegiate programs demand more and more of those who, as a result of extensive pre-college preparation, can qualify for the team. Swimmers are often in the pool up to four hours per day Monday through Friday, and year-round training, in one form or another, is common in most sports; the notion of a clearly demarcated "season" is becoming an anomaly. One obvious consequence is the decreasing number of students who play two or more intercollegiate sports. Another direct consequence is that the more broadly interested student who wants to play sports but also to do many other things is conflicted and may just opt out. We learned a great deal about these conflicts through talking with an Ivy League graduate who had been a star soccer player in high school. He spoke with great regret about his decision to limit his goal-scoring talent to intramural contests. "I just didn't think that I could spend the time that I would have had to in order to play at that [varsity] level, and still be able to cut it academically." What was fascinating was that this student saw his decision not to go out for the team to be *his* failing, rather than that of a program that placed such heavy demands on students who wanted to do more than just play soccer. In another scenario, this talented soccer player might have been able to enjoy the thrill of playing for his college, gotten the education that he wanted, and not blamed himself for failing to be able to do both at what the sports marketing brochures speak of as "the highest level of excellence."

The Athlete Culture: Campus Ethos

In part because of the increased degree of high-intensity "professionalization" that discourages ordinary students from competing, intercollegiate athletes have become a less and less central part of the main campus scene. This reality is of course attributable not only to changes in intercollegiate athletics. The broader changes in faculty cultures described at length in Chapter 3 (perhaps especially the greater emphasis on academic disciplines and specialized research accomplishments) have almost certainly made it harder for the highly focused athlete to feel truly welcome on many campuses. As we pointed out in the introduction to this chapter, it is the *combination* of greater intensity in athletics and greater academic intensity that has led to the growing divide between athletes and much of the rest of the campus community at many of the schools in this study.

The separateness of many athletes is most evident in the case of those playing High Profile sports at universities with big-time programs. Such students may be housed in athletic dorms, have their own tutors, and in large measure exist in their own world. But our research, and the work of others, suggests that an athlete culture has spread quite widely and can now be found in small coed liberal arts colleges and Ivy League universities as well as in Division IA universities offering athletic scholarships and other amenities. Social psychologists have documented these self-isolating tendencies in the norms and values of Ivy League athletes as well as in the ways that they spend their time, and we have tracked how male and female athletes are increasingly "banding together" in certain fields of study. The declining tendency for athletes, and especially High Profile athletes, to demonstrate their general interest in the school through financial contributions may be another harbinger of where current trends in athletics are leading us.

We have little direct evidence as to the effects of this culture on the rest of the campus community, and it would be a mistake to exaggerate them. At the same time, it would also be a mistake to be too sanguine, especially since differences in values and interests between athletes and other students continue to widen, women's athletic programs look more and more like those of the men, and athletes are increasingly being recruited on the basis of talent that differentiates them from other students.

Campus interest in attending sports events still serves as one way of bringing students, faculty, alumni/ae, and townspeople together under the school's banner. The long-term decline in student attendance at college sporting events reminds us, however, that this contribution of intercollegiate competition to the campus ethos has become less and less important. There is no denying the appeal of other activities, from playing recreational sports to spending time online, at the same time that aggressively marketed professional sports events are now available on too many television channels to count. Looking ahead, it would be a serious error to expect any resurgence of campus-based attendance at college sports events.

The Athlete Culture: Life after College

Including in the class a large number of highly recruited athletes has a number of other, less direct, effects on the rationing of opportunity since, as a colleague once put it, "people come in packages." In the case of men, in particular, we have seen that there is a strong correlation between being an athlete, having a strong interest in achieving financial success, seeing college as a means to this end, and pursuing careers in fields such as finance. The strong tendency for athletes to concentrate in the social sciences and to opt for business and communications majors (where they are offered) is clearly related to these goals, as is their subsequent tendency to enroll in MBA programs. More generally, the "athlete culture" has a set of norms, values, and goals that are coherent, largely independent of socioeconomic status, and different from those of other groups of students attending the same institutions. This culture has natural affinities with what University of Chicago economist Frank Knight has called the "business game." Games with clear goals and rules, where competitive instincts, team play, and discipline are rewarded, provide a link between the culture of sports and marketplace pursuits.

There is certainly nothing wrong with this confluence of the values of sports and those of the business world. Colleges and universities are surely right to take pride in the accomplishments of their graduates who succeed in the "business game." There are, however, two questions that give us pause and deserve consideration.

First, is there a risk that the focused career interests of many athletes will cause them to neglect the broader educational opportunities offered by schools that describe themselves as liberal arts colleges and universities? These schools want to educate business leaders, but they want to educate business leaders who will understand the complexities of the world in which they are working and the importance of participating effectively in shaping that world in positive ways. The utility of the strong competitive drives associated with athletics depends on the values and the ends to which these drives are directed. As Knight put it, "If . . . one adopts the view that the end of life is to get things done, the case for competition becomes much stronger; but even here misgivings arise. It is hard to avoid asking, *what things*. If it is thought to be important which things are done, competition may be entirely indifferent and unselective, equally effective as a drive toward worthy and unworthy ends."[4]

One of the great advantages of attending colleges that emphasize the liberal arts, as their catalogues properly proclaim, is that the breadth of the educational experience, and the emphasis on values and first principles, *can* help students harness their learning and their energies in ways that serve the broader goals of the society. This is, in fact, a core educational mission of these schools. It is not, however, a "treatment" that "takes" without the willing participation of those given the opportunity of learning in such an environment; in this regard, the decidedly weaker interest in gaining a broad liberal education expressed by the athletes is problematic. The debate at Yale over what kind of economics to teach (see Chapter 3) is one subtle example of how pre-professional business interests could affect the curriculum.

The second question focuses on the effects of athletic recruitment on the mix of students in the school. When recruited athletes make up such a substantial fraction of the entering class in at least some colleges and universities, is there a risk that there will be too few places for others who want to become poets, scientists, and leaders of civic causes? Is there a possibility that, without realizing what is leading to what, the schools themselves will become unbalanced in various ways? For example, will they feel a need to devote more and more of their teaching resources to fields such as business and economics that are disproportionately elected by athletes, in lieu of investing more heavily in less "practical" fields such as classics, physics, and language study? Similarly, as one commentator put the question, what are the effects on those students interested in fields like philosophy? Could they feel at risk of being devalued?

In an ideal world, we would suppose, schools would like to see a diversity of majors, values, and career choices among all subgroups of students. In our view, society is best served when the financial services sector "inherits" some students who have a deep commitment to understanding history and culture (rather than mainly those with a more narrow focus on earning a great deal of money as an end in and of itself). In the same way, academia benefits when some of those who pursue Ph.D.s also have learned some of the lessons about life that one gains on the playing fields (rather than just those with a more narrow focus on an arcane, if not obscure, realm of academic research). In short, the heavy concentration of male athletes, in particular, in certain fields of study raises real questions of institutional priorities and balance.

Allocating Financial Resources

If intercollegiate sports was self-financing and raised no resource allocation questions for colleges and universities, the issues discussed thus far would still be consequential. Unmeasured "costs," including especially the opportunity costs associated with admitting Smith but not Jones, matter enormously at academically selective institutions. But it is also true that intercollegiate athletics programs involve the expenditure of a great deal of money. We were surprised to learn how high the net costs are (after taking account of revenue offsets) at the vast majority of the schools in our study. An obvious question is whether so much money really needs to be spent to achieve the benefits of well-conceived athletic programs. This is an issue for colleges and universities of all kinds, not just for those that are academically selective.

Here we note only that students who might be interested in other extracurricular pursuits—putting out the school paper or acting on stage, for example—have no comparable, equally expensive, infrastructure supporting them. Each assistant football coach takes the place of the non-existent journalism coach who would indubitably make the campus paper even better than it is absent such coaching. Disproportionate funding follows disproportionate athletic recruiting and succeeds in enabling a level of professionalism—but only in one particular area. It is useful to remember that per-student expenditures on *all* student services combined (including core functions such as the admissions office) are in the range

of $2,000 to $3,000 at these institutions, as compared with athletic outlays of $8,000 per individual athlete in the Ivies, to take that one point of
comparison.

As he altered the university's funding structure to provide more
resources for the athletic program at Vanderbilt, Chancellor Joe Wyatt
acknowledged the reality of competing claims on scarce funds. As long
as unrestricted University funds are being used to subsidize athletics, he
noted, "the long-term effect may be to seriously impair Vanderbilt's ability to invest in some critical educational and research programs. And
there is little doubt that such an outcome could jeopardize Vanderbilt's
standing among the best universities in the nation." Wyatt also drew attention to the findings of a survey of parents of current students that
found that they placed the highest priority on the quality of teaching, the
quality of the faculty, the emphasis on undergraduate education, and
preparation for future employment. Parents were pleased with Vanderbilt's performance on these scales, but they were split on the question of
whether Vanderbilt was doing a good enough job controlling costs.
Although they were willing to pay more to improve educational quality,
Wyatt observed, "It seems safe to conclude that real or perceived increases in cost that do not contribute directly to the priorities related to
educational quality would not be well received by Vanderbilt parents."[5]

Commercialization

One way of limiting the expenditure of general funds on athletics is to attract revenues from commercial sponsors, and, as we saw in Chapter 11,
this is an approach that has proved increasingly attractive to schools—the
admonitions of the 1929 Carnegie report notwithstanding. At the schools
with big-time athletic programs, winning consistently in the High Profile
sports has very large financial consequences. There is no denying the
attendant incentives and pressures: on coaches, the admissions process,
academic programs followed by athletes who must stay eligible, scheduling of games, housing and training athletes, and on and on. Controlling
these pressures is not easy, and there is an obvious danger that the academic integrity of the institution will be corrupted.

These risks are greatest at private and public universities that both
compete at the Division IA level and have demanding academic programs. As President Emeritus Arnold Weber of Northwestern has
stressed, such issues are qualitatively different in Division IA than elsewhere. But these temptations and pressures are by no means confined to
the Division IA level of play or to athletic programs that generate large
amounts of revenue. The Princeton wrestling vignette illustrates the ten-

sions unleashed when alumni wish to substitute their financial support of a team for the support previously provided by the school. "Self-funded" teams, in the language used by the NCAA, can all too easily move outside the control of the institution. To whom will the coach paid by the "friends" group feel the most loyalty?

No revenues come without costs, some of which are less a threat to the budget than to the institution's mission. Selling students' uniforms as billboards to sneaker companies becomes tricky when an athlete decides that he or she objects to the labor practices of the company and refuses to wear the symbol. Letting boosters have an important say in the admissions process (sometimes subtly, through their relationships with coaches) represents another kind of infringement of material interests on the practices of the schools. These dangers are akin to similar dilemmas elsewhere on campus; one common example can be seen in how universities manage medical, scientific, or technological research with major commercial potential that is funded by external sponsors. It would be naïve to believe that financial inducements affect only the conduct of the athletic department; commercialization of athletics does, however, serve as a prism through which broader issues of institutional mission can be seen in clear relief.

In need of funds to carry out their mission, schools (and museums and zoos and orchestras) go into the marketplace. Sometimes, the revenue found there becomes habit forming, leading orchestras to perform Beethoven's Ninth night after night, magazines to resist commissioning investigative stories about companies that advertise in their pages, and colleges to offer just one more accounting class in place of one more course in philosophy. It is unrealistic (and, as Phillipe de Montebello of the Metropolitan Museum of Art said in a recent interview, unbecomingly righteous[6]) to deny a place in the museum for museum shops or to ignore entirely what prospective students want to study when designing a curriculum. Nevertheless, maintaining an appropriate balance between the pulls of the marketplace and the core educational values of colleges and universities produces a very real predicament: the more that colleges tell students and their parents that their $120,000 "investment" is the best one they will ever make, the greater the temptation to define the purposes of education in the currency of the marketplace.

It is abundantly clear that colleges and universities today face an array of market realities that are only partly—and in some schools, only in relatively small measure—the result of the increasing commercialization of athletics. In pursuing a wider and wider range of opportunities to earn income (the burgeoning interest in making lectures available over the Internet is a recent example), schools and other not-for-profits may be required to act like businesses: examples range from the fancy marketing brochures that schools distribute in their search for applicants to the highly professionalized fundraising machinery that now exists at almost all private and public institutions. More complex, and ultimately as important, are the financing and marketing of patented inventions and other forms of intellectual property. Done correctly, all of these activities can benefit the educational purposes of the host institution. But there is also the risk of what has been called "mission drift."

Economist Burton Weisbrod describes the threat to the mission of nonprofits in the marketplace:

When nonprofits seek opportunities to raise revenue by producing goods or services they can sell profitably, they enter the domain of the private, for-profit firm. There, the drive for profit demands attention to costs and revenues and, hence, to avoidance of activities that, however desirable they may be from a societal perspective, do not generate profit. What happens when nonprofits' pursuit of revenue drives them to act like private firms?

The answer . . . is not simple. There are dangers of goal displacement, as the social mission slips from sight in the drive for revenue. Aggressive marketing and merchandising produce almost inevitable conflict, sometimes forcing organizations to choose between "capitalist appetites" and . . . integrity.[7]

As always, the hard question is how to garner the resources needed to mount a scholarly exhibition or provide a good liberal education without subverting the mission of the institution in the process. An unavoidable question is whether the norms and values associated with an athlete culture end up having an overly commercialized impact on the campus ethos, and eventually, on how an institution interprets its mission.

Sending Signals

High school students, their parents, and their schools watch attentively for the signals that colleges and universities send. The more that leading colleges and universities signal *through their actions* how much they value athletic prowess, the greater the emphasis that potential applicants will place on these activities. The issuing of rewards based on sports accomplishments supports (and in fact makes real) the message that sports is the road to opportunity.[8] Young people in schools of all kinds—from prep schools to inner-city schools—are less likely to get a message that the way upward is to learn to write computer code or take chemistry seriously when it is not only the pros and the big-time schools, but also the Ivies and the most selective liberal arts colleges, that place a large premium on athletic prowess, focus, and specialization. Athletic scholarships and tickets of admission to non-scholarship schools provide a more powerful incentive than the promises contained in high-minded proclamations.

Henry Louis Gates, W.E.B. DuBois Professor at Harvard University, on just how clearly the signals are read among young African Americans:

The blind pursuit of attainment in sports is having a devastating effect on our people. Imbued with a belief that our principal avenue to fame and profit is through sports and seduced by a win-at-any-cost system that corrupts even elementary school students, far too many black kids treat basketball courts and football fields as if they were classrooms in an alternative school system. "O.K., I flunked English," a young athlete will say. "But I got an A plus in slam-dunking."[9]

Some of the clearest signals are those sent to secondary schools that rate themselves by their success in getting their students admitted to the most selective colleges and universities. The admission of talented athletes to these highly selective and academically oriented colleges and universities sends signals to many parties, as Peter Philip, former dean of admission and financial aid at the Hotchkiss School and now headmaster of the Tower School, explained in an interview:

Look first at the message sent to the athlete. She or he may well be confused as to the true reason for the offer of admission. Even if she had an excellent academic record, she might rightly conclude that she was admitted because she is an outstanding athlete. This cheapens her academic accomplishments and suggests that her athletic achievements in college will be more highly regarded than anything she accomplishes academically.

Look next at the message sent to a school community when a disproportionate number of admissions to the most selective colleges go to prominent athletes. Again, whatever the academic accomplishments of the admitted athlete, the community will read a mixed message. Needless to say, there are occasions when the admitted athlete is not a particularly successful student. This admission sends a very clear message. As students who have assembled virtually perfect academic records are denied by the most selective colleges while their peers whose athletic accomplishments have earned recognition are accepted, the perceived value of the academic program is diluted.

Finally, look at the message sent to the [secondary] school's administration. Especially if it is an independent school, it will naturally be concerned with its "college list." Like it or not, the fancier the college list, the more attractive the school will be to many families. When the school sees that many of its "most successful" college applicants are recruited athletes, it will . . . begin its own recruitment of athletes.

Taken together, this signaling process has a powerful impact. We were told of one specific situation in which almost *half* the students from a leading prep school admitted to an Ivy League university were either outstanding hockey or lacrosse players—and not particularly noteworthy students. When asked at a recruiting session in a large city about the success of his prep school in placing its students in the most prestigious colleges, the school's representative gave the absolute number of students admitted to this Ivy League school, hoped that no one would ask him how many of the admittees had been athletes, and went home with mixed feelings about his presentation. The real issue, however, is not about how forthcoming the prep school representative was in explaining his school's success in placing students than the nature of the reality that underlies that "success."

FORCES AT WORK SHAPING THE FACE OF ATHLETICS

The present-day face of intercollegiate athletics at academically selective colleges and universities is seen most clearly when it is juxtaposed with a corresponding snapshot taken in the 1950s. Much has changed, and it is important that those who grew up in those days understand how profound the changes have been. In 1955, the offensive linemen at Denison University averaged 196 pounds; in 1999, they averaged 251 pounds. In 1955, the 50-yard freestyle swimming record at Denison was 22.8 seconds; by 1999, it had dropped to 19.9 seconds. Much has changed, throughout the system. How has this happened?

Specialization, Athletic Recruitment, and Admissions

One of the most powerful forces driving these changes has been the increasing proficiency of high school athletes and the attendant increase in sports specialization by athletes at younger and younger ages. Outstanding goalies, lacrosse players, field hockey stars, squash and tennis players, golfers, swimmers, and runners (never mind punters and point guards) are identified much earlier than used to be the case. In Chapter 1, we cited an article describing how parents hire $70-per-hour batting coaches for their Little Leaguers. Stories abound about parents pushing children to excel in soccer or softball in the hope they will thereby gain admission to a good college and maybe even earn an athletic scholarship. The extent of the problem is illustrated vividly by a recent account of an effort by one thoughtful community leader to discourage a zealous basketball coach from starting a *second-grade* traveling team.[10]

This world of highly proficient and highly specialized young athletes calls out for a different kind of athletic recruiting than what sufficed before. Coaches must be sure that they enroll the right position players, that the prospective athletes they are recruiting can fit within the system they use, and that the right mix of talents is assembled. Lists of desired recruits drawn up by coaches are much more closely tailored to specific needs than they used to be. It is easier than in earlier years to know who is *the* most talented point guard or high school tennis player (thanks to camps, regional tournaments, and other structured ways of ranking individuals), and since the team's success now depends much more than before on the athletic skills that recruited athletes bring with them to campus, the pressure to admit the top-ranked athletes is strong indeed.

The most obvious consequence of this evolution in standards of performance and specialization of skills is that the coaches play a far more important role in determining *which* athletically talented applicants gain admission. It will not do to rely on the admissions office to look at a longish list of athletically talented candidates and then choose, say, half of them on the basis of criteria related marginally, if at all, to the very specific needs of the basketball or softball team. Assuming that the candidates on a coach's list are above the required academic threshold (defined by SAT scores, Academic Index requirements in the Ivy League, NCAA standards in the Division IA programs, and so on), admissions staff are understandably reluctant to override ("usurp") the coach's judgment as to which individual candidates will be the most valuable additions to the team.[11]

We infer that this changing model of athletic recruitment and admissions goes a long way toward explaining the changes that have occurred in the characteristics and performance of athletes over the time period covered by our study. Consider the women athletes in the '76 cohort. The mid- to late 1970s were still relatively early days for women's intercollegiate sports, and it is noteworthy that only a tiny number of women athletes in this cohort said that they had been recruited. We also know, however (as discussed in Chapter 6), that these women athletes enjoyed a considerable admissions advantage. Presumably the admissions offices identified fine athletes who were also attractive candidates for the school on other grounds, and it was the *combination* of qualifications that gave such candidates an edge in the admissions competition. We do not think it is coincidental that the women athletes in the '76 cohort ranked well in their class academically, did not underperform academically, and went on to earn advanced degrees in above-average numbers. In sharp contrast, large numbers of the women athletes in the '89 cohort reported having been recruited (especially in the Division IA programs and in the Ivies), and we surmise that coaches were playing more of a role, relative to the admissions staff, in deciding who made the final cut. This cohort of women athletes did not do as well in class, underperformed academically, and no longer enjoyed an edge in advanced degree attainment.

This same point can be made by comparing the male athletes in the '51 cohort with the male athletes in the '76 and '89 cohorts. The men in the '51 cohort were not nearly as actively recruited as their counterparts in the '76 and '89 cohorts, and their highly credible records in school and after college mirror those of the women athletes in the '76 cohort. Athletic recruitment for men intensified further between the '76 and '89 cohorts, and the differences in outcomes achieved by athletes in these three cohorts are consistent with what one would have expected to find, given the line of argument being developed here. However the data are analyzed (by gender, by sport, by level of competition, by cohort), there is at least a crude correlation between the degree to which athletes report having been recruited and the degree of academic underperformance. All of these effects are magnified in the Ivy League and the coed liberal arts colleges by an inescapable need to over-recruit. Because there are no athletic scholarships that bind recruited athletes to playing, a considerable number of first-year students may not continue with their teams. In order to allow for this attrition, larger numbers of athletes must be recruited initially.

The Well-Rounded Individual versus the Well-Rounded Class

We believe that the changes in the face of athletics between the 1950s and today can be related to a still broader shift in admissions philosophies. In the 1950s, much was said about the desirability of enrolling "well-rounded students." One consequence (among many others) was that athletes needed to have other attributes—to be ready to take advantage of the broad range of the school's academic offerings, to be interested in being part of the larger campus community (many of them were class officers, not just team captains), and so on. We suspect that the subsequent success of a number of the athletes of this era in gaining leadership positions, including positions as CEOs, owes something to their having had a strong combination of attributes.

Without being able to date the change precisely, we believe that, sometime in the late 1960s or the 1970s, this admissions philosophy was altered in major ways. At some of the schools with which we are familiar, the attack on the philosophy of the well-rounded individual came from faculty. For example, one group of mathematicians objected vehemently to the rejection of candidates who had extremely high math aptitude scores but were not impressive in other respects.[12] A new admissions mantra was coined: the search was on to enroll the "well-rounded class," rather than the well-rounded individual. The idea was that the super-mathematician should definitely be admitted, along with the super-musician and maybe even the super-gymnast. It was argued that, taken together, this array of talented individuals would create an attractively diverse community of learners. For some years now, most admissions officers at academically selective schools have talked in terms of the well-rounded class.

The former dean of admissions and financial aid at Hotchkiss, whom we quoted earlier, provides a sharp insight into how this new way of thinking about admissions has evolved:

> For years now, parents have heard college admission officers espousing the virtues of a well-rounded class over well-rounded students. Colleges believe that they can build a well-rounded class by assembling a group of students with particular talents in specific areas. These talents are often referred to as "hooks" and the students who possess them are called "spiky." The most visible evidence of this for many families is the admission of talented athletes to highly selective academically oriented colleges and universities. . . .
>
> Altogether the impact of the college admission office's search for "spiky" kids has become enormously significant. From the beginning of a child's high school career (and often much earlier) an increasing number of parents and children are concerned with building a "hook" rather than with getting the most out of the totality of the high school experience. As a result, there are more and more students concentrating their efforts in a particular field rather than experimenting with the broader range of available options. More and more students play only one sport in a given year, for example, instead of three. And more and more students concentrate immediately and precisely on theater or music instead of experiencing the full range of artistic disciplines. Of course, this early concentration is completely antithetical to the notion of a liberal arts education. The fact that liberal arts colleges are those most likely to be sending these messages to high schools, therefore, is particularly unfortunate.

In our view, the mathematicians who lobbied for the admission of high school students with off-the-scale mathematical potential were absolutely right. "Spiky" students of that kind belong in a great university that has a great mathematics department. We are much more skeptical that "spikiness" can be used to justify the admission of a bone-crushing full-back whose high school grades were over the academic threshold but who otherwise does not seem a particularly good fit for the academic values that colleges and universities espouse. There are many types of spikiness, and the objective, we believe, should be to assemble a well-rounded class *with a range of attributes that resonate with the academic and service missions of the college or university.* Looked at from this perspective, the arguments for spiky mathematicians and spiky golfers seem quite different. We also wonder how well some of the increasingly spiky athletes of the '89 (and later) cohorts will do in the long run. Not as well, we suspect, as their male predecessors in the '51 cohort and the women athletes from the '76 cohort, who appear to have had, as the saying goes, "more arrows in their quivers."

Competitiveness, Emulation, and "Fairness"

The forces described thus far operate primarily at the level of the individual athletics program within the individual school. But the broad changes in the intercollegiate landscape that have occurred at academically selective colleges and universities over the past 40 to 50 years (and especially over the past 20 years) have also been driven by system-wide forces. First among them is competitiveness. Although colleges and universities compete for faculty, for grants, and for talented (and tuition-paying) students, athletics can come to represent an arms race without end. Even winning is never enough, since there are always more levels to aspire to, more ways to excel, and, if all else fails, future seasons to think about. Part of the reason that sports is so alluring as a field for competition is that it is so results-driven and so quantifiable. Everyone knows (or can find out) who won the Rose Bowl, which women's basketball team is the national champion, and which Division III college was the swimming champion at its level. It is much harder to avoid endless arguments as to whether this program of study is superior to that one (although in recent years magazines such as *U.S. News and World Report* have sought to resolve those debates, too). There is also something about competition in sports that reminds people of courage and even victory in war. (It is not coincidental that the image of the arms race keeps reappearing in stories about intercollegiate sports.) Seeking anything but the top of the sports rankings may seem like surrender.

Resisting these pressures is made even more difficult by the frequent failure to distinguish between *levels of play* (which depend on how talented the athletes are, how much time and how many resources are devoted to preparing for a contest, and so on) and *vigorous competition* (which can occur, or fail to occur, at any level of play). A competitive cluster of like-minded schools "gets the competitive juices flowing" and contributes to the community spirit of a campus whatever the level of play—from Hamilton College field hockey to Penn State football. Heroes in uniforms help to build identity, and they help campus and alumni constituencies to coalesce under a common banner. That is clear. What is more difficult to understand is why it is so hard to convince people that, within the closed ecosystem of the conference, healthy competition and the concomitant benefits for school spirit do not depend on how expert the play is. A Denison-Kenyon swim meet from 1955 presumably inspired passion even though the times were seconds (or even dozens of seconds) slower than they are today.

Healthy competition requires a rough parity that makes the game worth playing, and sustaining such competition is anything but easy. Even among seemingly like institutions, differences that from a distance would be difficult to detect provide profound competitive advantages (or disadvantages). For example, within the Ivy League, student bodies of different sizes mean that it is much easier to absorb a few more athletes with lower qualifications in a relatively large school than in a smaller peer group. Professional teams recognize that such persistent advantages are detrimental to all and employ revenue sharing, salary caps, and draft pick systems to redress imbalances systemically.

Since the college equivalents of these measures (NCAA regulations and conference rules) never really end the race, an individual school will inevitably continue to act in ways that may make it 5 percent better off, although the whole system may end up 10 percent worse off. Building a new artificial turf field may help your team recruit, but only until the other schools in your league catch up. Then everyone has paid for a new field and its subsequent maintenance, but no one is any better off competitively. The classic example of this sort of behavior occurs when someone viewing a parade stands on his tiptoes to get a better view. Within moments the entire crowd will be on tiptoes and no one will see any better. No one wants to miss the parade, and the competitive dynamic in sports has unquestionably fueled the increases in expenditures on coaching and facilities at all levels of play. It has also put tremendous pressure on the admissions process. With the unimpeded flow of more and more information about the pre-college achievements of athletes, and the mobility of coaches between institutions, there seems to be no limit to the contagion of athletic expectations.

As important a driver as competition is in shaping the face of athletics, there is an equally (or almost equally) powerful force. It can be referred to simply as envy or emulation. It is not news that people tend to want what others have. And it is not surprising, therefore, that within the

Division IA scholarship schools the so-called "minor sports" of another day have sought to share as fully as they can in the attributes of the ambitious, well-funded High Profile programs. Many more specialized coaches have been hired, facilities have been improved, and scholarships have been provided. Such moves in the direction of equality are often urged in the name of "fairness." Because men who play football "get something," men playing other sports are said to "deserve," in the name of fairness, equal treatment. This same way of thinking is found within the Ivy League and the Division III coed liberal arts colleges. There is, for example, the recurring complaint among the football players in the Ivies or in the New England Small College Athletic Conference that, because members of all other teams have the chance to go to a national championship, "fairness" mandates that they be given this opportunity too. And, as we saw in the episode of the women's lacrosse team at Williams, part of the ethos of sport is to "refuse to lose"—to refuse to accept anything less than what anyone else has.[13]

The most widely publicized—and most consequential—arena for the application of the fairness doctrine is of course women's sports, and in Chapter 14 we say more about how this contentious issue affects many other questions of policy. At the present time, Title IX seems to be exporting to the domain of women's athletics all the salient characteristics of men's sports. An entirely understandable desire on the part of women to have the same opportunities that men enjoy is basic to this transfer of attitudes, policies, resources, and even values.

The women athletes of the late 1970s resemble the male athletes of the 1950s in their in-school and post-college success. It is only in the '89 cohort that we see the patterns for the women athletes that resemble those displayed by the male athletes in the '76 cohort and, even more strongly, by male athletes in the '89 cohort. The women swimmers on today's teams demonstrate the same dramatic gains in performance in the pool that are so evident in the case of the men. There are now many more coaches assigned to women's teams, and expenditures on women's athletics, although they still lag behind expenditures on men's teams, have grown dramatically.

In other words, with determined effort and considerable investment, it has been possible to increase the number of women playing intercollegiate sports and to improve the talent level of women athletes. But whether these developments provide access and opportunity to those women who are best able to take advantage of the resources of a selective college or university remains an entirely separate question. This too should be considered an issue of "fairness." To follow the men's approach to athletics is to follow historical precedent; but to do so unhesitatingly is to assume that history optimizes. We do not believe that this is necessarily true.

Directional Signposts

Comparisons over time, across institutional types, and between men's and women's athletic programs all lead to a single conclusion: intercollegiate programs in these academically selective institutions are moving steadily in the direction of greater intensification, increased tension with core educational values, and more substantial calls on the tangible and intangible resources of their host institutions. We cannot think of a single set of data that contradicts this proposition. Furthermore, the most recent cohort for which we have full data entered college more than ten years ago, in the fall of 1989. The limited data available for a much more recent cohort (the one that entered in the fall of 1999) suggest that the trends favoring the recruitment of highly specialized athletes have all continued—and, if anything, gained speed.

We are unable to identify any forces inside the system that—without considerable help—can be expected to alter these directions. On the contrary, there is an intergenerational dynamic that seems likely to accelerate the pace of the changes we see occurring. The more intensively recruited athletes of today, men and women, will become the next generation of alumni/ae, and in the fashion of their predecessors they can be expected to press for increased emphasis on supporting winning sports programs as they become trustees and assume other leadership positions. Two pieces of evidence that support this conclusion are the data on the priorities of former athletes who have become alumni/ae leaders and the data showing the effects of winning teams on the giving behavior of former athletes from the Division III coed liberal arts colleges. These may be no more than straws in the wind, but we believe that they should be taken seriously.

Institutionalization of Athletics in the Academy

Looking back at the history of college sports over the course of the 20th century, one of the most important changes can be seen clearly only with the help of a long-distance lens: intercollegiate sports have become institutionalized in institutions of higher education. Whereas athletics programs were once a wild stepchild held at arm's length from the schools, run mainly by the players themselves and their devotees, they have by now been thoroughly enfolded into the fabric of these institutions. In an effort to control excess and police the games, schools took charge. In doing so, it was assumed, the strength of the institution's discipline and sense of purpose would moderate the passions inspired by athletics. There was, however, always the risk that, having gained a solid foothold inside the walls, the troubling aspects of the athletics enterprise would affect the academy at the very time that the academy was working to control them. Sports once seen as merely an outlet for passions and energy or as a community-building ritual are now justified as a training ground for leaders, a school for character, or "the sweatiest of the liberal arts." While there are positive sides to taking sports so seriously, doing so also legitimizes a possible confusion between the dictates of the playing field and the lessons of the classroom.[14]

For years, people have understood that one can view life as a game. "Play the cards that Fate deals you," we are often told. But the country's leading colleges and universities have a special role to play in shaping the game of life, in setting the values (as opposed to the rules) of the game. The role of these institutions is not simply to be a facilitator of what each individual who "wins" the preliminary heats of the competition (the admissions game) sees the game to be. Colleges and universities are tax-favored, not-for-profit institutions because society agrees that they have a broader role to play in a far more consequential societal game. These institutions are charged to resist the narrow impulses of the marketplace, as well as ideological and political strictures of every kind: they are meant to live, as E. M. Forster once described the poet Cavafy, "at a slight angle to the universe." Pursuing their academic mission will produce better filmmakers, journalists, medical researchers, and yes, better bankers and lawyers too. But this will be accomplished by accepting those whom the schools believe will make best use of their educational resources and by insisting on the validity of their own missions.

In embracing intercollegiate athletics, colleges and universities gambled on their ability to "control the beast"—to harness the energies and many good qualities of sports to their own purposes, rather than to be subverted by them. The open question is whether this gamble was a good one: whether colleges and universities can rise to the challenge of rebalancing objectives and strengthening what we regard as the purer values of athletic competition. Leaders of these venerable academic institutions have difficult choices to make.

CHAPTER 14

Thinking Ahead: Impediments to Change and Proposed Directions

> A genuine assessment of the value of the current reform movement cannot be made by today's observers. The true test will be applied by historians of the future, because they will ask whether today's presidents employed their power wisely and chose well.
>
> —Knight Commission on Intercollegiate Athletics,
> *A New Beginning for a New Century* (1993)

THIS FINAL CHAPTER, more than any other, needs to begin with disclaimers. Readers seeking a summary of the book should not look here; Chapters 12 and 13, read together, serve that function. Even more important is our decision not to propose a detailed "blueprint" for reform. There are two reasons for this decision, neither of which derives from any reluctance to state our own convictions (which we have already done and will do again in the main part of this chapter).

First, we do not know enough. A main lesson learned from the extensive experiences of one of us in working to devise the Ivy League's Academic Index is that "the devil is in the details." Devising ways of regulating recruitment of athletes, even in that well-defined context (or in any other conference setting), depends on detailed knowledge of differences in the circumstances and needs of individual schools within the League, the predilections of various presidents and boards of trustees, the requirements associated with managing specific sports, and the implications of broader NCAA developments. To produce a credible set of proposals within any particular setting requires a different kind of research, and a different kind of process for arriving at conclusions, than the ones we have employed in writing this book. Our research will, we hope, provide a useful backdrop for the development of detailed proposals by knowledgeable people, but it cannot provide the highly specific guidance needed for concrete actions. It was never intended to serve that kind of prescriptive purpose.

Second, it would be presumptuous for us to think that we can provide specific advice on "what to do" to those who both know their own institutions far better than we could hope to know them and have their own priorities and values, which constitute the prism through which all of the data must be filtered. We hope that others will reflect on the findings and analysis presented in this book and design their own proposals, without feeling obligated to any one set of policy prescriptions.

Even though we are going to resist the temptation to produce anything resembling a blueprint for change, we will set forth general propositions that may conceivably encourage (or provoke) both thinking and action. First, however, we want to address a basic question that others keep asking us, and that we keep asking ourselves. If we are correct in arguing that the divide between the athletic enterprise and the academic enterprise continues to widen, and if we are right in believing that this growing divide is consequential, the obvious question is: why has so little happened to arrest this trend—never mind reverse it? Seeking to alter the course of college athletics is a sport for realists, if ever there was one, and anyone interested in it should enter the contest with eyes wide open.

IMPEDIMENTS TO CHANGE

In our view, the major impediments to change are the following: (1) a serious lack of the information that would lead to a clearer understanding of the issues; (2) fear of negative reactions from all quarters; (3) fear of revenue losses and hurtful effects on admissions, especially if any given institution were to contemplate "unilateral disarmament"; (4) the practical difficulties of acting in concert with suitable partners; and (5) the dominating effects of competing institutional priorities, combined with the power of inertia. Taken together, this is a formidable set of obstacles. They will yield only (if at all) to strong collective leadership on the part of trustees as well as presidents.

Lack of Information

As we saw in Chapter 11, it is extremely difficult to "unpack" financial statements in athletics, and many, many people misunderstand the full financial implications of decisions to compete at various levels of play. There appears to be a somewhat naïve view that playing big-time football and basketball will necessarily (or even probably) improve the financial fortunes of an institution.[1] Yet the evidence is all to the contrary.

There is even less understanding of the effects of athletic recruitment on admissions, the academic performance of athletes, the composition of the student body, and the ethos of the campus. This void is more understandable, since such data have generally been nonexistent, with the single exception of graduation rates. Moreover, trends within institutions (in what different groups of students view as important in college, what subjects they choose to study, what career paths they follow) are difficult for individual institutions to track on their own. We hope that, if it accomplishes nothing else, this study will close a large part of this information gap. Facts are necessary for a fair consideration of the true trade-offs associated with ever more intensive recruitment of athletes.

Fear of Negative Reactions

The kinds of vehement reactions described in the Princeton wrestling episode indicate that there is certainly some basis for a fear of negative reactions when tough choices are made concerning athletics. Nonetheless, while passions surely abound, it is important not to confuse the expressions of vocal minorities with the views of the overwhelming majority of those who support colleges and universities. One of the major lessons to be learned from the College and Beyond survey is that the graduates of these schools are far more interested in other aspects of college life (including especially the quality of undergraduate teaching) than in intercollegiate athletics. Alumni/ae of these schools—including notably the "big givers"—are, if anything, more in favor of reducing the emphasis on intercollegiate competition than increasing it.

Although any sensitive, emotion-laden subject must be addressed with care, we believe that in fact college and university leaders have more leeway than they may realize to consider what is really best for their institutions. Actions should, of course, follow extensive consultation and be rooted in a clear articulation of their relationship to the institution's educational mission. But we believe that sound decisions almost always speak for themselves, at least in the long run. Candid, thoughtful consideration of institutional policy toward intercollegiate athletics could well elicit a surprising amount of support.[2]

There are, to be sure, historical, institutional, and political realities that constrain the policy options that can be considered. This is especially true at leading state universities, where successful teams provide visibility and encourage legislative support. More generally, there is an "athletics establishment" that has clear vested interests in maintaining the status quo. Prior to the recent restructuring, NCAA conventions were perhaps the best illustration of how thousands of coaches, athletic directors, producers, marketers, suppliers, and representatives of the sports media have joined together to create an "industry" with power and reach.

Among all the groups with a "vote" on issues in athletics, trustees are the most consequential. Especially at private colleges and universities that do not have big-time programs, individual trustees can play powerful roles. Several commentators have cited personal experiences to illustrate this point. In the words of one former college president: "Trustees play many roles and can give generously of their time in areas where their advice is very welcome; suddenly they get oddly passionate about sports in a way that differs from their other interests. It can be very hard to disagree with or discount them."

Fear of Revenue Losses and Hurtful Effects on Admissions

At the Division IA level, in particular, any decisions that affect won-lost records could have an impact on revenues—although much would depend on whether institutions acted unilaterally or in concert with their peers. Decisions to withdraw from conferences that share bowl receipts and television revenues could have even greater consequences. (These propositions are, it should be said, fully consistent with the evidence in Chapter 11 showing that almost all athletic programs lose money; we are talking here about near-term incremental effects measured from a given starting point. It is entirely possible that, over time, any such losses in revenues would be more than made up by savings on the cost side of the ledger, depending on the kinds of changes that were introduced.)

Division III coed liberal arts colleges and Ivy League institutions have far less reason to worry about losing revenues, which are generally small if not nonexistent in the first place. But some of these schools, especially those that are less selective and admit high percentages of all students who apply, could worry about possible effects on applicant pools, and especially about losing applicants interested in playing on intercollegiate teams that may think of themselves as contenders for national championships in their division.

Whatever the level of play, the recurring image of the arms race suggests an obvious point: the more competitive the arena, the more important it is for institutions to act jointly, perhaps through the mechanism of a league or a conference. "Unilateral disarmament" is poorly suited to college sports. A decision by a single school to lessen the intensity with which it recruits athletes, or to reduce the support that it provides those whom it does recruit, would be very risky. Any such decision may not only threaten revenues or hurt admissions, it may also be interpreted more broadly as a lack of commitment to excellence in athletics—or, worse yet, as a more general lack of institutional will.

Practical Difficulties of Acting in Concert

Unlike arms races between nations—which eventually lead, through either open warfare or the economic ruin of one side, to a conclusion—the athletic arms races seem to have no built-in mechanism for either slowing or ending. This is true both because the race itself is portrayed as having little impact (due to the twin perceptions that sports makes money for the school and that there are no significant opportunity costs) and because the race to win is a race without end—there is always next season to worry about even if a team is the "winner" in this year's race.

Banding together, and acting in concert with the school's principal athletic rivals, is one way of countering such mindsets. However, it can be extremely difficult to muster the necessary support. As we observed in the previous chapter, differences in size of student body and in financial circumstances can create real problems in reaching agreement on policies even within a set of institutions as apparently coherent as the Ivy League. One of our commentators has suggested that asymmetries are far greater than most of us would realize within other groupings, such as those that include coed liberal arts colleges like Kenyon (which competes with Allegheny and Wittenberg, as well as Oberlin).[3] Similarly, Macalester and Swarthmore confront a very mixed set of rivals, some of which admit 85 percent of all applicants, have very different qualifications for admission, and do not have to be concerned about the opportunity costs of recruiting athletes—on the contrary, admitting large numbers of athletes may help these schools reach enrollment targets.[4] Realignment of competitive structures is sometimes possible, but it is not easy; associated costs (including travel) can be high, and there is often objection to disrupting old rivalries.

Competing Institutional Priorities and Inertia

This is the last of the impediments to change on our list, and it may be the most serious of all. Presidents, deans, and trustees of the institutions included in this study have a great many problems to consider, and they may just not get to athletics. Worries about how to pay for academic medical centers and scientific research, what to do about faculty recruitment and retention, how to finance doctoral education, and whether the dotcom world poses an opportunity or a threat may have higher claims on attention in the world of research universities. Leaders of coed liberal arts colleges have their own pressing concerns, including competing for the best students, sustaining healthy climates for learning in residential settings, and introducing and funding pedagogic changes made possible by new technologies. Since athletics is such a vexing subject, and since it is so hard to be confident that one can bring about real change even if that is the goal, there is certainly a case to be made for yielding to inertia. It is easy to understand why busy people might be reluctant to invest time and energy in what could turn out to be frustrating and fruitless tilting at windmills.

PROPOSITIONS

The existence of impediments to change, rooted both in mere perceptions and in realities, does not justify throwing up one's hands and accepting either the status quo or, more serious yet, the direction in which the athletics enterprise is moving. It is useful—indeed essential—to understand why the underlying issues are difficult to address, but such understanding should inform efforts to make things better, not immobilize us. In the balance of this chapter, we table for discussion nine propositions about the future of intercollegiate athletics that we believe deserve consideration.

> 1. *The growing gap between college athletics and educational values is a major, unavoidable, issue for the academy; it must be understood and addressed. The objective should be to reinvigorate the contribution of intercollegiate athletics to the achievement of educational goals.*

The tensions created by the ever-increasing intensification of intercollegiate athletics will not go away of their own accord. The "athletic divide" is widening, and decision makers have an obligation to get the relevant facts, even if some of them threaten "peace in our time." Then, once the facts are in, presidents, deans, faculty leaders, and trustees should find settings in which they can be discussed on a multilateral basis, not simply one school at a time. The goal would be to identify collective solutions that respect local circumstances and institutional priorities. In the absence of effective action, the underlying conflicts between college sports and educational values will only get worse. In the words of one commentator, "The wolf is at the door."

Whatever the particular approach or approaches tried, the objective should be to provide a rich offering of opportunities to play sports and to compete, both inside the school and beyond the campus—but without the pseudo-professional trappings and expectations that have come to dominate the college sports scene. The true educational value of participation in athletics might be realized more fully if larger numbers of "ordinary students" could play on teams, and athletes might then be less isolated from their classmates. In addition, the right signal could be sent to secondary schools and parents, as well as to young people interested in both a serious education and playing sports.

---

2. *Renewed efforts should be made to reduce the most blatant abuses of "the rules of the game," as well as to curb other threats to academic values; adherence to general standards of good conduct should be strongly encouraged. These problems are most pronounced in the High Profile sports of football and men's basketball, which in many ways occupy a world of their own.*

We have found, over and over, that recruitment patterns, admissions policies, academic outcomes, and revenue and cost structures are markedly different in the High Profile sports of football and men's basketball than they are elsewhere in intercollegiate athletics (although other sports, and especially women's basketball, seem to be moving rapidly in the same direction). This is not a coincidence. History, media attention, effects of competitive success on institutional status, and commercial factors all contribute to this outcome.

Given the great pressures to win, it is hardly surprising that it is in football and men's basketball that we find the most widely publicized scandals and other forms of bad behavior: cheating, falsification of academic records, point shaving, gambling, violence, and other blatant abuses that attract the attention of the media. Such incidents, even if infrequent and sometimes presented out of context, call into question the core values of the institutions where they occur and, most important of all, send wrong messages to aspiring athletes, high schools, coaches, members of campus communities, and society at large. The attendant bad publicity for higher education is a genuine concern, but the underlying challenges to educational values are of still greater importance.

Such incidents are reported most frequently in connection with big-time Division IA programs (and, as we have said, they carry the greatest risks for institutional reputation at this level of play). One irony is that the public may gain the impression that all is well, and perfectly "pure," at other schools simply because they are less likely than those with big-time programs to experience the most outrageous (and most highly publicized) scandals. However, versions of these problems can occur at every level of play and at every type of school.[5]

The NCAA itself devotes a tremendous amount of time and energy to achieving compliance with its volumes of regulations intended to protect intercollegiate athletics from at least some of these problems. It is widely understood that the most visible and embarrassing incidents have deep roots in underlying patterns of athletic recruitment, standards of admission, criteria for measuring academic progress, and failures to monitor the behavior of coaches as well as players. These patterns in turn lead to other problems, including erosion of academic standards, that may in the long run be of even greater consequence than the egregious behavior identified in today's headline.

Many individuals and many commissions have made conscientious efforts to address these deeper issues, which also sometimes affect Lower Profile sports. The Knight Commission on Intercollegiate Athletics, which worked hard on these and other problems in the beginning of the 1990s, reconvened in the fall of 2000 to continue its work—and perhaps to give additional attention to the ever-rising costs of intercollegiate sports.[6] It is surely important to chip away at this interconnected set of issues whenever and however it is politically possible to do so (for example, by continuing to question how many athletic scholarships are really needed in a sport like football). Various people have suggested additional reforms, such as ending the segregation of athletes in special dorms and reducing conflicts with academics by shortening seasons and limiting midweek games that involve travel. Measures of this kind, if carefully worked out and adopted, could have a significant across-the-board impact on college sports.

Developing and promoting such reforms is grinding work, and there are, we fear, few if any magic wands to wave. The most fundamental problems appear so intractable because they have deep roots in American culture. They are in large part the product of economic links between intercollegiate and professional sports, the ferocious competition to enroll high school students who possess exceptional athletic talent, the signals sent to aspiring athletes as to what really matters in life, and the seamier side of big-time athletics (which is influenced so strongly by the incentives given to coaches and the adulation heaped on often immature athletes). The history of attempts at reform suggests that it is excruciatingly difficult to make more than incremental progress—at best.[7]

There is now so much money involved (especially television dollars controlled by the NCAA and the major conferences and Division IA programs) that economic motivations are bound to loom large in the thinking of both the institutions that have invested so heavily in athletics and the thousands of coaches and administrators whose careers depend on the continuation of these programs in much their present form. It would take a veritable revolution in the financing of big-time sports, and a drying up of flows of television dollars from the Final Four basketball championships and the major bowl games, to permit any major rethinking of big-time football and basketball programs. There is no evidence of which we are aware that any such revolution is in the offing. Quite the contrary.[8]

It is also important to remember that successful football and basketball teams serve highly consequential institutional purposes for flagship state universities such as (in this study) the University of Michigan, Penn State, and the University of North Carolina at Chapel Hill. These universities depend heavily on the broadly based goodwill of their statewide constituencies and the legislators whom they elect. It is unlikely that residents of Michigan will relate viscerally to the tremendously important work in Asian studies, classical archaeology, and survey research that is done in Ann Arbor; but they certainly take pride in nationally televised wins by Michigan basketball and football teams. These political realities—which one must recognize but need not applaud—affect the emphasis placed on High Profile sports by the leading state universities. More than anything else, they can be used to justify viewing these sports as an appropriate avenue for institutional investment. Regrettable as such priorities may be, especially in states that depend on nationally acclaimed public universities for leadership in research and the training of the future workforce, it is within this context that reforms should be debated—not within an imagined world of truly "amateur" athletics that has not existed for a very long time, and in fact may never have existed.

---

3. *Wherever it is feasible, consideration should be given to lessening the emphasis placed on the High Profile sports, and, in particular, on winning national championships.*

We question whether there is as strong a case for placing heavy emphasis on the High Profile sports at the leading private universities as there is at the leading public universities—the political benefits are less important and the opportunity costs of no-holds-barred athletic recruitment are much higher because undergraduate enrollments are smaller and admissions tends to be more selective. *If* these private universities were truly free to chart their own course, there might well be grounds for wondering if places like Northwestern and Vanderbilt made the right investment decisions when they committed themselves to provide the facilities, scholar-ships, and highly expensive infrastructure needed to compete at the most demanding levels of play. But of course schools such as Northwestern and Vanderbilt are not really free to act alone. They are members of con-ferences, and so long as they belong to the Big Ten and the Southeast Conference, it is hard to see how they can "sit out" football. Nor would withdrawing from such high-prestige conferences (and forgoing the as-sociated revenues) be easy to do. These universities are, at least in some measure, captives of their histories and their present circumstances.

Other private universities, such as Duke, have addressed these prob-lems by investing significant resources in sustaining an outstanding bas-ketball program but refraining from making a comparable effort in foot-ball, which has much higher costs. Still, even national powerhouses can fall from grace. The Duke basketball program, long a model for athletic success while also successful in graduating its players, in 1999 faced its first experience with the phenomenon of talented players choosing to leave school for the rewards of the NBA, as not one but three players left early. Putting aside the implications of such choices from the individual's point of view, the episode makes it clear that no program will be able to rise above the big waves that wash over all programs. Football at Notre Dame is another revealing case in point. Less than stellar competitive results have combined with scandal to lead enthusiastic boosters to put pressure on the University to make even larger "investments" (academic as well as financial) in support of the football team.[9]

If we accept that tensions between the desire to excel in High Profile sports and the educational missions of leading Division IA universities are in large measure inevitable, there are still common-sense admonitions that may discourage the worst kinds of consequences (and mistakes). One experienced president, who has had wrenching encounters with the pres-sures to win in Division IA competition, offered these words of advice (in a personal letter to the authors):

> No administrative head of a university should ever announce publicly that he or she wants a national championship in football (or any other sport). . . . Shortly after I came here, my university played in and won a bowl game. In the next issue of the local newspaper, the sports editor wrote that the next major test is whether or not Coach . . . can now go to a major bowl and com-pete for a national championship. I said privately to my wife and other confidants, "Lord, I hope not!"
>
> Here are my tenets about football. If your school does not have it now, don't start it. If it has it now, make the best of it; it is hard to un-ring the bell. Making the best of it means following the rules and hoping for some win-ning seasons in the range of 7–4 or 8–3 records. A season or two of 11–0 or

10–1 records and high national ranking will change the culture of your institution and actually damage its academic reputation.

> 4. *Schools outside the orbit of Division IA, and especially the Division III coed liberal arts colleges, may be in a position to consider more far-reaching modifications in these High Profile sports.*

Football, in particular, raises very different questions for schools outside Division IA, but it poses a special challenge for them, too: football is a highly visible sport in almost every setting, and rosters are very large.[10] The number of male football players creates severe issues of gender equity in athletics for schools at every level of play. Colleges such as Haverford that do not play football have a much easier time complying with Title IX.[11]

Schools that do not play at the Division IA level have more choices regarding their football and basketball teams. The Ivies and the Division III coed liberal arts colleges are burdened by neither athletic scholarships nor the same expectations of national prominence associated with big-time football and basketball programs. In these settings, attempts to reconsider the appropriate level of commitment to the High Profile sports—while still an excursion into emotionally charged territory—may be less hostage to external forces than they are at the Division IA level.

Quite different approaches might even have appeal in some quarters, and one question is whether groups of schools (especially some of the small coed liberal arts colleges) might benefit from differentiating their programs. There is, for example, the "out-of-the-box" thinking of one admissions director who proposed a return to one-platoon football:

> What seems to be the obvious answer is to go back to one-platoon football—though the NCAA is opposed to it out of self-preservation. Doing so would solve two of today's biggest problems: it would make gender equity possible, and would open up another dozen spots in each entering class for the incredibly talented applicants that I have to turn away. But more importantly, it also has the appeal of being the same game that the earlier generations played and loved, so the alumni could buy in and still cheer for the team, and maybe even identify more strongly. Would it be the same game that Notre Dame or the San Francisco 49ers play? Of course not. But who says that Amherst or Bowdoin or Swarthmore should be trying to play that game?

Whatever the fate of such radical proposals pertaining to football (which are probably doomed to be judged "interesting"), other important questions abound, involving the recruitment of athletes, admissions philosophies, coaching assignments, and levels of expense. But these questions apply more generally to the full range of sports offerings at all the schools in our study, and we defer discussion of them until after we have considered athletic scholarships offered to athletes who compete in the Lower Profile sports at the Division IA universities.

---

5. *Awarding of athletic scholarships in the Lower Profile sports is, in our minds, difficult to justify. The most common justifications represent a misapplication of the concept of "fairness" and unquestioning devotion to "excellence in all things."*

Providing athletic scholarships to participants in the High Profile sports at Division IA schools is taken for granted in our society. Although such awards of course increase the costs of these programs, they are defended in terms of the critical role that these highly prized athletes play in allowing their schools to compete successfully on the football field and the basketball court. There was a movement some years ago to limit all financial aid in athletics to need-based awards, but that effort failed.[12] Providing some form of financial reward to High Profile athletes in Division IA schools is at least consistent with viewing support of these programs as an essentially inescapable institutional investment.

A different rationale must be found, it seems to us, to justify spending large sums of money on athletic scholarships in the Lower Profile sports. Putting to one side the complicating issue of gender equity, we wonder how one makes the case, on the merits, for awarding substantial numbers of athletic scholarships in sports such as tennis and lacrosse—and for spending, in total, $300,000 or more per year on such teams, quite apart from capital costs and their share of the costs of infrastructure? These outlays can hardly be considered institutional "investments" analogous to those needed to support big-time football and basketball programs. The standard arguments used to defend such large subsidies in the less visible sports invoke principles of fairness ("look what the football players got") and a commitment to the pursuit of excellence in all things ("a great university such as ours cannot accept mediocrity in any endeavor"). We find these arguments entirely unpersuasive.

Fairness is a concept we all respect; it involves treating equally individuals (or programs) *in the same circumstances* and *avoiding undeserved favoritism*. It is no requirement of fairness, however, that all individuals or all programs be treated alike. On the contrary, "fairness" requires assessing the resources devoted to each program in the light of what each *contributes to achieving the mission of the school*—and in the light of the other uses that could be made of the same resources if a more frugal approach were adopted. We know of no instance in which a school in fact acts as if it truly believes it has an equal obligation to promote excellence in every *academic* program it offers.[13] (Never mind extracurricular programs and auxiliary services of all kinds; should college dining halls strive to become Spago or Le Cirque?) Strategic choices must be made. The case for spending more or less on any activity has to be judged "on the margin," and in relation to what the activity means to the health of the institution and the broader educational purposes that it serves. Drawing distinctions requires courage as well as careful thought, but the alternative is an undisciplined sameness that no institution should seek and no one should applaud.

Does providing an athletic scholarship to a swimmer (or spending money on a full-time golf coach) advance the mission of an educational institution in a way similar to providing a fellowship to a graduate student or spending more on the library? We don't think so. The less visible sports presumably benefit mainly those who participate in them, and it is difficult to see the justification for large institutional investments in costly intercollegiate programs—which often require institutions to spend five to ten times as much per participant as they do on other extracurricular activities. Of course, the same issues of principle arise in considering the place of Lower Profile sports in the programs of non-scholarship schools. The fact that these schools do not provide scholarships does not mean that they do not "invest" in these sports. Targeted recruiting and providing advantages in admissions are themselves major investments, as are direct outlays on coaching, travel, facilities, and so on. In our view, justifications that invoke "fairness" and "excellence in all things" are no more persuasive in non-scholarship settings than in Division IA programs (setting aside, again, gender equity issues).

The few schools that are extremely successful in these Lower Profile sports do gain "bragging rights" that are made most visible through the rankings used to determine (at each level of play) the winners of the Sears Cup.[14] But there remain the questions of how much such recognition really contributes to the educational purposes of a college or university, how likely it is that any given school will "win" in this competition, and how much should be spent in pursuing such recognition.

6. *Colleges and universities should find ways of "rebalancing" the emphasis on athletics outside the big-time programs. Such efforts are likely to require*

> *a coordinated combination of changes in coaching assignments, recruiting, and admissions; other changes (in scheduling, for example) might then follow. A more radical approach would be to promote wider adoption of the club sport model.*

In academically selective institutions of all kinds, there is, we believe, a strong argument to be made for reducing substantially the number of students, male and female, admitted largely because they had athletic "spikiness" (to use the term of art introduced in the previous chapter). If nothing else, the evidence of significant and growing academic under-performance among athletes raises sharply the question of whether these students are taking full advantage of the educational opportunities that their schools are chartered to provide. Why should a Wesleyan or a Penn or a Smith favor a good baseball or softball player over an applicant more interested in academics and more likely to participate effectively in the life of the college? Why should these schools spend so much money providing special opportunities for the athletes that they do recruit? Present practice is, we submit, hard to justify on the merits. Moreover, all the early indicators warn us that these issues will only become more vexing with the passage of time.

If it were agreed that some substantial "de-intensification" of college athletics is in order, one place to begin would be with the size and character of coaching staffs. In 1970, one of the coed liberal arts colleges in our study had 10 full-time coaches and 3 part-time coaches; today, this college has 19 full-time head coaches, 2 part-time head coaches, and 24 part-time assistant coaches. One Ivy League university went from 27 coaches in 1970, full-time and part-time, to 54 in 1980 and 83 in 1996. Would it be possible to consider reversing the move to full-time coaches in more and more sports (a pattern that is now solidly in place in the Ivy League and a constant temptation for those Division III schools that are still holdouts), reducing the number of assistant coaches, and returning to the multitasking approach to staffing assignments that used to be the norm?[15]

This is a difficult suggestion to make for those of us who are close to the coaches of today, whom we value for their friendship, and whom we respect for their skills, their motivations, and their contributions. But there is no escaping the fact that it is the coaching and staffing configurations now in place (which are hardly the fault of the coaches themselves but rather reflect the expectations and policies of the schools that hired them) that drive the intensive recruiting that is more and more evident at these schools. Changes in the numbers and duties of coaches, as well as in explicit or implicit directives to "win big or move on," could have ripple effects on the entire athletic enterprise, especially if they were combined with reductions in recruiting budgets and a general move toward de-professionalizing college sports.

It seems equally clear that consideration should be given to changing the way in which at least some admissions offices approach the athletic side of the process of selecting a class. For reasons explained at length in the previous chapter, we believe that the admissions process should rely much less heavily on the coaches' lists, and that less weight should be given to raw athletic talent and what we can only call athletic "purposiveness" (single-minded commitment to a sport). Rather, admissions staffs could be encouraged to revert to the practices of earlier days when more weight was given to athletic talent *seen in combination with other qualifications that made the applicant attractive to the school, including the applicant's commitment to the educational purposes of the institution.* The exceptional records achieved both in school and after college by male athletes in the 1951 cohort and women athletes in the 1976 cohort reflect the presence then of the admissions approach we are advocating. Comparisons with the records of recruited athletes in the '89 cohorts are telling. Moreover, preliminary evidence suggests that recruited athletes in the '99 cohort, male and female, are still less likely than their classmates to take full advantage of their academic opportunities and less likely to contribute fully to the "community" ethos that is prized by residential colleges and universities.

These two suggested changes—in coaching and admissions philosophies—are the most fundamental. If they were agreed upon, many other changes could be considered, including length of seasons. To make sure that expectations and values were solidly framed, it might also be wise to reconsider institutional participation in NCAA national championships—thereby avoiding the stresses that sparked the Williams lacrosse saga. To be sure, students who play intercollegiate sports have come to expect the opportunity to compete in these championships, and there almost surely would be loud protests from both current athletes and those who want to attend one of these schools with participation in postseason play very much in mind. But these high-aspiration athletes could presumably be succeeded by other talented students, including athletes who want to go to the school in question for reasons more consistent with the institution's educational mission.

Another, more radical, approach would be to revert to the club sports model, which would entail providing only modest financial support to teams and eliminating paid coaches and recruiting advantages. Those who play on student-run clubs today certainly seem to enjoy themselves. Moreover, the club sport model has the advantage of encouraging student initiative, since participating students coordinate their activities with those of other clubs, agree upon rules and budgets, and generally take responsibility for their teams. To be sure, there are few fans; but, it needs to be said, there are few fans for most teams in most of the Lower Profile sports at most levels of play. Why not keep the pride of playing for one's school, but not require the institution to make the extensive investments that serve only to increase the level of play when few are watching? Moving to a club sport model would be a real paradigm shift, however, and it may be more practical to consider more modest modifications in present patterns of competition.

---

7. *Colleges and universities cannot hope to adopt the kinds of changes suggested here acting alone; they will need to act in concert, and perhaps to form new competitive groupings.*

Institutions that are in agreement about the appropriate balance between athletics and academics must act in concert. Within a conference, schools must recognize that there is *a strongly shared interest in achieving a reasonable competitive balance;* healthy competition, which benefits everyone, depends on there being no persistent doormats or consistent champions. But how is such a balance to be achieved—and maintained? Left to its own devices, each school is naturally inclined to play off its special strengths (bigger endowment, bigger student body, more forgiving academic standards, bucolic setting, urban location, and so on), thereby inevitably inciting a matching of bad bets when one school lets academic standards or a balanced budget slide. The result of such escalating competition is, however, likely to be disappointing all around, since an enhanced standard of play need not, in the end, improve one team's fortunes, even as it inevitably requires higher and higher levels of investment and sacrifice from all involved.

If those charged with promoting the well-being of these institutions agree with our analysis of the forces creating a larger and larger "athletic divide," then inter-institutional collaboration must be carried out in ways that go far beyond setting the next season's schedules. Those in leadership positions must join in common purpose with counterparts wearing other uniforms, and this includes not only deans and admissions directors, but presidents and trustees. Of critical importance is joint recognition that the collective self-interest is served by restraint rather than by seeking a temporary advantage in the name of fleeting water cooler bragging rights. Currently it is most often the presidents who are expected to work together, and yet presidents can be caught between the conflicting desires of different constituencies. There is no substitute for trustee collaboration in addressing these issues—in meeting together to endorse a common approach for restraining intensification, rather than only to celebrate their victories over each other.

History and geography conspire to complicate this already complex process by throwing together very different kinds of institutions. In some cases forming new conferences may be the right approach, since it is within conferences *of like-minded institutions* that a slowing of intensification could be possible. It may make sense to think again about the desirability of creating new national "confederations" of schools that have at least somewhat similar academic and athletic objectives. It might also help to reemphasize that competitive groupings may need to be defined on a sport-by-sport basis. At present, for example, the highly rated Johns Hopkins lacrosse team plays against teams from universities in Division IA while other teams at Johns Hopkins compete against coed liberal arts colleges in Division III. Getting the contours of the group set correctly is very important.

However much progress is made in bringing together like-minded institutions, some problems of unequal capacity to compete successfully will remain. Internal regulations of one kind or another that seek to redress differences in circumstances (like the Academic Index in the Ivy League) constitute one, highly imperfect, route to parity. A different, far more radical, route is the one that has been chosen by the professional leagues and the conferences that share revenues from bowl games: address asymmetries within a conference by taxing away natural advantages.[16] However implausible such far-out ideas may seem, they illustrate the need for creative thinking, coupled with the fact that sensible approaches will have to be tailored to specific situations. There is no denying the importance of confronting directly, in one way or another, the need to achieve as much healthy competition as can be managed. Some sacrifice in institutional autonomy is necessary—and can be justified by the implications of the alternative, which is the freedom to pursue mutually assured exhaustion.

---

8. *Title IX should be seen as providing an opportunity to rethink the organization and place of college sports on the campus; it should not be merely a stimulus to replicate the male model of college athletics in women's sports (including the current patterns of coaching, recruitment, and admissions).*

It is impossible to discuss the future directions of college sports without recognizing the revolutionary effects of Title IX. It is equally important to recognize that there is no obvious solution to the problem of how schools can reconcile the competing claims of fairness (which, we believe, *are* relevant here, if not in comparing one sport to another) and the need to "size" athletics properly within the setting of a college or university that has serious academic objectives. At present, colleges and universities generally attempt to comply with Title IX requirements by adding more and more women's teams and providing more and more athletic scholarships for women. Providing more opportunities for women athletes to compete, and better facilities and other forms of support for them, has unquestionably had major benefits—and not only for the athletes themselves. Perhaps especially at the formerly all-male schools that are now coed, highly visible support for women's teams has helped to send a signal that the schools take the aspirations of women seriously and that (at least on many campuses) there is a demonstrated desire to "play fair" in the treatment of women students. These are the right messages to send: they are consistent with an important aspect of institutional mission.

At the same time, we question the wisdom of continuing to emphasize the add-on approach, not because we are opposed to gender equity—we are not—but because we are skeptical that placing ever more emphasis on recruiting athletes of either gender is consistent with the broader educational objectives of these colleges and universities. The data on trends in women's athletics, which illustrate the tendency for women's programs to take on more and more of the characteristics of men's programs, certainly give one pause.

A more surgical (and much less costly) approach, but one that would surely be less palatable, would be for Division IA schools to eliminate all athletic scholarships for *men* outside football and basketball—and then to comply with the law by providing the number of women's athletic scholarships needed to counterbalance the number of men's awards in the High Profile sports.[17] If non-scholarship schools were to follow this same general approach, they would have to curtail support for many of their men's programs. Although a recent survey by the *Wall Street Journal* and NBC News indicates that cutting back men's programs in the service of gender equity would enjoy the support of a substantial majority of the American public,[18] we wonder if those surveyed have any idea of how substantial the redirection of athletic resources would have to be to comply with Title IX while retaining football. There would definitely be a huge outcry against any such approach, including vehement protests by the women athletes who would not want to be put in the position of appearing to curtail opportunities for men athletes.[19]

Nonetheless, before rejecting such thinking out of hand, careful consideration should be given to the longer-term implications of accepting the present add-on approach as the best that can be done. And there are, of course, middle paths that might be considered. For example, some further expansion of women's sports could be coupled with as much of a reduction in men's programs as political realities would permit (perhaps substituting more club sports). In any case, having to manage this extremely difficult balancing act may serve the useful purpose of compelling colleges and universities to address the basic issue of how much emphasis should be placed on intercollegiate athletics—for men and women—in institutions dedicated to educational goals. In this sense, Title IX can be seen as providing an impetus to rethink the entire athletics enterprise.[20]

---

9. *No consequential steps can be taken to rebuild the relationship between college sports and the core educational mission of these schools without a clear sense of direction and strong leadership from trustees, presidents, and key administrative officers.*

Americans prefer incremental change to radical redirection. And it is of course a series of incremental changes that has produced the trends in intercollegiate athletics that we have documented in this study. If it were possible to envision some "de-intensification" in athletic programs, these changes would probably also be incremental. In any event, however profound or modest any proposed change in direction, it would have to be led and managed. How this could be done is a huge subject all its own. A major question, beyond the purview of this study, is whether the non-scholarship schools, in particular, should continue to have a relationship with the NCAA, and, if so, what kind of relationship it should be. One commentator argues that "These institutions will almost always play a subordinate role in the NCAA and [they] offer a veneer of respectability to the organization that isn't otherwise warranted." Whatever the right set of organizational relationships, we believe strongly that efforts to pursue the *educational* objectives of the non-scholarship schools should not be constrained by regulations designed for other situations, or to meet other needs of institutions with different agendas.

One thing is abundantly clear: given the impediments to change noted at the start of the chapter, college and university presidents, along with key trustees, would have to play leading roles in encouraging new thinking. On this central point, almost everyone who commented on this manuscript is in agreement—and, protected by promises of anonymity, several have decried what they believe have been failures to acknowledge and address obvious problems in the athletic realm. One former president points out that a "visceral uneasiness or actual distaste for what is going on in intercollegiate athletics . . . results in a delegation of responsibility for watching over the intercollegiate athletics program to someone lower down in the organization"; he then goes on to argue that the president or provost should accept direct responsibility for what transpires.[21]

No one should underestimate the importance of those alumni/ae and trustees who care strongly enough about a school to express their opinions passionately; institutions need this sort of commitment to survive and to thrive. Earlier in the chapter, we noted that passionate "pro-high-intensity" trustees can impede consideration of new directions in athletics; key trustees can just as surely have powerful effects in promoting a rebalancing of priorities. The crucial governance issue, it seems to us, derives from the importance of making choices in the light of the mission of the institution. If, upon reflection, a college or university decides that a central part of its mission includes achieving a high standard of play and thus recruiting absolutely outstanding athletic talent—not just providing students with the opportunity to play—then this goal can understandably be pursued with the same energy that the college or university devotes to finding and supporting a great teacher of Shakespeare. But if the mission is defined in another way, then all those entrusted with guiding the ship should be prepared to row together.

The historian Ronald Smith has written of how in 1907 Swarthmore College was faced with an enormous dilemma: a Quaker heiress, aghast at the excesses of football, offered between $1 and $3 million to the school if it would agree to give up intercollegiate athletics. Although not unsympathetic to her concerns about the current state of sports, the president decided that he would not accept her gift, since to do so would be to give up the institution's freedom to make its own decisions.[22] We admire the president's resolve. Institutions should recall this lesson and be prepared to act independently of what isolated strong voices might advocate—from either side of the athletic divide!

New approaches might also strengthen the capacity of presidents and trustees to lead in this complex and emotional arena. Derek Bok, president emeritus of Harvard and a longtime observer of college sports, has suggested searching for a mechanism—such as an outside audit conducted by some organization other than the NCAA—that would force presidents and trustees to confront squarely what was going on in their athletics programs. "I was always amazed at the amount of wishful thinking and denial on the part of our fellow college presidents," Bok writes (in a letter to the authors). "Perhaps they would be more inclined to resist commercialization and intensification of athletics if they had to face the facts and discuss them periodically with trustees."

In setting out these propositions, our intention is to highlight what seem to us to be questions of compelling importance. We hope that others will consider these propositions, reflect on the findings and analysis presented in this book, and come to their own conclusions as to the desirable future shape of intercollegiate athletics. At the minimum, we would like to think that this study has helped de-mystify the current condition of college sports at academically selective colleges and universities. In turn, we hope that the findings will encourage more open and candid discussion of a subject that is often pushed aside, dealt with in a limited way, deferred for consideration to another day, or simply declared off limits.

The costs of intercollegiate athletics, financial and other, are real. If the leadership of an institution were to listen only to those voices that present themselves most forcefully—at alumni gatherings or in the letters to the alumni magazine—they might conclude that everyone believes in moving full steam ahead. But we know that this is not true. Those who feel differently should reflect upon the results reported here and voice their opinions as well. We have in mind those alumni/ae who might want to see their schools choose another path, those faculty and administrators (including directors of admissions) who are concerned about present trends, those exceptionally well-qualified applicants who do not enjoy the same admissions advantage as the recruited athletes, and those parents who watch as their grade school or high school children are swept up in high-stakes athletic competitions that can take the fun out of sports.

Tempting as it may be for presidents to leave athletics to the "true believers" (in the hope that they, in turn, will leave the rest of the college to them), that is not, in our view, the best approach. Intercollegiate athletics has come to have too pronounced an effect on colleges and universities—and on society—to be treated with benign neglect. Failure to see where the intensification of athletic programs is taking us, and to adjust expectations, could have the unintended consequence of allowing intercollegiate athletics to become less and less relevant to the educational experiences of most students and more and more at odds with the core missions of the institutions themselves. The objective, in our view, should be to strengthen the links between athletics and the educational missions of colleges and universities—to reinvigorate an aspect of college life that deserves to be celebrated for its positive contributions, not condemned for its excesses or criticized for its conflicts with educational values.

SCORECARD 2.1

Athletes as a Percent of All Male Students
(by Athlete Status, Cohort, and Division)

	Division IA Public Universities	Division IA Private Universities	Ivy League Universities	Coed Liberal Arts Colleges	Sector Composite
1951					
Students at large	92	92	80	67	81
Intercollegiate athletes	8	8	20	33	19
High Profile sports	3	5	6	13	8
Lower Profile sports	5	3	14	20	11
All men	100	100	100	100	100
1976					
Students at large	95	82	80	71	84
Intercollegiate athletes	5	8	20	29	16
High Profile sports	2	3	8	12	6
Lower Profile sports	3	5	12	18	10
All men	100	100	100	100	100
1989					
Students at large	95	91	73	68	81
Intercollegiate athletes	5	9	27	32	19
High Profile sports	2	4	8	11	6
Lower Profile sports	4	5	18	21	12
All men	100	100	100	100	100

Source: College and Beyond.

SCORECARD 2.2

Percent of Students Reporting That Being "Recruited" Was a "Very Important"
Influence in Choosing This Specific College
(by Athlete Status, Cohort, and Division, Male Only)

	Division IA Public Universities	Division IA Private Universities	Ivy League Universities	Coed Liberal Arts Colleges	Sector Composite
1976					
Students at large	6	11	18	18	13
Intercollegiate athletes	55	13	46	31	36
High Profile sports	n/a	n/a	71	38	n/a
Lower Profile sports	n/a	n/a	32	24	n/a
All men	8	11	23	20	16
1989					
Students at large	7	9	16	20	13
Intercollegiate athletes	81	78	67	65	73
High Profile sports	n/a	n/a	86	83	n/a
Lower Profile sports	n/a	n/a	59	56	n/a
All men	12	17	30	34	23

Source: College and Beyond.

Note: n/a indicates that cell sizes are insufficient for detailed breakdown.

SCORECARD 2.3

Average Combined SAT Score
(by Athlete Status, Cohort, and Division, Male Only)

	Division IA Public Universities	Division IA Private Universities	Ivy League Universities	Coed Liberal Arts Colleges	Sector Composite
1951					
Students at large	n/a	n/a	1185	1164	1173
Intercollegiate athletes	n/a	n/a	1145	1131	1137
High Profile sports	n/a	n/a	1114	1114	1114
Lower Profile sports	n/a	n/a	1161	1144	1151
All men	n/a	n/a	1176	1152	1162
1976					
Students at large	1110	1215	1299	1228	1216
Intercollegiate athletes	978	1109	1218	1164	1122
High Profile sports	911	1035	1150	1129	1063
Lower Profile sports	1014	1145	1263	1187	1156
All men	1104	1208	1282	1215	1205
1989					
Students at large	1154	1287	1337	1261	1263
Intercollegiate athletes	1009	1097	1270	1200	1145
High Profile sports	917	1003	1212	1126	1065
Lower Profile sports	1060	1165	1298	1235	1192
All men	1146	1271	1319	1244	1249

Source: College and Beyond.

Note: n/a indicates SATs not available from these schools for 1951.

SCORECARD 2.4

Percent of Students with a Father Who Has a Bachelor's Degree or Higher
(by Athlete Status, Cohort, and Division, Male Only)

	Division IA Public Universities	Division IA Private Universities	Ivy League Universities	Coed Liberal Arts Colleges	Sector Composite
1951					
Students at large	33	40	50	54	46
Intercollegiate athletes	25	35	50	58	44
High Profile sports	n/a	n/a	47	52	n/a
Lower Profile sports	n/a	n/a	51	60	n/a
All men	33	40	50	55	46
1976					
Students at large	53	67	60	72	65
Intercollegiate athletes	51	62	58	65	60
High Profile sports	n/a	n/a	45	52	n/a
Lower Profile sports	n/a	n/a	67	77	n/a
All men	53	67	59	71	64
1989					
Students at large	63	78	73	82	75
Intercollegiate athletes	58	63	73	78	69
High Profile sports	40	53	63	59	54
Lower Profile sports	67	75	78	87	78
All men	63	77	73	81	75

Source: College and Beyond.
Note: n/a indicates that cell sizes are insufficient for detailed breakdown.

SCORECARD 2.5

African Americans as a Percent of Male Students
(by Athlete Status, Cohort, and Division)

	Division IA Public Universities	Division IA Private Universities	Ivy League Universities	Coed Liberal Arts Colleges	Sector Composite
1951					
Students at large	n/a	1	1	1	1
Intercollegiate athletes	n/a	2	n/a	2	1
High Profile sports	n/a	3	n/a	3	2
Lower Profile sports	n/a	1	n/a	2	1
All men	n/a	1	1	1	1
1976					
Students at large	3	4	6	6	4
Intercollegiate athletes	7	12	7	7	8
High Profile sports	14	25	9	9	13
Lower Profile sports	2	4	5	6	4
All men	3	4	6	5	5
1989					
Students at large	4	5	6	5	5
Intercollegiate athletes	20	18	6	8	13
High Profile sports	35	39	10	17	26
Lower Profile sports	4	7	4	3	4
All men	6	5	6	6	6

Source: College and Beyond.

Note: n/a indicates that cell sizes are insufficient for detailed breakdown.

SCORECARD 2.6

Percent of Students Rating Themselves Pre-College as Liberal or Far Left
(by Athlete Status, Cohort, and Division, Male Only)

	Division IA Public Universities	Division IA Private Universities	Ivy League Universities	Coed Liberal Arts Colleges	Sector Composite
			1976		
Students at large	33	25	49	61	42
Intercollegiate athletes	25	22	22	34	26
High Profile sports	n/a	n/a	27	41	n/a
Lower Profile sports	n/a	n/a	39	53	n/a
All men	33	25	46	57	40
			1989		
Students at large	26	39	36	45	37
Intercollegiate athletes	25	22	22	34	26
High Profile sports	n/a	n/a	17	30	n/a
Lower Profile sports	n/a	n/a	23	36	n/a
All men	26	37	32	42	34

Source: College and Beyond.

Note: n/a indicates that cell sizes are insufficient for detailed breakdown.

SCORECARD 3.1
Six-Year Graduation Rates
(by Athlete Status, Cohort, and Division, Male Only)

	Division IA Public Universities	Division IA Private Universities	Ivy League Universities	Coed Liberal Arts Colleges	Sector Composite
1951					
Students at large	54	54	79	66	63
Intercollegiate athletes	77	73	90	85	82
High Profile sports	72	69	90	86	80
Lower Profile sports	81	78	91	85	84
All men	56	55	81	71	65
1976					
Students at large	73	75	82	77	77
Intercollegiate athletes	76	89	90	84	85
High Profile sports	69	87	86	81	82
Lower Profile sports	81	91	92	87	88
All men	73	76	84	78	78
1989					
Students at large	80	88	88	86	86
Intercollegiate athletes	85	85	91	93	89
High Profile sports	85	81	90	89	86
Lower Profile sports	84	90	92	95	91
All men	80	87	89	88	87

Source: College and Beyond.

SCORECARD 3.2
Mean GPA Percentile
(by Athlete Status, Cohort, and Division, Male Only)

	Division IA Public Universities	Division IA Private Universities	Ivy League Universities	Coed Liberal Arts Colleges	Sector Composite
1951					
Students at large	46	46	50	47	47
Intercollegiate athletes	50	42	50	49	48
High Profile sports	48	40	45	48	45
Lower Profile sports	53	45	51	50	50
All men	46	46	50	47	47
1976					
Students at large	47	49	51	50	49
Intercollegiate athletes	37	41	40	40	40
High Profile sports	32	32	31	37	33
Lower Profile sports	41	46	46	42	44
All men	46	48	49	47	48
1989					
Students at large	48	49	50	48	49
Intercollegiate athletes	34	28	37	37	34
High Profile sports	27	18	29	28	25
Lower Profile sports	37	37	42	42	40
All men	47	47	47	46	47

Source: College and Beyond.

SCORECARD 3.3

Percent of Students with GPA in Bottom One-Third of Class
(by Athlete Status, Cohort, and Division, Male Only)

	Division IA Public Universities	Division IA Private Universities	Ivy League Universities	Coed Liberal Arts Colleges	Sector Composite
1951					
Students at large	43	50	37	42	43
Intercollegiate athletes	26	44	41	31	35
High Profile sports	28	52	43	31	38
Lower Profile sports	23	37	39	30	32
All men	42	49	38	40	43
1976					
Students at large	40	39	35	37	38
Intercollegiate athletes	53	49	50	46	49
High Profile sports	67	61	65	52	60
Lower Profile sports	46	39	40	42	41
All men	41	40	38	39	39
1989					
Students at large	38	35	36	36	36
Intercollegiate athletes	57	66	54	54	58
High Profile sports	65	81	69	69	72
Lower Profile sports	53	53	47	46	49
All men	39	38	41	40	39

Source: College and Beyond.

SCORECARD 3.4

Percent of Male Students Majoring in Math or Engineering
(by Athlete Status, Cohort, and Division)

	Division IA Public Universities	Division IA Private Universities	Ivy League Universities	Coed Liberal Arts Colleges	Sector Composite
1951					
Students at large	15	27	14	4	14
Intercollegiate athletes	11	17	13	7	12
High Profile sports	8	15	16	8	12
Lower Profile sports	11	14	12	5	10
All men	14	26	14	6	15
1976					
Students at large	19	27	14	4	16
Intercollegiate athletes	12	20	15	5	13
High Profile sports	10	18	16	4	12
Lower Profile sports	12	22	15	5	13
All men	18	26	15	4	16
1989					
Students at large	21	23	23	5	17
Intercollegiate athletes	13	15	10	7	12
High Profile sports	13	9	10	3	8
Lower Profile sports	13	18	10	10	13
All men	20	21	17	5	16

Source: College and Beyond.

SCORECARD 3.5

Percent of Male Students Majoring in the Humanities
(by Athlete Status, Cohort, and Division)

	Division IA Public Universities	Division IA Private Universities	Ivy League Universities	Coed Liberal Arts Colleges	Sector Composite
1951					
Students at large	11	13	25	34	22
Intercollegiate athletes	11	11	22	35	21
High Profile sports	5	18	18	31	20
Lower Profile sports	16	11	24	37	23
All men	11	13	24	35	22
1976					
Students at large	7	12	27	37	22
Intercollegiate athletes	7	9	22	21	15
High Profile sports	4	11	17	13	11
Lower Profile sports	8	9	22	28	17
All men	7	12	26	34	21
1989					
Students at large	11	19	24	45	25
Intercollegiate athletes	13	14	27	32	21
High Profile sports	13	14	21	26	18
Lower Profile sports	13	15	30	35	23
All men	11	18	25	41	24

Source: College and Beyond.

SCORECARD 3.6

Percent of Male Students Majoring in the Social Sciences
(by Athlete Status, Cohort, and Division)

	Division IA Public Universities	Division IA Private Universities	Ivy League Universities	Coed Liberal Arts Colleges	Sector Composite
1951					
Students at large	8	14	22	24	18
Intercollegiate athletes	10	19	21	27	20
High Profile sports	7	21	22	25	20
Lower Profile sports	12	18	20	27	20
All men	8	15	21	24	18
1976					
Students at large	14	19	25	29	22
Intercollegiate athletes	17	25	34	45	32
High Profile sports	16	26	34	50	33
Lower Profile sports	16	26	34	39	30
All men	14	19	26	33	24
1989					
Students at large	20	29	24	31	26
Intercollegiate athletes	24	38	37	41	35
High Profile sports	27	39	44	58	42
Lower Profile sports	24	38	34	34	33
All men	21	31	30	35	29

Source: College and Beyond.

SCORECARD 3.7

Percent of Male Students Majoring in the Natural Sciences
(by Athlete Status, Cohort, and Division)

	Division IA Public Universities	Division IA Private Universities	Ivy League Universities	Coed Liberal Arts Colleges	Sector Composite
1951					
Students at large	11	10	14	19	14
Intercollegiate athletes	5	6	10	22	12
High Profile sports	7	6	9	23	13
Lower Profile sports	4	8	10	22	12
All men	11	10	13	19	14
1976					
Students at large	14	14	14	18	15
Intercollegiate athletes	10	9	10	18	12
High Profile sports	6	4	8	16	9
Lower Profile sports	12	11	11	20	14
All men	13	14	13	18	15
1989					
Students at large	13	13	14	12	13
Intercollegiate athletes	8	7	12	17	11
High Profile sports	4	6	10	12	8
Lower Profile sports	9	7	12	18	11
All men	12	12	13	13	12

Source: College and Beyond.

SCORECARD 4.1

Graduate Business Degree Attainment as a Percent of All Male Graduates
(by Athlete Status, Cohort, and Division)

	Division IA Public Universities	Division IA Private Universities	Ivy League Universities	Coed Liberal Arts Colleges	Sector Composite
1951					
Students at large	9	8	10	7	8
Intercollegiate athletes	11	7	12	10	10
High Profile sports	11	5	16	7	9
Lower Profile sports	12	9	11	10	10
All men	9	8	10	8	9
1976					
Students at large	13	17	14	12	14
Intercollegiate athletes	9	19	18	19	17
High Profile sports	6	11	16	21	14
Lower Profile sports	11	23	19	19	18
All men	13	17	15	14	15
1989					
Students at large	8	8	6	5	7
Intercollegiate athletes	7	7	11	5	7
High Profile sports	8	4	8	6	6
Lower Profile sports	7	8	12	5	8
All men	8	8	7	5	7

Source: College and Beyond.

SCORECARD 4.2

Medical Degree Attainment as a Percent of All Male Graduates
(by Athlete Status, Cohort, and Division)

	Division IA Public Universities	Division IA Private Universities	Ivy League Universities	Coed Liberal Arts Colleges	Sector Composite
			1951		
Students at large	7	13	14	12	12
Intercollegiate athletes	3	12	14	12	11
High Profile sports	2	10	9	17	11
Lower Profile sports	3	13	16	9	10
All men	7	13	14	12	12
			1976		
Students at large	6	12	12	10	10
Intercollegiate athletes	6	8	12	9	9
High Profile sports	3	9	9	9	8
Lower Profile sports	7	9	15	10	10
All men	6	12	12	10	10
			1989		
Students at large	12	7	9	7	9
Intercollegiate athletes	9	5	10	9	8
High Profile sports	0	4	8	6	4
Lower Profile sports	11	6	11	10	9
All men	11	7	9	7	9

Source: College and Beyond.

SCORECARD 4.3

Law Degree Attainment as a Percent of All Male Graduates
(by Athlete Status, Cohort, and Division)

	Division IA Public Universities	Division IA Private Universities	Ivy League Universities	Coed Liberal Arts Colleges	Sector Composite
1951					
Students at large	7	11	16	9	10
Intercollegiate athletes	7	9	15	7	9
High Profile sports	6	7	18	7	9
Lower Profile sports	7	7	14	6	8
All men	7	11	16	8	10
1976					
Students at large	8	15	20	15	15
Intercollegiate athletes	3	13	17	15	12
High Profile sports	1	11	12	10	9
Lower Profile sports	4	13	18	19	14
All men	8	15	19	15	14
1989					
Students at large	14	7	12	11	11
Intercollegiate athletes	10	7	11	9	9
High Profile sports	14	8	8	12	11
Lower Profile sports	7	6	12	8	8
All men	13	7	12	10	11

Source: College and Beyond.

SCORECARD 4.4

Ph.D. Attainment as a Percent of All Male Graduates
(by Athlete Status, Cohort, and Division)

	Division IA Public Universities	Division IA Private Universities	Ivy League Universities	Coed Liberal Arts Colleges	Sector Composite
1951					
Students at large	9	8	13	18	13
Intercollegiate athletes	6	4	8	15	9
High Profile sports	1	4	4	16	7
Lower Profile sports	8	5	10	14	10
All men	9	8	12	17	12
1976					
Students at large	4	7	11	11	8
Intercollegiate athletes	5	4	7	8	6
High Profile sports	2	7	7	6	6
Lower Profile sports	6	3	8	9	6
All men	4	7	10	10	8
1989					
Students at large	7	5	15	13	10
Intercollegiate athletes	5	2	6	10	6
High Profile sports	7	0	5	5	4
Lower Profile sports	3	3	7	11	6
All men	7	5	12	13	9

Source: College and Beyond.

SCORECARD 4.5

Any Masters Degree Attainment as a Percent of All Male Graduates
(by Athlete Status, Cohort, and Division)

	Division IA Public Universities	Division IA Private Universities	Ivy League Universities	Coed Liberal Arts Colleges	Sector Composite
1951					
Students at large	24	22	21	31	25
Intercollegiate athletes	23	17	17	29	22
High Profile sports	34	16	10	25	21
Lower Profile sports	16	17	21	33	23
All men	24	22	20	30	25
1976					
Students at large	17	19	24	27	22
Intercollegiate athletes	14	14	12	18	15
High Profile sports	15	15	8	16	14
Lower Profile sports	13	13	16	19	15
All men	17	19	21	24	21
1989					
Students at large	19	16	24	26	21
Intercollegiate athletes	15	12	15	24	16
High Profile sports	11	8	15	26	15
Lower Profile sports	16	11	15	23	16
All men	19	16	21	26	20

Source: College and Beyond.

SCORECARD 4.6

Percent of Full-Time Male Workers in Financial Services
(by Athlete Status, Cohort, and Division)

	Division IA Public Universities	Division IA Private Universities	Ivy League Universities	Coed Liberal Arts Colleges	Sector Composite
1951					
Students at large	12	10	11	9	10
Intercollegiate athletes	10	15	13	8	12
High Profile sports	10	23	15	5	13
Lower Profile sports	9	15	13	11	12
All men	12	11	11	8	10
1976					
Students at large	8	7	8	7	7
Intercollegiate athletes	4	10	14	11	10
High Profile sports	3	5	14	10	8
Lower Profile sports	4	15	14	11	11
All men	8	7	9	8	8
1989					
Students at large	14	15	20	9	14
Intercollegiate athletes	12	17	31	13	17
High Profile sports	13	13	31	12	16
Lower Profile sports	11	17	31	13	17
All men	14	15	25	11	16

Source: College and Beyond.

SCORECARD 4.7

Mean GPA Percentile of Men in Financial Services
(by Athlete Status, Cohort, and Division)

	Division IA Public Universities	Division IA Private Universities	Ivy League Universities	Coed Liberal Arts Colleges	Sector Composite
1951					
Students at large	55	48	43	39	45
Intercollegiate athletes	55	60	43	49	53
High Profile sports	47	59	33	36	44
Lower Profile sports	54	53	47	48	50
All men	56	51	43	38	46
1976					
Students at large	50	46	48	46	47
Intercollegiate athletes	32	46	37	43	41
High Profile sports	58	34	27	38	36
Lower Profile sports	25	46	40	47	42
All men	49	45	45	46	46
1989					
Students at large	54	43	52	56	51
Intercollegiate athletes	49	20	36	20	31
High Profile sports	44	26	33	26	34
Lower Profile sports	49	20	39	21	32
All men	53	38	43	48	45

Source: College and Beyond.

SCORECARD 4.8

Mean 1995 Own Earned Income
(by Athlete Status, Cohort, and Division, Male Only, in dollars)

	Division IA Public Universities	Division IA Private Universities	Ivy League Universities	Coed Liberal Arts Colleges	Sector Composite
1951					
Students at large	109,666	122,514	128,317	111,293	117,948
Intercollegiate athletes	117,339	131,733	135,127	128,547	128,187
High Profile sports	144,083	118,125	146,489	136,071	136,192
Lower Profile sports	104,603	140,656	129,839	123,279	124,594
All men	110,426	123,638	129,763	118,488	120,579
1976					
Students at large	84,248	106,311	108,172	92,770	97,875
Intercollegiate athletes	87,655	121,548	125,055	109,939	111,049
High Profile sports	80,243	117,468	119,295	106,465	105,868
Lower Profile sports	91,522	123,329	128,102	112,141	113,774
All men	84,408	107,412	111,887	97,343	100,263
1989					
Students at large	34,730	40,890	44,540	27,883	37,011
Intercollegiate athletes	40,610	39,300	53,744	37,228	42,721
High Profile sports	50,000	47,794	57,500	38,765	48,515
Lower Profile sports	36,437	35,942	51,779	36,591	40,187
All men	35,425	40,525	48,948	30,600	38,875

Source: College and Beyond.

SCORECARD 4.9a

Percent of Students Reporting as Freshmen That a "Very Important" Reason
for Going to College Is to "Make Money"
(by Athlete Status, Cohort, and Division, Male Only)

	Division IA Public Universities	Division IA Private Universities	Ivy League Universities	Coed Liberal Arts Colleges	Sector Composite
1976					
Students at large	55	50	45	29	44
Intercollegiate athletes	58	54	52	42	51
High Profile sports	n/a	n/a	64	47	n/a
Lower Profile sports	n/a	n/a	45	38	n/a
All men	55	50	47	32	45
1989					
Students at large	75	60	51	40	53
Intercollegiate athletes	79	72	64	53	65
High Profile sports	n/a	n/a	70	62	n/a
Lower Profile sports	n/a	n/a	62	49	n/a
All men	75	61	54	44	55

Source: College and Beyond.

Note: n/a indicates that cell sizes are insufficient for detailed breakdown.

SCORECARD 4.9b
Percent of Students Reporting as Freshmen That an "Essential" Goal Is to Be "Very Well Off Financially"
(by Athlete Status, Cohort, and Division, Male Only)

	Division IA Public Universities	Division IA Private Universities	Ivy League Universities	Coed Liberal Arts Colleges	Sector Composite
1976					
Students at large	18	20	15	8	13
Intercollegiate athletes	20	15	18	15	17
High Profile sports	n/a	n/a	21	20	n/a
Lower Profile sports	n/a	n/a	17	11	n/a
All men	18	19	15	9	14
1989					
Students at large	38	21	29	20	25
Intercollegiate athletes	49	37	36	28	33
High Profile sports	n/a	n/a	28	28	n/a
Lower Profile sports	n/a	n/a	36	27	n/a
All men	39	23	30	23	27

Source: College and Beyond.

Note: n/a indicates that cell sizes are insufficient for detailed breakdown.

SCORECARD 6.1
Athletes as a Percent of All Female Students
(by Cohort and Division)

	Division IA Public Universities	Division IA Private Universities	Ivy League Universities	Coed Liberal Arts Colleges	Women's Colleges	Sector Composite
1976	3	5	10	14	10	9
1989	3	6	15	19	12	11

Source: College and Beyond.

SCORECARD 6.2
Percent of Athletes Reporting That Being "Recruited" Was a
"Very Important" Reason for Choosing This Specific College
(by Athlete Status, Cohort, and Division, Female Only)

	Division IA Public Universities	Division IA Private Universities	Ivy League Universities	Coed Liberal Arts Colleges	Women's Colleges	Sector Composite
1976						
Students at large	2	1	3	2	4	2
Athletes	4	4	3	5	1	4
All women	2	1	3	3	4	2
1989						
Students at large	1	1	3	2	4	2
Athletes	57	52	42	9	3	29
All women	2	4	8	4	4	4

Source: College and Beyond.

SCORECARD 6.3
Average Combined SAT Score
(by Athlete Status, Cohort, and Division, Female Only)

	Division IA Public Universities	Division IA Private Universities	Ivy League Universities	Coed Liberal Arts Colleges	Women's Colleges	Sector Composite
1976						
Students at large	1064	1182	1264	1186	1206	1177
Athletes	1044	1165	1253	1173	1219	1167
All women	1063	1180	1263	1184	1207	1176
1989						
Students at large	1091	1243	1300	1213	1223	1217
Athletes	997	1138	1240	1193	1213	1159
All women	1089	1236	1291	1210	1221	1213

Source: College and Beyond.

SCORECARD 6.4
Percent of Students Reporting Themselves as in the "Top 10 Percent"
in terms of Intellectual Self-Confidence
(by Athlete Status, Cohort, and Division, Female Only)

	Division IA Public Universities	Division IA Private Universities	Ivy League Universities	Coed Liberal Arts Colleges	Women's Colleges	Sector Composite
1976						
Students at large	9	19	24	14	19	16
Athletes	6	7	20	17	5	11
All women	9	18	24	15	18	16
1989						
Students at large	13	27	26	18	18	20
Athletes	8	13	13	14	15	13
All women	13	26	24	17	18	20

Source: College and Beyond.

SCORECARD 6.5
African Americans as a Percent of All Female Students
(by Athlete Status, Cohort, and Division)

	Division IA Public Universities	Division IA Private Universities	Ivy League Universities	Coed Liberal Arts Colleges	Women's Colleges	Sector Composite
1976						
Students at large	5	7	10	8	6	7
Athletes	5	4	7	9	3	6
All women	5	7	10	7	6	7
1989						
Students at large	7	7	10	8	5	8
Athletes	4	11	6	4	2	6
All women	7	8	9	7	5	7

Source: College and Beyond.

SCORECARD 6.6
Attended a Private High School as a Percent of All Female Students
(by Athlete Status, Cohort, and Division)

	Division IA Public Universities	Division IA Private Universities	Ivy League Universities	Coed Liberal Arts Colleges	Women's Colleges	Sector Composite
1976						
Students at large	2	18	26	27	24	21
Athletes	0	26	37	37	27	28
All women	2	18	27	28	24	21
1989						
Students at large	9	22	34	29	34	28
Athletes	8	12	27	31	36	24
All women	9	22	33	30	34	28

Source: College and Beyond.

SCORECARD 6.7
Percent of Students with a Father Who Has Bachelor's Degree or Higher
(by Athlete Status, Cohort, and Division, Female Only)

	Division IA Public Universities	Division IA Private Universities	Ivy League Universities	Coed Liberal Arts Colleges	Women's Colleges	Sector Composite
1976						
Students at large	57	74	71	83	74	73
Athletes	72	80	79	82	84	80
All women	58	75	72	83	75	73
1989						
Students at large	65	80	81	80	78	78
Athletes	66	76	86	85	87	80
All women	65	80	81	81	79	78

Source: College and Beyond.

SCORECARD 6.8
Percent of Students with a Mother Who Has Bachelor's Degree or Higher
(by Athlete Status, Cohort, and Division, Female Only)

	Division IA Public Universities	Division IA Private Universities	Ivy League Universities	Coed Liberal Arts Colleges	Women's Colleges	Sector Composite
1976						
Students at large	37	54	58	64	57	55
Athletes	45	63	69	61	66	60
All women	37	54	59	64	58	55
1989						
Students at large	50	66	70	69	68	65
Athletes	52	60	68	73	73	65
All women	50	66	70	70	69	66

Source: College and Beyond.

SCORECARD 6.9a
Percent of Students Rating Themselves as Liberal or Far Left
(by Athlete Status, Cohort, and Division, Female Only)

	Division IA Public Universities	Division IA Private Universities	Ivy League Universities	Coed Liberal Arts Colleges	Women's Colleges	Sector Composite
1976						
Students at large	32	34	53	65	49	47
Athletes	20	21	41	54	50	37
All women	32	32	52	64	48	45
1989						
Students at large	28	38	44	56	53	46
Athletes	13	25	31	51	58	39
All women	27	37	42	55	54	45

Source: College and Beyond.

SCORECARD 6.9b
Percent of Students Rating Themselves as Conservative or Far Right
(by Athlete Status, Cohort, and Division, Female Only)

	Division IA Public Universities	Division IA Private Universities	Ivy League Universities	Coed Liberal Arts Colleges	Women's Colleges	Sector Composite
1976						
Students at large	15	22	11	7	14	13
Athletes	17	25	12	11	12	15
All women	15	23	11	8	14	14
1989						
Students at large	20	23	14	11	12	15
Athletes	29	38	19	12	15	21
All women	21	24	15	12	13	16

Source: College and Beyond.

SCORECARD 7.1
Mean GPA Percentile
(by Athlete Status, Cohort, and Division, Female Only)

	Division IA Public Universities	Division IA Private Universities	Ivy League Universities	Coed Liberal Arts Colleges	Women's Colleges	Sector Composite
1976						
Students at large	53	50	51	52	50	51
Athletes	54	51	51	50	49	51
All women	53	50	51	52	50	51
1989						
Students at large	54	52	55	54	49	53
Athletes	46	42	44	50	50	46
All women	54	52	53	53	50	52

Source: College and Beyond.

SCORECARD 7.2

Percent of Female Students Majoring in the Humanities
(by Athlete Status, Cohort, and Division)

	Division IA Public Universities	Division IA Private Universities	Ivy League Universities	Coed Liberal Arts Colleges	Women's Colleges	Sector Composite
1976						
Students at large	16	22	29	26	33	25
Athletes	15	28	32	34	39	30
All women	16	23	29	27	34	26
1989						
Students at large	16	25	36	41	37	31
Athletes	6	14	31	35	37	25
All women	15	24	35	40	37	31

Source: College and Beyond.

SCORECARD 7.3

Percent of Female Students Majoring in Math or Engineering
(by Athlete Status, Cohort, and Division)

	Division IA Public Universities	Division IA Private Universities	Ivy League Universities	Coed Liberal Arts Colleges	Women's Colleges	Sector Composite
1976						
Students at large	5	8	9	2	3	5
Athletes	5	11	8	1	4	5
All women	5	8	9	2	3	5
1989						
Students at large	7	10	6	5	4	7
Athletes	3	10	5	5	4	6
All women	7	10	6	5	4	7

Source: College and Beyond.

SCORECARD 7.4

Percent of Female Students Majoring in the Natural Sciences
(by Athlete Status, Cohort, and Division)

	Division IA Public Universities	Division IA Private Universities	Ivy League Universities	Coed Liberal Arts Colleges	Women's Colleges	Sector Composite
1976						
Students at large	7	13	11	10	13	11
Athletes	5	18	18	17	17	15
All women	7	14	11	11	14	11
1989						
Students at large	8	13	11	11	11	11
Athletes	8	11	11	12	16	12
All women	8	13	11	11	12	11

Source: College and Beyond.

SCORECARD 7.5

Percent of Female Students Majoring in the Social Sciences
(by Athlete Status, Cohort, and Division)

	Division IA Public Universities	Division IA Private Universities	Ivy League Universities	Coed Liberal Arts Colleges	Women's Colleges	Sector Composite
1976						
Students at large	16	22	29	26	33	25
Athletes	15	28	32	34	39	30
All women	16	23	29	27	34	26
1989						
Students at large	22	30	31	33	36	31
Athletes	25	30	38	41	35	34
All women	22	30	32	34	36	31

Source: College and Beyond.

SCORECARD 8.1

Mean 1995 Own Earned Income
(by Athlete Status, Cohort, and Division, Full-Time Female Workers, in dollars)

	Division IA Public Universities	Division IA Private Universities	Ivy League Universities	Coed Liberal Arts Colleges	Women's Colleges	Sector Composite
1976						
Students at large	54,491	72,943	77,239	58,478	69,400	65,889
Athletes	63,423	71,866	89,522	64,211	85,356	73,050
All women	55,293	72,659	79,144	59,258	70,360	66,539
1989						
Students at large	29,621	29,858	31,865	25,560	27,557	28,874
Athletes	28,142	30,151	30,392	26,230	28,053	28,551
All women	29,506	29,894	31,492	25,586	27,590	28,800

Source: College and Beyond.

SCORECARD 8.2

Mean 1995 Own Earned Income in the For-Profit Job Sector
(by Athlete Status, Cohort, and Division, Full-Time Female Workers, in dollars)

	Division IA Public Universities	Division IA Private Universities	Ivy League Universities	Coed Liberal Arts Colleges	Women's Colleges	Sector Composite
1976						
Students at large	60,814	82,526	88,426	69,464	80,492	75,777
Athletes	80,987	88,007	101,649	82,636	108,965	90,809
All women	62,134	82,575	90,744	70,371	81,533	76,701
1989						
Students at large	31,511	33,028	35,287	28,613	29,599	31,627
Athletes	25,410	33,555	31,882	29,096	33,878	30,332
All women	31,176	33,150	34,316	28,524	29,887	31,419

Source: College and Beyond.

SCORECARD 9.1

Percent of Freshman Rating Themselves in the Top 10 Percent of Peers on
"Leadership Ability"
(by Athlete Status, Cohort, and Division, Male Only)

	Division IA Public Universities	Division IA Private Universities	Ivy League Universities	Coed Liberal Arts Colleges	Sector Composite
1976					
Students at large	17	23	27	18	20
Athletes	19	23	34	21	23
High Profile sports	n/a	n/a	37	22	n/a
Lower Profile sports	n/a	n/a	33	21	n/a
All men	17	23	29	19	21
1989					
Students at large	23	30	29	20	25
Athletes	26	39	39	25	32
High Profile sports	n/a	n/a	55	28	n/a
Lower Profile sports	n/a	n/a	34	24	n/a
All men	23	30	32	22	26

Source: College and Beyond.

Note: n/a indicates that cell sizes are insufficient for detailed breakdown.

SCORECARD 9.2

Percent Reporting That "Competition" Has Been
"Very Important" in Life after College
(by Athlete Status, Cohort, and Division, Male Youth Leaders Only)

	Division IA Public Universities	Division IA Private Universities	Ivy League Universities	Coed Liberal Arts Colleges	Sector Composite
		1951			
Students at large	45	26	41	19	31
Intercollegiate athletes	63	71	29	28	48
High Profile sports	33	54	81	19	47
Lower Profile sports	88	67	0	30	45
All men	48	38	40	20	34
		1976			
Students at large	27	27	28	24	26
Intercollegiate athletes	46	48	43	33	42
High Profile sports	57	56	47	54	54
Lower Profile sports	40	40	36	15	31
All men	30	30	33	28	30
		1989			
Students at large	31	25	35	17	26
Intercollegiate athletes	55	58	39	26	45
High Profile sports	53	39	48	19	39
Lower Profile sports	53	62	34	29	45
All men	38	33	37	25	33

Source: College and Beyond.

SCORECARD 10.1

General Giving Rates

(by Athlete Status, Cohort, and Division, Male Only, percent)

	Division IA Private Universities	Ivy League Universities	Coed Liberal Arts Colleges	Sector Composite
——————————— 1951 ———————————				
Students at large	48	58	62	56
Intercollegiate athletes	48	62	70	61
High Profile sports	54	58	76	64
Lower Profile sports	43	64	69	60
All men	48	59	65	58
——————————— 1976 ———————————				
Students at large	49	48	63	54
Intercollegiate athletes	40	51	73	55
High Profile sports	29	49	69	49
Lower Profile sports	44	51	76	58
All men	49	49	68	55
——————————— 1989 ———————————				
Students at large	47	46	60	51
Intercollegiate athletes	33	47	62	48
High Profile sports	18	46	54	39
Lower Profile sports	53	48	65	56
All men	46	46	61	51

Source: College and Beyond.

SCORECARD 10.2

General Giving Rates

(by Athlete Status, Cohort, and Division, Female Only, percent)

	Division IA Private Universities	Ivy League Universities	Coed Liberal Arts Colleges	Women's Colleges	Sector Composite
1976					
Students at large	51	53	66	48	56
Intercollegiate athletes	45	60	75	75	63
All women	51	53	67	49	56
1989					
Students at large	50	50	63	38	53
Intercollegiate athletes	47	51	74	72	58
All women	50	50	66	40	54

Source: College and Beyond.

SCORECARD 10.3

General Giving Rates

(by Extracurricular Status, Cohort, and Division, Male Only, percent)

	Division IA Private Universities	Ivy League Universities	Coed Liberal Arts Colleges	Sector Composite
1951				
Extracurriculars	59	59	78	66
All others	38	60	65	56
1976				
Extracurriculars	40	73	76	64
All others	37	52	71	54
1989				
Extracurriculars	41	52	62	52
All others	37	44	57	43

Source: College and Beyond.

SCORECARD 10.4

General Giving Rates

(by Class Rank, Cohort, and Division, Male Only, percent)

	Division IA Private Universities	Ivy League Universities	Coed Liberal Arts Colleges	Sector Composite
		1951		
Top third	53	65	73	64
Middle third	50	59	62	57
Bottom third	43	52	56	51
All	49	59	64	58
		1976		
Top third	56	52	74	61
Middle third	50	49	69	56
Bottom third	41	44	59	48
All	49	49	68	56
		1989		
Top third	49	45	65	54
Middle third	48	45	60	51
Bottom third	41	39	50	44
All	46	43	58	49

Source: College and Beyond.

SCORECARD 10.5
Athletic Giving Rates
(by Athlete Status, Cohort, and Division, Male Only, percent)

	Division IA Private Universities	Ivy League Universities	Coed Liberal Arts Colleges	Sector Composite
1951				
Students at large	6	4	0	3
Intercollegiate athletes	25	25	5	17
High Profile sports	28	30	15	23
Lower Profile sports	24	23	2	14
All men	8	8	3	6
1976				
Students at large	3	2	1	2
Intercollegiate athletes	20	26	6	17
High Profile sports	18	25	7	16
Lower Profile sports	23	27	6	18
All men	5	7	3	5
1989				
Students at large	4	1	0	2
Intercollegiate athletes	10	17	11	13
High Profile sports	10	15	8	11
Lower Profile sports	14	17	12	14
All men	4	5	5	5

Source: College and Beyond.

SCORECARD 10.6

Athletic Giving Rates

(by Athlete Status, Cohort, and Division, Female Only, percent)

	Division IA Private Universities	Ivy League Universities	Coed Liberal Arts Colleges	Women's Colleges	Sector Composite
1976					
Students at large	2	2	1	n/a	1
Intercollegiate athletes	10	20	3	n/a	9
All women	2	4	2	n/a	2
1989					
Students at large	3	3	3	n/a	3
Intercollegiate athletes	5	15	12	n/a	10
All women	3	3	3	n/a	3

Source: College and Beyond.

Note: n/a indicates that cell sizes are insufficient for detailed breakdown.

SCORECARD 10.7

Average Size of Athletic Gifts
(by Athlete Status, Cohort, and Division, Male Only, in dollars)

	Division IA Private Universities	Ivy League Universities	Coed Liberal Arts Colleges	Sector Composite
1951				
Students at large	751	282	28	434
Intercollegiate athletes	1,439	154	24	574
High Profile sports	1,723	242	38	773
Lower Profile sports	281	112	11	149
All men	844	185	24	366
1976				
Students at large	157	38	41	88
Intercollegiate athletes	196	115	18	110
High Profile sports	433	77	14	183
Lower Profile sports	81	132	16	76
All men	163	107	27	104
1989				
Students at large	55	20	9	34
Intercollegiate athletes	22	73	16	35
High Profile sports	16	36	27	27
Lower Profile sports	27	111	13	47
All men	37	70	16	39

Source: College and Beyond.

SCORECARD 10.8
Average Size of General Gifts
(by Athlete Status, Cohort, and Division, Male Only, in dollars)

	Division IA Private Universities	Ivy League Universities	Coed Liberal Arts Colleges	Sector Composite
1951				
Students at large	386	775	1,031	751
Intercollegiate athletes	782	848	807	809
High Profile sports	533	801	838	727
Lower Profile sports	812	867	788	815
All men	442	763	972	743
1976				
Students at large	206	115	102	143
Intercollegiate athletes	100	211	112	136
High Profile sports	265	218	146	209
Lower Profile sports	79	217	89	122
All men	192	142	114	150
1989				
Students at large	29	40	23	30
Intercollegiate athletes	25	56	19	32
High Profile sports	22	29	17	22
Lower Profile sports	27	69	21	37
All men	29	46	22	31

Source: College and Beyond.

SCORECARD 10.9

Average Size of General Gifts
(by Athlete Status, Cohort, and Division, Female Only, in dollars)

	Division IA Private Universities	Ivy League Universities	Coed Liberal Arts Colleges	Women's Colleges	Sector Composite
		1976			
Students at large	78	98	75	104	86
Intercollegiate athletes	227	89	60	92	117
All women	86	98	71	102	87
		1989			
Students at large	22	37	15	20	23
Intercollegiate athletes	17	26	20	19	21
All women	21	37	17	20	23

Source: College and Beyond.

SCORECARD 11.1

Direct Expenditures on Football and Men's Basketball by Division
(in thousands of dollars)

	Division IA "Plus" Universities	Division IA "Standard" Universities	Ivy League Universities	Coed Liberal Arts Colleges
Football expenditures	9700	6100	1150	136
Percent of team expenditures	45%	45%	24%	13%
Percent of total expenditures	26%	29%	9%	10%
Men's basketball expenditures	1700	1800	350	52
Percent of team expenditures	8%	13%	7%	5%
Percent of total expenditures	4%	8%	4%	4%
Football plus men's basketball	11400	7900	1500	188
Percent of team expenditures	53%	58%	32%	18%
Percent of total expenditures	30%	37%	13%	13%

Source: Equity in Athletics Disclosure Act filings, 1997–98.

SCORECARD 11.2
Major Components of Expenditures in Football
and Men's Basketball by Division
(FY 1997–98, in thousands of dollars)

	Division IA Universities	Ivy League Universities	Coed Liberal Arts Colleges
Football			
Scholarships	2,300	0	0
Coaches	1,100	400	110
Recruiting	250	70	5
Operating expenses	700	200	30
Football—other	3,150	280	5
Total	7,500	950	150
Men's basketball			
Scholarships	300	0	0
Coaches	450	180	38
Recruiting	70	20	2
Operating expenses	300	100	15
Basketball—other	630	50	3
Total	1,750	350	58

Source: Estimates based on data provided by selected schools.

SCORECARD 11.3
Estimates of Average General Infrastructure Costs versus Total Expenditures
(in thousands of dollars)

	Division IA "Plus" Universities	Division IA "Standard" Universities	Ivy League Universities	Coed Liberal Arts Colleges
Total expenditures	38,000	21,200	9,000	1,400
Less team-specific costs	21,400	13,500	4,700	1,000
General infrastructure	16,600	7,700	4,300	400

Source: Estimates based on data from Equity in Athletics Disclosure Act filings, 1997–98.

SCORECARD 11.4
Average Numbers of Teams and Athletes by Division

	Division IA "Plus" Universities	Division IA "Standard" Universities	Ivy League Universities	Coed Liberal Arts Colleges	Division III Universities
All teams					
Average number of teams	25	16	30	21	17
Average athletes per team	30	27	29	25	35
Total athletes	726	422	850	535	601
Lower Profile teams					
Average number of teams	23	14	28	19	15
Average athletes per team	27	22	28	26	34
Total athletes	592	305	746	458	526

Source: Equity in Athletics Disclosure Act filings, 1997–98.

SCORECARD 11.5
Expenditures on Lower Profile Sports by Division
(in thousands of dollars)

	Division IA "Plus" Universities	Division IA "Standard" Universities	Ivy League Universities	Coed Liberal Arts Colleges
Team expenditures	10,000	5,700	3,200	830
Expenditure per team	456	426	126	42
Expenditure per athlete	17	20	4.5	1.6
Non-scholarship expenditure per team	255	208	126	42
Non-scholarship expenditure per athlete	10	10	4.5	1.6

Source: Equity in Athletics Disclosure Act filings, 1997–98.

SCORECARD 11.6

Sources of Revenues at Selected Schools
(in thousands of dollars)

	University of Michigan	Duke	Princeton	Williams	Division IA Average
Regular season	25,400	7,900	940	22	7,271
Postseason	4,700	1,900	n/a	n/a	2,782
Donor contributions	7,300	3,800	1,800	127	2,832
Sponsorship/signage/ licensing	8,000	[900]*	n/a	n/a	591
Endowed funds	2,100	700	360	n/a	n/a
Other	2,900	200	n/a	3	2,666
Total revenue	50,400	14,500	3,100	152	16,142

Source: Selected schools.
*Duke's licensing revenues are not credited toward the athletic department budget.

SCORECARD 11.7

Net Athletic and Student Services Expenditures by Division
(in dollars)

	Division IA "Plus" Universities	Division IA "Standard" Universities	Ivy League Universities	Coed Liberal Arts Colleges	Division III Universities
Estimated net expenditure	$0	$7,500,000	$8,000,000	$1,400,000	$1,500,000
Number of athletes	726	422	850	535	601
Net athletics expenditure per athlete	$0	$17,800	$9,400	$2,600	$2,500
Student services expenditure per undergraduate	$1,500	$2,000	$3,000	$3,000	$2,000

Source: Selected schools and Daniel L. Fulks, *Revenues and Expenses of Divisions I and II Intercollegiate Athletics Programs: Financial Trends and Relationships* (Indianapolis, Ind.: National Collegiate Athletic Association, 1997).

Appendix B: Supplementary Data

APPENDIX TABLE B.2.1

Mean SAT Scores by Cohort, Division, and Team (Male Only)

Team	Division IA Public Universities			Division IA Private Universities			Division IAA Ivy League Universities			Division III Coed Liberal Arts Colleges		
	1951	1976	1989	1951	1976	1989	1951	1976	1989	1951	1976	1989
Baseball	n/a	1000	1016	n/a	1069	1078	1020	1170	1248	1129	1111	1165
Basketball	n/a	970	949	n/a	1150	980	1094	1152	1230	1138	1161	1152
Crew	n/a	989	n/a	n/a	n/a	1367	1107	1288	1341	n/a	1292	1334
Cross-country	n/a	1049	1057	n/a	1218	1235	1117	1250	1261	1185	1300	1282
Fencing	n/a	1070	1157	n/a	1235	1310	1177	1309	1331	n/a	n/a	n/a
Football	n/a	871	892	n/a	1003	997	1073	1151	1213	1109	1112	1126
Lightweight football	n/a	n/a	n/a	n/a	n/a	n/a	1179	1347	1296	n/a	n/a	n/a
Golf	n/a	1015	1009	n/a	1148	1148	1162	1291	1348	1116	1192	1214
Gymnastics	n/a	1065	1020	n/a	1218	n/a	n/a	1290	n/a	n/a	n/a	n/a
Ice hockey	n/a	1037	960	n/a	1083	1213	1128	1093	1253	1062	1197	1193
Lacrosse	n/a	1036	1050	n/a	1148	1240	1127	1212	1278	1123	1185	1211
Soccer	n/a	963	1089	n/a	1192	1230	1005	1152	1264	1146	1152	1223
Squash	n/a	n/a	n/a	n/a	n/a	n/a	1202	1293	1315	1163	1329	1292
Swimming	n/a	1082	1134	n/a	1171	1270	1066	1209	1294	1104	1236	1234
Tennis	n/a	965	1094	n/a	1162	1179	1167	1282	1229	1150	1197	1118
Track	n/a	947	989	n/a	1149	1161	1078	1202	1294	1150	1170	1223
Volleyball	n/a	985	1028	n/a	1254	1215	n/a	1303	1365	1268	n/a	n/a
Wrestling	n/a	1028	946	n/a	1063	1144	1147	1212	1237	1230	1268	1264

Source: College and Beyond.

Note: n/a indicates that data are not available.

APPENDIX TABLE B.4.1

Mean 1995 Earnings by Years Played and Sport Profile
(by Division, 1976 Cohort, Full-Time Male Workers)

	Division IA Public Universities	Division IA Private Universities	Ivy League Universities	Coed Liberal Arts Colleges	Sector Composite
High Profile: 4 years	$88,824	$141,806	$143,895	$119,758	$123,571
High Profile: <4 years	$77,591	$110,287	$109,934	$102,216	$100,007
High Profile athletes	$80,243	$117,468	$119,295	$106,465	$105,868
Lower Profile: 4 years	$91,382	$116,607	$125,525	$124,940	$114,614
Lower Profile: <4 years	$91,575	$123,892	$129,077	$108,781	$113,331
Lower Profile athletes	$91,522	$123,329	$128,102	$112,141	$113,774
4-Year athletes	$90,591	$130,781	$131,895	$122,740	$119,002
<4-Year athletes	$86,613	$120,252	$122,462	$106,304	$108,908
Students at large	$84,248	$106,311	$108,172	$ 92,770	$ 97,875

Source: College and Beyond.

APPENDIX TABLE B.6.1
Mean SAT Scores by Cohort, Division, and Team (Female Only)

Team	Division IA Public Universities		Division IA Private Universities		Division IAA Ivy League Universities		Division III Coed Liberal Arts Colleges		Division III Women's Liberal Arts Colleges	
	1976	1989	1976	1989	1976	1989	1976	1989	1976	1989
Basketball	1017	911	1145	1010	1176	1201	1124	1201	1268	1183
Crew	n/a	n/a	n/a	n/a	1283	1299	n/a	1341	n/a	1189
Cross-country	n/a	905	n/a	1227	1313	1266	1213	1253	n/a	1217
Fencing	n/a	987	n/a	1180	1227	1250	n/a	n/a	n/a	n/a
Field hockey	1131	1046	1200	1188	1278	1219	1162	1169	1232	1208
Golf	1138	1035	1237	1160	n/a	1297	n/a	n/a	n/a	n/a
Gymnastics	975	1036	1111	n/a	1239	1193	n/a	n/a	n/a	n/a
Ice hockey	n/a	n/a	n/a	n/a	n/a	1223	n/a	n/a	n/a	n/a
Lacrosse	n/a	n/a	n/a	n/a	1276	1240	1173	1178	1226	1192
Soccer	n/a	n/a	1264	1219	n/a	1222	1269	1190	n/a	1212
Softball	1004	879	n/a	1191	n/a	1224	n/a	1277	n/a	n/a
Squash	n/a	n/a	n/a	n/a	1246	1257	1263	1224	n/a	1209
Swimming	989	1051	1146	1133	1247	1238	1238	1217	n/a	1183
Tennis	1031	1018	1070	1136	1202	1268	1167	1153	1230	1197
Track	1172	1006	1152	1138	1246	1240	1100	1199	n/a	n/a
Volleyball	1076	1030	1209	1131	1301	1203	1125	1166	1216	1182

Source: College and Beyond.

Note: n/a indicates that data are not available.

APPENDIX TABLE B.7.1
Ordinary Least Squares Regression Models Predicting Rank in Class at
Ivy League Universities
(1989 Cohort, Female Only)

	Model I		*Model II*	
	Parameter Estimate	Standard Error	Parameter Estimate	Standard Error
Intercept	**86.87**	**21.29**	**100.74**	**21.42**
Black	**−18.42**	**2.24**	**−13.07**	**2.18**
Hispanic	**−14.04**	**2.43**	**−15.10**	**2.32**
Asian	**−5.45**	**1.52**	**−5.35**	**1.45**
Other race	−10.39	5.96	−4.97	5.68
SAT increment	**0.075**	**0.006**	0.013	0.008
Average institutional SAT	−0.100	0.017	**−0.150**	**0.020**
Social science	−0.70	1.40	−0.86	1.35
Natural science	**−4.32**	**2.01**	**−7.83**	**1.93**
Math/engineering	**−13.07**	**2.40**	**−16.41**	**2.30**
Other major	**−5.95**	**1.89**	**−5.60**	**1.81**
Missing major	**−21.41**	**3.10**	**−21.27**	**2.95**
Parents' socioeconomic status (per $1000)	0.095	0.04	**0.13**	**0.04**
College athlete	**−8.91**	**1.71**	**−5.83**	**1.64**
High school GPA (A = 1; F = 12)			**−2.53**	**0.61**
High school rank-in-class			**0.58**	**0.11**
Achievement Test scores			**1.38**	**0.14**
Missing achievements			**84.53**	**9.88**
Number of observations	1763		1763	
R^2	0.2849		0.3541	

Source: College and Beyond.

Note: **Bold** coefficients are significant at the .05 level: other coefficients are not. The omitted categories in the model are white, non-athlete, humanities major.

APPENDIX TABLE B.9.1

CEO Leadership of Civic Activities

(by Athlete Status, Cohort, and Gender, percent)

	1951 Men		1976 Men		1976 Women	
	Athletes	Students at Large	Athletes	Students at Large	Athletes	Students at Large
Alumni activities	19	8	11	5	15	7
Arts activities	10	11	5	7	8	7
Community activities	13	7	8	7	8	12
Educational activities	13	10	10	10	8	11
Political activities	8	7	10	9	0	7
Professional activities	18	23	15	17	31	18
Religious activities	13	13	13	14	38	11
Social activities	16	13	7	8	15	8
Sports activities	9	2	16	12	0	4
Youth activities	9	6	25	20	8	9

Source: College and Beyond.

APPENDIX TABLE B.9.2

Institutional Priorities of Athlete Alumni/ae Leaders, Student-at-Large Alumni/ae Leaders, and All Other Alumni/ae (as Desired Emphasis minus Perceived Current Emphasis, by Cohort and Gender)

	1951 Men			1976 Men			1976 Women		
	Student-at-Large Alumni Leaders	Athlete Alumni Leaders	All Other Alumni	Student-at-Large Alumni Leaders	Athlete Alumni Leaders	All Other Alumni	Student-at-Large Alumnae Leaders	Athlete Alumnae Leaders	All Other Alumnae
Liberal arts	0.26	0.06	0.26	0.24	0.1	0.23	0.19	0.09	0.22
Intellectual freedom	0.21	0.13	0.22	0.42	0.15	0.44	0.35	0.21	0.41
Intercollegiate athletics	-0.24	0.04	-0.32	-0.13	0.46	-0.35	-0.17	0.42	-0.33
Other extracurriculars	0.11	0.25	0.1	0.31	0.54	0.33	0.31	0.44	0.36

Source: College and Beyond.

APPENDIX TABLE B.9.3

Institutional Priorities (as Desired Emphasis minus Perceived Current Emphasis, by Division, Male and Female Combined, 1976 Cohort)

	Division IA Public Universities	Division IA Private Universities	Ivy League Universities	Coed Liberal Arts Colleges	Women's Liberal Arts Colleges	Sector Composite
Teaching undergraduates	1.03	0.87	0.89	0.32	0.21	0.65
Intellectual freedom	0.55	0.46	0.40	0.36	0.21	0.40
Residential life	0.46	0.48	0.75	0.48	0.41	0.51
Diverse student body	0.45	0.42	0.13	0.59	0.14	0.38
Broad liberal arts education	0.41	0.34	0.25	0.06	0.03	0.21
Other extracurricular activities	0.21	0.37	0.38	0.35	0.50	0.36
Alumni/ae concerns	-0.30	-0.12	-0.19	-0.11	-0.08	-0.15
Faculty research	-0.37	-0.38	-0.46	-0.06	-0.13	-0.27
Intercollegiate athletics	-0.98	-0.46	-0.19	-0.15	0.21	-0.31

Source: College and Beyond.

APPENDIX TABLE B.11.1
Athletic Expenditures by Institution

	Division IA "Plus" Universities				
	University of Michigan	Penn State	Notre Dame	Stanford	Mean
Operating expenditures	$3,604,267	$3,932,792	$4,597,721	$3,473,361	$3,902,035
Recruiting	691,327	669,844	697,960	524,206	645,834
Student aid	7,629,296	4,576,117	5,893,757	8,716,662	6,703,958
Coaching/salaries	3,683,889	2,776,998	2,741,677	3,491,887	3,173,613
Other team expenditures	7,038,804	12,763,244	3,758,516	4,408,607	6,992,293
Subtotal (team expenditures)	$22,647,583	$24,718,995	$17,689,631	$20,614,723	$21,417,733
General infrastructure	24,721,306	14,782,159	12,060,443	15,100,704	16,666,153
Total intercollegiate expenditures	$47,368,889	$39,501,154	$29,750,074	$35,715,427	$38,083,886
Football expenditures	$8,925,114	$13,169,583	$8,525,473	$8,285,419	$9,726,397
Football revenue	23,390,257	22,999,193	23,740,540	10,976,458	20,276,612
Basketball expenditures (men)	$1,647,697	$2,158,331	$1,325,484	$1,700,621	$1,708,033
Basketball revenue (men)	5,389,526	4,613,275	1,380,150	2,245,688	3,407,160
Expenditures of Lower Profile teams	$12,074,772	$9,391,081	$7,838,674	$10,628,683	$9,983,303
Number of varsity teams	21	25	21	31	25
Number of varsity athletes	666	768	660	808	726
Number of undergraduates	23,939	31,667	10,300	6,639	18,136
Athletes as percent of undergraduates	3%	2%	6%	12%	6%
Expenditure per Lower Profile team	$635,514	$408,308	$412,562	$366,506	$455,723
Expenditure per Lower Profile athlete	22,826	14,978	15,250	15,249	17,076
Non-scholarship expenditure per Lower Profile team	362,180	277,873	220,785	159,610	255,112
Non-scholarship expenditure per Lower Profile athlete	13,008	10,193	8,161	6,641	9,501

Source: Equity in Athletics Disclosure Act filings, 1997–98.

APPENDIX TABLE B.11.1 *(Continued)*

	Division IA "Standard" Universities				
	Duke	*Northwestern*	*Vanderbilt*	*Tulane*	*Mean*
Operating expenditures	$1,723,454	$1,732,320	$1,512,606	$1,452,511	$1,605,223
Recruiting	399,322	538,561	409,344	370,258	429,371
Student aid	6,238,903	5,763,621	5,286,336	5,592,364	5,720,306
Coaching/salaries	2,577,889	2,367,325	1,981,882	2,188,383	2,278,869
Other team expenditures	1,228,642	5,300,764	5,207,668	2,192,767	3,482,460
Subtotal (team expenditures)	$12,168,210	$15,702,591	$14,397,835	$11,796,282	$13,516,230
General infrastructure	8,911,570	8,242,765	9,820,704	3,758,193	7,683,308
Total intercollegiate expenditures	$21,079,780	$23,945,356	$24,218,539	$15,554,475	$21,199,538
Football expenditures	$4,407,067	$6,767,842	$7,516,992	$5,535,138	$6,056,760
Football revenue	5,269,890	11,424,460	7,216,389	4,308,862	7,054,900
Basketball expenditures (men)	$1,818,780	$1,894,790	$1,788,209	$1,632,505	$1,783,571
Basketball revenue (men)	5,650,394	4,287,731	3,757,494	2,080,765	3,944,096
Expenditures of Lower Profile teams	$5,942,363	$7,039,959	$5,092,634	$4,628,639	$5,675,899
Number of varsity teams	21	17	13	12	16
Number of varsity athletes	587	410	383	306	422
Number of undergraduates	6,686	7,576	5,861	6,620	6,686
Athletes as percent of undergraduates	9%	5%	7%	5%	6%
Expenditure per Lower Profile team	$312,756	$469,331	$462,967	$462,864	$426,979
Expenditure per Lower Profile athlete	12,537	24,529	18,586	25,293	20,236
Non-scholarship expenditure per Lower Profile team	161,416	269,331	226,603	172,864	207,553
Non-scholarship expenditure per Lower Profile athlete	6,470	14,077	9,097	9,446	9,773

(continued)

APPENDIX TABLE B.11.1 *(Continued)*

	Columbia	University of Pennsylvania	Princeton	Yale	Mean
		Division IAA Ivy League Universities			
Operating expenditures	$919,895	$1,520,213	$1,882,350	$1,414,567	$1,434,256
Recruiting	381,418	411,661	351,906	570,328	428,828
Student aid	0	0	0	0	0
Coaching/salaries	1,822,485	2,167,822	2,282,847	2,413,198	2,171,588
Other team expenditures	778,216				
Subtotal (team expenditures)	$3,902,014	$5,812,000		$4,398,093	$4,704,036
General infrastructure	1,661,503				
Total intercollegiate expenditures	$5,563,517				
Football expenditures	$1,598,566	$1,510,000		$745,379	$1,284,648
Football revenue	246,396				
Basketball expenditures (men)	$285,979	$670,000		$220,345	$392,108
Basketball revenue (men)	106,658				
Expenditures of Lower Profile teams	$2,017,469	$3,632,000		$3,432,369	$3,027,279
Number of varsity teams	22	28	38	31	30
Number of varsity athletes	645	844	942	967	850
Number of undergraduates	7,265	9,484	4,600	5,230	6,645
Athletes as percent of undergraduates	9%	9%	20%	18%	14%
Expenditure per Lower Profile team	$100,873	$139,692		$118,358	$119,641
Expenditure per Lower Profile athlete	3,609	4,982		4,135	4,242
Non-scholarship expenditure per Lower Profile team	$100,873	$139,692		$118,358	$119,641
Non-scholarship expenditure per Lower Profile athlete	3,609	4,982		4,135	4,242

APPENDIX TABLE B.11.1 *(Continued)*

	Division III Coed Liberal Arts Colleges			
	Denison	*Kenyon*	*Hamilton*	*Oberlin*
Operating expenditures	$299,722	$234,558	$281,205	$180,912
Recruiting	57,138	38,054	1,931	16,123
Student aid	0	0	0	0
Coaching/salaries	437,001	544,500	1,083,110	397,544
Other team expenditures	45,125	7,514		
Subtotal (team expenditures)	$838,986	$824,626		
General infrastructure	632,255	374,605		
Total intercollegiate expenditures	$1,471,241	$1,199,231		
Football expenditures	$107,459	$152,385		
Football revenue	117,115	152,545		
Basketball expenditures (men)	$46,156	$53,255		
Basketball revenue (men)	46,923	53,334		
Expenditures of Lower Profile teams	$685,371	$618,986		
Number of varsity teams	18	18	22	16
Number of varsity athletes	527	472	554	327
Number of undergraduates	2,089	1,541	1,731	2,905
Athletes as percent of undergraduates	25%	31%	32%	11%
Expenditure per Lower Profile team	$42,836	$38,687		
Expenditure per Lower Profile athlete	1,568	1,502		
Non-scholarship expenditure per Lower Profile team	42,836	38,687		
Non-scholarship expenditure per Lower Profile athlete	1,568	1,502		

(continued)

APPENDIX TABLE B.11.1 *(Continued)*

	Division III Coed Liberal Arts Colleges (continued)			
	Swarthmore	*Wesleyan*	*Williams*	*Mean*
Operating expenditures	$196,950	$290,249	$325,849	$258,492
Recruiting	11,373	2,022	8,019	19,237
Student aid	0	0	0	0
Coaching/salaries	494,228	816,470	867,528	662,911
Other team expenditures	190,678	21,796	113,682	75,759
Subtotal (team expenditures)	$893,229	$1,130,537	$1,315,078	$1,000,491
General infrastructure		120,308	367,086	373,564
Total intercollegiate expenditures		$1,250,845	$1,682,164	$1,400,870
Football expenditures		$133,123	$149,681	$135,662
Football revenue		11,667	20,350	75,419
Basketball expenditures (men)		$47,698	$61,980	$52,272
Basketball revenue (men)		855	9,795	27,727
Expenditures of Lower Profile teams		$949,716	$1,103,417	$839,373
Number of varsity teams	22	25	27	21
Number of varsity athletes	457	691	715	535
Number of undergraduates	1,350	2,962	1,979	2,080
Athletes as percent of undergraduates	34%	23%	36%	27%
Expenditure per Lower Profile team		$41,292	$44,137	$41,738
Expenditure per Lower Profile athlete		1,586	1,780	1,609
Non-scholarship expenditure per Lower Profile team		41,292	44,137	41,738
Non-scholarship expenditure per Lower Profile athlete		1,586	1,780	1,609

APPENDIX TABLE B.11.1 *(Continued)*

	Division III Universities			
	Washington	*Emory*	*Tufts*	*Mean*
Operating expenditures	$548,804	$480,426	$325,097	$451,442
Recruiting	54,964	0	0	18,321
Student aid	0	0	0	0
Coaching/salaries	531,124	548,291	758,121	612,512
Other team expenditures		0		
Subtotal (team expenditures)		$1,028,717		
General infrastructure		506,174		
Total intercollegiate expenditures		$2,563,608		
Football expenditures				
Football revenue				
Basketball expenditures (men)		$112,120		
Basketball revenue (men)		112,120		
Expenditures of Lower Profile teams		$916,597		
Number of varsity teams	13	13	26	17
Number of varsity athletes	486	350	967	601
Number of undergraduates	5,152	5,608	4,718	5,159
Athletes as percent of undergraduates	9%	6%	20%	12%
Expenditure per Lower Profile team		$83,327		
Expenditure per Lower Profile athlete		2,820		
Non-scholarship expenditure per Lower Profile team		83,327		
Non-scholarship expenditure per Lower Profile athlete		2,820		

APPENDIX TABLE B.11.2

Sources of Revenues by Institution (thousands of dollars) (Selected Schools)

	University of Michigan		Duke		Princeton		Williams		NCAA Division IA Average	
Regular season										
Gate: football	$16,485	33%	$1,990	14%	$200	6%	$17	11%	n/a	0%
Gate: men's basketball	1,976	4	1,828	13	300	10	3	2	n/a	0
Gate: other sports	919	2	n/a	0	155	5	2	1	n/a	0
Subtotal	$19,380	38	$3,818	26%	$655	21%	$22	14%	$5,794	36%
Television/radio: football	$3,037	6	$1,694	12%	n/a	0%	n/a	0%	n/a	0%
Television/radio: men's basketball	1,706	3%	1,555	11	n/a	0	n/a	0	n/a	0
Subtotal	$4,743	9%	$3,249	22%	n/a	0%	n/a	0%	$1,150	7%
Advertising	$233	0%	$570	4%	$280	9%	n/a	0%	n/a	0%
Concessions	1,061	2	220	2	n/a	0	n/a	0	327	2
Total	$25,417	50%	$7,857	54%	$935	30%	$22	14%	$7,271	45%
Postseason										
Bowls: football	$2,998	6%	$700	5%	n/a	0%	n/a	0%	$591	8%
Conference tournaments: basketball	426	1	340	2	n/a	0	n/a	0	114	1

NCAA basketball	1,112	2		850	6		n/a	0		n/a	0		1,594	10
NCAA tournaments: other	119	0		n/a	0		n/a	0		n/a	0		483	3
Total	$4,655	9%		$1,890	13%		n/a	0%		n/a	0%		$2,782	17%
Sponsorship and licensing														
Sponsorship/signage	$2,270	4%		n/a	0%		n/a	0%		n/a	0%		$591	4%
Licensing	5,730	11		[900]*	0		n/a	0		n/a	0		n/a	0
Total	$8,000	16%		n/a	0%		n/a	0%		n/a	0%		$591	4%
Donor contributions	$7,321	15%		$3,800	26%		$1,800	58%		$127	84%		$2,832	18%
Endowed funds	2,140	4		673	5		365	12		n/a	0		n/a	0
Other	2,914	6		230	2		n/a	0		3	2		2,666	17
Total revenue	$50,447	100%		$14,450	100%		$3,100	100%		$152	100%		$16,142	100%
Total expenditures	47,369			21,080			11,000			1,682			17,586	
(Subvention)	$3,078			$(6,630)			$(8,000)			$(1,530)			$(1,444)	

Source: Selected schools and Daniel L. Fulks, *Revenues and Expenses of Divisions I and II Intercollegiate Athletics Programs: Financial Trends and Relationships* (Indianapolis, Ind.: National Collegiate Athletic Association, 1997).

*Duke's licensing revenues are not credited toward the athletic department budget.

Sources of Revenue, NCAA Divisions IA and IAA (thousands of dollars)

	Division IA			Division IAA		
	FY 1993	FY 1995	FY 1997	FY 1993	FY 1995	FY 1997
Regular season						
Ticket sales	$4,400 35%	$4,538 33%	$4,999 31%	$417 19%	$523 20%	$505 19%
Guarantees and options	862 7	917 7	795 5	107 5	143 6	136 5
Concessions	338 3	372 3	327 2	32 1	39 2	34 1
Television/radio	1,050 8	1,121 8	1,150 7	33 2	70 3	31 1
Program sales/advertising	131 1	94 1	103 1	24 1	31 1	31 1
Subtotal	$6,781 54%	$7,042 51%	$7,374 46%	$613 29%	$806 31%	$737 27%
General						
Student activity fees	$811 6%	$1,038 8%	$1,183 7%	$831 39%	$899 35%	$983 37%
Postseason						
Postseason competition	$974 8%	$553 4%	$1,188 7%	$18 1%	$29 1%	$34 1%
NCAA distributions	324 3	365 3	1,594 10	78 4	106 4	188 7
Conference distributions	483 4	1,105 8		46	43 2	
Subtotal	$1,781 14%	$2,023 15%	$2,782 17%	$142 7%	$178 7%	$222 8%

Contributions and sponsorship												
Donor contributions	$1,969	16%	$2,291	17%	$2,832	18%	$323	15%	$413	16%	$398	15%
Sponsorship/signage	240	2	439	3	591	4	74	3	81	3	131	5
Subtotal	$2,209	18%	$2,730	20%	$3,423	21%	$397	18%	$494	19%	$529	20%
Other												
Sports camps	$94	1%	$138	1%	$100	1%	$39	2%	$47	2%	$36	1%
Special events	67	1	81	1	59	0	27	1	14	1	24	1
Miscellaneous	768	6	787	6	1,221	8	101	1	141	5	153	6
Subtotal	$929	7%	$1,006	7%	$1,380	9%	$167	8%	$202	8%	$213	8%
Total (100%)*	$12,511	100%	$13,839	100%	$16,142		$2,150	100%	$2,579	100%	$2,684	100%

Source: Daniel L. Fulks, *Revenues and Expenses of Divisions I and II Intercollegiate Athletics Programs: Financial Trends and Relationships* (Indianapolis, Ind.: National Collegiate Athletic Association, 1993, 1995, and 1997).

*Excludes government and institutional support.

Prelude: Four Snapshots

1. As this book goes to press, it has become even clearer that the University of Michigan's budget problems in FY 1998–99 were not of the "once-in-a-lifetime" variety. According to recently published accounts, shortfalls in projected broadcasting revenues, licensing royalties, and gifts may produce a deficit in the $3 million range in the fiscal year ending June 30, 2000. Robert Kasdin, executive vice-president and chief financial officer, is quoted as saying that the newly projected deficit is "a predictable result of volatile revenue streams and fixed, inflexible expenses"; Fred Girard, "U-M Projects Another Deficit. Company Does Not Deliver Revenue for Sale of Broadcasts," *Detroit News,* March 7, 2000. On Michigan's successful commercialization of its image, see Dana Rubin, "You've Seen the Game. Now Buy the Underwear," *New York Times,* September 11, 1994, section 3, p. 5. For further background on the Michigan deficit and the effects it has been having, see Fred Girard, "Cuts Will Be Needed to Work on Deficit," *Detroit News,* June 24, 1999, p. C1; Fred Girard, "U-M's Bollinger: Costs of Athletic Teams Pose a Problem," *Detroit News,* June 24, 1999, p. A15; Jodi S. Cohen and Fred Girard, "U-M Sports Deficit Criticized: Regent Fears More Shortfalls. Athletics Director Vows to Watch Spending, Income More Closely," *Detroit News,* July 16, 1999, p. A1.

2. The detail on Williams lacrosse is taken largely from the correspondence exchanged between President Hank Payne and other members of the college community, including members of the women's lacrosse team. Also see Kris Dufour, "Eph Women Focus on ECAC; Can't Forget NCAA Turmoil," *North Adams Transcript,* May 11, 1996, pp. 13, 15. On the question of postseason play in NESCAC, see Welch Suggs, "Postseason Play Creates Tensions for an Unusual Athletics Conference," *Chronicle of Higher Education,* July 18, 1999. See also Douglas S. Looney, "Pure and Simple: In the New England Small College Athletic Conference, Athletes Compete for One Reason: Love of the Game," *Sports Illustrated,* October 31, 1994, pp. 68–80.

3. For more information on the team's successful season, see Tom Friend, "A Big Purple Haze Covers Hollywood," *New York Times,* December 31, 1995, section 8, p. 4; Malcolm Moran, "Northwestern and Its Fans Get to Stop and Savor the Roses," *New York Times,* November 27, 1995, section A, p. 1. On economic trickle-downs from football success, see Dan Bickley, "Cats Are Cashing In: Big Season Translates into Big Money for NU," *Chicago Sun-Times,* November 28, 1995, p. 86; Rick Telander, "NU's Bowl Economics Don't Trickle Down to General Fund," *Chicago Sun-Times,* November 29, 1995, p. 135. On the campaign for athletics, see Len Ziehm, "NU Begins Campaign to Renovate Its Facilities," *Chicago Sun-Times,* September 28, 1995, p. 92. On integrity in the face of success, see Tim Layden, "Now for the Hard Part," *Sports Illustrated,* May 6, 1996, pp. 62–66; Jim Naughton and Jeffrey Selingo, "A Point Shaving Scandal Rattles a University," *Chronicle of Higher Education,* April 10, 1998, p. A48.

4. On the decision to eliminate wrestling and its associated fallout, see Chris Edwards, "Princeton Continues to Grapple with Wrestling," *Trenton Times,* August 8, 1993, p. C6; Doug Lederman, "Tigers on Top: Princeton's Sports Program Is the Envy of the Ivies, But at What Price to the University and Its Athletes?" *Princeton Alumni Weekly,* November 6, 1996, pp. 12–22.

Preface

1. Data from four of the schools (Georgetown, Washington University, Tufts, and Emory) are used primarily in the chapter on finances. Student data concerning athletics from the latter three schools were not available for the 1951 cohort, and Georgetown's data were unique (and thus could not be merged with data for other schools) since it alone played big-time basketball but competed as a Division IAA school in other sports.

2. Supplementary data on giving patterns were collected from a subset of 15 institutions. For an extended discussion of the College and Beyond database, see William G. Bowen and Derek Bok, *The Shape of the River: Long-Term Consequences of Considering Race in College and University Admissions* (Princeton, N.J.: Princeton University Press, 1998), especially Appendix A.

3. The methods used to analyze data are similar to those described at length in Bowen and Bok, Appendix B. We try to use the simplest methods consistent with the objectives at hand, and ordinary tabulations and cross-tabulations often suffice. But we also employ multivariate regression analysis to isolate as best we can the effects of one independent variable (for example, whether or not a student played sports) on an "other-things-equal" basis. When the dependent variables are continuous, such as rank-in-class or income, we use ordinary least squares (OLS) regression techniques. When the dependent variables are binary, we use logit models; see Bowen and Bok, pp. 341–44.

Chapter 1   The Institutionalization and Regulation
of College Sports in Historical Perspective

1. The Yale statement is by the late Yale President A. Bartlett Giamatti; it served as the mission statement for the undergraduate college for many years. See http://www.yale.edu/accred/standards/s4.html. Recently it has been superseded by a new mission statement: "The mission of Yale College is to seek exceptionally promising students of all backgrounds from across the nation and around the world and to educate them, through mental discipline and social experience, to develop their intellectual, moral, civic and creative capacities to the fullest. The aim of this education is the cultivation of citizens with a rich awareness of our human heritage to lead and serve in every sphere of human activity." The statement is available online at http://www.yale.edu/accred/standards/s1.html. For the other mission statements, see http://circle.kenyon.edu/visitors/mission/; http://www.upenn.edu/audit/agenda.html; http://www.umich.edu/UM-Mission.html.

2. Hanna Gray, "The Leaning Tower of Academe," Bulletin of the American Academy of Arts and Sciences 49 (1996): 34–54; quote on pp. 52–53; emphasis in original.

3. We are indebted for much of the information about the early history of intercollegiate athletics to Ronald Smith, *Sports and Freedom: The Rise of Big-Time College Athletics* (New York: Oxford University Press, 1988).

4. This section borrows its name from the title the historian Frederick Rudolph gave to a famous chapter in his history of higher education, *The American College and University* (Athens: University of Georgia Press, 1990 [1962]).

5. Ibid., pp. 385–87.

6. Henry T. Fowler, "A Phase of Modern College Life," *Harper's New Monthly Magazine,* April 1896, pp. 688–95.

7. Howard J. Savage, *American College Athletics* (New York: Carnegie Foundation for the Advancement of Teaching, 1929).

8. Ibid., p. 102.

9. As historian John Thelin puts it, "The organizational revolution has been the ascent of the incorporated athletic association, a structure that has allowed athletic directors and boosters to create, basically on their own terms, a privileged entity attached to the university." *Games Colleges Play: Scandal and Reform in Intercollegiate Athletics* (Baltimore: Johns Hopkins University Press, 1994), p. 198.

10. Robert Maynard Hutchins, *Some Observations on American Education* (Cambridge: Cambridge University Press, 1956), pp. 67–68.

11. Ron Fimrite, "Once Regal, Soon to Be Razed," *Sports Illustrated,* November 25, 1956, p. R5 (originally published in the *New York Herald Tribune*).

12. Thelin, especially Chapter 2.

13. For the history and context of this reform effort, see Derek Bok, "Intercollegiate Athletics," in John B. Bennett and J. W. Peltason (eds.), *Contemporary Issues in Higher Education: Self-Regulation and the Ethical Roles of the Academy* (New York: American Council on Education, 1985), pp. 123–46; Arthur Padilla and Leroy T. Walker, "The Battle for Control of College Sports," *The Chronicle of Higher Education,* December 14, 1994, p. A56; Walter Byers (with Charles Hammer), *Unsportsmanlike Conduct: Exploiting College Athletes* (Ann Arbor: University of Michigan Press, 1995), especially Chapter 16.

14. 20 USC 1681(a). The associated language from the Code of Federal Regulations reads as follows: "No person shall, on the basis of sex, be excluded from participation in, be denied the benefits of, be treated differently from another person or otherwise be discriminated against in any interscholastic, intercollegiate, club or intramural athletics offered by a recipient, and no recipient shall provide any such athletics separately on such basis"; 34 C.F.R. 106.41(a).

15. Government regulation of course affects other parts of the campus as well. Chemical waste from the labs must be disposed of in ways that comply with OSHA regulations, for example. But the potential programmatic and financial consequences of Title IX, while still being defined, are substantial.

16. Guy Gugliotta, "On the Hill, Ex-wrestlers Go to the Mat for the Sport," *Washington Post,* April 30, 1998, p. A19; Bill McAllister, "Wrestler Wrider," *Washington Post,* July 2, 1998, p. A19.

17. It was in 1940 that television first attempted to bring college football from the cold outdoors into the comfort of our living rooms. By 1952, the NCAA had signed a contract with one of the networks on behalf of many of its constituent schools. The University of Pennsylvania and Notre Dame squared off against the

NCAA over the right of schools to set up their own television contracts. In the end, the Association won and over the next thirty years built up its own fortunes with a series of huge contracts with the major networks. The 1984 Supreme Court decision was made in response to a lawsuit brought by schools in the College Football Association (CFA). The CFA's own negotiations with the networks subsequently fell apart as Notre Dame defected and signed its own exclusive agreement with NBC; it was followed by the Southeastern Conference. For more detail, see Thelin, Chapter 4, and Andrew Zimbalist, *Unpaid Professionals: Commercialism and Conflict in Big-Time College Sports* (Princeton, N.J.: Princeton University Press, 1999).

18. "One of the biggest reasons for Vandy's football failure," one coach had said upon his departure in the mid-1980s, "is the continuous rise in academic standards." Vanderbilt also provides a textbook example of the difficulties in trying to compete in local entertainment markets and in the quest for support of the local community. In 1995, a *Sports Illustrated* article simultaneously celebrated Nashville's sports enthusiasm and blasted Vanderbilt athletics. The article portrayed Vanderbilt as plagued by "a uniquely arrogant defeatism." None of this was surprising coming from a sports magazine that sells its product by arousing sports passions; what was surprising to some people at Vanderbilt were the comments of the mayor of Nashville, who chided Vanderbilt as "an institution that has held itself very apart from the community." The mayor had sponsored the construction of a $125 million hockey and basketball arena, which was currently sitting empty awaiting either NHL or NBA expansion or a team purloined from another city; he also was hard at work crafting a deal to lure the NFL Houston Oilers to Nashville. He saw Vanderbilt's sports failures as a sign of contempt for his community. Vanderbilt Chancellor Joe Wyatt responded by pointing to the hundreds of doctors, nurses, and teachers who volunteered in the community. S. L. Price, "What's Hot, What's Not: In Nashville, the NBA, the NFL, and the NHL May Be on the Way In and Up, While Football at Prestigious Vanderbilt Is Down and Out," *Sports Illustrated,* November 27, 1995, p. 48.

19. The first sections of the original Ivy Group agreement of 1954 read as follows:

I. The subscribing institutions constitute themselves, for the purposes covered by this agreement, members of a group to be known as "The Ivy Group."

II. The Group reaffirm the basic principle of the control of athletics by the academic authorities of each institution.

III. A. The Group affirm their conviction that under proper conditions intercollegiate competition in organized athletics offers desirable development and recreation for players and a healthy focus of collegiate loyalty. These conditions require that the players shall be truly representative of the student body and not composed of a group of specially recruited athletes. They further require that undue strain upon players and coaches be eliminated and that they be permitted to enjoy the game as participants in a form of recreational competition rather than as professional performers in public spectacles. In the total life of the campus, emphasis upon intercollegiate competition must be kept in harmony with the essential educational purposes of the institution.

B. The Group conclude that these conditions and requirements can best be fulfilled by denying to the fullest possible extent external pressure for competitive extremes.

C. To this end, the Group will foster intra-group athletic competition in all sports. No member institution, however, shall necessarily field a team in every sport.

D. The Group approve a round-robin schedule in football and the principle of round-robin schedules in as many sports as practicable.

20. The best history of NESCAC was a report by Karin Vélez, commissioned by the conference in 1997, entitled *The New England Small College Athletic Conference, 1971–1997: A Retrospective*. We also benefited from a study written by Robert Edwards, president of Bowdoin College, entitled "A Reflection about NESCAC Football," appended to the Vélez report.

21. On the entertainment industry, see Michael J. Mandel and Mark Landler, "The Entertainment Economy," *Business Week*, March 14, 1994, pp. 58ff; Richard Butsch (ed.), *For Fun and Profit: The Transformation of Leisure into Consumption* (Philadelphia: Temple University Press, 1990).

Marketing has fed off (and into) the craving for sports as entertainment—and has also led to new complications for colleges and universities. In May 2000, Nike broke off talks with the University of Michigan on renewing a sports-equipment contract that could have been worth between $22 and $26 million. The dispute centered at least in part on differences between Nike and the university over the handling of "sweatshop" issues. Michigan's interim athletics director, William C. Martin, was quoted as saying: "Social change takes place at universities across the country. I think sometimes kids do a better job of understanding these things than adults do, and I'm proud of them. But it's one hell of an expensive stand"; Welch Suggs, "Abandoning Major Sponsorship Deal, Nike Plays Hardball over Sweatshops," *Chronicle of Higher Education*, May 12, 2000, online edition. Subsequently, Nike agreed to extend by one year its licensing agreement with the University—so that athletes would have uniforms and equipment for the next academic year. But it does not appear that this interim one-year contract represents any change of heart on the part of either party. See Martin Van Der Werf, "Nike Grants U. of Michigan a 1-Year Extension on Athletics-Apparel Contract," *Chronicle of Higher Education*, May 15, 2000, online edition. Earlier in the year, Nike had broken its contract to supply hockey equipment to Brown University, and Nike's chairman, Phil Knight, said he would give no more money to his alma mater, the University of Oregon, because of disagreements over similar issues. Such disputes illustrate how commercial, educational, and social values can become intertwined and lead to serious conflict when revenues from corporate sponsorship become so consequential.

22. For more on the intersection between television and college sports, see Murray Sperber, *College Sports, Inc.: The Athletic Department vs. the University* (New York: Henry Holt, 1990); Zimbalist, *Unpaid Professionals*.

23. Robert H. Frank and Philip J. Cook, *The Winner-Take-All Society: How More and More Americans Compete for Ever Fewer and Bigger Prizes, Encouraging Economic Waste, Income Inequality, and Impoverished Cultural Life* (New York: Free Press, 1995), p. viii.

24. Carolyn Hoxby, "The Changing Market Structure of U.S. Higher Education," unpublished paper (Cambridge, Mass.: Harvard University, 1997). For background on how the admissions offices of selective colleges and universities sought to diversify the type of student they admitted over the course of the 1950s, 1960s, and 1970s, see Nicholas Lemann, *The Big Test: The Secret History of the American Meritocracy* (New York: Farrar, Straus and Giroux, 1999).

25. The University of Michigan figure is courtesy of its news service. The others were calculated from data collected in 1998–99, published in *Peterson's Guide to 4 Year Colleges 2000* (Princeton, N.J.: Peterson's, 1999).

26. To illustrate, a partial listing of organizations organized by Yale students includes numerous publications: *Akili Newsmagazine,* Banner publications, the *Yale Course Critique,* the *Yale Daily News,* the *New Journal,* the *Yale Free Press,* the *Yale Herald,* the *Yale International Forum, Jormungandr,* the *Yale Journal of Human Rights,* the *Yale Literary Magazine,* the *Yale Political Monthly,* the *Yale Record,* the *Review of Politics, Yale Scientific Magazine, Splatter!* magazine, *Urim V'Turmim,* and Whirlpool Productions. In addition, Dwight Hall (the center for community service) lists 5 literacy groups, 12 arts organizations, 6 community development groups, 5 disabilities groups, 29 youth/tutoring programs, 4 programs for the elderly, 8 environmental groups, 7 gender-related groups, 26 health-related groups, 20 homeless and hunger groups, 8 legal groups, 14 political advocacy organizations, and 24 recreation or mentoring organizations.

27. For example, in the 1950s Yale attracted roughly 30,000 spectators per game, a figure that has dropped in the 1990s to the range of 10,000 to 20,000. Similar trends are observable at other schools in our sample.

28. Robert Lipsyte, "Backlash: The Entangled Web around Youth Sports," *New York Times,* May 23, 1999, section 8, p. 13.

29. George Orwell, *The Sporting Spirit* (New York: Harcourt, Brace & World, 1968 [1947]).

30. Dirk Johnson, "Seeking Little League Skills at $70 an Hour," *New York Times,* June 24, 1999, p. A1.

31. "Faster, Higher, Farther: Tracking Athletic Performance," *New York Times,* January 2, 2000, section 8, p. 9.

32. Jacob Viner, "Scholarship and Graduate Training," in his *The Long View and the Short* (New York: Free Press, 1958), pp. 378–79.

Chapter 2 The Admissions Game

1. Andree Brooks, "Heavy Angst When It's 'Ivy or Else,'" *New York Times,* March 30, 1995.

2. The NCAA uses the phrase "revenue sports," defined to include only football and men's basketball, and in some parts of our analysis (especially in Chapter 11, where we examine the finances of intercollegiate sports and use some NCAA data), we too treat football and men's basketball as a category all their own. In working with the student data for these selective institutions, however, and in recognizing the similarity of recruitment patterns, it seemed more appropriate to group men's ice hockey with football and basketball than to put the hockey players with, for example, the golfers. There is, of course, no exactly right

way to combine teams, and in some parts of the study we report data for other groupings of teams and occasionally even for particular sports.

3. These figures are taken from Scorecard 2.1, which shows the percentages of the male student body who played the High Profile and Lower Profile sports in each of the three generational cohorts and each divisional grouping (with a sector composite shown as well). The sector composite is a simple average of the values for each divisional grouping, with the divisional groupings in turn composed of simple averages of the values for each school within each divisional grouping. This approach emphasizes that it is the individual institution (and then the division, or type of school) that is the unit of analysis, *not* the individual athlete. We do not want to give larger weights to those schools (and divisions) that happen to enroll larger absolute numbers of athletes in particular sports or in all sports.

4. These numbers cannot be compared readily with the single-cohort numbers obtained from the College and Beyond database and presented in Figure 2.1. The single-cohort data tell us the number of students who won an award at any point in their college careers, and it would therefore be misleading to multiply these numbers by four to estimate the total size of the athlete population at any moment in time (which is what the EADA data report).

5. Savage, p. 240.

6. This account of recruiting practices in the 1950s, based on the recollections of former athletes, was confirmed by a memo made available to us by Thomas Wright, vice president of Princeton University. The memo recounts a lengthy conversation between Mr. Wright (who was working on an internal study of athletics) and Bill Edwards, the director of admission at Princeton through the 1950s and into the early 1960s. Mr. Edwards reported that the football coach at Princeton at that time, Charles Caldwell, was an early proponent of using alumni to contact prospective football players. Coach Caldwell also had excellent relations with the Office of Admission. He would bring to the director lists of prospective football players, ranked A, B, and C on the basis of their promise as athletes, and the two of them would then discuss the candidates, focusing on the A list. Mr. Edwards recalled that, in the words of the memo, "Coach Caldwell never put inappropriate pressure on the Director of Admission, and was 'just as interested' as Edwards was in seeing that young men who came to Princeton would do well and fit in well there." Perhaps ten students a year were admitted as a result of this process. Edwards also recalled that there was "a little" of the same sort of identification of players for basketball, also "a little" in ice hockey, "a very little" in track, and "others nil."

7. We present these data only for the Ivies and the Division III coed liberal arts colleges because the CIRP surveys were carried out more extensively at these schools; CIRP data are too limited at the Division IA private and public universities to permit presentation of meaningful numbers.

8. In order to judge how representative this school is of all the non-scholarship schools in the study, we calculated the difference between the mean (combined) SATs of all male athletes and of all male students at large at each of these schools in both the '76 and '89 cohorts. The resulting gaps are remarkably similar in size among the more selective institutions (in the 70 to 90 point range, in the case of the '89 cohort). They are somewhat smaller at some of the less selective liberal

arts colleges. In general, both the SAT gap and the admissions advantage are likely to be bigger, the more selective the school. For reasons explained in detail in Bowen and Bok, pp. 16–18, differences in average SAT scores are not a precise measure of the degree of advantage any subgroup of students enjoys in the admissions process. For present purposes, however, what is important is the consistency of the school-by-school pattern formed by the SAT scores. These data increase our confidence that the school for which we have the detailed data needed to calculate the admissions advantage is following admissions practices common to this set of schools.

Further confirmation of how representative these results are is provided by a recent article in the *Brown Daily Hearld,* which states that "the admit rate for recruited athletes is above 80 percent"; Emily Kimball, "For Athletes, Recruiting Requirements Jump-Start College Admission Process," September 13, 2000, online edition. According to *Peterson's Guide,* Brown University's overall admissions rate is 17 percent. In fact, this is an even larger crude admissions advantage (not controlling for SAT scores) than we found at the "representative institution."

9. These estimates of the admissions advantage enjoyed by various targeted groups were obtained by using a multivariate regression to predict the probability of admission, including SAT scores as control variables and dummy variables for legacy status, minority status, and recruited athlete status. The coefficients of all three dummy variables are easily significant at the 1 percent level. Of course some students fall into more than one of these categories. Roughly speaking, the advantages for them are additive; unfortunately, the number of such cases is too small to allow us to interact the dummy variables. The approach used here is by no means a perfect way of determining the degree of advantage enjoyed by all athletes, since some number of them may gain admission, and go on to play, without having been on a coach's list. Also, as one commentator pointed out, the underlying pools of targeted candidates are constituted in somewhat different ways. For example, if a college learns that a poorly qualified child of an alumnus is contemplating applying, the family may be counseled against completing the application and may be encouraged instead to consider other schools—but of course by no means all such candidates will be identified, and not all of those who are "counseled" will heed the advice. The prospective athletes on the coaches' lists are presumably the most carefully sifted of all those in targeted groups. In any case, the trend over time in these respective admissions advantages is unmistakable. Moreover, in one important respect, the method used to derive these estimates understates the true admissions advantage enjoyed by athletes. In using only SAT scores to control for precollegiate differences in academic qualifications, we tacitly assume that the athlete and the nonathlete with 1000 SAT scores were alike in other respects. In fact it seems likely that athletes are likely to have lower high school grades and in general to be weaker candidates than students at large *at any given level of SAT scores.* The reason is that those students at large with 1000 SAT scores who were admitted were presumably stronger candidates along these other dimensions than those students at large with 1000 SAT scores who were rejected. Athletes, on the other hand, are being singled out for a different set of skills, and so this is less likely to be true in their case. Data we

present later, when we discuss academic performance in college, are consistent with this interpretation.

10. Another question is to what extent the test score gap between students who play High Profile sports and other students is due mainly to associated differences in socioeconomic status (see the discussion in the next section). The short answer is that controlling for differences in socioeconomic status reduces the test score gap by perhaps 20 percent. The mean SAT scores of athletes in the High Profile sports are appreciably lower than the mean SATs of other students who come from similar socioeconomic backgrounds. For example, if we compare only High Profile athletes and other students whose fathers had advanced degrees, we find an average test score gap of 159 points; comparing High Profile athletes and other students without regard to socioeconomic status results in a test score gap of 198 points.

11. Crew is especially interesting in light of what the admissions dean had said about it being "the last of the amateur sports." The relative lack of recruitment of rowers is reflected in their higher average SAT scores.

12. The growing differences between athletes and other students in SAT scores are also reflected in self-reported differences in intellectual self-confidence, in self-ratings of mathematical and writing ability, and in their perceptions of whether they will graduate with honors or attain at least a B average (as expressed on the CIRP surveys).

13. These comparisons are based on the distribution of Verbal SATs among all male college-bound seniors in the '89 cohort. The results are very much the same if the Math SAT is used. National SAT data were obtained from the College Board.

14. In the '51 cohort, on the other hand, participants in the High Profile sports in the Ivy League schools and in the Division III coed liberal arts colleges came from essentially the same backgrounds as students at large; in the colleges, for example, 52 percent of the High Profile athletes had fathers with B.A.s or advanced degrees, as contrasted with 54 percent of the students at large.

15. Harry Edwards, "The Black 'Dumb Jock': An American Sports Tragedy," *College Board Review* 131 (Spring 1984): 8–13.

16. In the Ivy League schools, the corresponding percentages were 22 percent for the male athletes and 36 percent for the students at large (Scorecard 2.6). The pattern in the Division IA private universities appears to be similar, but not enough of these students participated in the CIRP survey to permit strong conclusions to be drawn. (Even fewer students in the Division IA public universities participated, and so we cannot report on their views.)

17. Not surprisingly, athletes also differ from students at large in the importance they attach to other goals. For example, in the Division III coed liberal arts colleges, 31 percent of entering students at large attach great importance to "developing a meaningful philosophy of life," as contrasted with 20 percent of athletes. In these same schools, 13 percent of entering male students at large state that one of their most important ("essential") goals is "writing original works (poems, novels, short stories, etc.)," as contrasted with 6 percent of athletes.

18. The results reported here are consistent with other research, including the study of athletes and other students at Amherst, Columbia, and Princeton carried out by social psychologists Deborah Prentice and Nancy Cantor. In a recent pa-

per titled "The Student-Athlete," the researchers sum up "how students describe themselves coming into college" (findings based on data taken from CIRP surveys): "Athletes . . . gave themselves lower ratings on academic attributes and higher ratings on social attributes, health-related attributes, and achievement-related attributes. So, compared to other students, athletes look to be more ambitious, more social, and, not surprisingly, healthier, but less academically focused, at least in the way they describe themselves." In high school, athletes reported "having spent more time exercising and doing sports [of course] . . . , but also more time socializing with friends and more time partying. They reported having spent less time studying, working for pay, doing volunteer work, and participating in student clubs and groups." Finally, with regard to goals, "athletes placed more value on being well off financially"; working paper presented to Princeton University's 250th Anniversary Symposium on "The Student Athlete," April 19, 1997, pp. 2, 5, 6. For another, somewhat fuller, account of this research, see Nancy E. Cantor and Deborah A. Prentice, "The Life of the Modern-Day Student-Athlete: Opportunities Won and Lost," paper presented at the Princeton Conference on Higher Education, March 21–23, 1996.

Chapter 3   The College Game

1. Welch Suggs, "Graduation Rates Hit Lowest Level in 7 Years for Athletes in Football and Basketball," *Chronicle of Higher Education*, September 10, 1999, p. A58.

2. This situation may be changing, however, as more highly visible athletes (especially basketball players) opt to leave school early to begin professional careers. Still, it is hard to view this kind of attrition as a decided negative for those athletes able to compete at the highest level.

3. The primary consideration in defining what "active" participation means is the amount of time required to participate. In some cases, simply belonging to a group (such as an orchestra) qualified a student as an active participant, since there is a high threshold of commitment that all group members must meet. In other cases that may not be true. For example, we would not want to include a student who occasionally contributes an article to a monthly magazine, even though he might consider himself a participant in that activity. Instead, we include only students who appear on the masthead of the student newspaper (since that implies a certain level of commitment) and only the officers or leaders of certain organizations.

4. These numbers are based on percentile rank-in-class. We use rank-in-class so that we can ignore differences among schools in grading scales. It is important to recall that since these percentages are means (or averages) of rankings spread out over a 100-point scale, the mean for the majority group (students at large) is inevitably going to be very close to 50 percent. (The average rank-in-class for men in general is slightly lower than the average for women, which is why the mean rank for the male students at large is below the 50th percentile.)

5. The record of academic performance is of course much more worrisome at Division IA schools that have to deal with serious charges of academic abuse. An English professor reviewed the academic records of 39 football players and

other athletes at the University of Tennessee and called attention to what is described as "a pattern of questionable practices, including many juniors and seniors who never declared a major, many altered grades, and a bunching of athletes in the urban studies department." Teri Bostian, "A Professor at Tennessee Cites Academic Abuses," *New York Times*, April 20, 2000, p. D3; Robert Lipsyte, "What Happens after the Whistle Blows?" *New York Times*, July 20, 2000, p. D1.

6. See Bowen and Bok for regressions based on data for the same schools and cohorts included in this analysis, and also for an explanation of the multivariate techniques used to produce the estimates shown.

7. These values are the coefficients of the dummy variables used to tag High Profile athletes and Lower Profile athletes in the multivariate regressions that control for SAT scores, major field of study, and socioeconomic status.

8. The differences between athletes and students at large in the distribution of SAT scores raise questions about the functional form assumptions that underlie these regressions. In the Ivies and the Division III coed liberal arts colleges, there are enough athletes and other students in each SAT interval to make it plausible to assume a linear relationship between SATs and rank-in-class; this assumption also seems reasonable when we look at the Lower Profile sports at the Division IA private universities; it is most questionable at the Division IA public universities and for the High Profile sports at the Division IA private universities. However, the use of other functional forms did not seem justified by the limited data available for specific groups of athletes at these schools—especially when we recognize differences in patterns of majors and other complicating factors noted later. We do not believe that this problem affects the general nature of the conclusions.

9. Athletes are not the only group of students at these schools who do less well academically than their test scores would predict. In *The Shape of the River*, Bowen and Bok found this same pattern among African Americans and to some extent among Hispanic students as well. In the epilogue to this chapter, we ask whether the same or different factors are at work in explaining performance gaps for the two groups, and we also raise the even more fundamental question of whether underperformance should be regarded in the same way for athletes and minority students.

10. This regression and others referred to in the text are available from the authors.

11. At the extremes, however, the extraordinarily heavy time commitments for athletes who participate in High Profile championship events are almost certain to affect academic performance. One commentator on the manuscript noted that "In winning the NCAA tournament this year, the Michigan State basketball team played 36 games in basically a four-month period.... Similarly, what appears to be irresistible pressure for a national football championship . . . will result in a parallel increase in the number of games in a more demanding physical competition."

12. A similar pattern, though more muted, is found among the students at the coed liberal arts colleges. In the Division IA universities, on the other hand, athletes playing High Profile sports were more likely than students at large to have a faculty mentor, a pattern attributable at least in part to the practice in some pro-

grams (Penn State football is an example) of assigning faculty members to individual athletes. Of course, the nature of the athlete-faculty relationship may differ across programs and schools.

13. When we look specifically at athletes, we find that those who reported having a faculty mentor had a class rank bonus ranging from 6 to 13 points (on an other-things-equal basis). (Regression not shown but available from the authors on request.) Of course, causation could go in both directions, with faculty mentors helping students to do better academically and with the more academically inclined students most likely to find faculty mentors. For a more general discussion of the relationship between mentors and grades, see Bowen and Bok, pp. 203–5.

14. Sara Conrath, "Choice to Quit Causes Tension in Varsity Sports," *Daily Princetonian,* October 21, 1999, online edition.

15. It is not necessary for large numbers of coaches to be like this for there to be strong effects. There is an analogy from the study of labor mobility. John Dunlop, a distinguished labor economist, liked to point out that the effectiveness of labor mobility does not depend on anything like all workers being prepared to move in response to incentives. If only a small fraction of the workforce responds to the incentives, a new equilibrium will be established. Similarly, if only a relatively small percentage of coaches think the way that the person described in the story thinks, the perceptions of students in general may be affected quite strongly.

16. This result is from a multivariate regression predicting rank-in-class for students from the Ivy League and the Division III coed liberal arts colleges. The –5-point penalty for having had a coach as a mentor is in addition to penalties of –11 points for being a High Profile athlete and –5 points for being a Lower Profile athlete. All of these coefficients are highly significant.

17. Cantor and Prentice; see especially p. 26.

18. Ernest T. Pascarella, Rachel Truckenmiller, Amaury Nora, Patrick T. Terenzini, Marcia Edison, and Linda Serra Hagedorn, "Cognitive Impacts of Intercollegiate Athletic Participation," *Journal of Higher Education,* January–February 1999, pp. 22–23. These observations follow a more general discussion of the presence of underperformance among male High Profile athletes at a group of schools that are more nationally representative than those in the C&B database.

19. We focus this part of the discussion on the Ivy League and the Division III coed liberal arts colleges because the consistency of the curricular offerings within these sets of schools allows us to pinpoint some evident changes over time in the field-of-study preferences of athletes versus other students. The range of majors offered in the Division IA universities includes so many other fields (such as business, education, and communications) that the same kinds of comparisons within the arts and sciences are difficult to make.

20. Jennifer Arthur, "Proposed Finance Major to Be Discussed," *Yale Daily News,* February 9, 1999, online edition.

21. "Preserve Liberal Arts Education in Economics," *Yale Daily News,* February 12, 1999, online edition.

22. Cantor and Prentice, p. 26.

23. Ibid., Tables 3 and 6.

24. George R. Goethals, Gordon C. Winston, and David J. Zimmerman, "Students Educating Students: The Emerging Role of Peer Effects in Higher Educa-

tion," Discussion Paper 50, Williams Project on the Economics of Higher Education, April 1999. This research team from Williams College, which is made up of one social psychologist (Goethals) and two economists (Winston and Zimmerman) is currently examining—for the first time—the effects that peers such as roommates and dormmates have on a person's academic performance. Their working papers can be obtained at http://www.williams.edu/wpehe/.

25. Regression not shown but available from the authors on request.

26. Bowen and Bok, pp. 53–90.

27. Claude Steele and Joshua Aronson, "Stereotype Threat and the Test Performance of Academically Successful African-Americans," in Christopher Jencks and Meredith Phillips (eds.), *The Black-White Test Score Gap* (Washington, D.C.: Brookings Institution, 1998), pp. 401–30.

28. One lesson learned in studying the subject of race-sensitive admissions was that many black students, feeling like outsiders on the campus of a traditionally white institution, were reminded of their outsider status when they encountered classmates who said things like "I've never met a black person before," as well as by becoming involved in, and distracted by, racially charged incidents. A key point is that no one decides to be black. All black students, whatever else may be said about them, are affected, albeit in different ways, by what Glenn Loury (in the foreword to the paperback edition of *The Shape of the River*) has called "this country's unlovely racial history." Athletes, on the other hand, choose their role. They can decide not to be athletes and thereby elect to "mainstream" themselves, or they can continue to participate in a valued activity. Due simply to facts of history, being an underrepresented minority student on a predominantly white campus is inescapably fraught with greater complications than being someone devoted to an optional (and usually enjoyable) athletic pursuit.

29. Signithia Fordham and John Ogbu, "Black Students' School Success: Coping with the Burden of 'Acting White,'" *Urban Review* 18(3) (1986): 176–206.

30. From a talk given at the Macalester College Forum on Higher Education, St. Paul, Minn., June 3, 1999.

Chapter 4   Men's Lives after College

1. This is not, however, a situation in which it is possible to parse out perfectly what is due to selection and what is due to treatment. We are not able to compare one randomly chosen set of mice with another randomly chosen set who were given 20 cups of coffee. What athletes accomplished in secondary school, and what they intended to do in life, were no doubt affected by both early-stage "treatments" and their expectations of what life as an athlete would offer them. When we distinguish "treatment" from "selection," we have in mind the added effects on individuals' outcomes associated with having played sports in college.

2. In this discussion, graduates are classified according to the highest advanced degree that they have earned. Thus those who first earned M.A.s and then earned Ph.D.s are counted among the Ph.D. recipients but not among the holders of M.A.s.

3. In much of the discussion that follows, the language that we use in describing the distribution of athletes and other students by occupation suggests that job

distributions reflect primarily the preferences of the job seekers. In reality, there is of course a demand side to the employment equation as well as a supply side; employers may be more likely to offer jobs to certain kinds of candidates than to others. Thus, at some points in the discussion, we speculate about the effects of employer preferences (for example, in explaining why so many athletes are in marketing jobs). Later in the chapter we consider at greater length the reasons why employers in certain fields may be especially interested in offering jobs to athletes. Some business schools also give athletes an extra edge in the admissions process, and such institutional preferences may affect the distribution of athletes and other students by advanced degree attainment in the same way that employer preferences affect occupational distributions.

4. The base for these percentages is all members of the cohort who were employed at the time of the survey. The particular occupational categories shown in the figure account for 89 percent of all the employed athletes and 92 percent of all the employed students at large.

5. The differences in the relative numbers of athletes and students at large in the higher education sector are less pronounced than we would have expected them to be on the basis of patterns of graduate study; one part of the explanation is that a large percentage of the former athletes working in this sector are either coaches or administrators.

6. Scorecards are not shown but are available on request from the authors.

7. Scorecards are not shown but are available on request from the authors.

8. Scorecards are not shown but are available on request from the authors.

9. This uptick in average class rank of students at large in the field of financial services is not attributable to any marked improvement in average class rank for the group as a whole; on average, they ranked in the 47th percentile in '51, the 49th percentile in '76, and the 49th percentile in '89. See Scorecard 4.7 for mean class rank data for athletes in financial services.

10. These data are for male full-time workers. The overall averages for "own income" of C&B respondents shown in Figure 4.4 are sector composites; that is, they are averages of the means within each set of C&B schools (Division IA public universities and so on) that are shown in Scorecard 4.8. The means for each set of schools are in turn averages of the means for the individual schools represented within each set (in the case of the Division IA public universities, for example, the University of Michigan, Penn State, Miami University in Ohio, and the University of North Carolina at Chapel Hill). As explained earlier, the advantage of this approach is that it treats the college or university as the unit of analysis and does not permit the overall summary figures (the sector composites) to be distorted by the presence of larger numbers of athletes within particular schools. Readers should be aware that all of the C&B earnings data are subject to "top coding"; that is, survey respondents at the top of the income scale checked the box "$200,000 or more." Using census data, we estimated that the average C&B respondent in this category could have been expected to earn $290,000 (see Bowen and Bok, p. 357). However, there could of course be differences in the earnings of athletes and students at large at the very top of the income scale, and any such differences will not be captured.

The national estimate is based on census data for men who were in the same age range as the C&B graduates in 1995, when the C&B survey was conducted (see Bowen and Bok, p. 124). The Bowen and Bok study contains an extended discussion of the problem of estimating the degree to which this earnings differential reflects selection (the high quality of the students admitted to these schools) versus treatment (the education they received and the connections they made).

11. See Bowen and Bok, pp. 131–42. As one would expect, earnings correlate positively with SAT scores, parents' socioeconomic status, class rank, and being white. Of these relationships, the one that may surprise some people is the large earnings advantage associated with a high class rank. Contrary to much folk wisdom, the student with the "gentleman C" did much less well in the marketplace than the classmate who earned better grades. On an "other things equal" basis (controlling for differences in field of study, type of school attended, advanced degrees attained, and sector of employment), "the typical male C&B matriculant who ranked in the top third of his class earned $21,000 more than a man in the bottom third" (p. 142).

12. These are sector composites for men working full time who identified (on the survey forms) the sector in which they were working as well as their occupation. For reasons that we do not understand, a smaller percentage of the members of the '51 cohort identified a sector, but these omissions do not appear to introduce any systematic bias into the analysis.

13. Earnings for members of both the '51 and '76 cohorts were measured in 1995 (when the C&B surveys were conducted), and of course the members of the two cohorts were at different stages of their lives in 1995. Most of the members of the '51 cohort were about 60 years old, whereas members of the '76 cohort were roughly 25 years younger. We are unable to estimate the "life cycle" effects on the earnings of the two groups, including differences in the earnings of those in the for-profit and not-for-profit sectors. The difficulty of handling this life cycle effect, combined with the more extensive data available for the '76 cohort, leads us to concentrate most of the rest of the analysis on the '76 cohort. The comparison shown here is useful mainly in demonstrating that the broad patterns for the two cohorts were similar.

14. There is also some (albeit limited) direct evidence indicating that earnings are affected by certain pre-collegiate attitudes that distinguish athletes from students at large. Self-perceptions and attitudes that students reported when they first entered college are associated with future earnings, *even after controlling for differences in advanced degree attainment and sector and occupation.* Two questions included on the CIRP surveys administered to incoming freshmen illustrate the approach. Freshmen who said that they regarded earning a high income as "very important" (5 on the 5-point scale) earned about $4,000 more than their classmates who regarded this objective as slightly less important (and thus checked 4 rather than 5). Conversely, those who attached the highest priority to "writing original works" paid an earnings penalty of about $4,500. Athletes were disproportionately interested in earning high incomes and less inclined than other students to attach a high value to the importance of writing original works. (These results are obtained from multivariate regressions not shown here but available

on request from the authors.) The student population analyzed in these regressions differs somewhat from the broader population because the pre-college data collected through the CIRP survey are available for only a portion of the students for which we have institutional records and C&B survey data (the sample size is reduced from about 9,000 to about 5,000).

15. The most basic multivariate model limits the population to males working full time in 1995 and controls only for the type of school attended (Division IA public universities, Division IA private universities, Ivy League, and Division III coed liberal arts colleges). The type-of-school controls are necessary for two reasons: both the relative numbers of athletes and students at large and the average earnings for all students vary appreciably by type of school. One could argue for including additional controls for pre-collegiate attributes such as race, socio-economic status, and SAT scores. An argument can also be made for controlling for college majors and advanced degrees earned. We experimented with a variety of specifications but concluded finally that the simplest model, which controlled only for type of school, provided the most useful way of looking at earnings advantages. The reasoning is simply that "athletes are who they are," and that when schools recruit athletes they do so knowing, for example, their pre-collegiate attributes. To compare athletes with other students after first "raising" the athletes' SAT scores to make them comparable to the SAT scores of the other students is to propose an artificial comparison. Similarly, it would be inappropriate, in our view, to control for measures of how athletes and other students did in college and then in graduate school, since the respective patterns of achievement are part of what we need to take into account in seeing how people do later in life. As we learned from earlier work in *The Shape of the River* (see note 22, p. 108, and note 24, p. 135), it is important to choose the controls included in a model on the basis of the particular question to be answered, and to avoid the temptation to "overcontrol." Since reasonable people can differ on the precise specifications that are "best," we should also note that including other groups of controls does not affect the tenor of the results. For example, when we add controls for pre-collegiate variables, advanced degrees, and occupations (in the for-profit regression), the earnings advantage for athletes remains at $13,000 (which is what it was in the simplest model). We believe that there is a better case for adding a set of occupational controls only, and when we do this, we obtain an earnings advantage for athletes of $12,000. The latter model (controlling for type of school and occupation) is the one we use generally. (Regressions are not shown but are available from the authors on request.)

16. The simple model used to pursue these occupation-specific questions (which involves interacting an athlete dummy variable with each occupation in turn) was suggested to us by Sarah Turner of the University of Virginia, who also suggested the test of statistical significance that we used. All of the results reported are based on multivariate regressions that control for type of school attended, but not (for reasons explained in the previous note) for pre-collegiate characteristics or other variables. The earnings advantage for athletes in financial services held up no matter what additional controls were introduced; similarly, the lack of a significant difference in earnings between athletes and other students continued to be observed. The regressions are available from the authors on request.

17. We should also record one finding from the '51 cohort to which we will return in Chapter 13. In the '51 cohort (although not in the '76 cohort), business CEOs who had been athletes enjoyed a statistically significant earnings advantage (of roughly $25,000) over other CEOs. As we argue in Chapter 13, we believe that this intercohort difference may be revealing, when interpreted in conjunction with changes over time in the nature of the admissions process.

18. We obtained the data needed to identify these individuals from the precollege questionnaires administered by the Educational Testing Service.

19. One possible interpretation of these patterns is based on the special recruiting efforts in athletics. Presumably most of the high-school-only athletes were not given the same degree of admissions advantage as those with more athletic talent; hence it can be argued that, although they may have had personal traits similar to those possessed by other athletic types, their norms and goals would be more akin to those of the usual applicants who were gaining admission without the boost given to recruited athletes. Survey data collected some 20 years later, when the C&B surveys were conducted in 1995, provide additional information concerning the views of the three groups. When asked about the importance of "high earnings" in thinking about a job, 47 percent of those who had played only high school sports responded with the highest ranking, as compared with 54 percent of those who had played college sports and 45 percent of those classified as "never athletes." Former high school athletes also held similar priorities in terms of the importance of "intellectual challenge" (very important for 85 percent of high school athletes, 79 percent of college athletes, and 84 percent of "never athletes"). High school athletes occupied a position between the other two groups on two other measures of "ambition" (importance of promotion opportunities and high-level responsibilities). These data indicate to us that, although former high school athletes differed from former college athletes in terms of their financial ambitions, they also may have lacked some of their determination and drive. Finally, despite affinities with the "never athletes" group in important job selection criteria, those who played high school sports sided with the college athletes in terms of the importance they attached to autonomy, flexible schedule, pleasant work environment, and job security.

20. See the bottom rows of Appendix Table B.4.1. These differences are roughly consistent by type of school or level of play. In general, the four-year athletes earned about 5 to 10 percent more than the athletes who earned awards in fewer than four years. The difference is 15 percent for the Division III coed liberal arts colleges, but this result is aberrational because it is driven by extreme values for two schools.

21. The conclusions concerning statistical significance are based on multivariate regressions of the kind described in note 15. These regressions are available from the authors on request. The actual dollar figures presented in Figure 4.9 and Appendix Table B.4.1 are sector composites (which are roughly equivalent to regression results controlling for type of school).

22. We group those who played two years and those who played three years to simplify the presentation and increase the cell sizes for those who played more than one year but less than four years. However, we also looked separately at those who played two years and those who played three years. Interestingly, the three-

year athletes in the High Profile sports not only earned far less than the four-year athletes, they earned less than the two-year participants and less than the students at large. In contrast, the three-year athletes in the Lower Profile sports earned more than the four-year athletes in these sports and more than the two-year athletes. The patterns relating earnings to years played are simply very erratic, which is the main point. The earnings increments given in Figure 4.10 use students at large as the reference group and are based on multivariate regressions of the kind described in note 15. These regressions are available from the authors on request.

23. The lack of a four-year premium for athletes outside the High Profile sports rebuts another hypothesis, namely that the four-year athletes should be thought of as analogous to the students who *graduate* from high school. Much research shows that finishing the 16th year of school (graduating) is worth more than, say, finishing the 15th year. Playing a sport for four years rather than three years is not, however, the same thing as graduating versus not graduating from high school, and this is presumably why we do not find a "graduation" premium in sports other than the High Profile sports. For a more extensive discussion of earnings premiums associated with graduating, see Bowen and Bok, pp. 68–69; David Card and Alan B. Krueger, "Labor Market Effects of School Quality: Theory and Evidence," in Gary Burtless (ed.), *Does Money Matter? The Link between Schools, Student Achievement, and Adult Success* (Washington, D.C.: Brookings Institution, 1996), pp. 97–140.

24. In these sports, the three-year participants had the highest average earnings, although the difference between their average earnings and the average for, say, the two-year participants is not statistically significant.

25. We interacted type of institution (Division IA public university, Division IA private university, Ivy League university, and Division III coed liberal arts college) with the dummy variables for athletes in High Profile sports (those who played four years and those who played less than four years) and for other athletes. None of the coefficients of the interaction variables was statistically significant.

Chapter 5   The Development of Women's Athletic Programs

1. 20 USC 1681(a). See Chapter 1, note 14, for the associated language from the Code of Federal Regulations, 34 C.F.R. 106.41(a).

2. Mary Jo Festle, *Playing Nice: Politics and Apologies in Women's Sports* (New York: Columbia University Press, 1996), pp. 111–13.

3. On the technical questions of substantial proportionality versus strict proportionality, see Walter B. Connolly, Jr., and Jeffrey D. Adelman, "A University's Defense to a Title IX Gender Equity in Athletics Lawsuit: Congress Never Intended Gender Equity Based on Student Body Ration," in Walter B. Connolly, Jr. (ed.), *A Practical Guide to Title IX: Law, Principles, and Practices* (Washington, D.C.: National Association of College and University Attorneys, 1995), p. 863. For a thorough discussion of the various statistical methods in use, see Mary W. Gray, "The Concept of Substantial Proportionality in Title IX Athletics Cases," *Duke Journal of Gender Law & Policy* 3(1) (1996): 185–88.

4. Rudolph also notes that "It is probably true, as Dean Briggs of Harvard suggested in a Wellesley commencement address in 1904, that the movement for col-

legiate education for women created the serious 'danger of intellectual unrest, of chafing, in the daily duties of later life, at the meagerness of intellectual opportunity' in the life that matrimony and motherhood were cut out for her." Rudolph concludes, however, that "when all the returns were in, the higher education of women was termed a success"; "The Education of Women," in *The American College and University,* p. 328.

5. Dimitri Pappas, "Women's Athletics Enjoys 23 Successful Years," *Daily Princetonian,* November 16, 1994, p. 10.

6. At the University of Tennessee, for example, the women's basketball team recently had annual attendance at its games approaching a quarter of a million fans, with nearly 17,000 per game. Indeed, this is one of the few women's teams in the country whose revenues exceed its expenditures. Nevertheless, the team remains the "Lady Vols," never just the "Vols" like their male counterparts. See Welch Suggs, "U. of Tennessee's Lady Vols Find Success—and Profit—on the Court," *Chronicle of Higher Education,* December 17, 1999, p. A54, online edition.

7. The presiding judge in a 1999 court decision made this point emphatically when she stressed that "women's attitudes toward sports are *socially constructed* [emphasis added] and have been limited by discrimination and gender stereotypes." The court's conclusion was that measures of the apparent *current interest* of women on campus in participating cannot justify failing to meet the "substantial proportionality" test of Title IX. U.S. Court of Appeals for the Ninth Circuit, ruling on a case involving the California State University at Bakersfield, as cited in Welch Suggs, "2 Appeals Courts Uphold Right of Universities to Reduce Numbers of Male Athletes," *Chronicle of Higher Education,* January 7, 2000, p. A64, online edition.

8. Paula Welch, *Silver Era, Golden Moments: A Celebration of Ivy League Women's Athletics* (Lanham, Md.: Madison, 1999), p. 9. For background on "play days" and, more generally, on the long history of women and athletics, see Allen Guttmann, *Women's Sports: A History* (New York: Columbia University Press, 1991). For more detail on men's views of the acceptability of women playing sports, see Donald J. Mrozek, "The 'Amazon' and the American 'Lady,'" in S. W. Pope (ed.), *The New American Sport History: Recent Approaches and Perspectives* (Urbana: University of Illinois Press, 1997), pp. 198–214.

9. Welch, p. 47.

10. Quoted in "Women's Basketball Pummels Penn," *Daily Princetonian,* March 7, 1997, online edition.

11. Festle, p. 138.

12. Ibid., p. 137.

13. For accounts of the NCAA takeover, see Festle, Chapter 8; Murray Sperber, "The NCAA as Predator: The Rape of the Association for Intercollegiate Athletics for Women," in *College Sports, Inc.,* pp. 322–32. See also the account by Merrily Dean Baker in Welch, pp. 60–64.

14. Linda-Jean Carpenter and R. Vivian Acosta, "Back to the Future: Reform with a Women's Voice," in D. Stanley Eitzen (ed.), *Sport in Contemporary Society: An Anthology,* 5th ed. (New York: St. Martin's Press, 1996); R. Vivian Acosta and Linda-Jean Carpenter, "Women in Intercollegiate Sport: A Longitudinal Study—

Twenty Three Year Update: 1977–2000," mimeograph, 2000. This study received substantial press coverage, including a *New York Times* article: Lena Williams, "Women Play More, but Coach Less," May 3, 2000, p. D8. It is available from the authors (retired from Brooklyn College) on request.

15. Jeffrey H. Orleans, "An End to the Odyssey: Equal Athletic Opportunities for Women," *Duke Journal of Gender Law & Policy* 3(1) (1996): 131–41; quote on p. 137.

16. Marvin Lazerson and Ursula Wagener, "Missed Opportunities: Lessons from the Title IX Case at Brown," *Change* 28(4) (1996): 46–52; quote on p. 47.

17. Executive vice president for alumni, public affairs, and external relations Robert A. Reichley, quoted in Debra E. Blum, "Brown Loses Bias Case," *Chronicle of Higher Education,* April 7, 1995, online edition.

18. "Defendant's Post-Trial Memorandum," in Connolly, p. 41.

19. In the 1999 ruling cited in note 7, the U.S. Court of Appeals for the Ninth Circuit refused to uphold an injunction issued by a lower court preventing California State University at Bakersfield from capping the rosters of men's teams (including wrestling) as part of their effort to comply with Title IX. The presiding judge wrote that the defendants' interpretation of Title IX "would have allowed universities to do little or nothing to equalize men's and women's opportunities if they could point to data showing that women were less interested in sports. . . . [But] a central aspect of Title IX's purpose was to encourage women to participate in sports: The increased number of roster spots and scholarships reserved for women would gradually increase demand among women for those roster spots and scholarships." This court ruling reminds us of one of the central points of this book: that the signals sent by colleges and universities to prospective students, their parents, and society at large can have a transformative impact on how individuals and other institutions act.

20. These data are from National Collegiate Athletic Association, *1997–98 NCAA Gender-Equity Study* (Indianapolis, Ind.: NCAA, 1999). We cite the data for the 1992–96 period because we are unsure how to interpret the more recent data (from 1997–98). These newer data show an enormous apparent decline in the operating expenses of men's sports (from $2.4 million to $1.4 million, with no such decline in the women's operating expenses. It must be remembered, however, that these data refer only to direct team expenses, and (as we will explain in Chapter 11) a good portion of the athletic budget resides in what we think of as the "black box" of administrative and infrastructure expenses. For this reason, we are skeptical that the substantial reported decline in spending on men's sports should be interpreted as an actual decline, as opposed to a recategorization of expenses. See also Marcia Chambers, "For Women, 25 Years of Title IX Has Not Leveled the Playing Field," *New York Times,* June 16, 1997, p. A1.

21. NCAA, *1997–98 NCAA Gender-Equity Study,* p. 33.

22. William C. Rhoden, "Ideals and Reality Collide on the Court," *New York Times,* July 21, 1997, p. C7.

23. Festle, p. 137.

24. Cindy Cohen, quoted in Mark Goodman, "A Squad with Few Equals," *New York Times,* April 27, 1997, p. S9.

Chapter 6   New Players

1. There are 18 schools in the database that had women students in the '51 cohort and that provided data for students in general for that year. Of these 18 schools, in only 6 cases were we able to tag women athletes. There were 220 identified athletes enrolled in these 6 schools, or just about 9 percent of all women enrolled. (However, the data for one of these 6 schools are of dubious validity, showing 46 percent of all women as having won awards for intercollegiate competition; if we exclude this school, the overall average falls to about 7 percent.) The roughly comparable composite figure for male athletes in the same types of schools (excluding the Division IA public universities, which show no women athletes) is 20 percent.

2. These numbers are comparable to those presented in Chapter 2 for the men, and they include the total number of participants (from all cohorts) in the single year in question, as opposed to the number of those in the one-year cohorts on which our study is focused who received awards at any point in their undergraduate careers. These data are taken from the Equity in Athletics Disclosure Act (EADA) filings for 1997–98. Since women's colleges are not required to submit these forms, we do not have comparable data for them. But we know from the College and Beyond database that in the '89 cohort 12 percent of the women at the women's colleges in our study were athletes, as compared with 19 percent of the women at the coed liberal arts colleges and 15 percent of the women at the Ivy League schools (see Scorecard 6.1). We interpret these differences as reflecting in large part the Title IX obligation to offer more sports for women at schools that have men's programs than at the women's colleges.

3. These data are restricted to the matriculants at the C&B schools who responded to the CIRP pre-college surveys. The cell sizes in the Division IA public and private universities are not large enough to yield entirely reliable data, and so we do not show results for these schools in Figure 6.1; in general, however, they follow the same pattern as the one shown for the Ivies.

4. Although these data are for one school only, we know from other data that the school that was able to supply these hard-to-obtain figures for all members of the applicant pool is very much "mainstream" among the academically selective schools that do not offer athletic scholarships (see discussion in Chapter 2).

5. As explained in Chapter 2, the method used to obtain these estimates of the admissions advantage enjoyed by various targeted groups is to predict the probability of admission on the basis of a multivariate regression equation that includes SAT scores as control variables and dummy variables for legacy status, minority status, and recruited athlete status. The coefficients of the dummy variables indicate the degree of advantage enjoyed by the group in question. The coefficients of all three dummy variables are easily significant at the 1 percent level.

6. It should be re-emphasized (see Chapter 2, note 9) that the measure of admissions advantage used here *understates* the true degree of advantage enjoyed by athletes since it relates admissions probabilities only to SAT scores. At given levels of SAT scores, women athletes in the '89 cohort presented weaker precollegiate academic credentials of other kinds (e.g., high school grades, achieve-

ment scores) than did other candidates. A more sophisticated prediction model that took account of differences in all of these pre-collegiate measures of academic potential would show an even greater difference in the probability of admission for recruited athletes on an other-things-equal basis.

7. Data for another school for which we have information concerning all applicants in the '89 cohort (including all recruited athletes) allows us to confirm the '89 part of the picture for women shown in Figure 6.1, just as these data permitted the confirmation of the similar pattern for men. At this second school, the admissions advantage enjoyed by recruited athletes in the '89 cohort was even greater than it was at the first school, and it was much greater than the advantage enjoyed by legacies and minority students. As we noted before, this approach is by no means a perfect way of determining the degree of advantage enjoyed by all athletes, since some number of them gain admission, and go on to play, without having been on a coach's list. Still the trend over time in these "advantages" is unmistakable. One commentator has pointed out that the yields (the percentages of those offered admission who decide to attend the school) also differ by targeted groups, with, for example, athletes and legacies having higher yields than minority students; and it is of course the absolute number of students in any category who enroll, not the number offered admission, that matters in terms of the composition of the student body. If a school sets an enrollment target for a particular group (such as football players), the higher the projected yield, the smaller the number of offers of admission that need to be tendered; and a large admissions advantage may seem less problematic if the number of offers of admission is not too large. Ultimately, however, yield does not matter because the school can adjust the number of offers to reflect whatever yield is expected.

8. One commentator on the manuscript who is very familiar with the women's colleges observed that, at least until recently (and perhaps this is still true), the recruiting process at the women's colleges has been "gentler" than the process at, for example, the Ivies. Thus prospective students with athletic ability may not even have known that they were on a coach's list and thus may not have thought of themselves as having been recruited.

9. The data on Figure 6.5 are sector composites, but the findings hold up at every level (Scorecard 6.4). At the Ivy League schools, where the SAT scores of women who do not play college sports averaged a very high 1300, and 26 percent rated themselves in the top 10 percent in terms of their intellectual self-confidence, the SATs of Ivy League male High Profile athletes were 88 points *lower* (1212) and yet they were 7 percent *more likely* to rate themselves in the highest category of intellectual self confidence.

Chapter 7   Women Athletes in College

1. As one would expect, students at these selective schools graduate at higher rates than students at all four-year institutions. Within Division IA, 69 percent of all female athletes who entered in the fall of 1992 graduated within six years, as compared with 62 percent of all female matriculants; National Collegiate Athletic

Association, *1999 NCAA Division I Graduation-Rates Report* (Indianapolis, Ind.: NCAA), p. 638.

2. The figures for male athletes used in this paragraph compare all male athletes (High Profile and Lower Profile) with male students at large.

3. These results are based on separate multivariate regressions by type of school (Division IA public universities, Division IA private universities, Ivies, Division III coed liberal arts colleges, and Division III women's colleges) in which we control for race, the student's own SAT score, broad field of study (humanities, social sciences, and so on), parents' socioeconomic status, and the selectivity of the particular institution attended within the category (measured by institutional SAT score). All of the control variables perform as expected (with both the student's own SAT score and parents' socioeconomic status significant predictors of rank-in-class, and with modest rank-in-class penalties associated with majoring in the sciences and with attending an especially selective institution). The coefficient of the dummy variable indicating that the person was an athlete is the point estimate of the degree of underperformance. The equation for women in the '89 cohort at the Ivy League schools is reproduced as Appendix Table B.7.1, Model I, to demonstrate what we have done; the other regressions of this kind are available from the authors on request.

4. To illustrate the set of regressions underlying the data in this figure, we reproduce the one for the Ivies as Appendix Table B.7.1, Model II; again, the others in this set are available on request.

5. The strongest evidence of academic *over*performance among women in the '89 cohort with heavy commitments to extracurricular activities other than athletics is found in the Division IA public universities, the Division III coed liberal arts colleges, and the women's colleges. The definition of "time-intensive extracurricular activities" and the regression model used to test for over- or underperformance are the same for the women as they were for the men (see Chapter 3). The results for the men and women are roughly comparable, with one exception: men in the '89 cohort in the Ivies with heavy extracurricular commitments *over*performed significantly, whereas the women with comparable commitments in the Ivies neither over- nor underperformed. Regressions are available from the authors on request.

6. See Sarah E. Turner and William G. Bowen, "Choice of Major: The Changing (Unchanging) Gender Gap," *Industrial and Labor Relations Review* 52(2) (January 1999): 289–313.

7. Turner and Bowen, Figure 2, p. 296. Much of the rest of the Turner and Bowen article is devoted to a formal decomposing of differences in the fields of study chosen by men and women into parts attributable to differences in math and verbal SAT scores and parts attributable to other forces (presumably "preferences," in the main).

8. Turner and Bowen, p. 310.

9. The percentages for all subgroups shown in this figure are lower than the percentages cited earlier in this section because here we are considering only women in the natural sciences, not women in the natural sciences plus mathematics and engineering.

10. This is an important reason why Turner and Bowen caution against relying on the usual systems of classifying majors (p. 309).

Chapter 8   Women's Lives after College

1. See sources cited in Gary S. Becker, "Human Capital, Effort, and the Sexual Division of Labor," in Ramon Febrero and Pedro Schwartz (eds.), *The Essence of Becker* (Stanford, Calif.: Hoover Institution Press, 1995), p. 444 (originally published in the *Journal of Labor Economics* 3 [1, pt. 2] [1985]: S33–S55). Another good source is Arlie Russell Hochschild, *The Time Bind: When Work Becomes Home and Home Becomes Work* (New York: Henry Holt, 1997).

2. Quotes from women athletes who attended Smith and the University of Pennsylvania in the '76 cohort.

3. Wendy Olson, cited by John Weistart, "The Path of Most Resistance: The Long Road to Gender Equity in Intercollegiate Athletics (Part 2 of 4)," *Duke Journal of Gender Law & Policy* 3(1) (1996): 61–71; quote on p. 66.

4. Donna Lopiano, "Equity in Women's Sports: A Health and Fairness Perspective," in Connolly, p. 164 (originally published in *Clinics in Sports Medicine*, April 1994).

5. Cynthia Fuchs Epstein, "Constraints of Excellence: Structural and Cultural Barriers to the Recognition and Demonstration of Achievement," in Harriet Zuckerman, Jonathan Cole, and John Bruer (eds.), *The Outer Circle: Women in the Scientific Community* (New Haven, Conn.: Yale University Press, 1992), pp. 239–58; quote on p. 253.

6. Logistic regressions used to predict advanced degree attainment for women in the '76 cohort confirm the tabular results presented in the text (regression not shown, but results available from the authors). For women in the '76 cohort, being an athlete increases the probability of earning a professional or doctoral degree after holding constant race, parents' socioeconomic status, type of school attended, field of study in college, rank-in-class, and whether or not an individual had aspired to earn an advanced degree before entering college. The dummy variable used to indicate whether a student was an athlete has a positive coefficient that is significantly different from zero at the 95 percent confidence level. In addition, all the control variables perform as expected. Not surprisingly, rank-in-class is highly correlated with attaining an advanced degree.

7. This supposition is supported by the results of logistic regressions used to predict advanced degree attainment for women in the '89 cohort. The dummy variable for athlete has a positive coefficient and is statistically significant (regression not shown, but results available from the authors).

8. These figures are sector composites; there are modest differences in percent married by type of school, especially in the '89 cohorts, with women in the Division IA public and private universities more likely to have married by the time of the survey than women from the other groups of schools (scorecards not shown). At the level of sector composites, the percentages of never-married women are also identical in the '89 cohort (59 percent for both athletes and other women) and similar although not identical in the '76 cohort (17 percent for athletes and 14 percent for other women). By definition, the residual category

(divorced, separated, widowed) is also the same in the '89 cohort and slightly different in the '76 cohort (3 percent of athletes were divorced, separated, or widowed, versus 6 percent of other women).

9. The Nobel Prize–winning economist Gary Becker, who has written extensively about how families make choices concerning the division of labor among husbands and wives, reminds us that how much to work (and who should do what) is a matter not simply of time, but also of energy: "If childcare and other housework demand relatively large quantities of 'energy' compared to leisure and other nonmarket uses of time by men, women with responsibilities for housework would have less energy available for the market than men would. This would reduce the hourly earnings of married women, affect their jobs and occupations, and even lower their investment in market human capital when they worked the same number of market hours as married men." Becker, p. 436.

10. The tabular data cited in this paragraph are all sector composites (scorecards not shown but results available from the authors). We have also made use of multivariate logistic regressions, as explained in note 12.

11. Stephen S. Hall, "The Smart Set," *New York Times Magazine,* June 4, 2000, p. 54.

12. A multivariate logistic regression used to predict the odds that a woman in the '76 cohort would have been working full-time when she was surveyed in 1995 shows that, other things equal, the odds of working full-time correlate positively (and strongly) with having received either a Ph.D. or a professional degree in law, medicine, or business. And, as one would expect, spousal income and the presence of children both correlate negatively (and strongly) with working full-time. The relationship between athletic status and full-time work remains positive after all of these other variables are taken into account, but the coefficient is no longer significantly different from zero. We conclude that the simple correlation between athletic status and full-time work is due in large part to the above-average tendency for athletes to earn advanced degrees.

13. The question on the CIRP survey that we are using here is: "How would you characterize your political views?" We then grouped those who responded "far left" or "liberal" (calling them "liberal") and those who responded "conservative" or "far right" (calling them "conservative"). The C&B survey contained a different question that also makes it possible to group respondents on the basis of the views they held when they were surveyed in 1995 (many years after college, in most cases). The C&B question is: "Thinking about your views concerning economic and social issues, where would you place yourself on the scale below?" Respondents were then given a five-point scale ranging from "very liberal" to "very conservative" and were asked to place themselves in terms of (1) economic issues and (2) social issues. (See Bowen and Bok, p. 328.) In using the C&B categories it is necessary to recognize that a person's post-college views are of course affected by what has happened to the individual since college, and for this reason we generally prefer to use the CIRP pre-college data, even though the universe of people covered by the CIRP data is smaller than the C&B set.

14. This result is confirmed by multivariate logistic regressions predicting the likelihood of working full-time. When we interact the dummy variables for being an athlete and holding conservative views, the interaction term is negative and

statistically significant (regression not shown, but results available from the authors). As an interesting aside, we can see very clearly in the C&B data how the presence of children and the passage of time affect one's political orientation—especially in terms of social views. A simple comparison of the presence of children, labor force status, and post-college statements of political views could lead to the conclusion that conservative former athletes are decidedly more likely than liberal former athletes to have children and to be out of the workforce entirely (at least at the time of the survey). But by using the CIRP measures of *pre-college* political attitudes, we see that the latter two findings are due to the fact that women with children and those not working are more likely, later in life, to classify themselves as socially conservative.

15. In addition to the particular self-ratings and attitudes described subsequently, we examined a number of other dimensions along which one can compare the views of women and men, athletes and other students. Although there are of course differences in what the various groups characteristically want in jobs, the similarities generally dominate the differences. We have already referred, early in the chapter, to one very important difference: the much greater importance that women attach to flexible work schedules.

16. We lack similar data on pre-college self-ratings of competitiveness for the '76 cohort because the CIRP survey in the fall of 1976 did not ask that question.

17. Among the men in the '76 cohort, 15 percent of the athletes and 8 percent of the other students checked "business" when asked, on entering college, about their "probable career"; among the women in this cohort, there was no real difference between the athletes and the others (3 percent of the athletes checked "business" versus 4 percent of the other women students). Of the men in the '76 cohort, 17 percent of the athletes and 14 percent of the other students said that it was "essential" for them to be "very well off financially"; among the women, 5 percent of the athletes and 7 percent of the other women thought achieving this financial objective was "essential." Our confidence that these differences, although modest in size, are of consequence is increased by the consistency of the patterns across categories defined by world view (liberal and conservative) and over time. The comparable figures for the '89 cohort show the same patterns, with, in some cases, greater differences between athletes and other students.

18. The gaps between athletes with children working part-time and other women with children working part-time who said that various factors were important in a job were as follows: intellectual challenge, 9 points; high level of responsibility, 9 points; and promotion opportunities, 11 points. In all of these cases, the response patterns of the athletes were much closer to those of the women who were working full-time.

19. All of the results reported in this paragraph are based on the same kind of multivariate regression model described in Chapter 4 (especially notes 15 and 16); we control for type of school attended, but not for pre-collegiate differences or for advanced degrees attained.

20. Put more colloquially, the proposition is that women athletes in the late 1970s were, in the words of the commentator, especially good at "playing nice in the sandbox." At that time, the argument goes, such temperaments and capaci-

ties were especially useful for women in making inroads into professions that had not been welcoming to them historically. We attempted to test this line of argument by comparing the earnings of those women who were high-school-only athletes with the earnings of both the college athletes and the "never athletes." However, the results are inconclusive. The high-school-only athletes appear to enjoy an overall earnings advantage over the "never athletes" of only about $1,000 (a difference that is not statistically significant); in addition, this relationship is not consistent across types of schools.

21. Multivariate regressions support the commonsense proposition that the disproportionate number of advanced degrees earned by women athletes from the '76 cohort boosted their earnings.

22. It is not surprising that we find no evidence among the women of anything comparable to the extra boost in earnings enjoyed by the small number of men who earned awards for four years in the High Profile sports (left-hand side of Figure 4.10). Women athletes in the '76 cohort certainly would not have expected to enjoy any of the kind of "celebrity effect" that we speculate may have accounted for the higher earnings of the most highly visible male athletes; the complete lack of any earnings boost for women four-year athletes provides some further support for the "celebrity" interpretation of the results for the men.

23. One reader of the manuscript asked us to test the proposition that the results showing a lack of association between earnings advantage and years played are misleading because we failed to take account of other factors—specifically, the reader suggested that the women athletes who played only one year (or one or two years) may have had lower SAT scores than women athletes who played for three or four years. The results of this test are straightforward. There are no significant differences in SAT scores by years of play: women in the '76 cohort who played for one year had an average SAT score of 1172, and women athletes in this cohort who played for four years also had an average SAT score of 1172 (both sector composites). Of course, the women who played for various numbers of years may have differed in other unobservable respects (interests, preferences, drive, and so on). But if there were such differences, they certainly do not dominate the earnings data.

Chapter 9 Leadership

1. Quoted in "Sports and American Society," *The Long Term View: A Journal of Informed Opinion* (Massachusetts School of Law at Andover) 3(2): 62.

2. Andrew W. Miracle, Jr., and C. Roger Rees, *Lessons of the Locker Room: The Myth of School Sports* (Amherst, Mass.: Prometheus, 1994), p. 94.

3. "House Speaker Put in Wrestling Hall," *AP Online,* June 3, 2000. In a similar vein, former University of Michigan Athletic Director Joe Roberson has stressed the importance of competition: "We are a very competitive people in general. Some might say competitiveness is the nature of people in general. But it can also be argued that it is particularly the nature of the American people because of the way our society functions. Politically and economically, competition is a very important part of what occurs in America"; Velvel, p. 21.

4. Mark Russell, "Competition Uber Alles," in Velvel, p. 32.

5. In a talk that Woodrow Wilson gave to the Princeton Class of 1909, at a time when he had been criticized for not "teaching character," he urged undergraduates to be aware that character is not something easily acquired: "I hear a great deal about character being the object of education. I take leave to believe that a man who cultivates his character consciously will cultivate nothing except what will make him intolerable to his fellow men. If your object in life is to make a fine fellow of yourself, you will not succeed, and you will not be acceptable to really fine fellows. Character, gentlemen, is a by-product. It comes, whether you will or not, as a consequence of a life devoted to the nearest duty; and the place in which character would be cultivated, if it be a place of study, is a place where study is the object and character is the result." President Woodrow Wilson to the Princeton Class of 1909, Princeton University archives.

6. We are unable to provide data for the Division IA public universities because too few of the High Profile athletes at these schools completed the CIRP questionnaire.

7. Figure 9.2 has more detail than Figure 9.1 because the C&B surveys, which are the source of these data, contain many more observations than the CIRP surveys. Scorecard 9.2 contains data for all types of schools, including the Division IA public universities, which are poorly represented in the CIRP surveys.

8. In the '76 cohort, 10 percent of male athletes and 12 percent of other male students worked in the governmental sector; in this same cohort, 16 percent of the women athletes and 14 percent of the other women working were in this sector. These and other occupational data in this chapter report on full-time workers only.

9. These calculated averages are subject to the top coding problem discussed in note 10 in Chapter 4.

10. Again, these figures are averages across all types of institutions in our study (i.e., sector composites). The most pronounced difference in earnings between women athletes and other women executives is in the Ivy League, where women executives who had been athletes earned $146,000, versus an average of $111,000 for other women executives who worked full-time in the for-profit sector.

11. These data are derived from multivariate regressions of the kind explained in Chapter 4. We measure an athlete's earnings advantage in a particular occupational category by subtracting the predicted earnings of the students at large in the category from the predicted earnings of the athletes who worked in the same field after adjusting for differences associated with type of school attended. To enhance comparability, the figures in the table for CEOs, other executives, people in finance-consulting, lawyers, and doctors are restricted to individuals who were either in the for-profit sector or self-employed.

12. Bowen and Bok, pp. 168–74.

13. Scorecards are available on request from the authors.

14. Andrew Ferguson, "Inside the Crazy Culture of Kids Sports," *Time,* July 12, 1999, online edition.

15. Gerhard Casper, president of Stanford, articulates a view held by many faculty and administrators when he emphasizes the ways in which teaching and research interact and strengthen each other in a "dialectical relationship"; "Transition and Endurance," State of the University Address, Stanford University, March 2, 2000.

16. A full set of data on all survey questions at each type of school is presented for the '76 cohort in Appendix Table B.9.3. These data are both interesting in their own right and comforting in that they pass the "face validity" test—that is, the differences by type of school are very much what one would have expected to find. For example, the preference for placing more emphasis on teaching undergraduates is strongest at the large public universities and least pronounced at the small coed liberal arts colleges, which are much more focused on undergraduate teaching in the first place. Similarly, graduates of the large universities (which offer much more work of a professional and pre-professional nature) are much more likely to want to see increased emphasis on providing a "broad liberal arts education" than are the graduates of the coed liberal arts colleges, which already emphasize this type of education.

Chapter 10 Giving Back

1. Most of the economics literature related to giving focuses heavily on income and price elasticities—that is, on how giving depends on income levels and on the "price" of giving (generally measured by the tax benefits of giving). Charles Clotfelter at Duke University has carried out the most broadly based work on charitable giving; see, for example, his *Federal Tax Policy and Charitable Giving* (Chicago: University of Chicago Press, 1985). There is, however, relatively little research on how factors such as intercollegiate athletic programs affect giving to particular types of colleges and universities—including giving by one group of students (say athletes) compared with giving by their classmates—largely because of the lack of data linking giving patterns to characteristics of individual donors and especially to what they did and how they fared as students.

The data show gifts by members of the '51, '76, and '89 entering cohorts. The giving data used in this chapter were provided by 18 private colleges and universities: 5 Division IA private universities (Duke, Notre Dame, Northwestern, Rice, and Vanderbilt); 4 Ivy League universities (Columbia, University of Pennsylvania, Princeton, and Yale); 6 coed liberal arts colleges (Denison, Hamilton, Oberlin, Swarthmore, Wesleyan, and Williams); and 3 women's colleges (Barnard, Bryn Mawr, and Smith). The gifts are categorized as follows: (1) for general purposes, (2) for capital purposes, (3) restricted to student aid, and (4) restricted to athletics. We generally lump together all nonathletics gifts, calling them "general gifts." As a rule, the giving data are available only for recent years when gifts were recorded in electronic form. For the '51 and '76 cohorts, we group gifts made during the five-year interval extending from 1989 through 1993; for the '89 cohort, we group gifts made during the five-year interval from 1994 through 1998.

2. Giving rates are defined as the percentage of a given group—such as athletes in the '51 cohort at Division IA private universities—who made one or more gifts for general (nonathletic) purposes during the five-year period being studied. We discuss sizes of gifts later in the chapter. The simple giving rates discussed in this section are useful indicators not only of the willingness to provide direct financial support to the school but also, indirectly, of attitudes toward the school.

3. The main results reported in this chapter are based principally on simple comparisons of the giving patterns of former athletes and the giving patterns of

other alumni/ae. Of course, any of the differences reported could be attributable, at least in part, to both selection effects and interrelationships with other variables, such as household income.

We explored the potential impact of selection effects (the possibility that the same personality characteristics that cause individuals to participate in intercollegiate athletics could cause them to be more likely than others to make gifts) by comparing the giving rates of those graduates who were high school athletes but did not win athletic awards in college with those of other graduates who did not play sports at *either* the high school or college level. In the case of the Division IA private universities, there is a mild positive relationship between having been a high school athlete and being a donor; there is, however, no statistically significant relation at the Ivy League schools or at the coed liberal arts colleges. These results cast doubt on the power of the selection effect in the case of giving, even though high school athletes are by no means a perfect proxy for college athletes.

To control for the potentially contaminating effects of other variables that might correlate with both the sports played by former students and their giving patterns, we ran a series of logit regressions that control for race/ethnicity, family background, type of secondary school attended, legacy status, academic achievement in college, and family income. The "other things equal" relationships between giving rates and athletic participation are highly consistent with the simple tabulations we present in the text, and for this reason we concentrate on presenting the simple tabulations and do not (except in rare cases) present adjusted probabilities or other more sophisticated measures. Among the control variables, household income is—as one would expect—by far the most powerful determinant of giving behavior. Legacy status also matters, principally at the Ivy League schools. The socioeconomic status of the parents of graduates has little effect, and the relationships with type of school attended are erratic. Minority students are less likely to be givers than are white students. The results of these logit regressions are available from the authors on request.

One final caveat should be introduced. We recognize that there is a "transactional" aspect to the making of a gift, in that the outcome depends not only on the inclinations of the individual graduate but also on how the school approaches the potential donor. We are unable, however, to look systematically at the effects of modes of solicitation.

4. Of course there are exceptions, which remind us of the danger of relying on anecdotal evidence. The press has reported that a recent Stanford graduate has made a substantial gift targeted to athletics; "Young Donor Establishes Fund for Stanford Athletes," *Chronicle of Higher Education,* August 4, 2000, online edition.

5. The data presented in earlier chapters documenting the growing gaps between athletes and other students in academic preparation, academic achievement, and interests and aspirations are bolstered by the rich in-depth data gathered by Cantor and Prentice. As we reported in Chapter 3, their findings (based on detailed studies of 1990s athletes at three selective colleges and universities) led them to conclude that "unlike members of social groups or performing artists, athletes reported that being a member of their group made it more difficult to make friends outside of the group and to spend time with new and different people. Across a diverse range of sports, athletes reported similar problems

in getting to know different kinds of people and having diverse experiences at college." Cantor and Prentice, p. 19.

6. There may be an analogy with trends in the professoriate. Many commentators have discussed the tendency for high-visibility scholars to think increasingly of their primary identification as with their discipline (molecular biology, European history, computer science) rather than their institution. See, for example, Oliver Fulton, "Unity or Fragmentation, Convergence or Diversity: The Academic Profession in Comparative Perspective in the Era of Mass Higher Education," in William G. Bowen and Harold T. Shapiro (eds.), *Universities and Their Leadership* (Princeton, N.J.: Princeton University Press, 1998), pp. 173–96.

7. These data, like those for the top-rated academic performers presented subsequently, are for men only. The reason is that the data for women in the '51 cohort are available for only a small number of schools and are hard to compare with other data. In the cohorts for which we have adequate data for women and men, the patterns are very similar.

8. Here again, selection effects may be part of the explanation. Students who participate actively in extracurricular activities could have personal characteristics that predispose them to be givers. However, these would have to be characteristics other than those measured by the variables included in the multivariate logit regressions, because holding constant variables such as race/ethnicity, socioeconomic status, one's own household income, and rank-in-class does not deprive the dummy variable for extracurricular participation of statistical significance. The simple associations reported in the text hold up well when control variables are introduced.

9. This relationship between rank-in-class and the likelihood of giving also holds up extremely well in the multivariate logit analysis. The coefficients remain highly significant after we control for the effects of other variables. This means, for example, that the high giving rates of the top-ranked graduates cannot be attributed to the fact that they are also likely to earn more money than other graduates. We find the strong association between rank-in-class and giving rates especially interesting when considered in the context of solicitation practices. One commentator has suggested that the high giving rates of graduates who were athletes or who were active participants in extracurricular activities may be due in part to the likelihood that such individuals will be well known to class fundraisers. But it seems dubious that the high giving rates of the more academically oriented students are due in any degree to this kind of "high visibility" effect. Put another way, if we were able (as we are not) to control for the characteristics of the solicitation process, the strength of the relationship between rank-in-class and giving would probably be even more impressive relative to the strength of the relationships between giving and athletic and extracurricular participation.

10. Generally speaking, rank-in-class correlates with giving rates for athletes as well as for all students. However, the relationship is not as consistent for the athletes, especially those in the '89 cohort. Most interesting is the pattern within the coed liberal arts colleges. At these schools, where rank-in-class correlates most powerfully with giving rates for students in general, the relationship for the athletes in the '89 cohort is essentially flat, with former athletes who ranked in the middle third of the class having the highest giving rate (scorecard not shown).

Our supposition is that the athletes within these colleges bonded well with their schools wherever they ranked in their classes, whereas the other graduates bonded much more strongly if they did well academically.

11. The figures for "average gifts" presented in this section are all obtained by taking the total gifts made by an individual over the five-year period we studied and dividing by 5; thus we show the "average annual gift." We also calculated medians, and the pattern of results does not change appreciably.

12. Cletus C. Coughlin and O. Homer Erekson, "An Examination of Contributions to Support Intercollegiate Athletics," *Southern Economic Journal* 51 (1984): 180–95.

13. The results reported in this paragraph are based on ordinary least squares regressions used to predict the average general gift of male graduates who were donors. Separate regressions were run for the '51 and '76 cohorts and for each of the three types of institutions that we are studying. Controls were included for race/ethnicity, legacy status, family socioeconomic status, extracurricular participation, type of secondary school attended, household income, and rank-in-class. The regressions are available from the authors on request.

14. There is also one piece of empirical evidence from the study of variations over time in "winning and giving" behavior summarized at the end of this chapter that suggests that, within a limited population of graduates, giving to athletics does substitute for general giving in certain circumstances. Former athletes from the '76 cohort who attended the Division IA schools show some tendency to substitute gifts to athletics for gifts for general purposes when the football program at their school improves its won-lost record. Sarah E. Turner, Lauren A. Meserve, and William G. Bowen, "On the Econometric Relationship between Year-to-Year Increments in Giving and Changes in Won-Lost Records," working paper, 1999, pp. 16–17.

15. We present these data for the male graduates because we do not have reliable figures for women in the '51 cohort. Among the men, the degree of concentration is very much the same by type of school in the '51 cohorts. In the '76 and '89 cohorts, giving to the coed liberal arts colleges is somewhat more broad-based than giving to the Division IA private universities and the Ivy League schools, but even within the colleges, the top 5 percent of donors contributed 55 percent of dollars received from members of the '76 cohorts and 40 percent of dollars from members of the '89 cohorts. The data for the women in the '76 and '89 cohorts are very similar to those for the men. They too show that giving is highly concentrated, although not quite as highly concentrated among women as among men. In the '76 cohort, 56 percent of female giving came from the top 5 percent of female donors (as compared with 62 percent for the men); in '89, the corresponding percentages are 42 percent for the women and 51 percent among the men.

16. In the '76 male cohort, athletes made up 19 percent of the big giver category, 21 percent of the other givers, and 18 percent of the nongivers. In the '89 male cohort, 21 percent of the big givers were athletes, as compared with 26 percent of the other givers and 24 percent of the nongivers. These relationships are all confirmed by logit regression analysis. Only in the '51 cohort is there a positive association between placement in the top giver category and having been an

athlete. Although very high household income (which is the most important single determinant of placement in the big giver category) correlates with both legacy status and rank-in-class, the legacy and rank-in-class variables continue to be highly significant predictors of big-giver status even after including controls for household income (and all of the demographic and other variables in the regression). The limited data available for the women—which can be studied only in the '76 and '89 cohorts and even then for only a subset of the schools—show patterns that are generally much the same as the patterns for the men.

17. The title of this section is taken from the title of the working paper by Turner, Meserve, and Bowen. The paper is an outgrowth of the same research agenda that has produced the present study and is the basis for the principal results reported in this section.

18. We do not have giving data for the public universities; thus all references in this chapter to Division IA apply to private universities only.

19. The findings in the Turner, Meserve, and Bowen paper are based on a standard multivariate regression analysis. The methodology employed is a fixed-effects model (which is computationally equivalent to including a dummy variable for each of the 15 institutions) in which year-to-year changes in the winning percentage of the football team are used to predict changes in aggregate measures of giving behavior. The study distinguishes the effects of athletic success according to the level of NCAA competition by including interactions between winning percentage and whether an institution plays in Division IA, Division IAA, or Division III; this approach yields what are, in effect, separate measures of the sensitivity of giving to winning by division. The model also includes a "campaign" dummy variable that indicates whether an institution was conducting a major fundraising campaign during the year in question and a year-fixed-effect specification that is intended to pick up the effects of any broad events that might have affected all institutions in a particular year (such as the timing of major reunions, which were the same for members of the '76 entering cohort at all of our schools). In this analysis, giving rates are defined as the average annual percentage of individuals in a category who made a gift. Thus, if 50 percent never gave and the other 50 percent averaged one gift every two years, the average giving rate would be 25 percent. This way of measuring giving differs from that used in the main part of this chapter, where we measure giving rates as the percentage of graduates making any gift within a defined period of time. The latter approach of course yields much higher giving rates. In the Turner study, giving levels are defined analogously to giving rates: as the average annual gift made by individuals in a defined category.

20. Turner, Meserve, and Bowen also used data on won-lost records for men's basketball, but they did not change the results, and so a decision was made to simplify the analysis by focusing only on football.

21. Refer to Scorecard 10.1. The Lower Profile athletes at the Division III coed liberal arts colleges in the '89 cohort continued to have higher giving rates than students at large, but their "advantage" in giving rates declined sharply between the '76 and '89 cohorts (from 13 percentage points to 5 points).

22. The most often cited study of this relationship that we have found was conducted by Robert E. McCormick and Maurice Tinsley of Clemson University;

"Athletics versus Academics? Evidence from SAT Scores," *Journal of Political Economy* 95(5) (1987): 1103–9. The authors found a positive correlation between membership in a big-time athletic conference and average SAT scores, on an "other-things-equal" basis; quantitatively, membership in one of these conferences was associated with an appoximately 3 percent increase in SAT scores (note 5 on p. 1106). Other studies of the relationship between athletic success and admissions include Franklin Mixon, "Athletics versus Academics? Rejoining the Evidence from SAT scores," *Education Economics* 3(3) (1995): 277–83. In general these studies also find that the relationship has the expected positive sign but is not very robust. Ancedotal evidence from Northwestern tells a similar story. Applications jumped 21 percent following the miracle Rose Bowl season, but the averge SAT score of the next entering class rose by only 5 points (information supplied by Northwestern).

Chapter 11   The Financial Equation

1. Welch Suggs, "Blue-Ribbon Panel on College-Sports Issues Will Reconvene This Fall," *Chronicle of Higher Education,* June 1, 2000, online edition.

2. See Zimbalist, *Unpaid Professionals,* and the large bibliography that he provides. See also Sperber, and Richard G. Sheehan, *Keeping Score: The Economics of Big-Time Sports* (South Bend, Ind.: Diamond Communications, 1996), Chapters 11 and 12.

3. Freshman eligibility was extended to other sports in the Ivy League through a series of incremental decisions that allowed freshmen to play varsity basketball in 1978 and that culminated in allowing freshmen to play varsity football beginning in the fall of 1993.

4. Quoted in John Weistart, "The 90's University: Reading, Writing and Shoe Contracts," *New York Times,* November 29, 1993, Section 8, p. 9.

5. These figures, and most of the other data on expenditures cited in this chapter, are taken from the forms prepared by individual schools to comply with the requirements of the Equity in Athletics Disclosure Act (EADA) of 1994. These forms are publicly available and were obtained from the individual colleges and universities; the relevant data were entered on a spreadsheet reproduced as Appendix Table B.11.1.

All coeducational institutions of higher education that receive federal funding for student aid or any other purpose, and that have intercollegiate athletic programs, must document participation by gender and also provide data that indicate the division of coaching complements, expenditures, and targeted revenues between men's and women's teams. In this chapter, our interest is in the overall dimensions of athletic programs. Women's colleges are exempt from these reporting requirements, and so they are not included in this analysis. There are manifold differences in ways of accounting for athletic expenditures (especially in the treatment of overhead costs and costs of maintaining facilities), and it would be a serious mistake to assume that anything like strict comparability exists across institutions. There are also major problems involved in interpreting data such as average salaries per full-time equivalent coach or staff member, because they do not take account of variables such as length of service. Moreover, all of the reported figures suffer from a failure to make adequate allowance for capital costs, a subject to which we return later in the chapter. Generic problems and anomalies notwithstanding, these EADA data are by far the best available source of information about the finances of intercollegiate athletic programs. As we hope to demonstrate, careful use of the FY 1997–98 reports can provide instructive profiles of patterns of expenditures. We expect that these annual reports will prove even more useful over time as improvements continue to be made in the forms and the accompanying instructions.

The NCAA publishes biannual reports—see, for example, Daniel L. Fulks, *Revenues and Expenses of Divisions I and II Intercollegiate Athletic Programs: Financial Trends and Relationships—1997* (Indianapolis, Ind.: NCAA, October 1998)—which have been the primary general source used by others who have written on this subject. While we too make some use of the NCAA summaries, they suffer from the serious limitation of providing only averages for very broad groupings of institutions. Historically, this use of averages was necessary to respect promises of confidentiality made to institutions that participated in the NCAA survey. Now, however, the public availability of the EADA forms for individual schools calls this approach into question.

6. As the detailed data in Appendix Table B.11.1 indicate, there are strong similarities in expenditure patterns within each of these five groupings, an attribute that permits us to describe each set of schools in terms of its average expenditures and other characteristics without introducing serious distortions into the analysis. However, this taxonomy omits the University of North Carolina at Chapel Hill, the University of Miami in Ohio, Rice University, and Georgetown University. The figures for these schools are shown in a separate section of the spreadsheet. The University of North Carolina at Chapel Hill probably belongs in the same category as Duke, but the EADA report filed by UNC has enough anomalies that we left it out to avoid distorting the averages for the group.

7. As already noted, the University of Michigan leads the pack with total expenditures of over $47 million; Penn State and Stanford were in the $35 to $40 million range, and Notre Dame spent roughly $30 million (Appendix Table B.11.1).

8. Lest anyone wonder if these schools are atypical, it is worth noting that their total expenditures are quite similar to the average for all Division IA schools. The average of total expenditures for all Division IA programs reporting to the NCAA for FY 1996–97 was $17.3 million; Fulks, *Revenues and Expenses of Divisions I and II Intercollegiate Athletic Programs,* p. 8. Our data are for one year later (FY 1997–98); assuming a continuation of annual rates of increase in expenditure for recent years, the two averages would be nearly identical.

9. There is reason to think, however, that the reported total expenditures of these more modest athletic programs understate their true costs by a relatively large amount because they are less likely than the more costly programs to be assigned shares of central costs or facilities costs. See the later discussion of the capital costs of athletics at Williams.

10. Under NCAA regulations, a school wishing to be classified in Division IA must "play at least 60 percent of their regular-season football games against other Division IA institutions; all but four basketball games . . . must be against

other Division I teams. Seven men's and seven women's, or alternatively, six men's and eight women's sports teams must be sponsored. There are also requirements for scheduling and financial aid"; Fulks, *Revenues and Expenses of Divisions I and II Intercollegiate Athletic Programs,* p. 90. Division IA teams must also meet the requirements of an attendance formula, which roughly prescribes a minimum average attendance of 20,000. Divisions IAA and IAAA (which are basically basketball schools) have their own requirements. No Division III schools provide athletic scholarships, nor do the Ivies, within Division IAA, by their own choice (in general, however, Division IAA schools do provide athletic scholarships).

11. It is tempting to adjust for differences among schools in the breadth of their programs by calculating expenditures per team or per student. At one point in our work we did precisely this, and the main lesson learned was that taking account of these differences in the extent of athletic activity barely makes a dent in the differences in total expenditures between the big-time schools in Division IA and the Ivies; nor do differences in the number of teams or number of participants do very much to explain why the Ivies spend so much more on intercollegiate athletics than the Division III liberal arts colleges and universities. Total expenditures per athlete averaged more than $50,000 in both of the Division IA groupings, just over $10,000 in the Ivy League, and about $2,500 in both of the Division III categories. Although the general point is correct (level of competition is a much more important driver of total expenditures on athletics than are number of teams and number of athletic participants), the actual figures per participant are essentially meaningless. The reason is that they are largely a function of two variables: (1) how much is spent on football and men's basketball and (2) how many other sports and intercollegiate participants the school supports. A school that has a more or less normal Division IA football program and only a small number of other sports will have a far higher average expenditure per athlete than a school with a similar football program but more other teams. Differences in average expenditure per athlete tell us nothing about the average cost of supporting a given set of teams. Thus we are convinced that adjusting mechanically for differences in number of teams and participants is a bad idea, so long as football and men's basketball are such large components of total expenditures. This is why we decided to analyze football and men's basketball separately and then look at expenditures on other sports.

12. According to Welch Suggs, "Alabama State Plans to Become First Black College in Division IA Football," *Chronicle of Higher Education,* May 15, 2000, online edition, Alabama State University's board of regents has voted to "elevate" its football team to Division IA status. The story recognizes that such a move would be dependent on the ability of the university's athletic department to raise approximately $90 million to upgrade its teams and facilities. The stated objective is to have the Alabama State University football team become "the first team from a historically black university to compete at the highest level of college football." The regents must of course come to their own decisions concerning priorities, but they should be aware of not only the start-up costs of entering Division IA in football but also the recurring costs of competing at this level.

13. Roger Noll, "The Business of College Sports and the High Cost of Winning," *Miliken Institute Review* (third quarter 1999): 24–37.

14. The correlation between competitive success and expenditures can also be seen, albeit in much more muted form, within the Ivy League. Princeton has had a highly successful men's basketball program, and its team has been invited to more holiday tournaments, in more exotic places, than many other teams. One consequence is higher travel costs. Similarly, when Division III schools are invited to compete in national championships, they incur expenses that exceed the reimbursements that the NCAA provides.

15. See the EADA forms, Table 6.

16. The EADA forms contain some but not all of the detail needed to estimate the sizes of these components, and we have supplemented the publicly available data with data obtained from individual schools. The figures shown should be regarded as no more than general indicators of how much is spent by schools operating at each level of competition. For this purpose, we have recombined Division IA "Plus" and Division IA "Standard" back into a single Division IA category.

17. The exact cost will depend on both the number of awards actually made by a school and the cost of each award, which in turn depends on tuition levels, room and board, and so on. (To illustrate the magnitudes, the average cost of a full grant-in-aid at Duke in FY 1997–98 was reported on the EADA forms to be nearly $31,000; at the University of Michigan, the average for in-state students was just over $14,000 while the average for out-of-state students was $28,000.) In general, private universities charge higher tuitions and therefore will have to plan on spending more on scholarships than public universities. This difference is often smaller than one might expect it to be, however, because all of the leading programs recruit nationally, which means that the heavily subsidized in-state tuition rates at the public universities apply to only a fraction of the recruited athletes.

18. Elizabeth A. Duffy and Idana Goldberg, *Crafting a Class: College Admissions and Financial Aid, 1955–1994* (Princeton, N. J.: Princeton University Press, 1998), p. 222.

19. The salary data available from the EADA forms are expressed in averages per full-time equivalent coach of men's and women's teams. These averages, in turn, drive formulaic calculations of total coaching costs. It seems safe to assume that average salaries are appreciably higher in the High Profile sports of football and basketball than in other sports included within the averages. Also, as is well known, total compensation of the best-known coaches in football and men's basketball includes endorsement contracts, television shows, and so on. Coach Steve Spurrier of the University of Florida, for example, is said to earn a base salary of nearly $170,000, plus approximately $1.9 million from other sources, including television appearances, promotional agreements with apparel companies such as Nike, and speaking engagements; see Zimbalist, *Unpaid Professionals*, p. 81. There is a continuing debate over how much of this total compensation ought to go to the coach and how much to the school.

We have also been told that costs of assistant coaches constitute one of the most rapidly rising components of athletic expenditures at Division IA and Division IAA levels, but we lack any way of testing this proposition.

20. On the EADA forms, recruiting expenditures are defined as "institutional expenditures associated with recruiting for the teams. . . . [and] include, but are not limited to: transportation, lodging, and meals for both recruits and institu-

tional personnel engaged in . . . recruiting; expenditures for on-site visits; and all other major expenses logically related to recruiting" (Table 5). The vagueness of this definition suggests that it would be a mistake to make too much of variations in reported figures.

21. George Vecsey, "Is It Only a Game?" *New York Times,* August 1, 1999, Section 4A, p. 28.

22. Another way of gaining some sense of the scale of the infrastructure used to support intercollegiate athletics is by counting the number of full-time equivalent noncoaching personnel (excluding students) employed by the athletic department. The EADA forms require schools to provide such data (right after Table 9), and they correlate with the dollar figures. The average number of noncoaching, nonstudent full-time equivalents employed by the athletic department is 108 at the four Division IA "Plus" schools in our study (reaching a high of 127 at the University of Michigan, which also reports the largest dollar expenditures on infrastructure), 54 at the Division IA "Standard" schools, roughly 40 at the Ivy League schools, and about 10 at the Division III liberal arts colleges.

23. Of course there are also some differences by school within our categories, but fewer than one might expect. With regard to number of teams and number of athletes, Stanford ranks above the three other IA "Plus" schools and is at the average for the Ivy League. Similarly, Williams, in spite of its much lower enrollment, is close to the average for the Ivies. (See Appendix Table B.11.1.)

24. The counting of teams is more complex than one might imagine. The numbers given here follow the EADA convention, which considers indoor and outdoor track and cross-country to be one team (in order to assess compliance with Title IX). The NCAA, on the other hand, allows schools to treat these as separate sports in demonstrating that they comply with the NCAA rule that schools in Division IA must field a minimum of 14 teams.

25. Data on numbers of teams and athletes may be found in Appendix Table B.11.1, which was compiled from the EADA reports submitted by the individual schools. Most of the data presented below on expenditures come from this same source, but in some instances we also use supplementary data supplied by individual schools.

26. The figures for the Division IA schools are taken directly from Table 10 of the EADA reports; the actual average of the figures for the eight Division IA schools on which this study concentrates is $1,067,000, with a large "clumping" in the $800,000 to $900,000 range. No one should treat the school-by-school differences as precise, since much judgment inevitably entered into the process of presenting these data. The figures for the Ivies and the Division III schools are our own estimates, based on detailed data supplied by five individual schools.

27. More surprising than the differences between the Ivies and the Division III schools are the differences between the Ivies and Division IA in expenditures per Lower Profile athlete (last line of Scorecard 11.5). These differences reflect the following factors: (1) much larger expenditures on women's basketball in Division IA; (2) the presence of athletic scholarships at the Division IA schools; (3) some (but only modest) differences in coaching costs; (4) some differences in operating and other expenses that reflect, in part, the easier time that the Ivies have in scheduling contests with neighboring schools that have similar programs;

(5) a "mix" effect, in that the additional teams that the Ivies field tend to be in relatively less expensive sports such as squash (the "mix" effect also explains why the average expenditure at the Division IA "Plus" universities is lower than the average for the Division IA "Standard" schools, which support fewer of the relatively inexpensive sports and devote relatively more money to women's basketball); and (6) the presence at the Ivies of more "self-funded" teams, such as wrestling, volleyball, and water polo at Princeton.

28. See Noll, Sheehan, Sperber, and Zimbalist, *Unpaid Professionals.*

29. Historically, the planned subvention to athletics at Duke has been related to the provision of a certain number of athletic scholarships. This convention is also followed at some other schools, but of course unanticipated events can cause the planned and actual subventions to differ—sometimes by quite a bit. Tying planned subventions to the number of athletic scholarships may become more problematic as the pressures to comply with Title IX increase.

30. For a good discussion of accounting conundrums in the reporting of "profits" and "losses" in athletics, see Andrew Zimbalist, "There's No Accounting for College Sports," *University Business,* June 1999, especially pp. 40–41, and *Unpaid Professionals,* pp. 152–57. Zimbalist concludes, and we agree, that oddities in accounting treatment almost always serve to understate the true costs of athletics.

31. Fulks, *Revenues and Expenses of Divisions I and II Intercollegiate Athletic Programs,* Tables 3.17, 4.1, and 6.1. As noted in the text, these figures reflect efforts to remove institutional subventions from revenue. It is unclear, however, if the NCAA has been completely successful in accomplishing this objective. From our own experience in working with the same data submitted to the NCAA by individual schools, we have learned to be wary about claims that all institutional funding has been identified. Schools are not always clear about this themselves, and we think it is prudent to assume that the frequency of deficits reported by the NCAA is a lower limit; in fact, we suspect that true deficits are much more common than these tabulations suggest.

32. Daniel L. Fulks, *Revenues and Expenses of Division III Intercollegiate Athletic Programs: Financial Trends and Relationships—1997* (Indianapolis, Ind.: NCAA, October 1998), p. 4.

33. The fact that financial "success" is so highly concentrated among a few schools has been recognized and emphasized by, among others, Noll, Sheehan, and Zimbalist, *Unpaid Professionals.* Zimbalist estimates that "perhaps a dozen top schools . . . are generating real surpluses year after year [and] . . . perhaps two or three dozen schools generate an occasional surplus when their teams perform well in postseason tournaments" (p. 164).

34. Of course, Stanford, Penn State, and Notre Dame have also done very well both competitively and financially, as have other schools that have had consistently successful big-time basketball programs; we have tried to check the detailed data from the four case-study schools against data for other programs whenever possible.

35. These figures include both conference and NCAA distributions of postseason revenues. It is obviously highly desirable to belong to a conference in which large numbers of member schools are successful in postseason competi-

tion—or to be so consistently successful standing alone that there is no need to rely on the success of others (as has been the case with Notre Dame for some years).

36. The postseason figure for Princeton is a modest understatement because Princeton, in company with the other Ivy League schools, does receive a distribution from the proceeds of the NCAA basketball tournament. In the Ivy League, however, these revenues are used to defray the expenses of the League office and therefore do not appear as revenues earned by individual schools. (In FY 1997–98, the eight Ivy League schools received a total of $3,210,922.)

37. These figures have been estimated by subtracting all revenues associated with men's and women's sports from total expenditures. These estimates will be high by the amount of non-sport-specific revenues raised for athletics. However, it seems unlikely that very many teams lacking top-flight competitive results can either command the support from sponsors or attract the level of general gifts from friends groups (gifts for specific sports are presumably in the revenue numbers) that are important at both Michigan and Duke. In filling out its EADA form, Northwestern comments at the end of its report that "99.3% of Northwestern's athletic revenue is derived from football and men's basketball."

38. We are indebted to Richard S. Myers, assistant provost and director of institutional research at Williams, for this painstaking analysis—and to Winston and his colleagues for the underlying analytical framework. For the latter, see the discussion paper by Gordon C. Winston and Ethan G. Lewis, "Physical Capital and Capital Service Costs in US Colleges and Universities: 1993," February 1996, available at http://www.williams.edu/WPEHE/publications.html. There is one other respect in which even this set of numbers underestimates the economic cost of intercollegiate athletics at Williams. Almost all of the Williams coaches also teach physical education, which holds down the costs of intercollegiate sports but almost surely increases the costs of physical education since, in the absence of a strong intercollegiate program, Williams could no doubt hire physical education staff at less than the prorated costs of head coaches of intercollegiate teams.

39. Zimbalist presents a particularly telling example of the false picture that can result from understating if not ignoring capital costs when he describes in detail the finances of the Mullins Center arena used by the basketball program at the University of Massachusetts at Amherst (*Unpaid Professionals,* p. 154). It is also true that most athletic budgets make grossly inadequate allowances, if any allowance at all, for the athletics share of central services. But this source of distortion, in contrast to failure to account for capital costs, is probably more important (relatively) at a college or university without big-time High Profile sports. The reason is that the athletic department at a university such as Michigan will have "internalized" more of these costs than will the department at a college or an Ivy League university. The infrastructure costs of the athletic department at Michigan include, for example, an investment in an information technology function of its own.

40. Noll, p. 28.

41. The data showing expenditures on student services are taken from the Department of Education's Integrated Postsecondary Education Data System (IPEDS) forms. The IPEDS glossary defines student services as follows: "Funds ex-

pended for admissions, registrar activities, and activities whose primary purpose is to contribute to students' emotional and physical well-being and to their intellectual, cultural, and social development outside the context of the formal instructional program. Examples are career guidance, counseling, financial aid administration, and student health services (except when operated as a self-supporting auxiliary enterprise)." Although no mention is made of intramural and recreational athletics, we know that some schools include this class of expenditures under this heading, and some of the Division III schools, at least, also include the expenses of intercollegiate teams. It is evident from the data, however, that the costs of big-time sports programs are not included here. It is also clear that the treatment of health expenditures varies markedly from school to school, and in arriving at crude averages for divisions we have excluded what appear to be clear outliers.

It is also possible, of course, to express the net costs of intercollegiate athletics per student, on the theory that all students may be presumed to benefit to some degree from the presence of the intercollegiate athletics program. But the trouble with this approach is that surely it is the tennis players who benefit primarily from the existence of an intercollegiate tennis program, just as it is the students who take classics who benefit mainly (although not exclusively) from the existence of a classics department.

42. Fulks, *Revenues and Expenses of Divisions I and II Intercollegiate Athletic Programs,* Table 3.17.

43. This is also the conclusion reached by Zimbalist, *Unpaid Professionals,* p. 160.

44. Steven Wine, "Plenty of Tradition, Empty Seats for the Orange Bowl," *AP Online,* January 1, 2000.

45. Although it is difficult (surprisingly so) to obtain historical data on attendance and gate receipts for the Ivy League schools, the figures that are available confirm the commonsense notion that not even more aggressive ticket pricing can reverse declines in attendance.

46. See, for example, Zimbalist, *Unpaid Professionals,* p. 151.

Chapter 12   Key Empirical Findings

1. Walter Camp Papers, Yale University Archives.

2. These summary figures and statements are based on data presented in Chapters 2 and 6; there are of course exceptions to all of these generalizations, which were mentioned in earlier chapters but cannot be repeated here (for, example, Stanford sponsors many more teams than Denison). Also, to minimize clutter, we will not continue to mention the chapters, figures, or scorecards that contain the actual data. We present only statistical highlights in this chapter; readers who want more detail (such as the numbers of athletes playing High Profile sports versus numbers playing other sports) or who are interested in more nuanced interpretations of the data, definitions of concepts, and discussions of measurement problems should consult the table of contents, lists of figures and tables, and index.

3. See Chapter 2 for a more complete explanation of this estimation method. The net effect of athletic recruitment on diversity is so small even in the case of

men for two reasons: (1) there are relatively few athletes, relative to other students, at those Division IA schools where large numbers of African American students play High Profile sports; and (2) white students are often more likely than African American students to participate in the Lower Profile sports such as tennis and crew.

Chapter 13   Taking Stock

1. Savage, p. 306.

2. Ibid., p. 294.

3. There is also evidence of academic underperformance among minority students (see Bowen and Bok), and—while some, but by no means all, of the causes are similar to those that apply to athletes—the issues involved in assessing underperformance are quite different (see the epilogue to Chapter 3).

4. Frank Knight, *The Ethics of Competition* (New Brunswick, N.J.: Transaction, 1997), p. 60.

5. Joe B. Wyatt, "Chancellor Responds to Athletics Committee Report," *Vanderbilt Register* 15(30) (1996): 8–9.

6. Judith H. Dobrzynski, "Hip vs. Stately: The Tao of Two Museums," *New York Times,* February 20, 2000, section 2, page 1.

7. Burton Weisbrod (ed.), *To Profit or Not to Profit: Commercialization in the Non-Profit Sector* (Cambridge: Cambridge University Press, 1998), p. 304.

8. The controversy over the suspension of St. John's point guard Erik Barkley for violating NCAA rules on accepting money from "athletic interests" to help cover prep school tuition provoked a number of revealing comments. *New York Times* columnist Harvey Araton has written about how discouraging it is for inner-city students with reasonable grades at schools like Kennedy High School in Paterson, New Jersey, to have to struggle constantly to figure out how they can possibly pay for college when athletes with much lower grades "will go to some college, somehow, some way, and free of charge." At this school, there was not a lot of sympathy for Barkley. Araton also calls attention to the eloquent pleas on behalf of Barkley by college coaches like Mike Krzyzewski at Duke, who preach about society's obligation to educate students like Barkley—provided, as Araton puts it, that "they can rebound and spot up for 3." Araton concludes: "Coach's sanctimony does not add up, or compute." "An Education Isn't a Game to Squander," *New York Times,* March 2, 2000, p. D1.

Similarly, in controversies over the initial eligibility standards that have been imposed by the NCAA, critics have complained that minority students will lose out on an education. Tulane University School of Law Professor Gary R. Roberts responds with outrage, "The notion that poor black kids are being denied opportunities . . . is nonsense. . . . I only wish that those who are so driven to allow schools to take academically unprepared black athletes would be more concerned about creating educational opportunities for minority students, whether or not they play basketball." David Goldfield, "Weaker NCAA Standards Won't Help Black Athletes," *Chronicle of Higher Education,* April 9, 1999, online edition.

9. "Delusions of Grandeur: Young Blacks Must Be Taught That Sports Are Not the Only Avenue of Opportunity," *Sports Illustrated,* August 19, 1991, p. 78.

10. Just as this book was going to press, an article appeared reporting an effort by parents in Wayzata, Minnesota, to resist the trend toward overscheduling of children's activities. Examples illustrate what is bothering the parents: "At Kristin Bender's house, where commotion of the 'I can't find my cleats' variety reigns as her three children rush to participate in three different sports simultaneously, she shoehorns in family time by having everyone meet near the sports fields for half an hour. Margaret Roddy's son Drew, 17, a basketball player, has been benched for taking a family vacation."

The reporter also points out that "Coaches and program directors are judged on their programs' success, creating pressure to schedule more practices and year-round playing seasons, and discourage talented children from cutting back." The tensions parents feel are all too real. "'In theory I support it [the cutback] 100 percent,' said Greg Rye, who said that because his 9-year-old son Michael's soccer takes up four days a week, the boy often eats 'on the fly.' But Mr. Rye worries that if Michael misses a season or does not play on the more competitive traveling teams, he may be denied opportunities later."

As always, competitive pressures are a concern. What if other towns do not follow the Wayzata example? "If the quality is going to go down [because of fewer practices, for example], you are going to have difficulty retaining [coaches] who want to excel." And less competitive programs, one person observed, "can hurt your chance for a college scholarship." Pam Belluck, "Parents Try to Reclaim Their Children's Time," *New York Times,* June 13, 2000, p. A18.

11. Coaches are very well aware of the academic thresholds that they must meet. Although, as one admissions director noted, coaches push things as far as they can go, they have no interest in wasting their own time pursuing candidates who will not be admissible under any circumstances. In this person's words, "They're very clear people. If you tell them, 'this is what you can have,' they accept it and do it. But I learned that it's impossible to let them have any gray area, because that's when they just can't stop testing to see how much they can get—how iffy a candidate, how many players. I made the mistake at one point of telling them that if they came up with a way to do well with the admissions process, I'd, in effect, reward them. But it was too gray, too jury-rigged. Each came up with some plan and then was angry when they didn't 'get' what Coach X had gotten. It only works when there are black and white boundaries. Gray they just push too hard." But within the boundaries, coaches are likely to feel that they "own" the admissions slots set aside for their teams.

12. In some instances, there were also issues of race, religion, and ethnicity involved. For instance, a disproportionate number of extremely smart students from schools like the Bronx High School of Science were Jewish. The shift from the notion of the well-rounded student to the notion of the well-rounded class also incorporated a greatly increased interest in enrolling diverse student bodies.

13. Another doctrine that has played a role in building the case for higher levels of athletic achievement and more generous funding is the idea that excellence for an educational institution carries with it the responsibility to seek excellence in *all* endeavors. This notion—which we discuss in some detail in the next chapter—leaves endless space for improvement in athletic programs at any one

institution, and the forces of competition and emulation then tend to spread such improvements system-wide.

14. This same tension is described vividly in a recent account of a high school basketball program. The head of the Montrose Christian School, Ray Hope, is quoted as expecting the big-time high school basketball program directed by Stu Vetter to increase the school's name recognition, enrollment, and revenue. To some degree, it has achieved these objectives. "Just as important to Hope," the author writes, "is the basketball team's role in helping the church [which operates the school] spread the word of God. As a Southern Baptist, Hope is unapologetic about his desire to convert people to Christianity, and the arrival of big-time basketball has given him the opportunity to preach the Gospel to a whole new group of potential converts. . . . According to some Montrose students, however, it's the basketball players who appear to be converting the school. 'Montrose used to be really spiritually oriented,' says Rob Gallalee, a senior who has been at Montrose for four years. 'But when you bring in all of these basketball players who aren't Christian, of course that changes the atmosphere of the school. Things are now ignored that didn't used to be ignored. Like cussing in the hallway. I know that wouldn't be a big deal at other schools, but it used to be a big deal at Montrose. Now, if a teacher overhears you cussing in the hallway, they'll look the other way." Jason Zengerle, "The Portable High-School Hoops Factory," *New York Times Magazine,* February 6, 2000, p. 56.

Chapter 14   Thinking Ahead

1. A number of athletics administrators at Division II schools are reported to feel that "moving up" their programs to Division IA will be a simple way to eliminate red ink. See Welch Suggs, "Football's Have-Nots Contemplate Their Place in the NCAA," *Chronicle of Higher Education,* June 30, 2000, online edition.

2. It is worth recalling the heated discussions at some of the schools included in this study of decisions to become coeducational—decisions that now, with the passage of time, seem obvious and are widely accepted. Even at the time, the vigorous opposition of some to coeducation had the useful effect of stimulating others to rally to the cause of the college or university. One supportive but heretofore quiet alumnus attending a particularly charged gathering came up afterward and said to one of the authors of this study: "Wow! Now I see that you guys really need my help."

3. In 1999, Kenyon lost to Allegheny 42–0 and to Wittenberg 48–3; in that same season, Kenyon beat Oberlin 49–7!

4. In 1999, Macalester lost games by as much as 0–74, always to rivals with admission rates of approximately 80 to 90 percent. Swarthmore, which admits only 30 percent of its applicants, finds itself facing rivals with admission rates as high as 83 percent.

5. For instance, the University of Pennsylvania had to forfeit a number of football games in the 1997 season because a highly acclaimed defensive tackle was found to have been ineligible because he was registered for only two courses. Even more disturbing in the minds of some was the attempt made to correct the eligibility problem by enrolling the student just weeks before the end of the term

in an independent study course taught by a faculty member who also happened to be the school's NCAA representative. The *Daily Pennsylvanian* carried an extensive series of articles on the case and, in an editorial titled "Betrayal of Ivy Academic Ideals" (December 2, 1997, online edition), suggested that "the most significant issue is: What value does Penn place on its academic integrity, and at what price can those principles be bought?" This is merely one, well-publicized example, and Penn is far from alone is struggling with such questions. More recently, the Council of Ivy Group Presidents stripped Brown University of recruiting slots and declared the school ineligible for the Ivy League championship in 2000 because of improper offers of financial aid to athletes. See Welch Suggs, "Ivy League Strips Brown U. of Recruits and Eligibility for Championship," *Chronicle of Higher Education*, August 2, 2000, online edition.

As this book was going to press, "Two star football players at the United States Naval Academy were charged . . . with raping a female midshipman. . . . The case could renew debate over what some critics view as a climate of privilege and leniency that surrounds the academy's most valuable athletes." Christopher Marquis, "Naval Academy Athletes Charged with Rape," *New York Times*, July 4, 2000, p. A11.

6. Knight Foundation President Hodding Carter III is concerned about the ways in which the athletic agenda can overwhelm that of the entire institution: "tails wagging the dogs." The original report suggested among other things a much stronger role for the leadership of university presidents in the administration of intercollegiate athletics. The commission now intends to take another look at its "one-plus-three" institutional recommendations, which suggest that presidential control should ensure "academic integrity, fiscal integrity, and an independent certification process to monitor both," to see if they have proven sufficient. Welch Suggs, "A Decade Later, Sports-Reform Panel Plans Another Look at Big-Time Athletics," *Chronicle of Higher Education*, June 16, 2000, online edition; *Reports of the Knight Foundation Commission on Intercollegiate Athletics, March 1991–March 1993* (Charlotte, N.C., 1993).

7. See John Thelin's *Games Colleges Play* for a fascinating account of the history of reform efforts throughout the twentieth century. Thelin concludes (p. 198): "When one looks at the debates and proposals that followed publication of each report [recommending reforms, such as the Carnegie reports], it also becomes evident that an equally durable legacy has been the capacity of athletics departments and their supporters to defer publicly to the rhetoric of reform while simultaneously diluting the intent of the new policies and proposals. 'Reform' all too often took the form of capitulation to and accommodation of professionalism. To argue that this has been a pragmatic and realistic adaptation to America's commercial and competitive culture conveniently explains away the right and the obligation of a college or university to offer a distinctive experience, including that of the genuine student-athlete."

8. Toward the end of 1999, the NCAA secured the latest in a series of multibillion-dollar contracts for the televising of its basketball championships. It will provide some $6 billion in revenue over its 11-year term, more favorable terms than those contained in the NBA's current four-year, $2.6 billion television agreement. Although the NCAA numbers are large, its president, Cedric W. Dempsey, points out that it is only a "myth . . . that college athletic programs make profits. . . .

The fact is that only 78 out of 1,000 programs generate more revenues than they spend." Welch Suggs, "CBS to Pay $6-Billion for TV Rights to NCAA Basketball Championships," *Chronicle of Higher Education,* December 3, 1999, online edition. As noted earlier, even these calculations are misleading because they exclude capital costs in what are highly capital-intensive activities.

There is, however, this irony, as one former university president has pointed out: "Certain invidious trends in intercollegiate athletics probably will solve some of the problems by carrying the commercial evolution of college athletics to its logical conclusion. For example, we now see many of the most talented basketball players leaving for the pros after their freshman or sophomore years. There is now a serious discussion of setting up a 'minor league' to spare these athletes the inconvenience of passing through a campus."

Former University of Michigan President James Duderstadt has recently proposed deregulating college sports and then disconnecting big-time High Profile programs from universities, making them professional franchises instead. At the same time, Duderstadt would take other remaining programs "that have any relevance to the educational mission of the university" and make them club sports. This seemingly radical proposal is the most thoroughgoing way of attacking the problems associated with commercialization and professionalization, but it may not make sense to trustees and others who want to believe that today's 250-pound linebacker is a replica of the "student-athlete" of earlier times. James Duderstadt, *Intercollegiate Athletics and the American University: A University President's Perspective* (Ann Arbor: University of Michigan Press, 2000).

9. We were shown a widely circulated e-mail copy of a letter allegedly sent by important Notre Dame alumni to the trustees that illustrates well the forces that are unleashed when high expectations are not fulfilled. Among other things, the writers of the letter call on the trustees to "reassess and, where appropriate, modify our admissions policies toward student athletes" and "show some flexibility in . . . core course requirements, and curriculum of the First Year of Studies."

10. It is, again, no coincidence that the Academic Index in the Ivy League, designed to constrain competition in recruitment and admissions, was applied only to the High Profile sports of football, men's basketball, and men's hockey, which is where the most serious issues were thought to exist.

11. Perusal of the EADA forms for 1997–98 confirms that Haverford has a much higher ratio of female to male participation in athletics (relative to female and male enrollments) than the liberal arts colleges in this study, with the single exception of Kenyon.

12. For a brief but helpful summary of the issues at stake in the need-based athletic aid debate, see Debra E. Blum, "Colleges Weigh Aid to Athletes Based on Need: Financial Problems Lead to Revival of an Old Idea, but Skepticism Remains," *Chronicle of Higher Education,* September 2, 1992, online edition. The revenue-generating capacities of the most successful football and basketball programs are often linked to the provision of athletic scholarships, and in recent years the only active debate has been over whether such athletes should be treated even better and paid salaries as employees. See Gary S. Becker, "The NCAA: A Cartel in Sheepskin Clothing," *Business Week,* September 14, 1987, p. 24. On the role of paying college athletes as a way of eliminating what he regards as hypocrisy,

see Sperber, p. 349. In a similar vein, Walter Byers (p. 379) has argued that "In today's commercialized marketplace, the NCAA has no right to dictate a standard grant-in-aid with a salary cap and then embargo the players' income for their entire varsity career."

13. Leading universities and top colleges routinely invest more heavily in one academic program than another—perhaps in part because of historical strength in a field such as mathematics or the performing arts, perhaps because it is more cost effective to maintain excellence in already strong fields than to build excellence in fields where there is less to build upon, and perhaps because of the conviction that the institution will benefit from establishing a standard of excellence in some areas that may prove to be a stimulus and benchmark for others.

14. The Sears Cup honors institutions for achieving success across a broad range of sports. In 1999–2000, two institutions in our study won the cup in their respective divisions (Stanford in Division IA and Williams in Division III). Adams State Colorado won in Division II, and Simon Fraser University won in the NAIA Division.

15. The pressure to move away from "old-style" coaching is also being felt in secondary schools. According to a story in the *Yale Daily News,* many parents are expecting professional coaches. Michael Kannealey, athletic director of the Milton Academy, notes that "Faculty coaches are looked at askance by parents." When professional coaches come in, "they often care more about their own careers than the games of the students," according to Andover's athletic director, Leon Modeste. Modeste also points out that "in the past, coaches would coach for 30 years or more [whereas] now, many seek promotions to the college level after only three or four years." Louise Story, "Prep Schools: The Leagues before the Ivy," February 3, 2000, online edition.

16. One commentator has suggested that, in the case of wealthier and poorer institutions, the wealthier schools could make direct payments to the poorer ones to balance out inequalities. His argument is that it would be hard to picture Amherst building a new hockey rink if it knew that it would have to pay for one for Bates as well!

17. Of course, reducing the number of athletic scholarships in football would ease the problem of complying with Title IX. It is the felt need to provide 85 football scholarships that often throws the ratio of male to female athletic scholarships so far out of balance.

18. "In a poll of 2,010 adults, 79 percent said that they approved of Title IX of the Education Amendments of 1979. . . . In a separate question, 76 percent of respondents said they approved of 'cutting back' on men's athletics to ensure equivalent athletic opportunities for women." Welch Suggs, "Most Americans Favor Cutting Men's Sports to Add Women's, Poll Finds," *Chronicle of Higher Education,* June 23, 2000, online edition.

19. Even while arguing that institutions have failed to hold men's participation opportunities stagnant at 1970 levels so that further funding of women's teams could achieve equity, Donna Lopiano (p. 167) insists that men's opportunities need not be downsized: "The answer is to reduce expenditures on men's athletics without damaging the participation opportunities for male students and to redistribute these funds to provide gender equity for female athletes. Institu-

tions, however, have been unwilling to reduce what many consider to be excessive expenditures on men's football and basketball, and are eliminating men's non-revenue-producing sports and blaming it on having to provide equal athletics opportunities for women."

Gymnast Treena Comacho, who sued UCLA in a Title IX case, is quoted as saying: "I don't think we want to shake things up. We just want to do what we like to do. We may not even know what else is happening." Debra Blum, "Mutual Respect at UCLA," *Chronicle of Higher Education*, February 9, 1994, p. A40.

20. We can imagine one other, much more radical, way of addressing the issue of gender equity in the context of a concurrent effort to restore a better balance between athletics and academics, but it is likely to seem so far out, and so impractical, that we relegate it to this endnote. If it were possible to think very freshly, and to contemplate radical changes in regulations, we believe that there is a potentially more attractive way of addressing the need to comply with Title IX. What the law seeks to promote, we presume, is genuine equality of opportunity for *all* men and *all* women students attending institutions receiving federal funds. Suppose institutions were to address this objective by recognizing the differential advantages enjoyed by men in High Profile athletics but then seeking to remedy the situation by a more broad-gauged effort to redress the balance. Could one imagine institutions choosing to create a special fund for "women's activities" that would be fed by the dollars needed to counterbalance the disproportionate expenditure of funds on men's athletic programs (including athletic scholarships)? Such a "Title IX Fund" might then be used to provide a whole range of additional opportunities for women, some in athletics, some in extracurricular pursuits, perhaps even some in foreign study. The entire population of women attending these institutions might be better off under this general approach than they are under present rules and regulations, which in effect require institutions to reproduce mechanically the men's intercollegiate programs (including their excesses) for the benefit of the women. The "extra" resources that otherwise would be beamed directly to women's intercollegiate teams could still be spent in exactly the same way *if that were what the institution wanted to do*—but there would also be the flexibility to allocate the resources so as to benefit women in other ways. There is appeal in allowing each educational institution to decide for itself how best to spend its resources in order to promote gender equity. But in the world that we inhabit, this more flexible approach is assuredly not going to happen—in part because it may seem too complex and too radical (and it would be devilishly difficult to administer), and in larger part because women's intercollegiate sports has now become as institutionalized as men's.

21. Accepting responsibility for what transpires is not of course the same as providing anything approaching day-to-day management of the athletics enterprise. As one experienced observer of the scene emphasized to us, a mistake that keeps getting made is to assume that presidents have the time, never mind the inclination, to actually design and implement a new order, either on their own campus or in an inter-institutional setting. The time-consuming and complex nature of such tasks requires the attention of others, but these "others" need to be given a clear charge by the president and the trustees.

22. Smith, pp. 209–12.

References

Acosta, R. Vivian, and Linda-Jean Carpenter. 2000. "Women in Intercollegiate Sport: A Longitudinal Study—Twenty Three Year Update: 1977–2000." Mimeograph.

AP Online. 2000. "House Speaker Put in Wrestling Hall." June 3.

Araton, Harvey. 2000. "An Education Isn't a Game to Squander." *New York Times*, March 2, p. D1.

Arthur, Jennifer. 1999. "Proposed Finance Major to Be Discussed." *Yale Daily News*, February 9, online edition.

Becker, Gary S. 1987. "The NCAA: A Cartel in Sheepskin Clothing." *Business Week*, September 14, p. 24.

———. 1995 [1985]. "Human Capital, Effort, and the Sexual Division of Labor." In *The Essence of Becker*, edited by Ramon Febrero and Pedro Schwartz, pp. 434–62, Stanford, Calif.: Hoover Institution Press.

Belluck, Pam. 2000. "Parents Try to Reclaim Their Children's Time." *New York Times*, June 13, p. A18.

Bickley, Dan. 1995. "Cats Are Cashing In: Big Season Translates into Big Money for NU." *Chicago Sun-Times*, November 28, p. 86.

Blum, Debra E. 1992. "Colleges Weigh Aid to Athletes Based on Need: Financial Problems Lead to Revival of an Old Idea, but Skepticism Remains." *Chronicle of Higher Education*, September 2, online edition.

———. 1994. "Mutual Respect at UCLA." *Chronicle of Higher Education*, February 9, p. A40.

———. 1995. "Brown Loses Bias Case." *Chronicle of Higher Education*, April 7, online edition.

Bok, Derek. 1985. "Intercollegiate Athletics." In *Contemporary Issues in Higher Education: Self-Regulation and the Ethical Roles of the Academy*, edited by John B. Bennett and J. W. Peltason, pp. 123–46. New York: American Council on Education.

Bollinger, Lee. 1999. Talk given at the Macalester College Forum on Higher Education, St. Paul, Minn., June 3.

Bostian, Teri. 2000. "A Professor at Tennessee Cites Academic Abuses." *New York Times*, April 20, p. D3.

Bowen, William G., and Derek Bok. 1998. *The Shape of the River: Long-Term Consequences of Considering Race in College and University Admissions*. Princeton, N.J.: Princeton University Press.

Brooks, Andree. 1995. "Heavy Angst When It's 'Ivy or Else.'" *New York Times*, March 30.

Butsch, Richard (ed.). 1990. *For Fun and Profit: The Transformation of Leisure into Consumption*. Philadelphia: Temple University Press.

Byers, Walter, with Charles Hammer. 1995. *Unsportsmanlike Conduct: Exploiting College Athletes*. Ann Arbor: University of Michigan Press.

Cantor, Nancy E., and Deborah A. Prentice. 1996. "The Life of the Modern-Day Student-Athlete: Opportunities Won and Lost." Paper presented at the Princeton Conference on Higher Education, March 21–23.

Card, David, and Alan B. Krueger. 1996. "Labor Market Effects of School Quality: Theory and Evidence." In *Does Money Matter? The Link between Schools, Student Achievement, and Adult Success,* edited by Gary Burtless, pp. 97–140. Washington, D.C.: Brookings Institution.

Carpenter, Linda-Jean, and R. Vivian Acosta. 1996. "Back to the Future: Reform with a Women's Voice." In *Sport in Contemporary Society: An Anthology,* 5th ed., edited by D. Stanley Eitzen. New York: St. Martin's Press.

Casper, Gerhard. 2000. "Transition and Endurance." State of the University Address, Stanford University, March 2.

Chambers, Marcia. 1997. "For Women, 25 Years of Title IX Has Not Leveled the Playing Field." *New York Times,* June 16, p. A1.

Chronicle of Higher Education. 2000. "Young Donor Establishes Fund for Stanford Athletes." August 4, online edition.

Clotfelter, Charles T. 1985. *Federal Tax Policy and Charitable Giving.* Chicago: University of Chicago Press.

Cohen, Jodi S., and Fred Girard. 1999. "U-M Sports Deficit Criticized: Regent Fears More Shortfalls. Athletics Director Vows to Watch Spending, Income More Closely." *Detroit News,* July 16, p. A1.

Connolly, Walter B., Jr. (ed.). 1995. *A Practical Guide to Title IX: Law, Principles, and Practices.* Washington, D.C.: National Association of College and University Attorneys.

Connolly, Walter B., Jr., and Jeffrey D. Adelman. 1995. "A University's Defense to a Title IX Gender Equity in Athletics Lawsuit: Congress Never Intended Gender Equity Based on Student Body Ratios." In *A Practical Guide to Title IX: Law, Principles, and Practices,* edited by Walter B. Connolly, Jr. pp. 75–162. Washington, D.C.: National Association of College and University Attorneys.

Conrath, Sarah. 1999. "Choice to Quit Causes Tension in Varsity Sports." *Daily Princetonian,* October 21, online edition.

Coughlin, Cletus C., and O. Homer Erekson. 1984. "An Examination of Contributions to Support Intercollegiate Athletics." *Southern Economic Journal* 51: 180–95.

Daily Pennsylvanian. 1997. "Betrayal of Ivy Academic Ideals." December 2, online edition.

Daily Princetonian. 1997. "Women's Basketball Pummels Penn." March 7, online edition.

Dobrzynski, Judith H. 2000. "Hip vs. Stately: The Tao of Two Museums." *New York Times,* February 20, section 2, p. 1.

Duderstadt, James. 2000. *Intercollegiate Athletics and the American University: A University President's Perspective.* Ann Arbor: University of Michigan Press.

Duffy, Elizabeth A., and Idana Goldberg. 1998. *Crafting a Class: College Admissions and Financial Aid, 1955–1994.* Princeton, N.J.: Princeton University Press.

Dufour, Kris. 1996. "Eph Women Focus on ECAC; Can't Forget NCAA Turmoil." *North Adams Transcript,* May 11, pp. 13, 15.

Edwards, Christ. 1993. "Princeton Continues to Grapple with Wrestling." *Times of Trenton,* August 8, p. C6.

Edwards, Harry. 1984. "The Black 'Dumb Jock': An American Sports Tragedy." *College Board Review* 131 (Spring): 8–13.

Edwards, Robert. 1997. "A Reflection about NESCAC Football." In *The New England Small College Athletic Conference, 1971–1997: A Retrospective.* New England Small College Athletic Conference working paper.

Epstein, Cynthia Fuchs. 1992. "Constraints of Excellence: Structural and Cultural Barriers to the Recognition and Demonstration of Achievement." In *The Outer Circle: Women in the Scientific Community,* edited by Harriet Zuckerman, Jonathan Cole, and John Bruer, pp. 239–58. New Haven, Conn.: Yale University Press.

Ferguson, Andrew. 1999. "Inside the Crazy Culture of Kids Sports." *Time,* July 12, online edition.

Festle, Mary Jo. 1996. *Playing Nice: Politics and Apologies in Women's Sports.* New York: Columbia University Press.

Fimrite, Ron. 1996. "Once Regal, Soon to Be Razed." *Sports Illustrated,* November 25, p. R5.

Fordham, Signithia, and John Ogbu. 1986. "Black Students' School Success: Coping with the Burden of 'Acting White.'" *Urban Review* 18(3): 176–206.

Fowler, Henry T. 1896. "A Phase of Modern College Life." *Harper's New Monthly Magazine,* April, pp. 688–95.

Frank, Robert H., and Philip J. Cook. 1995. *The Winner-Take-All Society: How More and More Americans Compete for Ever Fewer and Bigger Prizes, Encouraging Economic Waste, Income Inequality, and Impoverished Cultural Life.* New York: Free Press.

Friend, Tom. 1995. "A Big Purple Haze Covers Hollywood." *New York Times,* December 31, section 8, p. 4.

Fulks, Daniel L. 1998. *Revenues and Expenses of Divisions I and II Intercollegiate Athletic Programs: Financial Trends and Relationships—1997.* Indianapolis, Ind.: National Collegiate Athletic Association.

———. 1998. *Revenues and Expenses of Division III Intercollegiate Athletic Programs: Financial Trends and Relationships—1997.* Indianapolis, Ind.: National Collegiate Athletic Association.

Fulton, Oliver. 1998. "Unity or Fragmentation, Convergence or Diversity: The Academic Profession in Comparative Perspective in the Era of Mass Higher Education," in *Universities and Their Leadership,* edited by William G. Bowen and Harold T. Shapiro, pp. 173–96. Princeton, N.J.: Princeton University Press.

Gates, Henry Louis. 1991. "Delusions of Grandeur: Young Blacks Must Be Taught That Sports Are Not the Only Avenue of Opportunity." *Sports Illustrated,* August 19, p. 78.

Girard, Fred. 1999. "U-M's Bollinger: Costs of Athletic Teams Pose a Problem." *Detroit News,* June 24, p. A15.

———. 1999. "Cuts Will Be Needed to Work on Deficit." *Detroit News,* June 24, p. C1.

———. 2000. "U-M Projects Another Deficit. Company Does Not Deliver Revenue for Sale of Broadcasts." *Detroit News,* March 7.

Goethals, George R., Gordon C. Winston, and David J. Zimmerman. 1999. "Students Educating Students: The Emerging Role of Peer Effects in Higher Education." Discussion paper 50, Williams Project on the Economics of Higher Education.

Goldfield, David. 1999. "Weaker NCAA Standards Won't Help Black Athletes," *Chronicle of Higher Education,* April 9, online edition.

Goodman, Mark. 1997. "A Squad with Few Equals." *New York Times,* April 27, p. 59.

Gray, Hanna. 1996. "The Leaning Tower of Academe." *Bulletin of the American Academy of Arts and Sciences* 49: 34–54.

Gray, Mary W. 1996. "The Concept of Substantial Proportionality in Title IX Athletics Cases." *Duke Journal of Gender Law & Policy* 3(1): 185–88.

Gugliotta, Guy. 1998. "On the Hill, Ex-Wrestlers Go to the Mat for the Sport." *Washington Post,* April 30, p. A19.

Guttmann, Allen. 1991. *Women's Sports: A History.* New York: Columbia University Press.

Hall, Stephen S. 2000. "The Smart Set." *New York Times Magazine,* June 4.

Hochschild, Arlie Russell. 1997. *The Time Bind: When Work Becomes Home and Home Becomes Work.* New York: Henry Holt.

Hoxby, Carolyn. 1997. "The Changing Market Structure of U.S. Higher Education." Unpublished paper, Harvard University.

Hutchins, Robert Maynard. 1956. *Some Observations on American Education.* Cambridge: Cambridge University Press.

Johnson, Dirk. 1999. "Seeking Little League Skills at $70 an Hour." *New York Times,* June 24, p. A1.

Kimball, Emily. 2000. "For Athletes, Recruiting Requirements Jump-Start College Admission Process." *Brown Daily Herald,* September 13, online edition.

Knight Foundation Commission on Intercollegiate Athletics. 1993. *Reports of the Knight Foundation Commission on Intercollegiate Athletics, March 1991–March 1993.* Charlotte, N.C.

Knight, Frank. 1997. *The Ethics of Competition.* New Brunswick, N.J.: Transaction.

Layden, Tim. 1996. "Now for the Hard Part." *Sports Illustrated,* May 6, pp. 62–66.

Lazerson, Marvin, and Ursula Wagener. 1996. "Missed Opportunities: Lessons from the Title IX Case at Brown." *Change* 28(4): 46–52.

Lederman, Doug. 1996. "Tigers on Top: Princeton's Sports Program Is the Envy of the Ivies, But at What Price to the University and Its Athletes?" *Princeton Alumni Weekly,* November 6, pp. 12–22.

Lemann, Nicholas. 1999. *The Big Test: The Secret History of the American Meritocracy.* New York: Farrar, Straus and Giroux.

Lipsyte, Robert. 2000. "What Happens after the Whistle Blows?" *New York Times,* July 20, p. D1.

Looney, Douglas S. 1994. "Pure and Simple: In the New England Small College Athletic Conference, Athletes Compete for One Reason: Love of the Game." *Sports Illustrated,* October 31, pp. 68–80.

Lopiano, Donna. 1995. "Equity in Women's Sports: A Health and Fairness Perspective." In *A Practical Guide to Title IX: Law, Principles, and Practices,* edited by Walter B. Connolly, Jr., pp. 163–78. Washington, D.C.: National Association of College and University Attorneys.

Loury, Glenn C. 1999. Foreword. In *The Shape of the River: Long-Term Consequences of Considering Race in College and University Admissions*, paperback ed. Princeton, N.J.: Princeton University Press.

Lypsite, Robert. 1999. "Backlash: The Entangled Web around Youth Sports." *New York Times*, May 23, section 8, p. 13.

McAllister, Bill. 1998. "Wrestler Wrider." *Washington Post*, July 2, p. A19.

McCormick, Robert E., and Maurice Tinsley. 1987. "Athletics versus Academics? Evidence from SAT Scores." *Journal of Political Economy* 95(5): 1103–9.

Mandel, Michael J., and Mark Landler. 1994. "The Entertainment Economy." *Business Week*, March 14, pp. 58ff, online edition.

Marquis, Christopher. 2000. "Naval Academy Athletes Charged with Rape." *New York Times*, July 4, p. A11.

Miracle, Andrew W., Jr., and C. Roger Rees. 1994. *Lessons of the Locker Room: The Myth of School Sports*. Amherst, N.Y.: Prometheus.

Mixon, Franklin. 1995. "Athletics versus Academics? Rejoining the Evidence from SAT Scores." *Education Economics* 3(3): 277–83.

Moran, Malcolm. 1995. "Northwestern and Its Fans Get to Stop and Savor the Roses." *New York Times*, November 27, page A1.

Mrozek, Donald J. 1997. "The 'Amazon' and the American 'Lady.'" In *The New American Sport History: Recent Approaches and Perspectives*, edited by S. W. Pope, pp. 198–214. Urbana: University of Illinois Press.

National Collegiate Athletic Association. 1994, 1996, 1998. *Revenues and Expenditures in Intercollegiate Athletics*. Indianapolis, Ind.

———. 1999. *NCAA Division I Graduation-Rates Report*. Indianapolis, Ind.

———. 1999. *NCAA Gender-Equity Study, 1997–98*. Indianapolis, Ind.

Naughton, Jim, and Jeffrey Selingo. 1998. "A Point Shaving Scandal Rattles a University." *Chronicle of Higher Education*, April 10, p. A48.

New York Times. 2000. "Faster, Higher, Farther: Tracking Athletic Performance." January 2, section 8, p. 9.

Noll, Roger. 1999. "The Business of College Sports and the High Cost of Winning." *Miliken Institute Review* (third quarter): 24–37.

Orleans, Jeffrey H. 1996. "An End to the Odyssey: Equal Athletic Opportunities for Women." *Duke Journal of Gender Law & Policy* 3(1): 131–41.

Orwell, George. 1968 [1947]. *The Sporting Spirit*. New York: Harcourt, Brace & World.

Padilla, Arthur, and Leroy T. Walker. 1994. "The Battle for Control of College Sports." *Chronicle of Higher Education*, December 14, p. A56.

Pappas, Dimitri. 1994. "Women's Athletics Enjoys 23 Successful Years." *Daily Princetonian*, November 16, p. 10.

Pascarella, Ernest T., Rachel Truckenmiller, Amaury Nora, Patrick T. Terenzini, Marcia Edison, and Linda Serra Hagedorn. 1999. "Cognitive Impacts of Intercollegiate Athletic Participation." *Journal of Higher Education*, January–February, pp. 1–26.

Peterson's Guide to 4 Year Colleges 2000. 1999. Princeton, N.J.: Peterson's.

Price, S. L. 1995. "What's Hot, What's Not: In Nashville, the NBA, the NFL, and the NHL May Be on the Way In and Up, While Football at Prestigious Vanderbilt Is Down and Out." *Sports Illustrated*, November 27, p. 48.

Rhoden, William C. 1997. "Ideals and Reality Collide on the Court." *New York Times,* July 21, p. C7.

Rubin, Dana. 1994. "You've Seen the Game. Now Buy the Underwear." *New York Times,* September 11, section 3, p. 5.

Rudolph, Frederick. 1990 [1962]. *The American College and University.* Athens: University of Georgia Press.

Russell, Mark. 1995. "Competition über Alles." *The Long Term View: A Journal of Informed Opinion* (Massachusetts School of Law at Andover) 3(2): 23–33.

Savage, Howard J. 1929. *American College Athletics.* New York: Carnegie Foundation for the Advancement of Teaching.

Sheehan, Richard G. 1996. *Keeping Score: The Economics of Big-Time Sports.* South Bend, Ind.: Diamond Communications.

Smith, Ronald A. 1988. *Sports and Freedom: The Rise of Big-Time College Athletics.* New York: Oxford University Press.

Sperber, Murray. 1990. *College Sports, Inc.: The Athletic Department vs. the University.* New York: Henry Holt.

Steele, Claude, and Joshua Aronson. 1998. "Stereotype Threat and the Test Performance of Academically Successful African-Americans." In *The Black-White Test Score Gap,* edited by Christopher Jencks and Meredith Phillips, pp. 401–30. Washington, D.C.: Brookings Institution.

Story, Louise. 2000. "Prep Schools: The Leagues before the Ivy." *Yale Daily News,* February 3, online edition.

Suggs, Welch. 1999. "Postseason Play Creates Tensions for an Unusual Athletics Conference." *Chronicle of Higher Education,* July 18, online edition.

———. 1999. "Graduation Rates Hit Lowest Level in 7 Years for Athletes in Football and Basketball." *Chronicle of Higher Education,* September 10, p. A58.

———. 1999. "CBS to Pay $6-Billion for TV Rights to NCAA Basketball Championships," *Chronicle of Higher Education,* December 3, online edition.

———. 1999. "U. of Tennessee's Lady Vols Find Success—and Profit—on the Court." *Chronicle of Higher Education,* December 17, p. A54.

———. 2000. "2 Appeals Courts Uphold Right of Universities to Reduce Numbers of Male Athletes." *Chronicle of Higher Education,* January 7, p. A64.

———. 2000. "Abandoning Major Sponsorship Deal, Nike Plays Hardball over Sweatshops." *Chronicle of Higher Education,* May 12, online edition.

———. 2000. "Alabama State Plans to Become First Black College in Division IA Football." *Chronicle of Higher Education,* May 15, online edition.

———. 2000. "Blue-Ribbon Panel on College-Sports Issues Will Reconvene This Fall." *Chronicle of Higher Education,* June 1, online edition.

———. 2000. "A Decade Later, Sports-Reform Panel Plans Another Look at Big-Time Athletics," *Chronicle of Higher Education,* June 16, online edition.

———. 2000. "Most Americans Favor Cutting Men's Sports to Add Women's, Poll Finds," *Chronicle of Higher Education,* June 23, online edition.

———. 2000. "Football's Have-Nots Contemplate Their Place in the NCAA." *Chronicle of Higher Education,* June 30, online edition.

———. 2000. "Ivy League Strips Brown U. of Recruits and Eligibility for Championship," *Chronicle of Higher Education,* August 2, online edition.

Telander, Rick. 1995. "NU's Bowl Economics Don't Trickle Down to General Fund." *Chicago Sun-Times,* November 29, p. 135.

Thelin, John R. 1994. *Games Colleges Play: Scandal and Reform in Intercollegiate Athletics.* Baltimore: Johns Hopkins University Press.

Turner, Sarah E., and William G. Bowen. 1999. "Choice of Major: The Changing (Unchanging) Gender Gap." *Industrial and Labor Relations Review* 52(2): 289–313.

Turner, Sarah E., Lauren A. Meserve, and William G. Bowen. 1999. Working paper on the econometric relationship between year-to-year increments in giving and changes in won-lost records. Available from The Andrew W. Mellon Foundation.

Van Der Werf, Martin. 2000. "Nike Grants U. of Michigan a 1-Year Extension on Athletics-Apparel Contract." *Chronicle of Higher Education,* May 15, online edition.

Vecsey, George. 1999. "Is It Only a Game?" *New York Times,* August 1, p. 4A28.

Vélez, Karin. 1997. *The New England Small College Athletic Conference, 1971–1997: A Retrospective.* New England Small College Athletic Conference working paper.

Velvel, Lawrence (ed.). 1995. "Sports in America—A Distortion or Reflection of Life?" *The Long Term View: A Journal of Informed Opinion* (Massachusetts School of Law at Andover) 3(2).

Viner, Jacob. 1958. *The Long View and the Short.* New York: Free Press.

Weisbrod, Burton (ed.). 1998. *To Profit or Not to Profit: Commercialization in the Non-Profit Sector.* Cambridge: Cambridge University Press.

Weistart, John. 1993. "The 90's University: Reading, Writing and Shoe Contracts." *New York Times,* November 29, Section 8, p. 9.

———. 1996. "Can Gender Equity Find a Place in Commercialized College Sports?" *Duke Journal of Gender Law & Policy* 3(1).

———. 1996. "The Path of Most Resistance: The Long Road to Gender Equity in Intercollegiate Athletics (Part 2 of 4)." *Duke Journal of Gender Law & Policy* 3(1): 61–71.

Welch, Paula. 1999. *Silver Era, Golden Moments: A Celebration of Ivy League Women's Athletics.* Lanham, Md.: Madison.

Williams, Lena. 2000. "Women Play More, but Coach Less." *New York Times,* May 3, p. D8.

Wilson, Woodrow. Talk to the Princeton Class of 1909. Princeton University archives.

Wine, Steven. 2000. "Plenty of Tradition, Empty Seats for the Orange Bowl." *AP Online,* January 1.

Winston, Gordon C., and Ethan G. Lewis. 1996. "Physical Capital and Capital Service Costs in US Colleges and Universities: 1993." WPEHE Discussion Paper Series, February.

Wyatt, Joe B. 1996. "Chancellor Responds to Athletics Committee Report." *Vanderbilt Register* 15(30): 8–9.

Yale Daily News. 1999. "Preserve Liberal Arts Education in Economics." February 12, online edition.

Zengerle, Jason. 2000. "The Portable High-School Hoops Factory." *New York Times Magazine,* February 6, p. 56.

Ziehm, Len. 1995. "NU Begins Campaign to Renovate Its Facilities." *Chicago Sun-Times,* September 28, p. 92.

Zimbalist, Andrew. 1999. *Unpaid Professionals: Commercialism and Conflict in Big-Time College Sports.* Princeton, N.J.: Princeton University Press.

———. 1999. "There's No Accounting for College Sports." *University Business,* June, pp. 38–45.

Page numbers for entries occurring in figures are suffixed by an f; those for entries in notes, by an n, with the number of the note following; those for entries in scorecards, by an sc; and those for entries in tables, by a t.

James L. Shulman is Financial and Administrative Officer at The Andrew W. Mellon Foundation. He collaborated on *The Shape of the River: Long-Term Consequences of Considering Race in College Admissions* (Princeton).

William G. Bowen is President of the Andrew W. Mellon Foundation and was formerly President of Princeton University, where he was also Professor of Economics. He is co-author of *The Shape of the River* and many other works.